W0019649

THE NICEST FELLA
- The Life of Ben Johnson -
The world champion rodeo cowboy who became an Oscar-winning movie star

by Richard D. Jensen

iUniverse, Inc.
New York   Bloomington

The Nicest Fella

Copyright © 2010 by Richard D. Jensen

All rights reserved. No part of this book may be used or reproduced by any means, graphic, electronic, or mechanical, including photocopying, recording, taping or by any information storage retrieval system without the written permission of the publisher except in the case of brief quotations embodied in critical articles and reviews.

iUniverse books may be ordered through booksellers or by contacting:

iUniverse
1663 Liberty Drive
Bloomington, IN 47403
www.iuniverse.com
1-800-Authors (1-800-288-4677)

Because of the dynamic nature of the Internet, any Web addresses or links contained in this book may have changed since publication and may no longer be valid. The views expressed in this work are solely those of the author and do not necessarily reflect the views of the publisher, and the publisher hereby disclaims any responsibility for them.

ISBN: 978-1-4401-9678-2 (sc)
ISBN: 978-1-4401-9679-9 (ebook)

Printed in the United States of America

iUniverse rev. date: 01/07/2010

Appreciation

Thanks to my wife, Grenycherida Xavier de Freitas Jensen, who grew up riding bulls in the land of vaqueros in Limoeiro, Pernambuco, Brazil and came to America and fell in love with the world of American cowboys (and one cowboy in particular), with Colorado and with Oklahoma; and who assisted me on this project for hours on end, providing guidance, encouragement and constructive criticism.

Dedication

This book would never have been possible without the lifelong work of Helen Lee Johnson Christenson, who has spent more than three decades researching and archiving thousands of pieces of information and who interviewed and recorded on audio tape and video tape the recollections of the very people whose stories are heralded within these pages.

Because of her love of her father, Ben, Sr., and her brother Ben, Jr., called "Son" by those who knew him, and because the Tall Grass prairies of Osage County, Oklahoma are the essence of her blood and soul, Helen has single-handedly preserved not only the history of her famous father and brother, but also much of the history of the Tall Grass Prairie.

This book is dedicated to her. Her work is reflected herein, and it is a major part of the scholarship in these pages.

Foreword

I met World Champion rodeo cowboy, Oscar-winning actor, and perennial John Wayne co-star Ben Johnson in 1984 at a Western film festival in Knoxville, Tennessee. He had come as a guest of honor. My friend, Curtis Cook, and I went to spend time with the cowboy stars and watch some classic westerns. Both Curtis and I were active performers in wild west shows and lifelong cowboys. We were both excited about meeting one of our favorite real cowboy actors.

We found Johnson to be cordial, indeed amiable. When he discovered that both Curtis and I were cowboys – and that I was a professional film actor and card-carrying member of the Screen Actor's Guild and AFTRA, the two actor's unions, he became even more chummy. The festival was a bit slow and somewhat dreary, and by the end of the first day we were hanging out together, telling horse stories, discussing ranching and stock-raising issues. We also discussed the decline of Western movies both in popularity and in quality.

When it came time for dinner, we all piled into a rental car – followed close behind by a cadre of hanger-on festival organizers who were rather pushy – and went to a Bonanza steakhouse for dinner. As soon as we arrived, the restaurant became abuzz with excitement. We overheard people whispering, "John Wayne is here!" and "that guy who's in the movies with John Wayne is here!" One man walked up and said, "You're Ben Johnson, ain't ya?" Ol' Ben just nodded and smiled and chatted with the guy for a bit, then signed an autograph and posed for pictures. He never said no, always obliged, and always signed the same thing: "Always your friend, Ben Johnson."

Our waitress came by and asked, "Are you famous?" Ben shook his head and said, "Naw, I just hold John Wayne's horse a lot." When the checks came, Ben paid for everybody, which was a nice gesture indeed.

We saw a lot of Ben Johnson that weekend, and he was just a joy to get to know. I ran into Ben at several festivals thereafter, and Curtis visited him in Arizona on several occasions.

Ben Johnson was always quick to talk horses and cows and rodeo, not so much about movies and Hollywood. He loved his life, and he was devoted to Carol, his wife, and talked a lot about raising money for charity. He was patriotic, sincere and a true example of cowboy hospitality.

It was then, more than 25 years ago, that I decided that one day I'd write this book.

Ol' Son, I hope I got 'er right.

Prologue

The dead center middle of the United States of America is called the Great Plains.

During the early westward migration of white settlers this area was often erroneously called The Great American Desert, or the Great Desert.

In that region of what is now northern Oklahoma is an undulating landscape of blue stem grass, punctuated with staccato dashes of jack oak trees. It is a land of stark beauty, brimming with life. The prairie wind whispers its secrets incessantly.

The Osage Indians called this land home, and when whites came they paid homage to that heritage by referring to it as Osage country. When the State of Oklahoma was officially formed, this area was called Osage County, Oklahoma.

The cow hands who lived and worked in this region called themselves "tall grass cowboys." That handle has stuck even today. The prairie itself is the Tall Grass Prairie. Indeed, a more than 100,000-acre preserve under the auspices of the Nature Conservancy is called the Tall Grass Prairie Preserve.

This preserve is made up of many ranches, including the enormous Chapman Barnard Ranch. In its heyday, the over 100,000-acre ranch (72,000 deeded acres, the balance leased) was one of several monolithic cattle ranching operations located in northern Oklahoma.

The Chapman Barnard Ranch was a major cattle producer, shipping as many as 100,000 head of cattle to market each and every year from the 1920s until the 1950s. At any given time, the ranch kept from 20,000 to 30,000 cattle during the summer months.

The Chapman Barnard Ranch, along with the Drummond Ranch and others, were the lifeblood of the tightly knit ranching community of the Tall Grass Prairie.

Cowboy Johnny Cochran, who cowboyed at the Chapman Barnard Ranch from 1933 to 1937, said the ranch was vital to the survival of the people in the region when it was beset with twin catastrophes – the Great Depression and a severe drought. "The Chapman Barnard Ranch was one of the anchors of that time that gave the people in these small communities hope."[1]

While many ranches paid $20 a month plus room and board during the Great Depression, the Chapman Barnard Ranch paid $1 a day plus room and board. During such a calamitous time, this was a godsend to many families on the Tall Grass Prairie. By the late 1930s, the ranch paid $1.15 a day – an unheard of pay scale for the time.

"The Chapman Barnard Ranch was one of the best ranches around. The Chapman Barnard paid $35 a month," cowboy Trig Meeks said. "It was the best paying job I knew of."[2]

The ranch employed roughly two dozen cowboys in the summer. Only three cowboys were kept on the payroll during the winters as the ranch didn't winter cows. That policy changed in the late 1930s, when the number of year-round cows and cowboys increased.

James A Chapman was an oilman worth $75 million. His partner, Horace G. Barnard was an oilman and a cowman as well. Barnard was Chapman's wife's uncle.[3]

Neither man was known for his affability. Both were hard-nosed businessmen. They were tough but fair. They were respected – and if crossed were feared.

During the ranch's heyday, one man held the job as its foreman. The legendary Ben Johnson, Sr., three-time world champion rodeo cowboy, ran the Chapman Barnard during the Great Depression and through the World War II and Korean War years. His son, Ben, Jr., would become famous as a rodeo champion and Oscar-winning movie star.

To tell the story of the two Ben Johnsons, we must tell the story of the Tall Grass Prairie. The blood, sweat and tears of both men watered the ground of this beautiful region and the blue stem grass was in the marrow of their bones. Their bodies rest today beneath her fertile soil.

CHAPTER ONE
THE FATHER

For rodeo fans, especially older generations, Ben Johnson is a name that conjures up twin images: The iconic Ben Johnson, Sr. and his son, Ben Johnson, Jr. 'Ol Ben,' as he was called after his son became famous, was a champion steer roper who won Cheyenne Frontier Days (at that time considered the world's championship) in 1922, 1923 and 1926. His son, Ben Johnson, Jr. is remembered as the 1953 RCA World Champion Team Roper.

For Western movie fans, Ben Johnson, Jr. is simply Ben Johnson, also iconic, a true cowboy and rodeo champion turned movie star. Though he insisted he was a terrible actor, he was actually an actor of tremendous integrity who embodied Westerns movies in which he appeared with such realism that many mediocre films were elevated.

He made the greats of cinema, John Wayne, Henry Fonda, Marlon Brando, Alan Ladd – and so many more – look more authentic, both by acting alongside them and giving their movies an inherent credibility and by stunt-doubling them, making their portrayals of cowboys look more realistic.

This book is a biography of the famous actor Ben Johnson, whose name was actually Francis Benjamin Johnson, Jr., known as "Son" to his family and friends. To tell his story, however, we must tell the story of Ben Johnson, Sr. Their lives paralleled in some ways and diverged in others, but each impacted the other in many ways. Both were cowboys of the tall grass prairie at a time when there were few modern conveniences. Both could ride like the wind. Both could ride broncs and stick to them like glue. Son is seen in many films riding broncs, and there is even silent movie footage of Ol' Ben riding broncs on the Chapman Barnard Ranch. He does so with a casual, good-humored grace, a smile never leaving his face. Both men roped with lightning speed and true aim.

For purposes of clarity, Ben, Sr. is referred to as Ben throughout this book and Ben, Jr. is referred to as "Son." This is how they were referred to in life by those who knew them the best, and it makes the telling of the story easier for the reader.

Ben Johnson, Sr. was born February 19, 1896 in Harrison, Arkansas. He had three brothers and three sisters. His father and mother, Ralph and Annie Johnson, moved the family to Tulsa, Oklahoma.[1] Ben was four when the family made the move. Ralph had taken a job as a livestock auctioneer.[2]

Clearly Ben was fascinated with the cowboy life. An old family photo exists of young Ben, aged 10 or 11, dressed in traditional cowboy garb, including twin six guns, a single barrel shotgun and wearing a broad-brimmed Stetson. A lariat lays on the floor in front of him. The photo shows an early glimpse of Ben's sense of humor: Young Ben is also holding aloft a bottle of whiskey in his left hand and a cigarette dangles from his mouth![3] Ben began cowboying when he left home in the middle of the fifth grade, inspired by watching some of the earliest western films of cowboys, many of those films the first-ever footage of actual cowboys, which was shot at the 101 Ranch in Ponca City, Oklahoma.[4] Ben and his school buddy Ralph E. Barton took jobs at various ranches around Pawhuska and the tiny hamlets of Shidler and Foraker, Oklahoma.[5] These towns which were nestled in the bosoms of some of the largest ranches in Oklahoma and existed to serve the families of ranch hands.

By age 14, Ben had hired on with the famous 101 Ranch, owned by the Miller Brothers, Zack and George. At this time another cowboy worked at the ranch who would go on to become the highest paid and most famous cowboy star of the movies – Tom Mix. Nothing is recorded of their relationship, but the time line puts them in the same place at the same time, so surely they encountered each other and knew each other well. Both had broad smiles and expansive senses of humor, so one can imagine that they got along famously.

Young Ben was given various jobs, including riding fence, where a cowboy rides along the fence lines, either on horseback or in a wagon, inspecting and repairing broken fences. He also worked the cattle and, when the cowboys discovered Ben was good with a razor, became the defacto barber for the bunkhouse.[6] By the time Ben was 16, he had developed a reputation as a crackerjack barber, and his arsenal of barbering tools included four tempered steel German straight razors with wooden handles, which he kept in a soft leather carrying case which bore the inscription "Ben Johnson, 101 Ranch, Bliss, Oklahoma, March 1912."[7]

Ben was a hard worker, a trait he would retain until his death. Daughter Helen Johnson Christenson remembered her father coming in from a day on the range exhausted, covered in dust and sweat. He was a top hand, and his reputation as a steer roper was considerable. By 1918 he was supplementing his cowboy income by competing in rodeos, earning prize money with regularity. A wonderful photo, dated 1920, shows Ben and his roping partner, Fred Beeson, as they prepared to compete at a roping contest. It is a rare photo because Ben is wearing jeans. Throughout his life, he preferred baggy khaki pants tucked into the tops of his ornate cowboy boots. He is sitting on a dark horse with a large blaze on its face and two rear stockings. His right hand is raised high over his head, his loop built. His underarm is stained with sweat. Throughout his life, Ben was constantly photographed with his right hand raised, his cowboy hat held high. In all of these photos his exuberance is apparent. "He put more living into 56 years than most people cram into a lifetime," Helen said.[8]

Beeson sits to Ben's right in the photo, astride a dark horses with a snip on its nose and a white stocking on it's right foreleg and another right rear leg. His saddle is ornate, most likely a prize from a rodeo contest. He has also built his loop and is holding it high. To their left is a Ford Model T, likely a truck.

It is easy to picture Ben if you are a fan of his son. Imagine the movie image of young Ben Johnson, starring in John Ford's *Wagonmaster*. Then make him taller and thinner. The two men are mirror images - son and father.

Ben was the epitome of the American cowboy of life and legend. He was part Owen Wister's *Virginian* and part *Bret Maverick*. He was larger than life. D.E. "Gene" Waters wrote, "Ben Johnson, Sr. ... was a real cowboy in the full meaning of the word."[9]

Tall and rangy, with a big loopy grin and flashing eyes, he was gregarious and affable, but stern and direct when crossed. When he ascended to the post of manager of the enormous Chapman Barnard Ranch, he was widely respected as a solid, dependable ranch boss. He was a leader of men who were not easily led. To have the respect of the toughest cowboys on the range, he had to be just a little bit tougher. He was, in many ways, the leader of the entire Osage prairie. When problems arose, Ben Johnson often solved them – and did so with a smile on his face. He was single-handedly the backbone and inspiration of the entire community.

On Saturdays, when all the cowboys and ranchers and their families came to town to shop and socialize, Ben was the life of the party. He held court in the café, swapped stories on the benches outside the stores, roped steers at the fairgrounds – and usually won. He raced horses – and won then, too. He gambled on anything, from horse racing to betting on which way a horse would swish its tail first. He won with a grin and lost with a grin. He was cheerful when times were good and equally cheerful when times were hard.

Ben had an expression that he used whenever he was highly pleased, whether it be from winning a horse race or watching kids play baseball. He'd yell, "Hot Dang!" It was as much a part of his inherent exuberance as was his penchant for raising his hat high into the air with his right hand whenever his picture was taken.[10]

Ben was widely believed to be the best square dancer in Oklahoma. Not only that, he was famous for his ability to call the dances in his booming voice as he danced, no easy feat. He could tell stories that held the listener in rapt attention. He doted on children – anyone's children – buying them candy or a soda pop. He would often forget the child's first name, but he always remembered what family the child belonged to, and would holler a greeting. Edna Mae Barton Olsen recalled that Ben would drive by or ride by on a horse and holler, "Hello, little Barton."

He *loved* children, not just his own but any child. He bought them soda pop and ice cream. If he walked into a general store and saw a child, he'd toss a coin on the counter and tell the clerk, "Give that youngster a pop."

He would drop what he was doing and pitch a baseball to kids playing ball on the street.

Ben Fowler remembered Ben Johnson's kindness and impish humor. "When I was 6 or 7 my brother, Chuck, and the two youngest Pontius boys would keep watch for the Chapman and Barnard pickups and trucks to come through Foraker going out west of town to haul alfalfa out to the ranch for the horses," Fowler said. "And, of course, they would stop at the little store for a bottle of pop and [Ben] was right in the middle and when he would see us come in he would say in that big voice of his, 'You boys want to work today, all I can pay you is a Grapette. Well, get you one and get in the back of my pickup.' And boy would we pile in.

"About 5 miles down the road was Salt Creek and Ben would stop and tell us boys to strip down to our shorts and he would shoot the turtles off of the old tree trunks and we would dive in to see who could come up with the biggest turtle," Fowler said.

"After about an hour of that Ben would say that he had to get to the hay field and he would reach into his pocket and pull out a handful of money and tell us to split it up among us and he would be back in about an hour and pick us up. We would all pile in or on the running boards and he would torment us all the way back to town.

"Nobody worried about us because somebody saw us leave town with Ben and they knew that he would take care of us," Fowler said.[11]

Every Christmas, Ben would attend the Christmas pageant at the tiny Pearsonia School, the rural school nudged between the Chapman Barnard Ranch and other adjoining ranches. Ben's daughter Helen attended school there, riding the six miles to school on her horse every day. Ben would assign the role of Santa Claus to one of the Chapman Barnard cowboys. The children would put on a Christmas play that told the story of the birth of the baby Jesus and then a second play that featured Santa Claus. After the plays, Ben would give every child in the play $5.

Frances Jo Brooks, a childhood friend of Helen Johnson and a classmate at Pearsonia School, said while Ben would give $5 to the kids, the Chapman Barnard Ranch, known for its tightwad owners, gave each child a mere dollar.[12]

Brooks was the recipient of Ben's largesse when she burned her hands in an accident. "Dad would drive out and meet Frances Jo and her family on the road when she had a doctor's appointment," Helen recalled. "Her dad, Red Brooks, worked for the ranch. Frances Jo burned her hands very badly and Red had to take her to the doctor for weeks getting skin grafts. She said Dad would always meet them on the county road, have his arm waving out the window for them to stop, would ask Red, 'Do those girls have any money?' Of course, the little girls would be shaking their heads, 'No.' And, Dad would give them, I think it was, $10."[13]

When the Pearsonia School held its annual Halloween costume contest, Ben would attend and give the winner a dollar. One year Helen won and Ben felt so sad for the other 19 contestants that he ended up giving all 20 children in the contest a silver dollar.

"He was literally loved by everybody," Nita Jones, whose father was a cowhand at Chapman Barnard and other ranches, said. "He was the most generous person I knew."[14]

Ben's notoriety as a square dancer and square dance caller spilled over into his love for children. He'd pull kids onto the dance floor during the Saturday square dances and encourage them to dance.[15]

Paul McGuire remembered Ben Johnson's kindness to him when McGuire was a child. "Way back in 1916 a kindly neighbor gave me a ride to the Dewey (Oklahoma) Roundup, but he neglected to give me an admission ticket. It was up to my own ingenuity to see the rodeo, so I wandered aimlessly down to the barn where they had the roping horses, thinking I might wander through an open gate and follow a cow horse on into the show.

"The cowboys were cinching saddles, coiling ropes and taking up collections for one thing or some other, at least most of them had hand fulls of bills they passed around to one certain fellow who didn't look like much of a roper.

"I got about halfway down the pens when a big fellow grabbed me and said, 'Sonny, you shouldn't be in here, it's pretty rough for a little feller like you, some of the wild ones might trample on you.'

"Ben Johnson lifted me up and set me back of Henry Grammar, telling him to throw me off in the quarter stretch. In a few more minutes I had part of a grandstand seat and a bottle of red pop. I then saw one of the wildest, roughest and biggest paid-off rodeos that ever happened in this part of the country.

"Later, when I knew Ben Johnson better, I learned that incident was typical of him. He liked kids and always had a kind word or some little something else for them. Everyone liked Ben and he always had time to say at least a few kind words in passing by," McGuire said.[16]

This story is one of the earliest stories of Ben's association with Henry Grammar, one of Ben's good friends. Grammar was an Osage county rancher, cowboy and, some say, desperado. Grammar was famous (and infamous) in the Tall Grass Prairie for his purported exploits, which some say included robbery, moonshine liquor, gambling and prostitution.[17]

Oklahoma was wide open to vice in the 1920s and 1930s, and a lawless element thrived. During the Prohibition of the 1920s and the Great Depression of the 1930s, the state was familiar stomping grounds for such legendary gangsters Machine Gun Kelly, "Baby Face" Nelson and the infamous Bonnie Parker and Clyde Barrow, also known as Bonnie and Clyde.[18]

Ben's sense of humor was legendary. He was a prankster par excellence.

In the 1920s, large events were often captured on film by photographers who took panorama photographs. A large company of people were stood side-by-side and the photograph that resulted was shallow in height but very wide. This was accomplished by the photographer taking multiple images and then merging them side-by-side.

Ben was at a large rodeo – some believe it was the then gigantic Dewey, Ok. Roundup – when he made a bet with his fellow cowboys that he could be in both ends of the line in the same panorama photo. When the photographer took the photo of the left side of the group, Ben was to the far left on the image. Then, while the photographer reloaded his box camera, Ben ran around to the other side of the group and was standing to the far right of the image of that group. The result is two Ben Johnsons in the photo![19]

Cowboy Trig Meeks said that whenever Ben was around there was "lots of slappin' and kickin' and practical jokes."[20]

Cowboy Dallas Poteet remembered a practical joke gone awry during the early 1920s. He was working at the Chapman Barnard at the time, and Ben decided it would be fun for the cowboys to rope some of Chapman's prized greyhounds, which the rancher used to chase down wolves during wolf hunts and to chase jackrabbits.

"Ben lived on Pearce Brooks' old place at the time, just south of Foraker," Poteet said. "I saddled a pretty black mare and we started out. Ben decided he'd rope the greyhounds, and I decided to rope one too. Sure enough, the dog ran under my horse and that horse turned wrong side out."[21]

Ben was so dazzling a personality that everyone he knew liked him and many went out of their way to spend time with him.

"Ol' Ben, well he was as good a fella as I ever worked for," Meeks said. "He was good to everybody. He treated everybody alike. If you treated him right he was a good friend to you."[22]

Ben was a man's man, and he was a ladies man. He commanded the respect of the men who he encountered, friend and foe, and he caught the roving eye of many a lady. After his divorce from his first wife, Ollie, Ben was the number one bachelor on the Osage prairie. That said, all evidence suggests that while women flocked to him, he was always courtly and respectful with his attentions.

"Ben Johnson was a friendly, happy-go-lucky cowboy who liked horses and people," Aleta Lutz recalled in 1964. "Ben had the natural build of a cowboy, broad shoulders, long arms and superb confirmation."[23]

Holton Payne, an Osage County rancher who knew Ben well, said, "Ben was a gentleman. He'd dance with the girls but he was a gentleman."

Ben's horsemanship was legendary. He could ride any horse and he was a superior judge of horseflesh. As were many cowboys and ranchers in the Tall Grass prairie, Ben liked to play the horses, betting on match races and roping events every weekend.

During the early days of Oklahoma, each county had weekly horse races and roping competitions. They were held on Saturdays. Ranchers and farmers and their employees came to town to go to the store, the bank and to socialize. Saturday evenings were reserved for big square dances, usually at a local nightclub which was located in an old oil company building.

"The Big Beaver Night Club was about three miles from where I lived out in the country," Payne recalled. "We're in an oil field area. A pipeline company built these pump station every eight miles. The night club was in one of these old pump stations. Ol Ben was a square dancer and he'd call them dances."[24]

Cowboy Dallas Poteet, who worked for the Chapman Barnard Ranch alongside Ben from 1923 to 1926, recalled another incident in which Ben showed his true grit.

"I was young and ignorant," Poteet said. "I rode the rough string. A rough string rider is as tough as a boot and as ignorant as a boot." Poteet said that he was conscripted to act as bouncer during one of the weekend square dances in Pawhuska. "I was so ignorant they made me bouncer. I was so big, I think I weighed 150 pounds.

"These dances would have oil field workers, Indians from Shidler and from Pawhuska, and cowboys from all of the ranches. That was the perfect place to get in trouble if you were silly enough to take the job as bouncer," Poteet said.

"There were these two brothers, Bud Hall who was foreman of the Drummond Ranch and Todd Hall, who would get drunk at the dances and pull a knife.

"One night Todd pulled a knife on me and Ben came up behind him and put his arms around Todd and talked him out of usin' that knife. That saved my life."[25]

Most of the women wanted to dance with Ben, who was known for his gift of gab and his allure to the ladies. Many times Ben would finish the square dance and spend the balance of the evening holding court at Brown's Café. The eaterie was owned by "Blondie" Jackson. Ben always referred to the café as "Blondie's."

Nita Jones, tells a story of her father, Sol Salmon, a cowboy who worked for most of the big ranches in Osage County. Jones, a lifelong friend of Helen, recalled that Ben used to tell the children that if his horse won at the races he'd taken them to the café.

"Ben'd always say, 'I'll take you to Blondie's if we win,' but win or lose he'd take us to supper there. It was a hopping place." Jones said.[26]

Payne recalled that very late one night after a square dance he peered in through the window of Brown's Café. "Ben and Bill Bowers were inside visitin' with Blondie and her sister, 'romancing' the girls," Payne said. "Well they got 'em to open the café and up and let us in."[27]

The weekend shivarees gave the men a chance to get haircuts and stock up on their fill of liquid spirits – and to gamble their pay, and often their horses, on races and steer roping.

Ben was a voracious gambler and was famous for his lucky streak.

Match races often pitted cash-strapped cowboys against each other, and sometimes the only thing of value they had to bet were the very horses they were racing. A cowboy could – and often did – win or lose in a big way. The winner rode away leading a new, fine horse, while the loser walked away on foot.

"There was guy in Fairfax named Skinner Neff. He owned a horse named Monty Williams. Everybody knew that Monty could outrun Leo short." Holton Payne recalled. "It was questionable if he could outrun him longer. Ol' Ben bought her and matched her two races, one at 2:20 and one at three and won him both. And he was judge at Newkirk Race Track and he'd be up there for them to get ready to run a race and he'd holler out, 'I've got $100 to bet on a horse.' Nobody questioned his decision when he'd made one."

For spectators, the money was won by betting. Ben was a master at judging horses, and he won money and horses often. Whenever he was racing one of his own horses, he bet heavily on his entry and usually won big. He had one rule: The race had to be fair or else.

During one race, Ben had hired a young, black jockey to ride his horse. Rumors began spreading that the jockey was going to throw the race. Ben went to see the jockey and showed the jockey his pistol. As the jockey stared wild-eyed at the gun, Ben told him that he'd better not slow the horse down during the contest. He was to run all out.

When the race began, the jockey rode the horse to victory and when the horse crossed the finish line the jockey leapt off the galloping steed and ran for the hills, never to be seen again.[29]

Payne remembered a dispute in the late 1940s over a horse race that almost ended in violence. A horse named War Star was matched against a horse named King Bee. Ben and Bill Roe and another man whose name is lost to history were the judges of the race. When King Bee was judged the winner, War Star's owner took offense.

"This guy had a bad rep," Payne said. "He'd killed somebody and we all had heard about it. Well, he looked at Bill Roe and told him that he was a 'goddamn liar.' Then he turned to Ben and Ben gave him a cold look and said, 'King Bee won, and if you doubt it, put up your money and we'll run him again.' The fella backed down. He'd intimidated Bill Rowe but he didn't intimidate ol' Ben." Payne said he was glad Ben stuck to his guns that King Bee had won the race. "I had sold my milk check and I took it and bet it all on King Bee. My friend said 'you ought not to' and I said, 'whatever ol' Ben did I was on his side. King Bee won.'

"Ben'd bet on anything," Dallas Poteet said.

" He was a gamblin'est fella ya ever saw," Payne recalled. "I don't care what you could do and they have about 40 men working Chapman Barnard and Ben would bet you that there's one of them beat you at whatever you could do. A guy named John Barhan told me that him and Ben were close at that time.

"One day Ben asked John, 'You got any money?' John said, 'Uh yeah.' Ben said, 'Give it to me. They're starting a crap game.' Ben won enough to win a wagon and he and John hauled pipe to the oil fields."[30]

It is hard to say which trait about Ben Johnson is best remembered - his boundless exuberance and friendliness; his rodeo championships, his leadership skills managing a crew of wild and wooly cowboys during his years as a foreman of the Chapman Barnard Ranch; his square dancing or his luck at gambling.

By the early 1920s, Ben's speed and skill at steer roping was already legendary. He won big prize money competing in steer roping at a time when organized rodeo was in its infancy.

He competed throughout the west, in rodeos big and small, and in 1922 won Cheyenne Frontier Days, which at the time was considered the rodeo world's championship. He won it again in 1923 and 1926 and seemed destined to do so for years to come.[31]

At the time there were no horse trailers, so cowboys had to ship their horses by train in boxcars fitted with stalls. A group of cowboys would load their horses onto a boxcar and leave one of their group with the horses to care for them. The other cowboys would pile into a Model T truck, and later a Model A, and drive to the rodeo.[32]

Ben toured the rodeo circuit with Barton Carter, Ike Rude, Irby Mundy and Bright Drake, all Osage County, Oklahoma cowboys.

By the 1930s, horse trailers were in use and the men would pull the trailer behind a Model A roadster, lashing their saddles to the hood of the car. They traveled the rodeo circuit as far east as Memphis, Tennessee and as far south as Mesquite, Texas, and every rodeo in the Midwest they could reach, including Dodge City, Kansas and the enormous Dewey, Oklahoma Roundup.[33]

A photo of Ben and his rodeo compadres, circa late 1920s thankfully contains the names of the cowboys written next to them, saving for posterity their identities. Some names are blurred, and beside these the author has noted with a question mark. They are Gary Schultz, Eddie Burgess, Ed Sublette, Tommy Grimes, Gary (?), Henry Grammar, Red Carter, Jeff McCall (?) and Frank Prue. In this photo Ben is wearing a dark shirt, buttoned to the neck in traditional cowboy fashion, and dark pants. Most of the other cowboys are dressed nattily in suits and many are wearing ties. He and his fellow cowboys would soon eschew the suits for white shirts, khaki pants stuffed into their boots, but the ties would remain. Indeed, it wasn't until the 1940s that rodeo cowboys stopped wearing white shirts and neckties while competing.

"They wore khaki pants tucked into boots and those smaller roper-style cowboy hats," Nita Jones, Sol Salmon's daughter, said. "Dad never wore the tie as much as the other cowboys as he was a bull rider and a bronc rider – and never any flowery shirts. He liked long boots though. He had fun with those. Plus he liked nice belts and big buckles."[34]

Two photos exist of Ben when he won the 101 Ranch Rodeo at the legendary ranch in Ponca City, Ok. He is nattily dressed in khaki pants, a white shirt and tie and his trademark roper's cowboy hat as he accepts his winning pin from Hugo Milde.

In 1927, Ben set the world's record in steer roping at the Pendelton, Oregon Roundup, roping and tying his three steers in an average of 18 seconds.[35]

An interesting article about Ben's rodeo career appears in the May 1941 issue of *The Ranchman*. Rodeo commentator Fog Horn Clancy recalls watching Ben compete. He tells of how he liked to watch Ben, but "I got a bigger kick out of watching his wife while Ben was roping. She could qualify as America's number one roping rooter when her hubby was dabbling a loop on a steer or calf. Ben used to park his car next to the arena where she could watch him work without leaving the car, Mrs. Johnson used to stand upon the fender while Ben was roping, and no Osage, Chickasaw, Seminole or any other breed of Indian were able to put more action in to a stamp or war dance than Mrs. Johnson put in to that dance she always did on the fender of the car as Ben roped in the arena."[36]

While Clancy's article doesn't use a name other than "Mrs. Johnson," it is clear from the time line that this was during Ben's marriage to Ollie Workmon. By the time Ben was married to second wife, Aileen, he was no longer competing in rodeos.

Ben had become a rodeo star, known throughout the west, and at home in Oklahoma he was treated as a local hero. Small town newspapers never failed to mention his comings and goings and those of his relatives, including his brother Ralph, who was assistant postmaster in Tulsa. One article even mentions, "his mother, Mrs. Annie Johnson, lives at 1224 North Elwood Avenue, Tulsa."[37]

On June 16, 1923, Ben's cowboy pal Henry Grammar was killed in a car wreck near Shidler, Ok. Grammar was a colorful figure, casually moving from one side of the law to the other. He was reputed to be a quick-draw artist, robber and gunman, but he was also a top hand with cattle and horses.

Holton Payne recalled that Grammar was found dead in a car accident.

The Ponca City News reported that "Grammar was killed when a motor car in which he was returning home from Shidler turned turtle when it struck a sharp curve in the road just west of DeNoya. John Mayo of Osage county was driving the machine and his wife was an occupant. Both Mayo and his wife were thrown clear of the car but Grammar was pinned beneath, his body being crushed. Mayo and his wife reported held by Shidler authorities for investigation."[38]

There was much controversy over Grammar's death because there was a suspicious hole in his back at the time of death that could have been a bullet hole.[39]

Grammar was notorious in his day, a colorful, gun-toting cowboy who was somewhat dangerous. He was a top hand at the 101 Ranch Wild West Shows and toured Europe, playing for King Edward of England, Kaiser Wilhelm of German and other European royalty.[40]

CHAPTER TWO
BEN SETTLES DOWN

Little is known about Ben's courtship with Ollie Workmon. The daughter of John David Workmon and his wife, Cynthia Myriah ne' Hendrickson, who was called Mae.[1] Ollie had two sisters, Emma and Elizabeth, and two brothers, Ruben and Will.[2]

The photos of Ollie from that time period show that she was a small woman with thick, dark hair and expressive brown eyes. She had high cheekbones and a wide forehead, and a wide nose and full, sensuous lips. Many old-timers in Osage County remember her as having Osage blood, which her appearance tends to support. She was a markedly striking, indeed earthy woman.

Ben married Ollie at a small family gathering on May 5, 1917 in Tulsa. The ceremony was officiated by Lewis D. Barton, a Methodist minister. The ceremony was likely held in Tulsa because most of Ben's family lived there. The couple settled in Foraker, in close proximity to the Drummond and Chapman Barnard Ranches, where Ben worked.

A photo exists from the 1920s of Ben and Ollie. It is a formal portrait, taken in the fashion of the time in a studio. Ben is seated in a heavy wooden armchair, nattily dressed in a three-piece suit and a bow tie. He is wearing custom-made cowboy boots and his pants are tucked into them. Ollie is wearing an open-collar dress popular in the 1920s. She is sitting on the right arm of the chair. They look happy and somewhat prosperous. Another family photo from the 1920s of Ollie and her children is also a formal portrait. In it, Ollie sits to the right of Son. Daughter Mary, called "Sis," stands in front. Ollie's thick hair is cut short, just below her ears. Her dark eyes stare straight at the camera, a languid look. Son and Sis look off to their right, most likely looking at the photographer. Son is dressed in a suit and bow tie. Sis is wearing a dress with ruffled collar and ruffled shoulders. Her hair is cut chin length with straight bangs, a style popularized by film star Constance Moore at the time.[3]

The son who would be called Son and would one day become even more famous than his famous father was born Francis Benjamin Johnson, Jr. on June 13, 1918 in the tiny hamlet of Foraker.

Ollie was at home and the hospital in Pawhuska was too far to drive as Model T's had trouble navigating the primitive dirt roads. When she went into labor, Ollie sent Ben off to find an old Osage woman who lived nearby. The woman, whose name is lost to history, was well-known as a mid-wife and she came and assisted Ollie in giving birth.

The young Johnson was immediately dubbed "Son."

Ben was gone from home a lot during Son's first thirteen years. Between rodeoing throughout the west and cowboying throughout the Tall Grass Prairie, Ben came home usually one day a week – Saturday – the day all the cowboys came to town. Sunday, Ben would spend some time with Ollie and his small family and then rush back to work.

Ben's marriage to Ollie was strained from the beginning. Ben never sat still long enough to be a devoted husband to Ollie and his absences were lengthy.

In 1924, they divorced.[4]

The legend of Ben Johnson has it that Ben was fond of the ladies during his rodeo days, straining and eventually breaking the bonds of his marriage to Ollie.

Ben had been cowboying on many of the large ranches, but his main employer at the time was the Chapman Barnard Ranch. It had nearly 72,000 acres of deeded land, and another 28,000 acres of leased land, for a total of over 100,000 acres. Dale Christenson recalled that the number was 101,000 acres, which was widely reported at the time, but many believe that this number was often stated out of a sense of competition with the Miller Brothers 101 Ranch, which was located to the west of Chapman Barnard near Ponca City, Oklahoma.[5]

The Chapman Barnard Ranch was owned by James A. Chapman and Horace G. Barnard. Chapman had made his money in the oil business. Barnard was a well-respected rancher. Their partnership produced one of the most successful cattle ranches in Oklahoma history. During World War II, the ranch was a major supplier of beef to the country, and instrumental in the war effort.

The best anyone can remember, Ben Johnson was promoted to foreman of the Chapman Barnard Ranch sometime in late 1929 or early 1930.

As much as Ben had made a name for himself in the rodeo world with his three world championships in 1922, 1923 and 1926, and his many victories at rodeos throughout the west, he was also highly in demand for his ranching skills.

The Chapman Barnard Ranch wanted to lock in Ben's employment. He was so respected for both his ranch skills and his people skills that he was clearly the best man for the job.

There was just one problem - he was prone to run off and start rodeoing whenever he got the itch.

Ben was offered the job with one hitch - he could not rope competitively. He had to quit roping steers in rodeos if he wanted the plum job.

With the advent of the Great Depression and economic insecurity the worst in U.S. history, Ben took the manager's post without hesitation, giving up any further glory as a rodeo competitor. He did so without so much as a hint of reservation.

With such respect and admiration from the cowboys, their wives and children, the ranch owners, the cattle buyers, indeed nearly everyone with whom he had daily contact, Ben Johnson was the perfect choice for manager of the Chapman Barnard Ranch. He was the largest larger-than-life cowboy in a world of larger-than-life cowboys.

"He never asked anyone to do anything he wouldn't do himself," Helen said. "If he wanted you to do a job, he'd be right in there with you."[6]

Chapman needed Ben Johnson as his manager. Noted for his brusque, often rude manner, Chapman needed a ranch manager who people respected – and liked.

"Mr. Chapman was short-tempered," Leon "Puny" Martin, Chapman's driver, recalled. Conversely, Ben was "a good guy to work for. He never met a stranger."[7]

Ben was a task master who got a full days work out of his men. He had a rule that each day after breakfast, he'd join the cowboys at the horse trap and he would choose their mounts for them. This was because the cowboys had favorite horses they liked to ride – usually the better broke horses who didn't pitch as many fits and buck as much. Ben knew that this meant the green-broke horses with lesser training – and the meaner horses – weren't getting as much work and experience. Ben wanted the rougher horses rode so they'd get gentler with more handling.

"Ben'd point out the horses he wanted each cowboy to ride," rancher Frederick Drummond recalled. "He made sure that rough string got rode. I tell you, it was like a rodeo, roping, bucking, dust flying, horses squealing."[8]

Ben rode those rough horses, too. He'd pick out a mean one for himself and ride it to a standstill. He never shirked hard work even when he was foreman. Indeed, he went out of his way to do even the most menial task – leading by example.

"Ben had an unwritten rule that all of the men knew," Frederick Drummond said. "Ben'd always open the first gate, that way the cowboys would open all the other gates." Drummond said he saw this occur when he was a young man, and he adopted that practice for his ranch.

"I tried to do the same thing for 47 years," Drummond said. "I learned that from Ben."[9]

Ranch life was fraught with risks.

Oliver Knuckles, known as 'Knuck,' worked for more than 30 years at the ranch. He recalled one heavy snowstorm that caught a crew of hands out in the dangerous winter weather.

"I remember the month of January in 1946. We had terrible weather that month. We lived down at Blackland southwest of headquarters. We went out to feed that morning and it was starting to sleet. We had to feed with a wagon and team in those days. We started in the north Blackland pasture. By the time we got to the Reed, there was two inches of snow on the ground. The snow had increased to about five inches when I and Har' (Johnson) finished feeding the calves in the West Daily Pasture. When we got to the East Daily the cattle were walking in the storm. The snow flakes were so big the cattle could hardly walk through the snow. ... Anyway, by then the snow was too deep. We had to turn the horses loose because they couldn't pull the wagon. We couldn't get back to the house, either, so we built a great big fire.

"The next morning... we started out walking. The snow was three or four feet deep, and we could just barely see the tops of the fence posts. We followed the fence until we got to the railroad and then followed it home.

"When we got back to the house, my wife had a fire built in the cook stove, but she didn't have one going in the other room. The snow had blown through the cracks in the walls and the divan was completely covered with snow. My wife was afraid the snow would all melt if she lit the stove.

"Since we didn't have a phone, we had to go to the railroad station to call. The man there would call the dispatcher in Muskogee who would get a hold of Ben Johnson, the ranch foreman. We finally got through to Ben and told him that six of the crew men were lost in the snow storm. He told us that there wasn't anything we could do.

"We found all but one of those men. We couldn't find a Montana cowboy named Joel. He finally came back though. Har' and me were out splitting wood one day when we saw someone walking along the railroad. About 30 or 45 minutes later, he came walking up to the house. He had made himself a bed down in a ditch and spent a couple of nights there with his coon dog," Knuck said.[10]

Oscar Wright recalled that prairie fires were a constant threat. The Chapman Barnard Ranch was at the forefront of prairie fire control efforts, including the use of controlled burns, where prairie grass was intentionally burned to lessen the growth of grasses that could fuel a catastrophic fire.

To start these fires, the cowboys developed a surefire way.

"We'd take gunny sacks with soaked kerosene oil, light them and they'd become fire balls and we'd drag them behind horses," Wright said. "We'd drag them five miles before they burned out."[11]

Working for Chapman Barnard was hard work, and keeping both Chapman and Barnard happy was a full-time job. Many a day with the boss turned into an incident that resulted in a humorous tale told for decades to come.

Chapman and Barnard were both tight wads, counting their books to the penny. Chapman never learned how to drive. He kept Leonard "Puny" Martin on the payroll as his driver for years.

One day when Puny was not at the wheel, a load of 1,700 heifers was delivered from the King Ranch in Texas. Chapman wanted to see the heifers so Ben was pressed into dual service as foreman and chauffeur. Oliver Knuckles came along for ride down to the pens to see the heifers as they were unloaded from the train. Ben drove Chapman's station wagon.

When they arrived to inspect the herd, they saw that one heifer had somehow gotten her hoof stuck in a pipe collar.

"We knew we couldn't just walk up to her and take it off of her foot, so Mr. Chapman said, 'We'll run her awhile and wear her out and then, Knuck, you reach out there and knock her down with this ballpeen hammer,'" Knuck said.

"Back then, every car came with a tool kit, and there was this hammer in it. We were supposed to get out there on the running board and get that heifer down," Knuck said.

To the surprise of both Ben and Knuck, Chapman decided he'd drive the station wagon while the two men tried to knock the heifer down.

"Mr. Chapman was going to drive while Ben and I took care of the heifer," Knuck said. "There was only one bad thing about the whole set up. Mr. Chapman had never touched a steering wheel in his life. So when he got to the edge of the hill, Mr. Chapman just kept on driving. Ben and I got that heifer down and got the pipe collar off her foot when Mr. Chapman came walking up the hill. When Ben asked Mr. Chapman why he didn't stop before he went over the hill, Mr. Chapman replied, 'That's what I've got you for, you're the driver.'"

Knuck was sent back for a team of mules to pull the car out of the ditch while Chapman caught a ride back to the headquarters with a ranch hand's daughter.

Ben and Knuck used mules to pull the car out of the ditch, but the radiator had sprung a leak during the mishap. "We filled the radiator with water using Ben's hat. He drove the car and I drove the team back..." Knuck said.

Knuck said the next day Chapman's only comment about the incident was "'this is the last time something like this is going to happen."[12] Cowboy Oscar Wright recalled an incident years later when Son decided to repeat his father's stunt and bulldogged a steer from a moving car.[13] Son would often set out to repeat his father's deeds, a pattern that would continue throughout his life.

In 1932, Ben was talked into turning his popularity into a political career. It seemed a likely path for him to take, and his reluctance to enter the seamy world of politics was balanced with his desire to benefit the community.

He qualified as a Democrat and ran for the office, but it was a short-lived campaign. He lost to Dick Conner, who received 3767 votes to Ben's 2188 votes. Conner ended up serving as sheriff for a decade. Ben was openly glad when it was over and he'd lost.[14]

"Ben Johnson was friendly with everyone and always wore a broad smile, except once when he ran for sheriff," Paul McGuire recalled. "He had a picture taken without even a grin. Ben wasn't elected sheriff only because of some unpopular backers that he wouldn't disown, but he was runner-up in a field of seven candidates some of whom are still campaigning for the office. The children have always been happy that he stayed out of politics although he might have gone a long way had he been interested in making another try for a different office. He had more friends than any man in the county."[15]

CHAPTER THREE
THE SON OF THE FATHER

Son began life as any typical Oklahoma kid of his day amongst his peers – the kids of local ranchers, farmers and their hired help. He was a typically inquisitive kid, but rather shy and reserved – especially at school.

"I was always afraid the kids would laugh at me if I couldn't answer the teacher's questions," Son said.[1] When he was young, he fell and broke his left arm. The bone wasn't set correctly. When he began competing in rodeos as an adult, he believed his left arm hampered his performance and cost him valuable seconds. He never discussed the matter until late in life.[2]

Son grew up aware of his father's reputation as a mythic hero, a rodeo champion and leader of men. It was something he had to contend with early on.

"I felt defeated because I couldn't produce what was expected of me."[3]

All that changed when Son became the target of a bully.

"Icem Stumbull, the biggest bully in our school who was forever runnin' over all the smaller ones, hit me in the school auditorium in front of 200 or 300 kids, busting open my head and embarrassing me pretty bad. And I just couldn't take it. After that I had one thought in mind, and that was to destroy. I laid for Icem, plottin' for a way to kill him. I succeeded in almost literally doin' so a few days later. While Icem was in the hospital, every day word came to our house, 'Icem took a turn for the worse,' or 'he may not live.' Just hearing that did somethin' to me. I learned that if somebody flies off the handle so he wants to kill somebody, that's pretty bad. And then I started to straighten up and be somebody. And it was fortunate thing. Otherwise, I might have ended up in prison or someplace worse."[4]

Growing up amongst cowboys in the middle of the tall grass prairie was a life of hard work in the outdoors. But it was also a life of mythic proportions. It was the true cowboy existence. Working cattle, riding bucking horses, fixing fences, harvesting and hauling hay – all of this was hard work.

Boys grew to manhood quickly.

Son began working for Ben on the Chapman Barnard Ranch at 11 years of age.[5] He was hired to work cattle and he spent many a day riding through the thick bluestem grasses of the Osage prairie looking for strays.[6] He also learned to ride broncs and train horses. Ben showed Son no favoritism. He required Son to work just as hard as the other men. Period.

And Ben worked hard. He never lead his men from on high. He was right there with hem. After his divorce from Ollie, Ben threw himself into his work as foreman of the Chapman Barnard Ranch and lived on the ranch full-time.

He followed his usual pattern of working all week and then coming to town on Saturday for the rodeos, match races, square dancing and socializing with the ladies. Then, he fell in love.

No one knows for sure when Ben met the lovely Aileen Vinsant, but she would become his second wife.

She was one of ten children born to Willie Davis Vinsant and her husband, Othello Moreno Vinsant.

Born Sarah Aileen Vinsant in Crawford County, Arkansas on September 16, 1906, she was called Aileen, or Allie.

The Vinsant family moved to the Pawhuska area in the spring of 1926. Othello Vinsant worked for a local dairy and farmed sweet potatoes on a small patch of land he'd purchased. The Vinsant brood made an immediate impression in the Pawhuska schools. There were so many of them that none of the local kids picked on them, as the fear of reprisal from the entire Vinsant contingent was considerable. That said, the Vinsant kids were known as good, respectable children who did well in school and excelled in sports.[7]

Sometime in late 1936 or early 1937, Aileen Vinsant caught Ben's eye. She was a vivacious, chestnut-haired beauty, and she worked as a registered nurse at Pawhuska Hospital.

They had a whirlwind courtship and were married on June 16, 1937 in Kay County, Oklahoma. Ben applied for the marriage license earlier that day, listing his age as 41 and Aileen's as 30. He listed his home town as Foraker, Oklahoma and Aileen's as Pawhuska. He wrote that his father was "Jim Johnson" and that

Aileen's father was "O.M. Vinsant." The application was accepted by deputy clerk B.B. Snouffer and court clerk O.E. Hodges. Later that day the Rev. L.L. Roberts of the Newkirk Christian Church married Ben and Aileen in the presence of Mrs. M. Walker and Mrs. L.L. Roberts, both of Newkirk, Oklahoma.[8]

It is unknown if the newlyweds had a honeymoon, but it is unlikely, considering it was the height of the summer ranching season and Ben was foreman of the enormous Chapman Barnard Ranch. One thing is certain, contemporaneously with their marriage they conceived their first child – and she would arrive in a most dramatic way.

A brutal February blizzard slammed northern Oklahoma, covering the ground with thick, hard-packed snow. The incessant prairie winds blew deep drifts over the fences, vehicles, pastures and dirt roads, and the people of the Osage prairie hunkered down to ride it out.

Ben and Aileen were living at their ranch near the Chapman Barnard Ranch, roughly 20 miles from Pawhuska.

As the blizzard raged outside, Aileen suddenly doubled over with labor cramps. Her due date was three weeks to a month away, but Aileen was certain she was in labor. Ben realized he had to get Aileen to the hospital. The only way to get there was via the snow-covered dirt roads. Ben bundled Aileen up and put her in a ranch truck and rustled up a handful of cowboys, who donned heavy coats and climbed into the back of the truck. They headed out into the blinding blizzard, stopping often so Ben and the cowboys could bail out and shovel drifts out of the road by hand. It took hours, but Ben and his cowboys saw Aileen safely to Pawhuska Hospital – more than 20 miles away.

Helen Lee Johnson was born on February 22, 1938. She was a mere two and a half pounds at birth. Doctors and nurses worked feverishly to keep the tiny girl alive. Ben called her his "sparrow," as she was so tiny the doctors could hold her in one hand. The nurses used to bring Helen to the window for Ben to see her, carrying her in their hands on a swatch of cotton.

Helen stayed at Pawhuska Hospital for three months as she grew strong enough to leave and venture out into the world.[9]

She was taken home to live with Ben and Aileen sometime in early May, 1938. For a brief time Son and Sis came to stay with them, a move prompted by the fact that Ollie had married Francis Watkins, a man Son did not like. Indeed, Helen Johnson stated years later that Son thereafter dropped his first name of Francis completely, and referred to himself only as Ben Johnson, Jr.[10]

The Johnson household settled in and Helen grew ever stronger. Before long she was a perky toddler, getting into everything.

Aileen discovered early in 1939 that she and Ben were pregnant with her second child. Sadly, tragedy soon struck.

Aileen Johnson was in the early stages of her second pregnancy when she developed an infection.[11]

The infection was incurable, as there were no antibiotics at the time.

Aileen was rushed to Pawhuska Hospital and died on July 28, 1939. The death certificate states that Aileen died of septicemia and "partial abortion."[12] While the records no longer exist, the indication is Aileen had a spontaneous miscarriage and failed to expel the fetus, resulting in a severe pelvic infection which took her life.

Ben was devastated. For the first time in his storied life, the familiar Ben Johnson grin and effervescent personality were not on display.

The funeral was held at 4 p.m. on a windswept Saturday, August 4, 1939 at Johnson Funeral Home Chapel. The Rev. J.B. Cooprider conducted the service. Ben solemnly buried his wife on the grassy hillside at Pawhuska City Cemetery.

The shock of losing Aileen was numbing. And it put Ben in a pickle. He had a toddler daughter to raise, and no wife to help him. A single dad responsible for running an enormous cattle ranch, Ben had to find someone to take care of Helen.

Helen had several caretakers after Aileen's death, women who worked at the Chapman Barnard and the wives of cowboys at the ranch. She eventually went to live with John and Nora Mounts and their six daughters. Helen said years later that she was treated as "the seventh Mounts daughter."

When Helen married Dale Christenson on March 18, 1956, John Mounts gave her away.[13]

Son stayed with Ben and worked alongside him on the Chapman Barnard Ranch. By this time he was a strapping 20 year old, the spitting image of his father. The difference between Son and his father was

Son dreamed of making a lot of money, and working as a cowboy for $1 a day was not going to make that happen. While Ben loved his life in the Osage prairie, Son dreamed of more.

"My dad and Son looked quite alike," Helen Johnson Christenson recalled. "My dad and Son were very genuine in that the 'affected personality' probably would not have enjoyed being around either of them for a long period of time. There was not one iota of put-on to either of them. What you saw was what you got. That may have been one of the reasons Son chose to live his life pretty solitary and outside the presence of Hollywood scene. They both had magnetic personalities, but for different reasons."[14]

"Uncle Ben and Ol' Ben were a whole lot similar except that Ol' Ben was a lot more outgoing," Ben's grandson and Son's nephew John Miller said. "Uncle Ben didn't stand on the street corner laughing out loud. He was quite a bit more reserved than Ol' Ben. Ol' Ben was a take charge guy, he wanted to be the main cog in the wheel and Uncle Ben didn't necessarily want to have everything rely on his shoulder.

"I have a feeling he was ready to do something else than work for his father," Miller said. "I just sense that. He never said anything, just he put things in perspective. Also, it had to be a problem trying to live up to daddy's standard. And, also, he had too much ambition to be a $3 a day cowboy."[15]

CHAPTER FOUR
A BILLIONAIRE STEPS IN AND CHANGES HISTORY

The legend of Ben Johnson contains the story that Son arrived in Hollywood in 1940, yet he is found in cast lists for films made in 1939. This conflicting information stems from numerous articles and interviews with Son which recite that at some point in 1940, Son went to work on reclusive billionaire Howard Hughes' pet project, a movie called *The Outlaw*. Son clarified the time line in a 1993 television interview, confirming that in fact he went to Hollywood in 1939 when Hughes bought horses from the Chapman Barnard Ranch for the film and Son went with them.[1]

"They shipped those horses by train. Someone had to feed and water them and see that they got there all right. I came to Hollywood in a box car with that load of horses for Howard Hughes," Son said.[2]

Son's arrival in Hollywood was heralded by a tremendous thunderstorm. He was to deliver the horses to Fat Jones. In the heyday of Hollywood Westerns, the studios needed an inexhaustible supply of horses and there were two stables that supplied the bulk of them – Fat Jones' Stables and Hudkins Brothers Stables. Jones' ranch was located in the eastern San Fernando Valley near the hamlet of Sun Valley. Hudkins was located in Burbank, a stone's throw from Warner Brother Studios.[3]

Fat Jones was actually Clarence Y. Jones, and his stable was located at 11340 Sherman Way, North Hollywood, California. For years his business card was a colorful illustration of a stagecoach and horses with the words "Fat Jones Stables, Inc." in letters that look like wood logs. The phone number, 765-0795 was printed at the bottom. Fat Jones ran his movie horse stable from 1912 until his death in 1962. The stable was initially located in Edenville, now Silverlake, near the Mixville studio set up by Tom Mix. In the 1920s, the stables moved to the northern edge of North Hollywood, right at the border of the suburb of Sun Valley.[4]

Carol Elaine Jones, Fat Jones' daughter, met her future husband on the day that Hughes' horses arrived.

"It was raining hard that day, so we drove right up to the track to keep from getting wet. They slung the train door open and here's this guy running back and forth telling those hands what to do and giving orders. I asked my friend who that guy was. He acted like he owned the railroad," Carol recalled.[5] "I didn't like him then. He acted like a big shot. But, when I got to know him, I thought he was gorgeous!"[6]

When Son arrived in Hollywood, he and Hughes hit it off. Not known for socializing or making friends,

Hughes liked Son and decided to keep him around – on the payroll as a wrangler.

Son's pay for this work was $175.00 a week, a large sum in 1940 and more than quadruple his monthly pay as a working cowboy.[7] "I was making $30 a month at the ranch. The first week I was out there, I made $175. I wasn't very smart, but I knew that was worth more than $30 so I just stayed with it."[8] "I thought I got rich in a hurry," Son said.[9]

Son recalled that Hughes "was a great guy. Seemed like he was a little afraid of people. He'd get away from the office and come over and visit me once in a while."[10] Son said Hughes was clearly unhappy. "He was always a very lonely guy," Son said. "A prime example of where money didn't make a man happy. He used to sneak off and come and look at the horses when nobody would know about it."[11]

One day Son was training horses for *The Outlaw* when Gary Cooper came by to visit Hughes, bringing with him noted director Howard Hawks. Cooper, who grew up on a Montana ranch and was a real-life cowboy, and Hawks, a director known for his machismo, took a liking to Son and decided to vouch for Son's application to the Screen Actor's Guild. The three men signed letters of recommendation for Son's admission to the guild.[12]

Son realized that working for Hughes left him plenty of free time. His status as a wrangler of movie horses put him in contact with other movie cowboys, many of whom worked as stuntmen. This led to Son's first job on camera, as a stunt double in a George O'Brien western called *The Fighting Gringo*, which was made

Richard D. Jensen

in 1939. O'Brien was a muscular leading man popular with audiences for his easy-going charm and better-than-average acting skills. Long before bodybuilding became a popular sport and decades before Steve Reeves made a name for himself in Hercules movies and Arnold Schwarzenegger became a movie icon, O'Brien was the first true adonis of film, and he worked mainly in Westerns. He had started out as a crew member in Tom Mix westerns in the 1920s, where he met fellow Irishman John Ford, who directed several of Mix's most popular films.

Ford chose O'Brien over Mix for his 1924 masterpiece *The Iron Horse*, launching the charismatic O'Brien's career as a leading man.

When Son reported to work at Iverson's Ranch in Chatsworth, California for *The Fighting Gringo*, he met O'Brien, and found him to be a congenial man. O'Brien would later become a valuable conduit to Ford and to one of Ford's proteges - John Wayne. In addition to his stunt scenes, Son was given the part of a Mexican bar patron, an uncredited background role. Lupita Tovar, a famous Mexican actress known for her work in the acclaimed 1932 Spanish version of *Dracula*, played the lover, Nita.

One interesting tidbit: Also working on the film were Hank Bell and Sid Jordan. Bell was a short, feisty cowboy with a huge, drooping handlebar mustache and the inspiration for the cartoon character Yosemite Sam. Bell had worked with Tom Mix on dozens of films, where he met O'Brien, then a crew member. Sid Jordan was one of Tom Mix's closest friends. Jordan was from Dewey, Oklahoma, a stone's throw from

Son's hometown of Pawhuska. Jordan had served with Mix when both were lawmen in Oklahoma. Jordan followed Mix into the movies, helping Mix develop his famous stunt-laden films.

The Fighting Gringo was released on August 8, 1939.

Immediately after finishing his work with O'Brien, Son was hired to stunt-double Charles Starrett, who would become legendary in B Westerns. Indeed, Son doubled Starrett for the initial film of the series known as *The Durango Kid*. The musical act in the film was the Sons of the Pioneers, the cowboy musical group that rose to prominence along with Roy Rogers. The group was popular and found work in dozens of B Westerns and in John Ford's A Westerns. *The Durango Kid* was released on August 15, 1940 and was followed by a string of sequels over the following decade.

CHAPTER FIVE
STUNTMAN AND MOVIE COWBOY

Working as a movie wrangler and nascent stuntman gave Son a sense of a future. He was making more money than he could have dreamed possible when he was a ranch hand in Oklahoma – and now he was in love.

On August 31, 1941, Son and Carol Jones married. Their marriage would last 53 years until Carol's death in 1994.

Life for the Johnsons was a daily routine of horses, movies and stunt work. The Jones and Johnson contingents were providing most of the horses to the Hollywood studios for their Westerns. And Hollywood was in its second decade of the B Western craze. B Westerns were those hour-long matinee features, designed to fill the theaters all day on Saturday with kids while moms went shopping.

War was raging in Europe, but America had stayed out, uneasily standing on the sidelines as the nation supplied the English with ammunition and materiel to fight the Nazi onslaught.

The die was cast for the United States on December 7, 1941 when the Japanese attacked Pearl Harbor Navy Base in Hawaii and destroyed America's Pacific Fleet. The declaration of war by President Franklin D. Roosevelt resulted in the enlistment of many able-bodied men.

Patriotic and full of vigor, Son joined many Hollywood cowboys at the enlistment station. Gene Autry had signed up, as had James Stewart and Glenn Ford. Clark Gable would soon follow, as would Robert Montgomery and many others. Son tried to enlist, but he was declared 4-F due to flat feet. Also, Son's left arm had some limited range of motion, the result of the bad break which was set improperly when he was a child. Additionally, Son had a weak right ankle, which had been injured many times while doing ranch and, later, stunt work.

Helen Johnson Christenson recalled that Son had expressed regret that he was declared 4-F because he had flat feet.[1]

As the American war effort got underway, Hughes took a long time preparing his new western because he wanted to showcase his new discovery, a buxom brunette named Jane Russell. When filming started sometime in 1942, in addition to his duties as a wrangler, Son was hired as a stuntman for *The Outlaw*. He worked alongside Richard Farnsworth, who was a reliable stuntman in Western movies for decades. Like Son, Farnsworth went on to become a highly regarded actor, and was nominated for a Best Supporting Actor

Oscar in 1978 for *Comes A Horseman* and for a Best Actor Oscar in 2000 for *Straight Story*.

Hughes was a hands-on director. For a billionaire who only dabbled in movie-making, Hughes was passionate about his movies – and his horses.

"That movie Hughes was making in Monument Valley, *The Outlaw*, had a scene where the government had rounded up something like 4,000 horses," Son said years later. " Well, Hughes owned this palomino stud named Cherokee Charlie, which he also used in that movie. He had an enormous insurance policy on that horse, and he said to me, 'When they start moving that herd, whatever you do, do not let Cherokee Charlie get into the middle of that bunch of horses.' Well, of course, as soon as the herd starts to run, the first thing that palomino does is start running toward the bunch, so I took off after it and roped it real fast. I'd been doing that all my life, but it imprinted on Hughes' mind so much that he became a pretty good friend of mine. He liked to come out and go riding with me all the time, and he'd roll up a hundred dollar bill and tuck it in my shirt pocket. I thought that was pretty good."[2]

There is a funny story about the first time Son saw actress Jane Russell on the set of *The Outlaw*. Son is rumored to have said to the assembled cowboys, "look at those tits!"[3] *The Outlaw* languished on the shelves of Hughes' film vault for seven years while censors insisted it was indecent. It wasn't released until June 13, 1948.

The Herculean national effort to win World War II brought with it an explosion of factory jobs.

Son's mother, Ollie and her new husband, Fred Rider, moved to California sometime in 1942 or 1943 to seek factory work. Son was working steadily in the movie business, and it seemed natural for Ollie and Fred to follow him there. Fred got a job as a machinist at Adell Precision and Ollie found work as a detail assembler at Lockheed, where she worked on P-38 fighter planes.[4]

In addition to the work, Ollie was able to bask in Son's association with Hollywood stars, and she was often seen accompanying Son and Carol to the movie studios and to various Hollywood premieres and parties.[5]

In late 1942 Son doubled for Russell Hayden in *Riders of the Northwest Mounted*, a B Western. Hayden had gained fame playing Hopalong Cassidy's sidekick in the mid and late 1930s. He went on to star in his own features and then star and produce some of the earliest Western television shows. The film featured a rare appearance on screen by the famous Texas swing music band of Bob Wills and the Texas Playboys. The film was shot on location at Big Bear Lake, California and contains some great action and beautiful scenery.

Riders of the Northwest Mounted was released on February 15, 1943.

Making a name for himself as a Western movie stunt double, Son was hired to double Tom Tyler in the popular Three Mesquiteers series at Republic Studios. His first film for the series was *Riders of the Rio Grande* (1943). Stunt legend Yakima Canutt, himself a rodeo champion and who, along with John Wayne, invented the modern style of film fisticuffs, appeared in the film as a deputy. Son would work with Canutt many times over the years, and would be there when Canutt worked on his last film, *Breakheart Pass* (1975). *Riders of the Rio Grande* was released on May 21, 1943.

Son went from that production to another Republic film entitled *Bordertown Gun Fighters* (1943), starring Gordon Elliott, popularly known by fans as "Wild Bill" Elliott. Son doubled for Elliott in the dangerous stunts, though Elliott did most of his own riding. A real cowboy like Son, Elliott didn't need someone to do his riding for him, so Son was given a bit part as a messenger.

It was Son's first time uttering a line on film.

In the script, Son was to gallop up on his horse, dismount and run into an office and say the line, "I have a telegram for you from the United States Treasury Department."

Son was terrified, and he recalled. "I studied that line for eight days and eight nights, and then muffed it. I messed up the shot about three times before I could remember my line," Son said.[6]

Bordertown Gun Fighters was released on July 8, 1943.

Son next found work at Universal, doubling for singing cowboy Tex Ritter in *Arizona Trail* (1943). Nearly 30 years later, the two men would be in contention for the coveted role of Sam the Lion in *The Last Picture Show*, a role for which Son would win the Oscar. Ritter got along well with Son, as both men had grown up in the hardscrabble world of ranching in the Great Plains.

Also doubling on that film was veteran stuntman Cliff Lyons, who worked steadily on John Wayne films at Republic. Son would work with Lyons often thereafter.

From there Son went to low budget studio Monogram to stunt double in *Blazing Guns* (1943) a Trail Busters series western starring Ken Maynard and Hoot Gibson, two giant cowboy stars in the waning days of their careers. Maynard was a silent movie icon who was actually the first singing cowboy, even before Gene Autry, and Gibson was the second most popular cowboy star of the 1920s, surpassed only by Tom Mix. Gibson's films tended toward more humor than action. Like Son's dad, Gibson was a world champion rodeo cowboy and had cowboyed in Oklahoma along with Mix, later following Mix to Hollywood.

Son reported to Corriganville, the Western studio location in Simi Valley, California owned by cowboy star Ray "Crash" Corrigan. It is unclear whether he doubled either Maynard or Gibson, or merely doubled villains. As doubles are supposed to match the stars in build, and Son was lanky and both Maynard and Gibson had grown fat with old age, it is hard to tell. *Blazing Guns* was released on October 8, 1943.

Stepping away from Westerns, Son was then hired to do stunts at RKO for *Tarzan's Desert Mystery* (1943), starring the iconic Johnny Weissmuller. By this time Son had worked for most of the studios and was credible enough as a stuntman to get work in non-Western films, even if the film was shot in that very Western location of Alabama Hills in Lone Pine, California.

Richard D. Jensen

By this time the Tarzan series of films was in its second decade with Weissmuller as star. The former Olympic gold medalist had jumped from sports stardom to movie stardom as the King of the Jungle in 1932. The initial films in the series had been for MGM, but the studio dropped the contract when World War II broke out because more than half of the series' box office revenues had been from European theaters.[7]

Producer Sol Lesser, with RKO Studios, snapped up the contracts and immediately updated the Tarzan stories to contemporary times, including having Tarzan fight the Nazis in *Tarzan Triumphs* (1943), the first in the RKO Tarzan films. When Nazi agents try to kill Tarzan and kidnap his son, Tarzan grabs his knife and glowers, "Now, Tarzan make war!" Audiences throughout the United States rose to their feet and cheered Tarzan's assault on the Nazis in the film and it was used by the United States government as propaganda to provide encouragement to U.S. theater-goers.

The success of *Tarzan Triumphs* made an impression on Lesser, who immediately rushed into production a follow-up called *Tarzan Against the Sahara*. The film had Tarzan crossing the scorching desert and coming into conflict with a German spy and rushing to the aid of an American magician who is helping a sheik (Lloyd Corrigan). Problems arose during production when the producers tried to inject a budget-saving mess of stock footage into the film, including some science fiction footage of dinosaurs. Then Tarzan does battle with the Nazi spy and kills him by throwing him into the web of a giant spider. By the time the picture was finished, the film had been retitled *Tarzan and the Sheik* and then retitled again to *Tarzan's Desert Mystery*. Released on December 8, 1943, only 11 months after the release of *Tarzan Triumphs*, the film was panned by critics.[9] Still, it drew millions of kids to the cinema to watch their jungle hero whip the Nazis.

One of the most intriguing photos of Son's long career is the photo of him, dressed as an Arabian sheik, standing with Weissmuller. Son is young, his expression a little shy, as if he feels slightly out of place in a sheik's robes.

It's simply a great photo and a great piece of cinema history. This photo was long believed to be lost, but appears in the photo section of this book, published for the first time in over 60 years.

Son told a reporter in 1948 that the toughest stunt he ever did was when he stunt-doubled Weissmuller in the movie. "I was on a stair landing, 16 feet above an alleyway. With 35 head of loose wild horses comin' through, I jumped onto this one certain horse – to catch him, y'understand."[10]

Son did that jump in a loincloth, which is little protection for one's private parts, especially when one is landing on the withers of a running horse from 16 feet up. It is no small wonder that Son viewed this stunt as his toughest to date.

Stuntmen never look at whether or not a film is low budget or big budget. Work is work and Son had a strong work ethic, born of a desire to never work for $1 a day ever again. As soon as his stint with Tarzan was finished, Son reported to PRC Studios.

The lowest rung studio on the stretch of Gower Boulevard in Hollywood known as Poverty Row was

Richard D. Jensen

PRC. PRC stood for Producers' Releasing Corporation. The micro-studio, barely able to finance and release films, had somehow gotten a hold of two popular cowboy stars, Dave O'Brien and Tex Ritter.

O'Brien was a Texan, born David Fronabarger, who had come to Hollywood and worked as a stunt man before becoming an actor. He would later become a comedy writer and work on Red Skelton's Emmy Award-winning comedy show. Ritter was an authentic Texan and popular singing cowboy.

Son signed on to do stunts in *The Pinto Bandit* (1944), which was shot in Simi Valley, California at Corriganville. The film starred O'Brien, James Newill and Guy Wilkerson.

Son stunt-doubled and played the bit part of a mail race contestant. Son is clearly seen in this early screen appearance. He is tall, fresh-faced. He is dressed in black hat, a tan shirt, in an outfit often worn by Tex Ritter when Ritter worked for PRC. The king of budget cutters, PRC would reuse the footage of Son riding in future Tex Ritter films for the studio. Son is astride a bay horse with a star on its forehead and a snip on its nose. When the mail race starts, Son spurs his horse into a dead run, leaving co-star Guy Wilkerson and villain Jack Ingram in the dust. As the race continues, the contestants are shot close up from a camera car. The riders are at a dead run, and soon Son is clearly holding his horse back so as not to pass Wilkerson and Ingram. Later, when the crooked mail riders attack O'Brien and try to steal the mail bag, we clearly see Son charging in, trying to grab the mail bag. It is a terrific B Western chase sequence, and a wonderful early glimpse of Son in the earliest stages of his film career.

Kermit Maynard, brother of Ken, also did stunt work on the film, along with Bob Kortman, a film villain who appeared in hundreds of Westerns as far back as the early silent movies, including many with Tom Mix. *The Pinto Bandit* was released on April 27, 1944.

In 1944, Son's career took a serendipitous turn when he was hired to stunt double John Wayne in *Tall In The Saddle*. The film is one of Wayne's best early A Westerns, made only five years after Wayne became a major star in *Stagecoach* (1939). Wayne was just three years away from critical acclaim as a serious actor with a string of performances in Howard Hawk's *Red River* (1948) and John Ford's *She Wore A Yellow Ribbon* (1949).

Son reported to the set of *Tall In The Saddle* in Agoura Hills, California in April 1944. His job was to stunt double Wayne in some terrific action scenes. He was also given a bit part as a townsman. It was Son's first film working alongside Fred Graham, a stuntman who worked with Wayne for decades. They would work together often after that. Production was competed in June 1944.

Tall In the Saddle was released on September 29, 1944 and was a big hit.

After completing work on *Tall In the Saddle*, Son went back to Universal for stunt doubling Rod Cameron in *The Old Texas Trail* (1944), a run-of-the-mill film. It is interesting to note that in the cast of this film was silent movie icon William Desmond, now working in

Richard D. Jensen

character parts in Westerns. Further, Son again worked stunts with Cliff Lyons, one of John Wayne's favorite stuntmen.

Son then worked again with stuntman Fred Graham on *Nevada*, which starred a newcomer named Robert Mitchum, who had attracted the attention of producers while playing villains in Hopalong Cassidy Westerns at Paramount starring William Boyd. Mitchum would become a major movie star, with a career lasting four decades.

Also in the cast of *Nevada* was Guinn "Big Boy" Williams, a drinking buddy of John Wayne's, and a roistering he-man of an actor who was as strong as a bull and as affable as a puppy. Williams was known as an unstoppable freight train of a guy, a man who was unfazed by pain and unafraid of getting hurt. Years later, Williams was cast by Wayne in *The Alamo*, which was Wayne's pet project. During one of Williams' scenes, he was to ride into the Alamo to give a report to William Travis, played by British actor Laurence Harvey. When Williams rides into the shot, his horse unexpectedly rears, tossing Williams to the hard, west Texas ground. Williams merely stands up and continues the scene. Wayne left the sequence in the picture and it lends realism to the scene. Williams, like many he-man actors of the early days of movies, was unfazed by the incident. If such an event occurred today, most modern movie actors would insist on a trip to the doctor and a call to their lawyers, and production would likely shut down for weeks.

RKO released *Nevada* on Christmas Day, 1944. Studios release film on Christmas that they expect to be big hits. *Nevada* didn't disappoint.

After finishing *Nevada*, Son reported for work on *Corpus Christi Bandits* (1945) starring Allan "Rocky" Lane, who gained fame as Red Ryder and then went on to star in dozens of Republic Studio Westerns before becoming the voice of the talking horse in the Mister Ed television series. Son did stunts on the film while Tom Steele doubled Lane. Lane was a notorious ass, an egomaniac of grandiose proportions. One wonders how he and Son got along during filming, as Son detested self-important Hollywood types. *Corpus Christi Bandits* was released on April 20, 1945.

On May 7, 1945, Nazi Germany surrendered, ending the European theater of World War II. As victory celebrations erupted all across the nation, Hollywood prepared for a new era of prosperity. Some of Hollywood's biggest stars, Gene Autry, Clark Gable, James Stewart and Robert Montgomery to name a few, would soon return to the states and begin work on their new films. A sense of optimism began to take hold again.

After finishing *Corpus Christi Bandits*, Son was hired to stunt drive a horse and coach in a Bud Abbott and Lou Costello comedy called *The Naughty Nineties* (1945). The comic duo, known as "Abbott and Costello," was second in popularity only to Stan Laurel and Oliver Hardy. The raucous film also featured Joe Sawyer, a favorite film villain, silent movie icon William Desmond, and western favorite Rex Lease. It was released on July 6, 1945 and was yet another hit film for the beloved comedic duo.

Son immediately went to work on *Santa Fe Saddlemates* (1945), a Republic B Western starring Sunset Carson, the incredibly tall young cowboy star which Republic was grooming to take John Wayne's place in their B Western stable.

Carson was a genial fellow who could ride like the wind but couldn't act to save his life. Despite his lack of acting skills, audiences in the southern United States flocked to see his films. Once again, Son worked alongside Fred Graham. It is likely that the unaffected Carson got along well with Son. Rex Lease who had just worked with Son on the Abbott and Costello comedy, was also in the film. The film was released on June 2, 1945.

Son and Sunset's paths would cross often over the next 40 years at various functions, including Western movie festivals and charity events.

The Japanese empire surrendered on September 2, 1945 after the devastating nuclear bomb attacks by US bombers on Hiroshima and Nagasaki.

Jubilation erupted nationwide, and Americans breathed a sigh of relief now that the forces of tyranny were defeated.

Studios began making big plans to ramp up their output, and this included a steady stream of both A and B Westerns. For Son, this meant a wealth of opportunity for stunt work.

Republic Studios continued to groom Gordon "Wild Bill" Elliott as a new John Wayne for A pictures and the studio began beefing the budgets of his Red Ryder films, adding more production values. In just two years the studio would place Elliott in longer, big budget A films. In late 1945 Son was working hard at Republic, stunt doubling Elliott in the Red Ryder film *California Gold Rush* (1946), which co-starred Bobby Blake, who grew up and became a television icon under the name Robert Blake. Blake would later fall from grace when he was accused of murdering his wife. While acquitted of her murder, Blake was tarred by the media and left Hollywood to live in seclusion. Monte Hale, an actor who was best friends with Gene Autry and appeared in hundreds of Westerns, was also in the cast.

California Gold Rush was shot at Iverson Ranch in Chatsworth, California. The film was released on February 4, 1946.

Son jumped back into A Westerns with *Badman's Territory* (1946), starring Randolph Scott, an major star who was capable of carrying both Western and non-Western films. Scott rivaled John Wayne in popularity for over a decade. During the 1950s, Wayne was over-committed and hired Scott to take his place and star in *Seven Men From Now* (1956), considered one of the best Westerns ever made. (One wonders how that film would have been had Wayne played the lead role. It certainly would be a more famous film, as Scott retired from films in the early 1960s and modern movie fans don't know of him as well as they know of Wayne.)

In the late 1940s Scott was making a series of highly popular and highly profitable Westerns for producer Nat Holt, and *Badman's Territory* proved to be a hit with audiences.

Richard D. Jensen

The film is a who's who of cowboy stars and stuntmen, many of them former silent movie cowboy stars, including Kermit Maynard, Buddy Roosevelt, Tom Tyler and Neal Hart, and even silent movie comic icon Snub Pollard and the first-ever movie Tarzan, Elmo Lincoln. In the film, Son is a member of the posse accompanying the marshal played by Morgan Conway. He was even given a couple of lines of dialog. *Badman's Territory* was released on April 1, 1946.

By this time, Son was increasingly entrusted with small speaking parts. Within a year, he would get feature roles working for legendary director John Ford.

After working with Scott on *Badman's Territory*, Son went to work for Twentieth Century Fox on location in Utah for *Smoky* (1946), starring Fred MacMurray, based upon the classic Will James novel. In the cast of *Smoky* was Bruce Cabot, the star of the original *King Kong* (1933) who now kept busy playing villains in Westerns, often working with his close pal and drinking buddy, John Wayne. *Smoky* was released in July 1946 and was a big hit. MacMurray would ever-after be grateful to Son for stunt-doubling the actor in his tough riding sequences, especially the scene where the horse drags the hero by his arm to safety. The two men would work together again in *The Swarm* (1978), only by that time Son was an Oscar-winning actor with a resurgent career and MacMurray's career was in decline..

Republic summoned Son to Chatsworth to stunt double for actor Monte Hale in *Out California Way* (1946). The film was planned as an all-star B western production and as a promotion for Republic's stable of cowboy heroes. The film featured Roy Rogers and

Allan "Rocky" Lane as well as Robert Blake. Once again Son worked with stuntman Fred Graham. Released on Christmas Day 1946, the film was a popular B Western entry.

Son got his second chance to work with John Wayne again in 1946 when Wayne produced *Angel and the Badman*, his first effort as producer/star. The film is remarkable, an uncharacteristic anti-gun Western that features Wayne as a gunman reformed by the love of a Quaker girl, played by Gail Russell.

Son was hired to double Wayne, who hired his pals Paul Fix, Bruce Cabot and his mentor, Harry Carey. Wayne also hired Hank Worden, a real cowboy-turned-actor. Worden would work steadily for Wayne for the next thirty years. His most memorable role was that of "Old Mose" in John Ford's *The Searchers*.

During the filming of *Angel and the Badman*, the 39 year-old Wayne began a brief but torrid affair with the 22-year-old Russell, a breath-taking beauty who was as insecure as she was head-over-heels in love with Wayne. When the film ended, Wayne had Russell cast in his sea epic *Wake of the Red Witch* (1948), but broke off the relationship when the film finished production. Russell was despondent. She descended into alcoholism. Nearly a decade later, Wayne tried to save her life and career by giving her a leading part in *Seven Men From Now (1956)*. Russell, who still loved Wayne, had married Western star Guy Madison in 1950 but divorced him four years later. Russell's drank herself to death in 1961. She was 36 years old.

Angel and the Badman is one of Wayne's best films. It has a pace and crispness to it that is memorable, and the texture of the film is wonderful. Released on February 15, 1947, the film was a flop. A horrid TV remake of this classic was released in 2009 with Lou Diamond Phillips in the role of Quirt. It is virtually unwatchable and makes the original all the more special.

Son then went to Zion National Park in Utah to stunt double Joel McCrea in *Ramrod* (1947). McCrea was a real-life rancher and was widely considered that among actors, McCrea was the best horseman in Hollywood. A funny story about McCrea's horsemanship involves John Wayne.

During the filming of *Comancheros*, a John Wayne Western, director Michael Curtiz made a joking derogatory comment about Wayne's riding. Wayne, always quick to chafe at criticism, hollered to stuntman "Bad Chuck" Roberson, "Who's the best horseman in Hollywood?" To Wayne's dismay, Roberson immediately responded, "Joel McCrea!"

Ramrod's cast included another real cowboy turned actor, a man from Wyoming named Hal Taliaferro Alderson, who gained fame in silent Westerns as "Wally Wales," and later, as Hal Taliaferro, forged a lengthy career as a character actor in both B and A Westerns, including such classics as *Red River*. *Ramrod* was released on May 2, 1947 to good reviews and successful ticket sales.

Immediately after *Ramrod*, Son went back to Republic and stunt-doubled Gordon "Wild Bill" Elliott in *Wyoming*, one of the big budget A Western designed by the studio to groom Elliott to replace John Wayne. The film, released on July 28, 1947, was popular and added luster to Elliott's reputation as Wayne's heir apparent.

The film gave Son the opportunity to work with Fred Graham and a brand-spanking new stuntman named Chuck Roberson, who would eventually become John Wayne's favorite stunt double. Roberson would later earn the nickname "Bad Chuck," which was bestowed upon him by John Ford. Ford already employed another stuntman named Chuck Hayward. Ford dubbed Roberson "Bad Chuck" mostly because of Roberson's notoriety as a ladies man, and Hayward became known as "Good Chuck."

Roberson recalled in his autobiography that at his first encounter with Son he could tell that Son was a top stuntman. Roberson realized immediately that "a young fella by the name of Ben Johnson" was the man to emulate.

"I watched every move he made to see what I might have to do. I didn't do much of anything but get in the way." Roberson said.[11] Roberson was given the task of falling off a horse, a stunt called a "saddle fall," where a stuntman falls from a running horse as if shot out of the saddle. Roberson was so inexperienced that he rode the horse at too fast of a gallop and failed to prepare his landing spot by digging up the dirt so soften his landing. After the stunt, Son told a shaken Roberson to talk to Fred Kennedy about how to properly do the stunt.[12]

When the production company moved to Kernville, California for the location filming, Roberson shared a room with Son. "He gave me a few pointers on how to make it in the picture business. Ol' Ben knew what he was talking about, and he was a master at getting what was owed to him."

"'Bout the hardest stunt I know is collectin' your pay. Ever' once in a while you might have some feller forget just how much you done during the day. You just gotta keep remindin' him,'" Son told Roberson.

"In Kerrville we did some pretty hairy chase scenes; through big boulders, down hills and around scrub oaks. When it came time to collect I let Ben do the talking, and I'll be damned if he didn't get seventy five bucks a day for each of us. That was more money than I had ever seen in my whole life. This stunt business was something else!"[13]

CHAPTER SIX
FINALLY AN ACTOR

Thanks to John Wayne, Son was hired by director John Ford to stunt double Wayne, do a variety of other horse stunts, and play a small part in a new A-Western that Ford was planning to shoot in Navajo country. His pay was a whopping $1,000 a day.

Son arrived on location in Monument Valley, Utah in mid-August, 1947. The name of the film was *War Party*, a story of an egotistical cavalry colonel who causes an Indian war. The film was based on James Warner Bellah's short story, *The Massacre*.

Ford took immediate notice of Son's work as stunt double for co-star John Agar. Ford told Wayne one afternoon, "no one looks better than that kid on a horse."

Wayne replied, "His name is Ben Johnson. He's married to Fat Jones' daughter."[1]

During the filming of an Indian attack, a stunt went awry when a team of horses panicked and ran away, overturning a wagon filled with stuntmen. Son raced to the rescue and stopped the runaway team.

Richard D. Jensen

Son recalled the incident with his usual humility in a 1951 interview. "There was three guys doing a chase in a covered army wagon. They took a curve a little too fast and turned over. They were all hung underneath that wagon, and the horses were dragging it toward some big rocks. I just ran my horse into the team, piled them up and got them stopped. I stopped them about 16 feet before they got to the rocks. Had they reached the rocks first it would have killed them all. Just lucky, all around, I guess."[2]

Ford was grateful, telling Son he would "be rewarded for life."[3]

After the location shots were finished in Monument Valley and around Moab, Utah, the production returned to Corriganville, where the film's fort sets were built.

When *War Party* wrapped in late September, 1947, Son hoped it would be the beginning of a long-term working relationship with Ford. Ford was a major director of A features. He was a multi-Oscar-winner, and he had tremendous clout in the film business. Fortune had smiled upon Son.

Ford called Son to his office and tossed a contract at him and told him to take it to his agent. Son read it, saw that it was a seven-year contract at $5,000.00 a week, and signed it on the spot. Now that Son was making good money – equal to Clark Gable's pay when he was the top star at MGM, he went out and bought a sleek new car, a Studebaker.

Harry "Dobe" Carey, Jr. said this type of contract was typical of Ford. "Ford never dealt with agents. You just heard that Ford was making a picture and you'd just go down and see if he had a part in it for you."

One thing was certain, Son liked working with John Wayne, who was supportive of Son's career. Son also felt like his relationship with John Wayne was a big part of his newfound success. Son said John Wayne "was a great guy for us to work with. He was just like we was around John Ford. He was just as scared of John Ford as we was."[3]

"I doubled for Duke way back in the 1940s, right after I first came out [to Los Angeles]. He was very professional and a great guy to work with," Son said.[4]

"John Wayne would always give you an opportunity to do your thing. If you had a memorable scene to do, he'd always give you plenty of time to do it. He didn't try to upstage you or cut you short. As far as I was concerned, he was a great guy to work with."[5]

Wayne's had a high opinion of Son's skills as well. "Ben Johnson can sit a horse better than any actor I've ever seen," Wayne said.[6]

The film which was shot as *War Party* was released on March 9, 1948 under the title *Fort Apache*. It was an immediate hit and is considered a Western classic.

Most of the John Ford stock company of actors appears in the film, including Victor McLaglen, Dick Foran, Ward Bond and many others. Also, Movita, the actress who would later become the live-in lover of Marlon Brando, appeared as a Colonel Thursday's cook. Son would co-star with Marlon Brando in *One-Eyed Jacks* 12 years later.

With the security of being under contract to Ford and the freedom to work for other studios while Ford was between pictures, Son went back at work as a stunt man and part-time actor.

Son, however, didn't think he could act at all.

"I was doubling for people like John Wayne, Jimmy Stewart and Joel McCrea, and I would watch the way they did things," Son said. "But you know, I never really had a desire to be an actor. I always had something else to do I didn't sit around waiting for the phone to ring. I could always make a living working on a ranch or in a rodeo."[7]

His first gig was at Republic on a Gordon "Wild Bill" Elliott western called *The Gallant Legion*. Still working to groom Elliott as the next John Wayne, Republic studio boss Herbert Yates was pouring money into Elliott's films and this was no exception. Shot on location in Vazquez Hills in Agua Dulce, California, the film had higher production values than Republic's standard B-Westerns. Elliott was an actor who also owned a cattle ranch and was a pretty sturdy hand as a cowboy. He was well-liked by the cowboys who worked with him, but his career lasted only about a decade. His taciturn acting style was never quite dynamic enough to rise above B-Westerns.

In the mid-1930s, Yates hired the best actors and stuntmen available, but he always trying to get them on the cheap. Yates was notorious for paying only $75 a week to his actors, no matter how famous. The policy came about after William Fox nearly went broke paying Tom Mix $20,000 a week during Mix's heyday at Fox. When Yates merged his Consolidated Film Laboratories with Monogram and Lone Star Pictures to form Republic, he swore he'd never pay actors more than base pay. Actors were, in Yates' opinion, a dime a dozen. Yates knew that actors were always clamoring for work, and he took advantage of that fact. By the late 1940s, Yates was having to pay higher salaries. Son was earning as much as $75 a day just as a stuntman.

The Gallant Legion features Son as a Texas Ranger in an un-billed part. The cast included a who's who of actors who all worked steadily with John Wayne and John Ford, including Bruce Cabot, Andy Devine and Grant Withers. It also featured an actor Son would work with often in the future, most notably Indian actor Iron Eyes Cody, who would become famous in the 1960s as the "Keep America Beautiful" Indian in the TV commercials. Cody would make several more films with Son over the next forty years. Also on board for *The Gallant Legion* were real life cowboys Hank Bell and Hal Taliaferro. The stunt team included Son and stunt legends Tom Steele, Dale Van Sickel, and Kermit Maynard, who also had a role in the film..

When *The Gallant Legion* was released on May 24, 1948, Republic Studio brass felt they had a new John Wayne. Alas, the studio was not counting on a competitor that would soon put it out of business – television.

John Wayne saw to it that Son was hired by Howard Hawks for the epic Western entitled *Red River*. Production of *Red River* took place from September 1946 to November 1946 in Elgin, Arizona.

The film was based on a Borden Chase story published in the popular Saturday Evening Post magazine. It was essentially the *Mutiny on the Bounty* saga transplanted to the American West. At the time of its release on September 30, 1948, it was heralded as Wayne's arrival as a serious actor. It was, and is, one of

Richard D. Jensen

the best Western films ever made, and many believe it is the best.

Son wasn't given a speaking part in the film, but he stunt doubled on it and worked alongside Wayne, Harry Carey, Jr. (known as "Dobe" to his friends because of his adobe-colored hair), fellow real cowboys-turned actors Hank Worden and Hal Taliaferro, and stunt legend Richard Farnsworth. The only Western film that rivals the scope of *Red River* is the classic *Lonesome Dove* (1989), which nearly every critic believes is the finest Western film ever made.

From the sublime to the ridiculous, Son finished *Red River* and went to MGM to stunt double Frank Sinatra in *The Kissing Bandit* (1948), a turkey that Sinatra bristled at the mention of for the rest of his life. Son made Sinatra's horseback scenes look good, and doubled other actors in action scenes. Mildred Natwick, who would work with Son on *Three Godfathers* later that year, was also in the cast. When *The Singing Bandit* was released in January 1949, the gales of laughter and derisive comments were heard nationwide. Sinatra spent nearly four decades trying to live that film down.

CHAPTER SEVEN
STARRING WITH A GORILLA

Life is stranger than fiction. How else could a cowboy from Oklahoma, making a living as a stuntman in Westerns, suddenly become the star of a *King Kong*-style adventure film?

The answer is simple: John Ford was as good as his word.

Grateful for Son's heroics during the *Fort Apache* shoot, Ford made sure that Son was cast in early 1948 as the cowboy hero in *Mighty Joe Young*, which was produced by Ford's Argosy Pictures. Son co-starred with the comely actress Terry Moore and worked alongside many of his cowboy stunt pals, including Richard Farnsworth and Kermit Maynard, who appeared as a cowboy, and stunt legends Joe Gray, Fred Kennedy, Carey Loftin, Eddie Parker, David Sharpe, Tom Steele, and Dale Van Sickel.

Also appearing in the cast was a young actor named William Schallert as a gas station attendant. Schallert would later become president of the Screen Actor's Guild. Also Ellen Corby, who would become famous forty years later as Grandma Walton on TV's *The*

Richard D. Jensen

Waltons, appeared as a woman in an orphanage and Irene Ryan, who 20 years later would become famous as Granny on TV's *The Beverly Hillbillies*, appeared as a girl sitting at a bar.

Mighty Joe Young is similar in many ways to the classic *King Kong*, mixing live action with stop-action animation. Son is cast as a rodeo champ who signs on to help a promoter capture wild animals for a Broadway act. While on the Dark Continent, they encounter a giant gorilla. Trying to capture the enormous gorilla without killing it, Son and his cowboy pals try roping it like a wild horse. This action sequence is one of the highlights of the film. Son, along with Kermit Maynard and other cowboys, ride hell-for-leather in an action sequence that still packs a punch, even 60 years later. The stop-action animation, courtesy of Ray Harryhausen, is superb. Harryhausen would become famous for this animation in the 1950s, when he created the special effects for various sword and sorcerer epics.

A unique feature of *Mighty Joe Young* is the tinted sequence during the fire at the orphanage. A technique used in the silent movies to enhance a scene, tinting took black and white film and gave it the punch of color. It's akin to modern colorizing of old black and white movies, and in this sequence is has a striking effect. Son does his own stunts on the burning building, and the scene is good old-fashioned Hollywood thrill-making.

The film was shot at RKO Studios, and Son worked hard to turn in credible performance as the hero cowboy.

During production, Son was a bit overwhelmed by the publicity. Just when he thought it was all a bit too much, he had a welcome surprise visitor. Horace Barnard, one of the partners at Chapman Barnard Ranch, flew to Hollywood to visit Son.

The reunion was highly publicized by studio public relations men. Son told Barnard that despite all of the hoopla over his stardom, he was still a cowboy first. He told Barnard that he was investing his money in ranching and had that to fall back on if his film career ended. Barnard jokingly told Son that he could always have his job back at the Chapman Barnard Ranch.[1]

Mighty Joe Young has one spectacular scene in a nightclub in which the gigantic gorilla trashes the place. More than 50 stuntmen were hired to do the scene. The stuntmen were paid $55 a day for such work.[2]

Son handles the heroics with great competency, and his acting is reminiscent of a very young John Wayne, easy-going and personable, even charismatic.

When *Mighty Joe Young* was released on August 29, 1949, the Hollywood Reporter said Son was "lean and lanky" and "charming."[3]

Ford told reporters that Son was "a young Gary Cooper. He's the best thing to come out of Oklahoma since Will Rogers."[4]

The film was heavily promoted, and Son was given the star treatment, complete with publicity tours, photo sessions, magazine and newspaper articles, live appearances, all designed to make him – and the *Mighty Joe Young* – a household name.

Publicists and photographers took photos of Ben and Terry Moore, and tried to hint at a "romance." Son would have none of it. He insisted the publicists photograph him and Carol at home, out on the town,

Richard D. Jensen

on the ranch. He also had them photograph him with his mother, Ollie.

When asked about Moore, Son told reporters that Moore was "a pretty little critter, but she makes me more nervous than a bucking horse."[5]

This made for some confusing PR, and Son thought the entire situation was rather ridiculous. He approached his newfound fame with a mixture of excitement and chagrin. To Son, the movies were a job, and he wanted to work and make money and invest that money in ranching. All the Hollywood silliness that came with fame was meaningless to him.

Now flush with cash and a salary equal to Clark Gable's at MGM, Son began buying ranches in California. He hired three former Oklahoma hands to help him run his operation - Joe Crow of Bartlesville, Bob Errington of Oklahoma City and Dick Crow from Pawhuska. (One article on Son's ranch lists the men as Bob Clark, Doe Elliott and Dick Crew.)

Mighty Joe Young had just wrapped in the fall of 1948 when Ford offered Son work in a new Western.

Ford was about to begin production of *Three Godfathers* and decided to hire Son in May 1948 to do double duty as stunt man and actor.

In his autobiography, Dobe Carey recalled that he first met Son during rehearsals for *Three Godfathers*, but it was likely during *Red River*.

In *Three Godfathers*, Son was to double Wayne in the scene where Dobe's character is shot off his horse during the escape from the bank robbery early in the film.[6] Son was also to play a member of the posse.

Three Godfathers was to be Ford's first color Western. It had been eight months since Son completed his work on *Fort Apache* and he had just finished *Mighty Joe Young*.

Son reported for work on *Three Godfathers*, and recalled that during the filming "Duke was real good to me."[7]

The filming took place from mid-May 1948 until mid-June 1948 in the broiling Mojave Desert.[8]

Son recalled the experience years later. "One of the toughest pictures I have ever been on was *Three Godfathers*. We were working in the sand dunes all the time. Sometimes I thought Ford was trying to destroy us."[9]

Three Godfathers is an excellent Western, technically superb, full of breath-taking action and awe-inspiring visuals.

The film contains some remarkable moments, including some terrific horsemanship, especially by Son and actor Pedro Armendariz, Jr.. In the initial robbery scene, Armendariz's horse rears and does a roll back while fully vertical. Armendariz continues shooting his pistol and never loses his seat – a testament to his horsemanship. Few actors – indeed few stuntmen – could have sat a horse during such an event.

Son doubles Dobe in the initial robbery sequence, then plays a posse member in the initial chase when Sheriff Pearlie Sweet (Ward Bond) gives chase on a buckboard. Son stands behind the buckboard seat, rifle in hand, during this full gallop chase. Here Son is clearly a stuntman playing a featured part. Actors turn their face to the camera and cheat for camera time.

Richard D. Jensen

Stunt men turn their faces away from the camera, a habit born of standing in for recognizable actors. In his scenes, Son keeps his face away from the camera. He has not yet begun to think of himself as an actor.

Son began to think of ways to use his success in movies as a way to help the folks back home in Oklahoma. It was a pattern he would follow for the rest of his life.

Immediately after wrapping production on *Three Godfathers*, Son grabbed Republic Studios producer Lee Van Atta for a road trip to Pawhuska. Son wanted to convince the producer that Osage County's tall grass prairie was suitable for shooting Western movies. They arrived on July 17, 1948 and Son took Van Atta to the Chapman Barnard Ranch. While in Pawhuska, Son took Van Atta to the International Roundup Cavalcade, which was held from July 23 through 25 in Pawhuska.[10]

This was one of many efforts Son made throughout his career to steer film-making to Oklahoma. Son knew that film productions brought enormous sums of money and jobs to a community, and Son wanted to do what he could to spread the wealth to his friends and neighbors from his hometown.

When it was released on December 1, 1948, *Three Godfathers* received mixed reviews. It was not as big a hit as Ford and his cast had hoped it would be. Released just after Thanksgiving and before Christmas, the film's religious message should have struck a chord with film audiences. Instead, many found it preachy and somewhat creaky in tone. Ford had made this same film twice before, and it was one of his favorite stories, but post World War II audiences had become more cynical in the wake of the global impact of the war.

As uneven as the reviews for *Three Godfathers* were in 1948, it has since become considered a Western classic. As is often the case with movies, *Three Godfathers* has aged well, like a fine wine that needs the passage of time to turn from grape juice into a fine vintage.

Ford was planning another cavalry Western entitled *She Wore A Yellow Ribbon*, and he decided to give Son a big part in the star-laden film.

Son didn't believe Ford wanted him for his acting skills. "I think Ford chose me because I rode a horse better than just about anyone else, and that's pretty much what my role required to do. I had no aspirations to be a great actor and I think Ford knew that because Wayne told me, 'Watch out, you'll be the new whipping boy," but Ford treated me so well, it was a bit unnerving."[11]

After *Mighty Joe Young*, Son was, for the time, Ford's newest discovery. As *She Wore A Yellow Ribbon* began production, Ford did the same thing he did when he made John Wayne a star – took full credit for everything.

Ford and Son's relationship would eventually sour during the making of *Rio Grande*, but during the production of *She Wore A Yellow Ribbon*, Son was the new star rising in Ford's universe.

Son played the part of Sgt. Tyree, the trooper sent out to scout for Indians on the warpath. In the film, Ford's second color Western, Son has a wonderful scene in which he is chased by marauding braves across the spectacular Monument Valley, Utah landscape. Son rides like the wind, including leaping a horse over a deep chasm. The chasm is accomplished by a glass shot, where the chasm is made to look deeper. The jump is reminiscent of Tom Mix's jump over the Newhall Gap in *Three Jumps Ahead* (1923), also directed by Ford. In addition to his role, Son did plenty of stunt doubling along with Fred Graham and Richard Farnsworth.

She Wore A Yellow Ribbon was filmed during November and December of 1948.[12] At this time of year, Monument Valley, Utah was often bitterly cold. And like any outdoor film, production has considerable risks. This is especially true with Westerns, where even the most trained movie horses can have a bad day with disastrous results.

During the filming of the scene in which Wayne, as Sgt. Brittles, drives a herd of horses by waving his cavalry coat, Wayne's horse began to panic. The horse bucked and the saddle cinch broke and Wayne was thrown beneath the horse. He was knocked cold right as the horses began to stampede.

Wayne recalled the event years later with relish. "Now there's about fifty horses tear-assing at me. I came out of the blackout to hear the Old Man, Mr. Ford, yelling and there was general hysteria, but a wrangler with guts, he ran out and headed off the stampeding horses, which were within a few feet of tromping me to death."[13] The identity of that wrangler is lost to history. Some credit Son with the rescue, but if it had been Son, Wayne would likely have given him credit.

Son did double duty on *She Wore A Yellow Ribbon*, stunt-doubling other actors and playing Sgt. Tyree, which was a major character. Son assumed it was because Ford thought of him as easily replaceable.[14] He didn't complain though, as his salary was $5,000 a week, a far cry from a $1 a day as a cowboy.

At various times, production of *She Wore A Yellow Ribbon* was hampered by weather or other factors. While the cast and crew waited for conditions to improve, the actors often debated politics. Ford was a notorious reactionary – though a downright centrist in comparison to the arch-right wing politics of actor Ward Bond. Wayne and others were equally far to the right. One day, Dobe Carey was complaining about the state of the union under Franklin D. Roosevelt's presidency and, of late, that of Harry S. Truman, both Democrats. Several actors took the position that Truman was a Communist.

Ford angry at the weather delay, growled, "I don't what you're talking about. You all became millionaires under Roosevelt."[15]

Rather than waste time waiting for the weather to improve, Ford ordered Son to do some hard riding in front of the cameras. "Whenever Ford didn't know what to shoot, he'd film Ben riding over a mountain with Indians after him," Harry "Dobe" Carey, Jr. recalled.[16]

During his scenes, Son was especially good. His had grown so comfortable in front of the camera doing dialog – despite his innate belief that he couldn't act or remember his lines – that his scenes smack of realism. His banter with John Wayne, as Capt. Nathan Brittles, are some of the best dialog sequences in the film, especially Son's constant and memorable use of the phrase, "that ain't my department."

Dobe Carey said Son was nervous during his dialog scenes. At one point, Ford said to him, "All right, here we go. Nice and easy now. Ready, Ol' Ben. You're Johnny Reb giving these guys the lowdown, okay?"

"I'll try, Mr. Ford," Son replied. "But I'd sure rather fall off a doggoned horse or come flat-out down one of them hills than say this here dialog. You jes' point out the hill you want me to come off, an' let some other actor say them words."[17]

Son was nearly killed during the film's climactic stampede sequence when the cavalry drive a herd of horses through an Indian village.

"Well, during the stampede I'm in dust and all of those horses and I can't see and my horse falls down. Fortunately, I hold onto him and when he falls down I get back up with him and go out of the scene and nobody even knew I fell because they couldn't see me and I couldn't see either," Son said.

Carey was on the set that day, and added, "After it was over, he said, 'My horse fell' and I said 'How come you're still here?' And he said, 'He got back up and I rode him out.'"

Ben was lucky and he knew it. "Fortunately, those other loose horses didn't run over me."[18]

An interesting bit of trivia, fellow Oklahoman Tom Mix was in a similar wreck in the silent film *The Man From Texas* and did the same thing, held on to the horse and rode it out of the scene. In Mix' case, the event was captured on film close up.

One of Son's fondest memories about working on *She Wore A Yellow Ribbon* was working with veteran character actor Victor McLaglen. Ford loved McLaglen, who liked to nip at a bottle of whiskey all day long as he worked. The two men had earned Oscars working together on *The Informer* (1935). Ford forbade drink during working hours, and kept vigil over McLaglen. To get around this forced prohibition, McLaglen conspired with Son to have Son carry the whiskey flask in his shirt pocket.

"Ford knew I didn't drink," Son said. Son carried McLaglen's flask, and whenever McLaglen wanted a nip he'd sidle up to Son, take a hit, and hand it back. The ruse worked and Ford never figured out who was stashing McLaglen's hooch for him.

The result of this was humorous. The tipsy McLaglen, when not on camera, would fall fast asleep on the set, often snoring so loudly that he would interrupt the scene, whereupon Ford would shout for someone to wake McLaglen up to stop his snoring.[19]

"I really enjoyed working in *She Wore A Yellow Ribbon*. It was a good movie, a good clean movie, something you can take your family to see. We had an awful lot of fun doing it. I got a lot of pleasure running from the Indians in that one."[20]

Dobe Carey recalled in 1994 that when he and Son finished work on *She Wore A Yellow Ribbon* they were taken by car to Flagstaff, Arizona to wait for the train back to Los Angeles.

"Our arrival in Flagstaff, after spending three hard weeks in Monument Valley, was the equivalent of arriving in, say, San Francisco," Carey said. "Flagstaff seemed like a metropolis."[21]

Carey said the production had thoughtfully booked hotel rooms for he and Son to relax in while awaiting the train. "Ben and I went up to our room to take our first real shower in three weeks. We had that red dust in our hair, our ears, our eyes, and ground into our skin. One shower wasn't going to get it all, but it would make us presentable."

Carey said that it was commonplace for actors to dress up when they left home as they knew the public would be watching. He said he generally did not dress Western style, preferring the casual clothes of the Hollywood set, blue blazer, grey slacks and Bass Weejuns loafers. "Ben used to call my clothes 'jellybean clothes.'"

Son, however, was always a cowboy. "Ben was different. He wore a western-cut suede jacket, a cowboy shirt, and a tie. He had on $50 boots and a $50 cowboy hat," Carey said. "Those last two cost way over $200 each today, and Ben still dresses the same way. I dress Western style nowadays, too. For some reason back then, I thought you had to be a champion roper to wear Western clothes."[22]

As was his habit, whenever not working on a film, Son would head to one of his ranches or to a rodeo. Son continued to compete in rodeos in as much of his spare time as possible, with top notch results. He set a calf-roping record in Oregon at the Pendleton Roundup when he roped and tied a calf in 12.5 seconds with a 60-foot rope. "I really thought I was something," says Ben.

CHAPTER EIGHT
JOHN FORD - CONFLICTS, INNER AND OUTER

For all the work that Ford was giving him, Son didn't want to be a part of the sycophantic group of actors working with Ford. These actors worked in all of Ford's productions and were affectionately - and sometimes derisively - called "the John Ford Stock Company." The group existed because Ford held the purse strings, and held the livelihoods of these actors in his tight, often mean-spirited fists. Ford was a notorious bully, notorious even for striking actors – and sometimes actresses, as he once did to Maureen O'Hara, his favorite female star.[1] Ford was as petty and self-loathing an Irish drunk as ever existed, one of the heaviest binge drinkers in Hollywood, and that's saying something. Iconic actor James Cagney, one of Hollywood's biggest stars in the 1930s and 1940s, said Ford was filled with "malice."[2]

That said, he was a brilliant director who won four Best Director Oscars. His films made money because he made lyrical and highly commercial films on tight budgets, shooting fast and using only camera angles he wanted in the film. While other directors shot multiple takes, Ford edited his films in the camera, shooting only the setups he wanted, keeping his costs down and his artistic vision intact.

Ford's reputation allowed him the luxury of hiring the biggest stars in Hollywood, many of whom were willing to tolerate his abuse in order to work for him. His image was burnished by studio publicists during his lifetime and has been romanticized over the decades since his death, especially by many actors who have written autobiographies of their careers under Ford's tutelage. In truth, Ford was notoriously impossible to deal with, and often insisted that his actors submit to his feudal lordship.

Stuntman Chuck Roberson recalled that his first time working on a Ford film was on *Rio Grande*, and he was appalled when Ford fired a crew member merely for whistling. Ford was superstitious and he believed whistling was bad luck.[3]

In her 2004 autobiography *Tis Herself*, O'Hara, the fiery redhead Irish actress who was Ford's favorite leading lady, laid bare the truth about Ford's violence, his physical abuse of both the men and women in his circle. She reveals that Ford even slugged O'Hara during a drunken rage and his verbal and emotional cruelty towards those who loved him.

O'Hara also alleged that Ford's over-done machismo and bullying was to compensate for his closeted bisexuality. No other source for this allegation has ever surfaced, and O'Hara chooses to avoid naming others who witnessed an alleged encounter during the filming of *The Long Gray Line*, when the actress accidentally caught Ford in a clinch with a gay actor. O'Hara's co-star on the film was closeted gay actor Tyrone Power, whose identity she only alludes to.

"[I] went to Ford's office to show him the revised sketches for my wardrobe. My arms full of the sketches, I walked into his office without knocking and could hardly believe my eyes. Ford had his arms around another man and was kissing him. I was shocked and speechless. I quickly dropped the sketches on the floor, then knelt down to pick them up. I fumbled around slowly and kept my head down. I took my time so they could part and compose themselves. They were on opposite sides of the room in a flash. The gentleman Ford was with was one of the most famous leading men in the picture business. He addressed a few pleasantries to me, which were forced and awkward, then quickly left. Ford and I went on with our business. Not a word was said, and I played it out as if I hadn't seen a thing. Later, that actor approached me and asked, 'Why didn't you tell me John Ford was homosexual?' I answered, 'How could I tell you something I knew nothing about?.'"[4]

O'Hara explains that she had noticed Ford's overdone machismo and it had caused her to wonder about his sexuality. She recalls that she often wondered about Ford's harsh treatment of his wife, Mary. She remembers that Ford and his wife did not share a bed, nor did they ever express or display affection for one another.[5]

Indeed, O'Hara details that her brother, Jimmy Fitzsimmons, a tall and good-looking Irishman, had been told by the stunt men on *Rio Grande* to never be around Ford after dark. Just why, O'Hara and her brother didn't know until that day she caught Ford in the arms of a man.[6]

O'Hara's revelation is intriguing because Ford's depiction of men and women on film portray the typical traditional machismo of the time. His films are all dominated by strong, manly men who eschew women for male camaraderie, usually in communal violence and riotous drunkenness. Women are often depicted as matronly or annoyingly shrewish. O'Hara's depiction of Ford warrants further investigation, something Ford would dislike, especially when one considers his mantra - "When the legend becomes fact, print the legend."

O'Hara believes that Ford was sexually conflicted, so much so that it lead to his abusiveness and his descent in to alcoholism.[7] She recalled that Ford often wrote letters to her when he was drunk, one of which included this passage:

> "Father – I love my man dearly
> "I love him above my own life
> "But, Father – my soul hurts me –
> "I've never been in the same bed with him –
> "And I want him heaven knows –
> "Father, dear – what shall I do —
> "Oh, what shall I do."[8]

The revelation also begs the investigative question - why did John Ford take long sailing trips on his yacht, Araner, in the early 1930s, always in the company of so many male actors, including a very young and handsome unknown actor named John Wayne? Was it male bonding, as has been recorded by history, or was it closeted affection. Ford often took actor Lloyd Nolan, a closeted homosexual, who was also Ford's first choice for the part of Ringo Kid in *Stagecoach* (1939). Ford later gave the role to John Wayne, making him a superstar.

Contrast this with notorious ladies man Errol Flynn, who spent months aboard his yacht in the company of scores of comely, and often under-aged, females. Consider, too, that Flynn was a closeted bisexual as well.

Indeed, Wayne was the most famous of all actors who sucked up to Ford, and he did it for 45 years. Other actors, most notably Henry Fonda, Robert Montgomery, William Holden and Richard Widmark, bristled under Ford's treatment and refused to be cowed by him or socialize with him.

Wayne was so grateful to Ford for making him into a major star that the big actor was willing to be belittled by Ford at Ford's whim. Wayne was given his first job in the movies by Tom Mix, the biggest silent movie cowboy star of the time, but it was Ford who put Wayne on film first, as a goose-herder in *Mother Macree* (1927). And it was Ford who gave Wayne his first starring role in an A Western called *Stagecoach* (1939).

Wayne had a habit of adopting older men as mentors and as surrogate fathers. He latched onto Ford and to silent Western icon Harry Carey. Wayne was the child of a loveless marriage between a frail and sickly – but devoted – father and a cruel, emotionally abusive mother.

Richard D. Jensen

Wayne idolized his father, who died when Wayne was in his early 20s. Indeed, it is clear from the record that Wayne's vile mother drove Wayne's father to an early grave. This childhood impacted his self-image and his ability to have long term romantic relationships with women. He spent his entire life deriding homosexuals and sissies, often without provocation. He was fanatical about it. Despite this, he spent all of his free time in the company of men.

This was because Wayne was determined to never be perceived as weak as his beloved late father was often accused by Wayne's shrew mother. Wayne was paranoid about appearing unmanly, even lecturing his children about his mannerisms to prove to them that these mannerisms were macho.[9] He adopted stuntman and rodeo champion Enos "Yakima" Canutt's sauntering walk, and even practiced holding his cigarette in the cleft of his first and second finger, near the palm, in what he believed appeared to be a more manly manner.[10]

Determined to be more of a man than his sickly father, and determined never to be derided by a woman's sharp tongue, Wayne also walled himself off from his women, thrice marrying Latin women because in the Latin culture women accept the dominance of the husband in the household. In all three marriages, when Wayne's wives began to assert some independence, the marriages failed. Wayne's most successful relationship was a long-term elicit affair with Marlene Dietrich, a bisexual. She and Wayne were both married to other people the entire time. Wayne liked the fact that Dietrich smoke, drank, caroused and played cards like a man. She was "one of the guys."

While Wayne credited Ford with making him a star, in reality Ford allowed Wayne to languish in low-budget westerns for more than ten years before finally casting Wayne in *Stagecoach* (1939), the film which launched Wayne as a major star. Despite that, Ford used Wayne only once for nearly another decade, in a version of Eugene O'Neill's *The Long Voyage Home* (1940) and didn't cast Wayne in a major role until *Three Godfathers*. It was only after Wayne became thought of as a serious actor with his success in Howard Hawks' *Red River* that Ford began using Wayne with any regularity. Further, Ford claimed publicly thereafter that he was the one who discovered Wayne and made him a star.

Privately, Ford often assailed Wayne for his lack of talent, his lack of machismo.

Why did John Wayne, who was big enough to kick Ford's butt anytime, take so much taunting and verbal abuse – and even physical abuse – from Ford through their entire working relationship? Why did Ford often make disparaging comments about Wayne's penis, often while holding up his pinky, to which Wayne never once responded?[11]

Wayne, later in life, candidly admitted that Ford was "the cruelest man I know."[12]

Son didn't like to talk badly about anyone, but he candidly stated that Ford was " a mean son of a buck."[13]

For his part, Son held to the code of the Oklahoma cowboys and he wanted no part of kissing up to Ford. He never traded his dignity for work or favoritism and he didn't take guff off of any man. "I didn't really want to be a part of the Ford family, and when he invited

Richard D. Jensen

me to play cards at night, which was a tradition on his films, I made sure I played so lousy he never asked me again. But there was Duke Wayne playing cards every night – and Duke was a great card player – but he had to lose so as not to upset the old man. Duke would do just anything to keep Ford happy."[14] Indeed, Son knew of the crew's warning to never be around Ford after dark, and surely this played into his reactions to Ford later, when the two men would have a falling out.

All that said, Son was Ford's favorite new actor, and Son was pressed into the starring role in Ford's new epic *Wagonmaster*.

The film is considered by many Ford scholars as a masterpiece, a simple story of a wagon train and Mormon settlers. Lyric, almost elegiac in tone, with all of the elements of Ford's classic Westerns, the movie features Son and Dobe Carey as Travis and Sandy, two cowpokes who join the wagon train.

Ward Bond and many of the John Ford Stock Company are on hand, including Shakespearean actor Alan Mowbray, Jane Darwell (who Ford immortalized as Ma Joad in *The Grapes of Wrath*) and even Indian Olympic champion Jim Thorpe, who played a Navajo brave. Young James Arness, who would later star in the iconic television series *Gunsmoke*, is on hand.

When Ford began casting *Wagonmaster* in 1949, he had already decided to cast Son as the young, chivalrous cowboy hero. Son had just played the lead role in *Mighty Joe Young* and Tyree in *She Wore A Yellow Ribbon* and this was clearly to be a Western film of great importance. Son was nervous about the film. He and Dobie Carey were both hired for the movie, and they both felt considerable optimism about their respective futures, but this was a huge opportunity. Stardom!

Oddly, it was during the making of *Wagonmaster* that Ford began taking chances with Son's safety in order to get certain scenes on film.

During the filming of *Wagonmaster*, Ford decided he wanted to spice up a dialog scene by having Son ride a wild bucking horse in the middle of the scene.

"We were about halfway through the picture and he says, 'Ben, can you ride a bucking horse?' And I said, 'Yes, sir. I'll try.' So, he puts me in on a buckin' horse. So we get the shot and I buck off at the given point and the wrangler runs in and ruins the shot so I have to do it again," Son recalled.

"Alan Lee was the wrangler," Dobe Carey said. "And he ran in and said, 'Ben, are you all right?'" Ford ordered several more takes, and on the last one asked Son to land, then get up saying his dialog. "It was a vicious horse," Son recalled. "It was one of Andy Reggie's broncs."[15] Son landed hard on the take and the wind was knocked out of him. Still, he rose from the ground, trying to say his dialog.

The scene in the completed picture is a mix of various angles from different takes, and the dialog is from a pickup shot, implying that Son didn't get the lines out after landing.

Ford played one of his typical practical jokes on Son during the filming. At one point, Ford asked Son to help him plan a sequence where the wagon train comes down a steep gorge. Ford wanted the scene to look rough, but for no actors or stuntmen to get hurt.

He asked Son to ride along the gorge and figure out the best route for the wagons to take.

Son rode off on horseback and scouted the location carefully.

The next morning, Ford asked Son if he was ready to do some dialog scenes that day and Son said he was. He added, "I'm not worried about any dialogue right now anyway, but I think I've figured out a way for you to do that shot you were a-tellin' me about."

Ford gave Son a look of feigned aggravation and said, "Jesus! So, now you want to direct the picture!"[16]

Wagonmaster was the first film in which Son was flown to the location. Most film studios used trains and cars to move actors during this period. Airplane travel was considered expensive and risky. Additionally, many distant locales didn't have suitable airports.

Son didn't like the idea. Indeed, Dobe Carey said Son was terrified of flying.

"Ben Johnson was a fearless cowboy and stuntman, but he was deathly afraid of airplanes," Carey said. "We were sitting in one that was to take us to Moab [Utah]. Ben had a window seat and was hanging onto my left arm as though I could do something if we got into trouble.

"The plane was a DC-3. In those days, that was what you flew on short hops. For years, it was known as the safest plane ever built. When I told Ben I had flown across the Pacific Ocean in one, he countered with, 'Yeah, Dobe, but that there was over water where a fella' might have a chance, if he could swim. We're goin' over them big high mountains.' To be honest, I was not feeling that secure, either."[17]

Carey said that Ford sat at the front of the plane smoking a cigar, unconcerned, even when the plane hit turbulence. Son, on the other hand, was sweating bullets.

"We started over the mountains and that little plane started bucking and pitching like a bronc. 'Dobe,' Ben drawled, 'this son a' bitch is a'gonna fall for sure."

Carey said that when the DC-3 landed, it was a rough landing, and the plane nearly skidded off the edge of a mesa.

"'Ol' Dobe,' Ben said, following a long look at where we had ended up, 'you remember what I done told you about them Brahma bulls? Well, I'll ride one of them bastards any day before I'll take another plane ride like this.'"[18]

During the shooting of *Wagonmaster*, Son became involved in a wild drunken brawl after a day of shooting. Film locations often have moments of tension-breaking revelry, where actors and crew get out of control. Son usually stayed clear of such shenanigans. He rarely drank, and this is one of the few moments in his life when he was embroiled in a drunken brouhaha.

One Saturday afternoon, as was his custom, Ford wrapped shooting at 4 p.m. Alan Mowbray, the English-born, Shakespearean actor who, prior to entering films had been a decorated war hero in World War I, was a favorite of John Ford's. The director loved injecting Mowbray into his films to contrast the cultured Shakespearean actor with the ruggedness of the frontier. This one particular evening, Mowbray invited the cast and stuntmen to his hotel room for a cocktail party. During the heavy drinking that occurred that night, burly stuntman Freddie Kennedy got into a shoving match with another stuntman, a cowboy pal of Son's named Eddie Jauregui. Kennedy was notorious for walking up to everyone and punching them in the chest, leaving huge bruises. Son and Carey saw this as a chance to get some licks in on Kennedy and jumped into the fray. The party erupted into a brawl and only the intervention of stuntman Cliff Lyons prevented the night from turning out badly.[19]

Son's celebrity in Hollywood reverberated back home. Son's reputation began to eclipse his father's. For decades Ben Johnson was the top dog in Osage County. He was larger than life. He was a rodeo champion, indeed a three-time world champion. At the time of *Wagonmaster's* premiere, Ben had begun to notice that his Son's notoriety was eclipsing him. Ben could no longer ignore that his Son was now the biggest hero in Osage County, Oklahoma. The Son now outshone the Father.

The newspapers heralded Son's comings and goings, repeating over and over the legend of Son going to Hollywood in a box car with horses, the $1 a day cowpoke who'd become a star. These articles often footnoted that Son's father was a three-time world champion rodeo cowboy, but Ben was pretty much shoved to the margins of the stories.

This all came to a head in April 1950 when Son returned to Pawhuska for the premiere of *Wagonmaster* at the Kihekah Theater. Son brought Dobe Carey and cowboy and songwriter Stan Jones, composer of the anthem *Ghost Riders In the Sky,* with him. The three became good friends while working together on *Fort*

Apache, Three Godfathers and *She Wore A Yellow Ribbon*. Dobe appeared with Son in *Wagonmaster* and Jones wrote four songs for the score.

Son and Dobe had much in common. Both were famous sons of famous fathers. Both had the same names as their fathers. Son was a rapidly rising Hollywood actor and the son of a three-time rodeo world champion. Dobe was the rising star son of famous cowboy actor Harry Carey, one of the original Western heroes of silent film who had become an iconic character actor in the 1930s and 1940s.

Son and Dobe arrived late in the day at the Chapman Barnard Ranch and after warm greetings and a hearty dinner they bunked in at the foreman's wing on the east side of the main house. It is not clear if Jones stayed in Pawhuska in a hotel or joined Son and Dobe at the ranch.

The next morning Ben arose before dawn, as was customary. Son and Dobie slept in.

Ben went to breakfast with the hands in the main eating room and, seeing that Son and Dobe were absent, went looking for them. When he found them still asleep, he blew up.

The story goes that Ben chided his Son and Dobe, making disparaging remarks about the laziness of movie cowboys. Daughter Helen, reflecting on the incident, said she thought that Ben may have been embarrassed. The Chapman Barnard cowboys knew that the men had to be up and ready to work at dawn, and laziness was the cause of much derision. It is likely that Ben was somewhat embarrassed by Son's and Dobe's apparent sloth.

Clearly, Son and Dobie slept in because they were on vacation. It is certain that neither intended to rise before dawn with the crew of working cowboys to spend the entire day doing grueling ranch work.[20]

"I was thinking ... about Dad not liking Hollywood. I cannot put my finger on why I think he did not have a high regard for Hollywood other than he did not talk about it," Son's sister, Helen, recalled. "He seemed pleased if Son came back to Oklahoma but I don't he had any illusions about wanting to visit Hollywood. He fit perfectly into the ranch scene. He loved every minute of it. Perhaps to him the movies were just a fantasy of what 'being a cowboy' really was.

"I never heard him say a bad word about what Son did for a living but I don't think Dad would have traded an hour of his life for a month of life in Hollywood," Helen said.[21]

While Ben didn't have much to say about the film industry, and his lack of appreciation for the industry was a cause of some friction between he and Son, they adjusted as best they could.

While Ben was proud of Son, he had no great love for the easy life of the movie business. To Ben, ranching was his life, and he could think of living nowhere else than the Tall Grass of northern Oklahoma.

It is uncertain, but it is likely that Ben's dim view of Hollywood was all the more palpable because the World War II years made ranching all the more vital to the cause of America's liberty.

While Son fell off of horses and played actor in the movies, the Chapman Barnard Ranch and others provided millions of pounds of beef to feed the war effort to defeat the Axis powers that threatened the world. Ben's role as foreman of the Chapman Barnard put him on the front lines of that effort, and he was responsible for shipping 30,000 head of cattle a month from the Blackland Pens to slaughterhouses nationwide.

The attitude Ben had for the movie business may have been further exacerbated by the fact that Son's mother, Ollie, had left Oklahoma and was also living in Hollywood. While Ben toiled on the ranch in the searing heat of summer and the frigid cold of winter, and while the nation was beset with a world war that threatened all of humanity, the newspapers and magazines were chock full of publicity photos of Son and Carol and Ollie at various movie premieres and other Hollywood events.

When the Oklahoma premiere of *Wagonmaster* was held a few nights after the embarrassing morning at the ranch, Helen recalled being in the audience. The entire community of Pawhuska seemed to be in attendance, and Son and Dobe Carey were hailed as heroes.

Helen said Son took the stage when he was introduced and yelled, "Where's my sister?" Helen said she cried out, "I'm here!" She said the moment filled her with pride to be hailed by her brother, now a famous movie star, in front of the hometown crowd. "We just idolized him," Helen recalled.[22] Frances Jo Brooks, a lifelong friend of Helen's, was there. "We didn't get to town much, but when a Son Johnson movie was playing, we'd come to town."[23]

Wagonmaster was released nationwide on April 19, 1950 to mixed reviews.

Son, Dobe and Jones made a highly-publicized appearance at the Bartlesville, Oklahoma's Arrow Theater on August 20, 1950 for the Oklahoma "premiere." They appeared on stage and had a sing-a-long before the movie.

Just like *Three Godfathers,* the reputation of *Wagonmaster* has grown with time

Film historians have long included the movie in their list of "best Westerns," and many have called it a small masterpiece.

Film historian William K. Everson cites Son's performance as one of his best, comparing it favorably to Ford's classic *Stagecoach*. "Ben Johnson and Joanne Dru, a dull actress who came to life for Ford, were Ringo and Dallas from *Stagecoach* all over again. Johnson, one of Ford's best players, gave an especially appealing performance."[24]

Everson, further praises *Wagonmaster,* calling it "a lovely, leisurely movie, a deliberately romanticized invocation of the pioneer spirit, all beautiful images and stirring ballads."[25] He adds, that *Wagonmaster* "get(s) better with each viewing."[26]

Sadly, perhaps because Son was not a major star, *Wagonmaster* did poorly at the box office.

CHAPTER NINE
STANDING UP TO FORD – BUT NOW AN ACTOR

John Ford began preparing the third of his cavalry epics in 1950, a film entitled *Rio Grande*. More somber than *Fort Apache* and *She Wore A Yellow Ribbon*, the film focuses on the relationship of a cavalry colonel (John Wayne), his estranged wife (Maureen O'Hara) and their son (Claude Jarman, Jr.).

Ford had moved his production company to Republic Studios, a studio more known for Roy Rogers and Gene Autry B Westerns than for quality productions. As television loomed on the horizon as a serious threat to movie attendance, studio head Herbert J. Yates began attracting directors known for A pictures to his studio. He lured Orson Welles to Republic for a low-budget, but highly effective version of William Shakespeare's *MacBeth*, and now he had Ford.

Son, feeling that his new career as an actor was well underway, splurged and bought a 1950 Studebaker, a beautiful cream-colored sedan. When he arrived at the gates of Republic Studios to begin work on *Rio Grande*,

Richard D. Jensen

the gate guard recognized him and waved him on through. Ironically, Son's co-star – and now best friend – Harry "Dobe" Carey, Jr. was denied entrance. Dobe said thereafter that it was because he had driven up in a 1947 Plymouth coupe, while Son had driven up in a sleek new car. Additionally, Son parked his Studebaker in the VIP parking lot and Dobe had to park in the general parking.[1]

During the first pre-production meeting, Ford told Son and Dobe that Jarman would be playing Wayne's son, and that Ford wanted all three of them to learn how to Roman ride for the film. Roman riding is where one horseman stands on two side-by-side horses, with a foot on each horse's back, and the horses work in tandem.

Son stepped up and told Ford that you couldn't just use any horses for a Roman ride, that the horses had to be trained to work in tandem. Ford immediately ordered Son to go to Fat Jones' stable and have some horses – and the three actors – trained.

Dobe insisted that he could never learn how to trick ride, but Son told him, "Dobe, you're gonna be one now, or you'll be damn sure out of a job."[2]

Fat Jones, Son's father-in-law, assigned Kenny Lee to train two teams. One team was a pair of sorrel horses. The other team was a pair of thoroughbreds. In less than a week, the team was performing well, with only an occasional problem, but the thoroughbred team was still prone to acting up and even bucking. Dobe recalled that he and Son went out to Fat's stable to watch the training and Son seemed anxious to try it. Dobe was not so enthusiastic. Son spent the afternoon aiding Lee and talking about the finer points of Roman riding, including how much rein pressure was needed by the rider to control the horses.[3]

About a week later, Fat's secretary, Connie, called Dobe and told him to be at Fat's stable at 9 a.m. the following morning. When he arrived, Son was there. The two men had their first lessons in Roman riding. The ring was so small that the horses had to lope in a tight circle. By the end of the day, the strain of crouching on the backs of the horses was too much for both men. They could hardly walk. Son and Dobe went straight to a spa on Vineland Boulevard, a favorite with stuntmen because it had whirlpool baths.[4]

Shortly thereafter Jarman arrived for training and within two weeks all three actors could Roman ride. The sequence is a highlight of the film.

Rio Grande was shot from mid-June 1950 until the end of July 1950 in Moab, Utah, which is similar to Monument Valley in appearance but an easier location at which to film due to proximity to town. That said, there were few modern hotels and other facilities. The cast lived in simple motels, as they did on location in Monument Valley.[5]

Much of the film was shot at the George White Ranch. The first shot of the film was the roll call sequence. The scene is where Victor McLaglen is playing a drill instructor and he's bellowing at Son, Dobe and Jarman, among other recruits. It is typical of Ford's Irish humor, and it has some wonderful dialog. McLaglen is delightful.[6]

Chuck Roberson remembered a funny incident that occurred during the filming of *Rio Grande*. He and Son were to gallop their horses toward the camera and when their paths intercepted, Roberson was to take a spectacular horse fall. The scene was to be shot at a canter - what cowboys call a lope – a slow gallop that looks faster on film because the cameraman slows the camera speed down three to four frames per second so that when the film is shown at regular speed the action looks faster. Roberson decided – without telling Son – that he thought that if the stunt looked good at a lope, it would look even better at a full gallop.

Ford yelled "Action!" and the two men began riding toward each other at a lope. Roberson suddenly urged his horse to a full gallop. Son began shouting, "dammit, slow down!"

"I kept right on going as hard as I could go. I left Ben in the dust, but when I reached the spot where I was supposed to fall that old horse, I just kept right on going past the camera."

"'Shit!' I yelled, as the horse finally came down fifteen feet past the mark; I rolled through a row of folding chairs like a cannon ball, we scattered the crew to hell and gone and as I dusted myself off and looked for a sympathetic face I could see that I was looking for something that wasn't there."

"Ben came up to me and said, 'What the hell were you doing? There's nobody can make a horse fall from that speed.' Of course, at that time he was right."[7]

Carey recalls that Ford shot the *Rio Grande* at a leisurely pace, referring to it as a "vacation" picture.[8]

The phrase refers to a film made in a location where either a director or star wants to film just so he can be in a certain locale. Many actors take roles in films merely to visit the locations on which the film is made. Oscar-winner Michael Caine has often joked that he took a certain film because he'd never visited whatever country in which the film was shot.

The *Rio Grande* schedule was simple: Three weeks of shooting in Moab and one week at Republic's Studio City, California backlot.[9] Despite the leisurely pace, Ford was ahead of schedule for most of the shoot. When he drifted over, he didn't care. He simply made up the time by shooting one take of a scene, usually in a medium shot where all of the actors were in the scene, and then yelling "print!"

It was this leisurely, and seemingly lackadaisical shooting – so out of the norm for Ford – that indirectly caused Son's relationship with the dictatorial director to sour. Son noticed during the filming that Ford seemed distracted, like he wasn't taking the film as seriously as others.

Son had an altercation with Ford during dinner one night on location in Monument Valley. The location was primitive, with limited hotel and dining space at Goulding's Lodge, right in the middle of the Navajo Reservation. Many of the actors lived in hotel rooms and trailers and the cast and crew ate meals together in a big dining room. Ford always took the third table from the door.[10]

The story is widely told. During the dinner, Son mentioned to Dobe Carey that the day's filming seemed to consist of a lot of riding and shooting, but with no real cohesion. "It seemed to me that Ford wasn't taking the film as seriously as he normally did. He seemed to be sort of easier to work with. Not much shouting and

Richard D. Jensen

abuse. Except for one time I made a comment to Dobe that there'd been a lot of shooting going on that day, but not many Indians had bitten the dust."

Son and Dobe both remembered years later that it was actually actor Grant Withers, a notorious loud mouth, who made a comment that Ford heard and found offensive.[11]

In any event, as luck would have it, the room grew silent and Ford's head popped up and he fixed a withering gaze on Son. "What did you say?"

Trying to avoid a confrontation, Son deflected the question by answering, "I was talking to Dobe, Mr. Ford."

Ford grew angrier and said, "I know that. What did you say?"

Again, Son tried to avoid a confrontation with Ford, answering, "I was talking to Dobe, Mr. Ford."

Dobe tried to come to Son's defense. "Uncle Jack, Ben didn't say nothin.'"[12]

Ford lost his temper and shouted, "Hey, stupid, I asked you a question."[13]

Son and Dobe also remembered that Ford said, "You mind your own business."[14]

Ford, however, had made a huge mistake. Ben "Son" Johnson was an Oklahoma cowboy from the tip of his hat to the soles of his boot heels. In his world, it was rude for someone to interrupt a conversation and asks what was being said in private, but it was fightin' words to call another man "stupid." Ford was accustomed to being able to insult everyone on his set without fear, mainly because he held the livelihoods of his cast and crew in his hands.

It didn't matter to Son that Ford was writing him a check. He had just been insulted, and Son would not let that go without a response.

"There was about 200 people in the dining room all gettin' around close so they could hear me get chewed out," Son said.[15]

With a steely glint in his eyes, Son rose cooly from the table and walked straight to Ford, and bent down, whispering in his ear.

"The old man said something pretty bad to me and I proceeds to tell him what he can do with his picture and I guess I shouldn't have done that but that was my way of gettin' even with him," Son said.[16]

The exact words aren't known, as neither Ford nor Son would repeat what was said, but Son recounted years later that "... as I passed Ford, I whispered to him what he could do with his damn picture. I could see Duke and Maureen (O'Hara) with their jaws dropping to the ground."[17]

Son then left the mess hall without another word.

Dobe Carey said that there was "no doubt in anyone's mind that he was ready to kill!" Carey said after Son spoke the room was filled with a "deadly silence."[18]

Son refused to speak to Ford the rest of the evening and most of the next day.

O'Hara remembered that the incident substantially changed her opinion of Ford, whom she now viewed with increasing discomfort – indeed alarm. She said that after this incident she began to see chinks in Ford's armor.[19]

Ford was in a pickle. He needed Son to finish his part in the film and Son refused to speak to Ford. The director needed to finish the movie without expensive retakes with another actor, and to do so he had to have Son on the set. So, forced to eat crow, Ford made nice with Son and spent the entire rest of the shoot treating Son with an over-exaggerated courtliness. Many on the set knew that such treatment by Ford signaled the end of that actor's working relationship with the director.

True to form, after the filming was over, Son didn't work for Ford for more than a decade.

"So, he lets Dobe and I finish the picture but don't hire us – he don't hire Dobe for eight years and he don't hire me for 11." Son said.[20]

Son avoided the Hollywood gossip over the incident and tried to put the best foot forward.

"That John Ford, I worked for him for six years. I mean, he was a mean old bastard, but if you listened to him, you could learn something," Son said years later.[21]

O'Hara recalled the *Rio Grande* fiasco years later, pointedly stating that Son was a "total professional" and noted that years later Son won his Oscar for *The Last Picture Show* "without Ford"'s help.[22]

Despite the run-in that would cost Son work with Ford for eleven years, he remembered working on *Rio Grande* fondly, mostly because he enjoyed working with the cast, and especially the famous Roman riding scenes with Dobe Carey and Claude Jarman, Jr.

"We had quite an experience with the Roman Riding. I always like to ride a horse and did a lot of riding in that picture."[23]

Rio Grande was released on November 15, 1950, to praise from leading film critics.

CHAPTER TEN
IN THE WILDERNESS

Son's phone suddenly stopped ringing.

John Ford had either passed the word, or it simply floated on the ether, but suddenly Ben Johnson was no longer in demand as an actor – at least as far as Ford was concerned.

As the year 1951 began, Son worried that he'd have to go back to ranching. If he was lucky, he might continue his dual life of stuntman moonlighting as an actor.

After several nervous months, film-makers not beholding to Ford came calling. Their films weren't the top quality Westerns Son had made for Ford, but it was work. By mid- summer, director John Rawlins was looking for a co-star to give some credibility to his new low-budget Western called *Fort Defiance*. For his lead actor, Rawlins had hired Dane Clark, a popular TV actor known more for gritty gangster roles – not Westerns. Rawlins knew Son was the perfect actor to bring some authenticity to the film.

Son signed on to play co-star opposite Clark and Peter Graves, the actor who would later star in TV's

Fury and *Mission Impossible*. Graves was the younger brother of James Arness, John Wayne's protégé. The film was shot in Gallup, New Mexico.

Fort Defiance has in its cast Son's frequent co-star Iron Eyes Cody and popular Dennis Moore, a Warner Brothers's singing star in the 1940s whose career was slipping badly. A run-of-the-mill Western, *Fort Defiance* was released on October 9, 1951.

When Son finished *Fort Defiance*, he was surprised – and relieved – to be immediately cast in the lead role in the low budget B Western *Wild Stallion*. Shot at Monogram Pictures, one of the lowest ranked independent studios in Hollywood, the film was a far cry from the heady A-list films of John Ford, but it was work and a paycheck and a starring role.

Released on April 27, 1952 and shot in color, the movie is only slightly glossier than normal B-Western. That said, the cast is quite good, especially Martha Hyer, who would later marry director Hal Wallis and would later co-star with John Wayne in *The Sons of Katie Elder* and co-write *Rooster Cogburn* for Wayne. Stalwart character actor Edgar Buchanan is on hand, as well.

Such roles were good for two reasons, it kept Son working and kept a paycheck coming in and it added to his reputation as an actor more so than a stunt man. A great many directors and producers in Hollywood thought of Son as a stuntman who could act. As he grew older, Son wanted the industry to view him as an actor who could do his own stunts.

Why? Because actors made more money than stuntmen. Lots more.

Son was perfect for Westerns because he was a real cowboy. His mannerisms were 100% authentic. No actor sat a horse better than Son, and there were darn few actors who could actually cowboy. When Son played a cowboy, he could ride and rope and work cows or herd horses. Whenever Son spoke, his voice rang with a true Oklahoma accent. Ben Johnson was the real deal.

Hiring Ben Johnson gave a producer an actor who would save that producer the expense of a stuntman or wrangler to double for Son. Son gave a producer reduced costs and added authenticity.

This is what lured one of the finest directors in Hollywood to hire Son for his newest movie.

Throughout 1950 and 1951, director George Stevens was planning a film adaptation of Jack Schaeffer's classic Western novel *Shane*. It is the story of sodbusters who move into a valley controlled by ruthless cattle barons. Besieged by daily and nightly attacks, the farmers are about to give up when into their midst rides a lone gunman who comes to their aid.

Initially, Stevens had cast Montgomery Clift to play Shane, William Holden to play Joe Starrett, the beleaguered rancher, and Katherine Hepburn to play Starrett's wife. Production delays resulted in all three actors being unavailable, so Stevens went looking for new leads.

Alan Ladd, his career badly in need of a hit, was cast as Shane and Van Heflin was cast as Joe. Jean Arthur agreed to play Marian. Son was cast as Chris Calloway, one of the ranch hands who goads Shane into a violent saloon brawl.

Richard D. Jensen

The film was shot in Jackson Hole, Wyoming between July and October, 1951. It was not released until April 23, 1953 because Stevens kept obsessively reediting the film until he felt it was perfect.

The shooting of the movie was fraught with odd problems. Ladd was terrible with guns. It took over 116 takes for the fast-draw scene to be shot. Jack Palance, whose performance as the evil hired gun made him a star, was terrified of horses. He could not mount a horse without looking afraid and clumsy. Stevens was exasperated. He asked Son to help Palance with his horsemanship, but to no avail.

Eventually, Stevens shot Palance dismounting a horse and played the film backwards to get the required shot.

The famous fistfight between Shane and Chris is an iconic moment of Western film. It too was difficult to film for one reason. Ladd was incredibly short and Son was nearly as tall as John Wayne.

Son stood well over six feet tall and weighed slightly over 200 pounds. Ladd was just over five feet tall and was of slight build. In order to make the fight believable, Stevens had a walkway built over the floor of the saloon to make Ladd as tall as Son. Son recalled later that filming the fight scene was a painstaking process because he had to brawl with Ladd without knocking him off the platform. The cameraman had to shoot at odd camera angles to make Ladd look bigger and Son look smaller.

The end result is a thrilling fight scene, in which the diminutive Alan Ladd bests the much bigger Ben Johnson.

Because of the delays in the shooting schedule, Son had plenty of time to do some fishing with Ladd and Heflin, both avid anglers.

"We fished, sure," Son said. "We filmed *Shane* up around Jackson Hole, Wyoming, and there's the Snake River there and a lot of lakes. We had a lot of fun. Caught a lot of good fish too – trout, rainbow trout. I love any kind of fish, bass but I prefer trout. I like to put lemon and butter on them and put them in the broiler. And I, myself, like to use a little cornmeal once in a while."[1]

Shane is a marvel of color photography and staging. The film is dazzling from the opening shot of Shane, framed in the antlers of an elk, to the final shot of Shane riding away as the young boy (Brandon DeWilde), who worships Shane as his hero, cries for him come back.

Son is especially charismatic in the film, bringing added dimension to his character and making his character, ostensibly a bully, almost likeable at times. He is taller and better looking than Ladd, and he is far more "western" that Ladd. His costume is quintessentially cowboy, and he exudes realism, where at times Ladd struggles to be believable as the notorious gunfighter. One wonders what would have resulted had Son been cast in the title role!

Film historian William K. Everson praised the performance of the entire cast, "with Ben Johnson especially effective among the supporting players, displaying a subtlety of acting style as a three-dimensional villain that had not been apparent in his effortless playing of his straightforward and likeable heroes for Ford."[2]

Richard D. Jensen

Around the time of Shane's premiere, Hubbard Keavy wrote an article for Bob Thomas' Hollywood, lauding Son as Hollywood's true cowboy. "Do you know who the best cowboy in all Hollywood is? Ben Johnson, that's who." Keavy wrote. Keavy noted that both Joel McCrea and Wild Bill Elliott were the other two real cowboys starring in movies at the time.[3]

Son had high praise for Shane's director. "George Stevens was one of the greatest directors I've ever worked for," Son recalled.

When not working on a film, Son hated the Hollywood scene and stayed as far away from it as he could while maintaining enough contact to keep working. He kept his film life separate from his real life, so much so that he refused to have a phone at his ranch. "When I'm in town, it's for business. When I'm at the ranch, I come up here to get away from everything, the telephone especially. Everybody makes fun of me, but I get up there to relax, go fishing, hunting or horseback riding. I don't like to take my work home with me," Son said.[4]

The year 1952 arrived and it turned out to be a difficult year for Son. His film career was nearly derailed again by Ford and, more importantly, his beloved father died.

It was in 1952 that Ford began to soften a little about Son and put out the word that he might want Son to star in a movie entitled *The Sun Shines Bright*, a remake of Ford's film *Judge Priest* (1933).

The absolute worst thing that could have happened to Son subsequently took place. Upon hearing of Ford's plan, Son's agent called Ford and named a high price for

Son's services. Ford was notorious for dealing directly with actors, setting their salaries without negotiation, and freezing out agents in the process. Ford wanted the actors beholden to him for their work, not believing their agents had beaten Ford into a deal.

When Son's agent made his demands, Ford lost his temper, ripped the phone off the wall and swore neither he nor any other director would ever hire the ungrateful Ben Johnson.[5] Ford cast Charles Winninger in the lead in the less-than-memorable film. The role would have been a plum starring role for Son. Ford's resolve to blacklist Son was steeled.

As bad as this news was for Son professionally, there was even worse news from back home. Back in Oklahoma, Ben Johnson was dying and didn't even know it.

Ben had stomach cancer. It started with a stomach ache in the early part of 1950 and gradually grew worse. Ben thought the sharp stomach pains were indigestion. Many others thought Ben had an ulcer.

By 1952, Ben suddenly fell so ill he could not work.

The family took him to the nearest hospital, the Snyder Clinic in Winfield, Kansas. Dr. Cecil Snyder knew Ben well, and often went to the Chapman Barnard Ranch to hunt quail with him. The two men became close and had made a pact: If Ben was ever fatally ill, Dr. Snyder wouldn't tell him. Ben wanted to live each day to the fullest.

When Snyder operated on Ben, he realized Ben had an advanced case of stomach cancer. Helen was at the hospital when Snyder finished the exploratory surgery. Snyder told Helen the bad news.

Richard D. Jensen

Helen said that she and Snyder agreed to abide by Ben's pact with Snyder. They agreed to keep the extent of Ben's illness from him. Helen said she later regretted that decision. Years later Helen said she believed that the wrong decision was made. She said her father might have had more to say to his children had he known his end was near. It is clear that this still causes Helen great sadness.[6]

"Dad couldn't understand why he wasn't getting better," Helen said. "It was a bad thing."

As his condition worsened, Ben hated being in the hospital. Helen arranged for Ben to live in the quaint Sonner Motel in Winfield. Dr. Snyder provided full-time nurses to attend to Ben the entire time. James Chapman paid for everything.

Ben perked up at the improved surroundings, and received visits from Helen and other family members. Son came as soon as he heard of his father's grave condition and stayed by his side during his final weeks.

Ben rapidly lost weight and strength and died on Monday, September 15, 1952. He was 56 years old.

Helen, Sis and Son made arrangements to have their father transported back to Pawhuska, where news of his passing spread like wildfire among the close-knit ranching community.

Ben Johnson's funeral was held at 4 p.m. on Wednesday, September 17, 1952, at Johnson Funeral Home in Pawhuska. The building was packed with mourners, all of whom came to pay their last, somber respects to the man who was the life of the party and the rock of their community. Larger than life, the gregarious Ben Johnson's death seemed inconceivable. He was too young, too virile, too vibrant, too happy. For Ben to die so young seemed, to those in attendance, incomprehensible.

After the service Ben was laid to rest next to Aileen on a windswept, grassy hillside in a community that seemed somehow less alive with his passing. Ben was buried with his favorite boots on, his favorite lariat in his hand.[7]

CHAPTER ELEVEN
SON GOES BACK TO HIS ROOTS AND ROPES

Ben Johnson's untimely death clearly drove Son back into rodeo. He never discussed it, but it is likely that Son went back to his roots to find some peace with the staggering loss of his father.

Surely returning to a world of cowboys – many of them close friends – eased Son's grief. Son was devastated by his father's untimely death at age 56. It is certain that the blacklisting of Son by John Ford had taken it's toll on Son's income and prospects in Hollywood. He had some money put aside, so why not?

Son candidly told a reporter in 1972 that he felt like he never measured up when his father was alive. "I felt defeated because I couldn't produce what was expected of me," Son said.[1] "I decided to take the whole year and see if I could do it – and I did. I had to try because my father had been world champion five or six times. I'd heard championship all my life to the point I decided, if my father can do it, I'd like to try to do it. And then

I really didn't care if was the championship of playing marbles or whatever. I just wanted to be the best too."[2]

He left Hollywood and struck out on the rodeo circuit.

Son bankrolled his rodeo career with the money from his movie work. "I got in a position where I could afford to travel, so I decided to see just what I could do," Son said. He jointed up with pals Andy Jauregui and Buckshot Sorrells in the team roping.

"To him, it was an 'If dad did it, I want to do it, too.' I think Dad's passing away made it possible and he had some money then and he was able to hit the road," Helen said.[3]

The years growing up under the tutelage of his roping champion father paid off. Son was a top-flight roper and quickly rose in the ranks. By the season's end, Son was competing for the world championship. Sadly, the Rodeo Cowboy Association (now the Professional Rodeo Cowboy Association) did not keep detailed statistics during the 1950s, so there are few records of his winning times or earnings.

Son, with typical modesty, said his world championship was merely a matter of luck. "That was the year everybody else had hard luck," Son said.[4]

Casey Tibbs, the legendary rodeo champion who won seven world titles, said, "Ben could have been one of the greatest ropers of all time if he had done it full-time."

Ever the pragmatist, Son realized that his rodeo championship had left him broke.

"When I finished up that year, I had a worn out pickup, a mad wife and exactly $3 in my pocket. I went back to the movie business where the money was a little better. I was very fortunate they let me back in," Son said.[5]

With all the acclaim and awards Son would win in years to come, his championship buckle meant the most to him.

"That big silver buckle they gave me means more to me than that Oscar," Son said.

Son returned to his ranch north of Los Angeles and vowed to restart his film career yet again.

CHAPTER TWELVE
AN ACTOR AGAIN FROM SCRATCH

After winning the RCA World Championship in team roping, Son was flat broke. He was so broke he "couldn't even pay attention."

And taking a year off from Hollywood to rodeo had robbed his movie career of necessary momentum. He knew that if he wanted to work in the film industry, he'd have to remind producers and directors that he was still in the business.

To his chagrin, the many actors, directors and producers aligned with John Ford acted as though Son did not exist. Ford's boycott was nearly complete.

With little acting work being offered, Son jumped at the chance to do stunt work again, only this time the Western movie he signed up for was also the hottest and most anticipated musical of the decade.

Oklahoma! was originally a play by Lynn Riggs entitled *Green Grow The Lilacs*, which opened on Broadway in 1931 starring Texas cowboy star Tex Ritter. Broadway composers Richard Rodgers and

Richard D. Jensen

Oscar Hammerstein revamped the play into a musical and in March 1943 the retitled *Oklahoma!* was an immediate smash hit, running for an amazing 2200 performances.

As was always the case with Broadway musicals, Hollywood brought the play to the screen.

James Dean and Paul Newman were both considered for the lead role of Curly, but neither man could sing and neither was very good in light, musical-comedy roles. The producers considered Frank Sinatra and even Howard Keel, who starred in the London production of the show, but instead chose the marvelous Gordon MacRae. There was some discussion of Broadway actress Joan Roberts reprising the role of Laurey, but producers cast a newcomer named Shirley Jones, who became a huge star when the film opened on January 9, 1956.

Son had no lines, no visible on-camera role, and was hired to stunt-double MacRae, a singer with little experience with horses, and make the singer look good in the action sequences.

Son, ever on the lookout for ways to make money behind the scenes in movies, rented the producers his herd of longhorn cattle from his Escalon, California ranch to be used in the movie. Virgil Berry, an old friend of Son's from Bartlesville, Oklahoma, was Son's ranch manager. He assisted Son with the cattle during production.[1]

The film was shot on location in the Arizona towns of Nogales and Amado, and the famous train station sequence, where Gene Nelson signs and dances the famous song, "Kansas City," was shot at the train station in Elgin, Arizona, where Son had worked on *Red River.*

The famous corn field used in the opening number, where Curley sings, "Oh What A Beautiful Morning!" was created just for the scene. Arizona Agriculture Department botanists planted corn in pots and cultivated the field carefully to ensure the corn stalks would grow 16 feet high.

Having finished his stunt work on *Oklahoma!*, Son was able to wrangle a bit part in a low-budget Western starring John Payne. Produced by Aubrey Schenck and Howard Koch for their company, Schenck-Koch Productions, *Rebel In Town* opened on July 30, 1956 and was a forgettable Western. Son had little to do in it but stunt double Payne in the riding sequences and play a bit part. After the heady days of working for John Ford and the winning of a world championship in rodeo, this demotion to stunt man was hard to take, but it was work. And Son wanted to work. He had bills to pay and dreams of owning bigger and bigger ranches – and donating more of his time to charity work and rodeos. He also wanted to commemorate his father's life and career. When the Osage County Cattlemen's Association proposed the idea of an event celebrating Ben's life, Son signed on.

In June 1954, Pawhuska rancher John Tillmon put together and staged the first-ever Ben Johnson Memorial Steer Roping. The event raised money for charity and was held in Ben's honor. Son attended and roped, but didn't win the competition.

The event has been held each year in mid-June at the Osage County Cattlemen's Convention ever since.

Richard D. Jensen

Like many actors in the 1950s, Son recognized that the number of films being made for theaters was rapidly declining, but television was booming – and most of the new shows were Westerns.

America, gripped in the uncertainty of the Cold War and with constant anxiety over the possibility of nuclear war, focused its collective energy on entertainment with traditional themes, and Westerns provided TV audiences with that comfort.

Son, eager to work steadily as an actor, began accepting parts in both films and television, something many actors would not do. There was a fear running rampant in Hollywood at the time that an actor who worked in film would lose film roles if he accepted work in television.

Son bucked the trend and began seeking out and landing roles on television.

To Sons's surprise, John Ford alumnus Ward Bond decided to risk Ford's censure and called. He was about to star in a TV episode of the popular *Cavalcade of Stars*. The show was like many series of that day, focusing on new stories and new characters every week. The show had a script entitled *Once A Hero*, written by Jack Schaefer, the author of *Shane*. *Once A Hero* was about a boy and his father, a reputed legendary rodeo cowboy. Bond insisted that the producers hire Son to play a champion rodeo cowboy. Son was grateful to Bond for the vote of confidence, which came at some risk. John Ford had a long memory and violent temper, and Bond's gesture could have caused Bond some discomfort.

That said, Bond had become a staple on television, and his popularity had soared. *Once A Hero* aired on December 11, 1956. The following year Bond would be cast in the lead role of Major Seth Adams in *Wagon Train*, a TV adaptation of the 1950 Ford film *Wagonmaster*. The series premiered on September 18, 1957 and roared to the top of the ratings. Bond was hailed for his work on the series, but his hard living and boisterous lifestyle caught up with him on November 5, 1960 when he died at age 57 of a heart attack while in Dallas, Texas to attend a college football game.

Bond's death stunned the inner circle of the John Ford Stock Company, and John Wayne – Bond's closest friend – was never the same. Wayne's devil-may-care optimism transformed into a dark fatalism that would sour his demeanor with increasing severity over the rest of Wayne's life.

Meanwhile, Aubrey Schenck and Howard Koch were preparing a new Western and, having liked Son's affable personality and no-nonsense approach to stunt work, wanted to hire Son for an role.

The film, entitled *War Drums*, starred Lex Barker, the handsome, muscular actor who had succeeded Johnny Weissmuller as Tarzan. Barker had switched to Westerns and *War Drums* was the beginning of a 20-year period of productivity where the actor would eventually make Westerns in Europe, even before Clint Eastwood went to Italy and became famous in the "spaghetti Westerns."

Son has a speaking role, playing bad guy Luke Fargo, while Barker plays Mangas Coloradas, the hero. The film was shot in color in the gorgeous colored deserts around Kanab, Utah. Released on March 21, 1957, *War Drums* made a small profit, then disappeared from theaters. It mattered little to Son, who was back in the movies in speaking roles.

His career as an actor back on track, Son was cast in *Slim Carter*, an odd film about a country singer (Jock Mahoney) who becomes a famous cowboy star. Son plays Montana Burris, the real-life cowboy hired to stunt double the movie star. Released in November, 1957, the film is light entertainment, and somewhat enjoyable. Son adds credibility to the story as the real cowboy, allowing Mahoney, himself a former stunt double for Gene Autry, to focus on his singing. Mahoney does his own stunts in the film.

Son enjoyed working with Mahoney, and the two men would remain friends for many years.

For the third time in two years, Aubrey Schenck and Howard Koch came calling and offered Son yet another role in a Western. This time Son was offered the lead in *Fort Bowie*, a calvary Western. Shot on location in the deserts around Kanab, Utah, the film was cast with largely unknown actors. It was released on February 1, 1958 and Son was happy to let family and friends now he was back playing leading roles in Westerns.

Television production began to outpace film production in the late 1950s, and Son took advantage of the need television producers had for a dependable cowboy/actor.

Son appeared on the popular *The Adventures of Ozzie and Harriet*, in an episode entitled *Top Gun*. Son played a cowboy named Tex Barton and the episode aired on April 2, 1958.

Son then appeared in a TV show called *Navy Log*, in an episode entitled *Florida Weekend*. In the show, Son played a border patrol agent. The episode aired on August 21, 1958.

Son was then cast as a sheriff in the TV show *The Restless Gun*, in an episode entitled *No Way To Kill*. The episode aired on November 24, 1958 and starred John Payne.

Movie suspense master Alfred Hitchcock's successful TV series offered Son the role of a sheriff in an episode of *Alfred Hitchcock Presents* entitled *And The Desert Shall Blossom,* which aired on December 21, 1958.

The opening introduction, for which Hitchcock was famous, has the corpulent British director standing in front of a fake cactus and wearing a black Tom Mix Stetson. It's quite funny.

The episode starred William Demarest and Roscoe Ates, two long-time character actors. The opening desert shots are of stock footage of the Arizona desert, then the scene dissolves to a studio "exterior" of a desert cabin.

Son is quite good as the sheriff. In the opening scene, the sheriff tries to convince two old prospectors to move into town where they can live in a retirement community with other senior citizens. They refuse, and insist that they can survive in the desert. The sheriff tells them that the town council wants the two oldsters off of their claim, and the prospectors bet the sheriff they can make a bush bloom with roses in less than a month to prove they can survive in the desert. After the sheriff leaves, a gangster arrives and threatens the old men, who turn the tables on him.

The sheriff returns to search for the gangster, and he is suspicious of the story the two men concoct about the gangster having merely stopped by and fled. Son conveys the right amount of skepticism and authority.

Demarest, a seasoned character actor who became famous as Uncle Charlie in TV's *My Three Sons*, chews scenery as an angry prospector. Ates is a marvel. His calm, sincere performance as Ben the prospector is brilliant.

The plot is typical Hitchcock, and the bush thrives because of the dead gangster's body buried beneath it.

Son then appeared in the TV series *Border Patrol* in an episode entitled *Everglades Story*. The show aired on March 10, 1959.

The popularity of Westerns on TV was enormous, and Son found a ready market for his talent guest-starring on the numerous Western series of the time.

Laramie was a hit series starring Robert Crawford, Jr. and Robert Fuller, who also starred on TV's *Wagon Train*. John Smith co-starred. The show was set in Wyoming. Crawford and Smith are brothers who open a stagecoach station on their failing ranch in an effort to save their land in the wake of their father's death. The premise gave the show ample opportunity to introduce new characters each week for new episodes. Son was cast in an episode entitled *Hour After Dawn*, which aired on March 15, 1960.

In 1960 Son had the opportunity to work with a young director named Andrew MacLaglen. MacLaglen was the son of beloved actor Victor MacLaglen, with whom Son had worked – and conspired to stash whiskey – on John Ford's cavalry trilogy.

MacLaglen was directing an episode of the popular TV series *Have Gun Will Travel*, which starred Richard Boone as Paladin, an adventurer who traveled the west righting wrongs. The episode in which Son was signed to appear was entitled *A Head of Hair*, and was written by Harry Julian Fink. Less than a decade later MacLaglen and Fink would both work often with John Wayne, as would Son.

The episode, which aired on September 24, 1960, also co-starred George Kennedy, who would win an Oscar for his performance in the Paul Newman film *Cool Hand Luke* in 1967. Stuntman "Good" Chuck Hayward, with whom Son had worked on several Ford Westerns, also appeared in the episode.

Son then jumped back to the movies when he was cast in a Walt Disney film entitled *Ten Who Dared* (1960).

The film was shot around Moab, Utah. Indeed, it was the ninth film Son had made in Utah in 14 years. *Ten Who Dared* starred Brian Keith, with whom Son would work again in *The Rare Breed* (1966) and James Drury, who would star in the smash hit TV series *The Virginian*. Son became close friends with Drury and would guest star often on *The Virginian* in the next decade. Drury would often appear at charity roping events organized by Son over the next two decades.

Character actor L.Q. Jones also appeared in the episode and Son would work with Jones often in the next 20 years, including on the classic *The Wild Bunch*.

Richard D. Jensen

The film also featured old pal Stan Jones, the park ranger turned songwriter who wrote the anthem, *Ghost Riders In The Sky* in 1949 while working for the National Park Service in Death Valley, California and who had accompanied Son to Pawhuska for the premiere of *Wagonmaster*.

Ten Who Dared was released on November 1, 1960.

Son was back on the set of the TV series *Laramie* almost immediately after finishing *Ten Who Dared*. He was cast as a stagecoach driver in an episode entitled *A Sound of Bells*. Dick Foran, the Irish-American actor who often appeared in John Ford Westerns in bit parts and was known for his marvelous singing voice also appeared. At one point Foran was groomed as a singing cowboy to compete with Gene Autry, but his career focused more on musicals. The episode aired on December 27, 1960.

For Son, the television work was uneven. Some roles were major feature parts, while others were merely bit parts. It didn't matter. He took whatever work he was offered. He had no desire to go back to ranch work, and he had bills to pay and ranch payments to make.

Son's acting career got a gigantic boost when he was cast in one of the most controversial Westerns ever made, a film entitled *One-Eyed Jacks*, starring, partially written, produced and directed by Marlon Brando.

Brando was everything Ben "Son" Johnson was not. Son was down-to-earth, a true cowboy who would rather spend his days away from Hollywood-types and their egos. Son was Joe Everyman, more comfortable drinking coffee in a truck stop or country café than swilling martinis with the jet set.

Brando was all about the Hollywood scene. A "method actor" who had risen to fame on Broadway with his explosive portrayal of Stanley Kowalski in Tennessee Williams' *A Streetcar Named Desire,* Brando took Hollywood by storm in the 1950s and changed the landscape of film acting.

The leading actor of his generation, and the most notorious practitioner of the Stanislavski method of acting, Brando unofficially lead the invasion of Broadway actors who moonlighted in the new medium of live television into Hollywood stardom.

Brando's caché in Hollywood was typical of actors who rise to the zenith of critical and popular acclaim. He demanded – and got – outrageous perks, misbehaved during the production of movies – and got away with it. The demise of the studio system, where actors were mere employees of the studio had much to do with this. Actress Olivia deHavilland had sued and won a court battle against the studio-system.

Television had cut into the profit margins of movie studios. Actors now had the ability to work on TV and shirk the yoke of studio contracts. Studio moguls were used to operating like any other factory in a one-industry town, literally running actors' lives. By the mid-1950s actors were demanding big paychecks, percentages of the box office gross, and creative control of their movies.

Brando was one of many actors who took advantage of this newfound power.

Richard D. Jensen

In 1957 Brando was demanding that he be allowed to produce and star in a project called *A Burst of Vermillion* – and it was a Western. Brando wanted to adapt Charles Neider's novel, *The Authentic Death of Hendry Jones*, a fictional version of the relationship between William Bonney ("Billy the Kid") and lawman Pat Garrett.

Brando's Pennebaker Productions hired the screenwriter and director who had bought the rights to Neider's book for $40,000.00. His name was Sam Peckinpah, and he agreed to draft a screenplay and direct the film, which was to be shot in Mexico.

Peckinpah was born in rural California and had a tough childhood on a working cattle ranch. His life was upended when the ranch was sold and he was ever-after a soul adrift. Searching for a life on the edge, he enlisted during World War II and served in the South Pacific. Peckinpah was a hard-driving dynamo who drank, fought and whored his way through life. He was as macho as macho could be. He was obsessed with making lyrical movies about violent men – especially Westerns.

"The outlaws of the West have always fascinated me. They had a certain notoriety, they were supposed to have a Robin Hood quality about them, which was not really the truth. In a land for all intents and purposes without law, they made their own. I suppose I'm something of an outlaw myself, I identify with them," Peckinpah said in 1969.[2]

During the pre-production casting of *A Burst of Vermillion,* Brando cast Son to play the part of Bob, sidekick to Brando's tortured bank robber, Chris. It is Bob who turns Judas and betrays his friend at the climax of the film. This was a juicy part for Son, who had been languishing in TV roles for nearly a decade since his blacklist by Ford. Son was rescued from the wilderness by, of all people, Marlon Brando.

Ironically, six months into the pre-production of the project, Peckinpah had a falling out with Brando and was fired. Brando initially hired Stanley Kubrick to direct, then fired Kubrick and directed the movie himself.

Relocating the film's production from Mexico to Big Sur, California, the cast and crew assembled for what was to be a 60-day shoot. Brando, determined to film his vision at all costs, dragged filming on for six months. The actors spent half a year on salary, on a movie that was shot at a pace so slowly that it was maddening.

Brando would sit for hours with his camera crew and cast at the ready, watching the waves crash into the shore, waiting for the best waves to film. He cast a young Mexican actress named Pina Pellicer as the love interest, Louisa, and then spent hours coaxing a performance out of her. She was inexperienced, neurotic, terrified – and in love with Brando. At times she was so overwhelmed with the pressure of working on the film that she became catatonic and Brando would terrify her to get a reaction on film. During a scene in which she was supposed to show surprise and fear, Brando shot a pistol next to her with the camera rolling just to get her reaction on film.

For the cast, the one saving grace was that Brando had changed the production to Big Sur. Had Peckinpah

Richard D. Jensen

had his way, the actors would have been stuck in rural Mexico for a half a year. Son was thankful that Brando had hired fellow rodeo alum Slim Pickens, otherwise he'd have spent six months in the company of Brando's beatnik compadres.

The film finally wrapped production and it took another six months to edit. When Brando turned in his final edit of the film, it was five hours long!

The Paramount Studios brass was apoplectic. How in God's name, they screamed, could Brando deliver a film more than three times longer than the average American film?

The studio took the film away from Brando and recut it to only 141 minutes. Brando was furious and spoke openly about how he'd been robbed of his masterpiece. In fits of pique similar to those of film wunderkind Orson Welles (whose masterpieces *Citizen Kane*, *The Magnificent Ambersons* and *Touch of Evil* were gutted by studio editors) Brando disavowed any responsibility for the film.

The movie, renamed *One-Eyed Jacks*, premiered in New York City on December 31, 1960 and opened nationwide on March 30, 1961. Critics savaged the film and it bombed at the box office, but many film fans declared it a masterpiece.

One-Eyed Jacks is actually a very good movie. It has aged well and is far better than critics claimed at the time of its release. Sadly, the five-hour version was completely destroyed by the studio. One wonders what masterpiece may have been lost forever at the hands of studio bureaucrats.

Despite the film's lackluster showing at the box office, Son's career was resurrected. He had co-starred in a major Hollywood film with the biggest star of the new generation of film actors. Brando's hip fans, who would never otherwise see a Western because they viewed the genre as cliched and square, saw Son for the first time. Son, smartly, roughed up his look in the film, growing facial hair and played the traitorous Bob Amory with a greasy, smarmy menace.

Most importantly, Son had come to the attention of young Sam Peckinpah, the up-and-coming writer-director.

Peckinpah would thereafter hire Son for all of his major films of the 1960s. Working for Peckinpah would give Son something he'd never achieved in show business – critical acclaim for his acting skills.

Son's association with Peckinpah would make him the darling of the hip, anti-war generation. Son's situation was similar to that of country singer Johnny Cash, whose career had faltered until his friendship and collaboration with folk-rock icon Bob Dylan exposed Cash to a new generation of fans – and lengthened his career by decades.

Son's acting career was back in gear, and he continued to invest his movie money in more traditional businesses, such as real estate development and ranching.

Son even went into business with John Wayne, buying cattle with the Duke as far back as 1946.

Wayne co-owned a ranch in Arizona with Louis Johnson, a life-long rancher. Son was involved in cattle-breeding as well. At various times, Son and Wayne bought and sold bulls and did business together.

"I spent time with him in various cattle operations. That's how I know that Duke was an honest man," Son said. "I watched him make a lot of deals and a lot of swaps, and he was always an honest man."[3]

Rancher John Hughes of Pawhuska, Oklahoma explained that Wayne used his celebrity to boost prices at bull sales and swaps. He recalled a 1969 bull sale held by Pawhuksa rancher John Oxley, which Wayne attended.

"Wayne co-owned the Bar 20 in Arizona with Louis Johnson, and Oxley had a ranch here in Pawhuska," Hughes said. "Oxley would buy a Bar 20 bull and all the Bar 20 had to do was reciprocate. All they had to do was for John Wayne to show up.

"For example, Oxley would go to the Bar 20 sale and buy a bull and to reciprocate, all Wayne had to do was show up to Oxley's bull sale." Hughes said.

"You see, you buy a $10,000 bull and you buy two $5,000 heifers and no money changes hands. It boosts the sale average and it makes the people who buy at those sales feel better about paying half that much," Hughes said.[4]

Son dealt in the cattle business with Wayne because he believed that Wayne was honest. "It's a shame there aren't a lot of people around today like Duke. A lot of younger people don't even know what honesty means." Son said.[5]

CHAPTER THIRTEEN
IN THE WILDERNESS, STILL

One-Eyed Jacks did not launch Son back into the pantheon of character actors as he had hoped, but it did expose him to a new generation of film fans. And it landed him a major role in a small-budget Disney film called *Tomboy and the Champ*, a forgettable effort. Released on April 1, 1961, the film co-starred rodeo champion Casey Tibbs and featured singing cowboy legend Rex Allen, now making a living doing folksy voice-over narrations for Disney's live- action nature films.

As soon as he was done with *Tomboy and the Champ*, Son was back slugging it out from 1961 through 1964 in guest-star roles on TV, including a flurry of episodes of TV Westerns *Laramie, Have Gun Will Travel, Route 66, Bonanza, The Virginian, Stoney Burke* and *Gunsmoke*.

It is interesting how, during this period on the outs with John Ford that John Wayne did not once hire Son to work with him in a movie. The 1950s and 1960s were a period of significant productivity by Wayne, who had formed his own production company, Batjac. Wayne was chief, cook and bottle-washer on these films,

Richard D. Jensen

controlling all aspects of the films, from story to cast, to directors, crew, locations. Every detail was under Wayne's control. Son was in the cattle buying business with Duke, but he didn't make an effort to hire Son for his movies until 1969, when Ford was bedridden and had lost most of his power in Hollywood.

Did Wayne fear angering Ford? Was Wayne afraid of losing Ford's mentorship and affection?

Son never held it against Wayne, and indeed spoke only highly of him. The two men weren't close friends. They had little in common. Wayne was an actor who lived in Encino, California and later on the ocean in Newport Beach, California. Son lived part-time in Los Angeles and the rest of his time on his California ranch, or on ranches in Arizona or Oklahoma. The two men invested in the cattle business together and remained on good terms, but it was years before they worked on a film together.

Working as hard and as often as he could, Son was cast in an episode of *Laramie* entitled *Widow In White*, which aired on June 13, 1961. He then headed straight to another episode of *Have Gun Will Travel* entitled *The Race*, which aired on October 28, 1961.

Son was then hired by director David Lowell Rich for an episode of the trendy series *Route 66*, which starred George Maharis and Martin Milner. The episode was entitled *A Long Piece of Mischief,* and co-starred Slim Pickens and Denver Pyle, who had worked with John Ford a great deal in the 1950s when Son was ostracized by Ford. The episode aired on January 19, 1962. Rich got along well with Son on the production and would hire Son for a movie entitled *Runaway* a decade later.

Producer David Dortort's hit series *Bonanza* was in its third season. The show eventually became one of the longest-running and most popular programs in the history of television. Its theme song is one of the most recognizable pieces of music in modern culture.

Dortort was casting an episode entitled *The Gamble* and the director for the installment was William Witney, the veteran director of hundreds of B Westerns, mostly at Republic. Witney cast Son as a deputy sheriff. The story revolves around the Cartwrights being falsely accused and convicted of robbery and murder. In the episode, which aired on April 1, 1962, Son plays a corrupt deputy sheriff working for a dirty sheriff played by Charles McGraw. The episode is tense, directed with Witney's sure hand. The scenes are well-photographed, and the sequence where Little Joe Cartwright (Michael Landon) stalks Son down the dark street is as cinematic as the nighttime gunfight in Howard Hawks' *El Dorado*. Little Joe captures Son and threatens to hang him unless he comes clean. The episode is one of the best of the long-running series, more drama and less slapstick comedy that often occurred on the program. Long time Western character actors I. Stanford Jolley and Morris Ankrum both appear in the episode as a townsman and banker respectively.

Son would return to work on *Bonanza* in the future, and in several resurrected sequels after that.

Son then went back to work for director Andrew MacLaglen again for an episode of *Have Gun Will Travel* entitled *The Fifth Bullet,* which aired on September 29, 1962.

Richard D. Jensen

The television show *Stoney Burke* prepared an rodeo-themed episode entitled *Point of Honor* and director/writer Leslie Stevens cast Son and fellow rodeo great Casey Tibbs for the program, which aired on October 22, 1962.

When Universal Studios and NBC adapted Owen Wister's iconic Western novel *The Virginian* for TV, the plan was to make the highest quality television Western ever. The first season was well underway and the show was an instant hit with audiences when Son was cast in an episode entitled *Duel At Shiloh*. Brian Keith also co-starred, as did DeForest Kelley who would shortly thereafter achieve fame as Dr. McCoy on *Star Trek*. The episode aired on April 27, 1963. Son would come back to Shiloh Ranch and the hit show often during its nine-year run.

Son then headed for the mythical Dodge City of the hit TV series *Gunsmoke*, already in its eighth year. The episode, entitled *Quint-Cident,* aired on April 27, 1963. It featured Burt Reynolds, who played the character Quint on the show. Reynolds would soon quit *Gunsmoke* and in 1969 become an "overnight success" with the film *Deliverance*. Son would work with Reynolds again in 1975 in *Hustle*.

Son then made a quick appearance on the hit lawyer show *Perry Mason* in an episode entitled *The Case of The Reckless Hound*. The episode was shot in Bronson Canyon in Los Angeles, a famous cave set used in hundred of Western movies, and aired on November 26, 1964.

CHAPTER FOURTEEN
THE OLD MAN CALLS – CHEYENNE AUTUMN

By 1963, Ford was in failing health. He had begun to slip as a director. His tendency toward sentimentality had earned his films the reputation of being old hat. Warner Brothers had agreed to finance Ford's latest Western, an homage to the American Indian called *Cheyenne Autumn*. Ford summoned many of the fabled stock company for the film – including Dobe Carey and Son.

Both men were surprised to get the call, assuming that they'd never work for Ford again. As was Ford's method, he told neither men what their part would be, telling them they would be informed upon arrival on set.

When they reached the Moab, Utah location for the film, both discovered that they were to be basically extras, the background actors who fill the scenes behind the lead actors. Neither had a major part. To dig the knife in deeper, Ford also refused to give either man screen credit for their work.

Richard D. Jensen

On top of that, rather than quartering Son and Carey with the rest of the cast at Goulding's Lodge, they were housed in a mobile home a mile away from the rest of the cast.[1]

It is unknown why both men swallowed their pride and worked on *Cheyenne Autumn*. It is possible that they felt a sense of nostalgia about Ford, now 69 years of age and in terrible health. For Dobe, Ford had been his godfather, his "pappy." Ford had been instrumental in the rise of Dobe's father, Harry Carey, Sr., to superstardom in the silent movies. Ford had been a part of the Carey extended family before the senior Carey's death.

For Son, perhaps it was a similar sense of reunion. Ford had lifted Son from the ranks of the stuntman and placed him into the pantheon of actors, only to shun him to near oblivion.

Perhaps both Son and Dobe realized that their acting careers were a constant struggle for work, lurching from good parts to small parts, both earning a steady but modest living as featured actors guesting on TV Westerns. They may very well have considered that if they had aroused Ford's ire again, he might very well have ruined the remainders of their careers.

Whatever the reason, it must have been bitter pills for both men to swallow, having once played leads in Ford's halcyon Westerns, they were now reduced to glorified extras – and without billing at that.

Ford was his usual cantankerous self, as seen during the filming of a scene in which the mounted troop is riding in a narrow canyon. Ford liked to shoot the dialog in wide shots without closeups. He liked to finish scenes quickly, without retakes.

Assistant director Wingate Smith assembled the cast by calling their names out over his bullhorn. "Dick Widmark, Pat Wayne, Dobe Carey, Ben Johnson! Come to the camera!" Wingate is alleged to have shouted. It's important to note that Richard Widmark hated to be called 'Dick,' and even came to blows with John Wayne over it during the production of *The Alamo*. If, indeed, Smith used the name Dick, it was likely to get under Widmark's skin.

As the actors rode up, Ford pointed, "When you get out there, Dick, you yell out, 'Troop, halt!'" Then Ford looked at Pat Wayne and said, " Pat, you wait til the echo dies, then you yell, (using a lower key) 'Troop, halt!'" Ford then stuck his cigar back in his mouth and the actors rehearsed it. "Ok," Ford said, "remember to wait til the echo dies, Pat." Ford then turned to Son and Dobe. "When Dick yells, you two advance within six feet of him. Get the idea?"

Son and Dobe looked at each other, then at Ford, clearly confused. "Huh?" Ford asked.

Son and Dobe both said, "Yes, sir," in unison.

"Ok," Ford said, rubbing his hands together. "Come at a fast trot, Dick. It's fairly early on in the story and the horses are still fresh."

After shooting the initial master shot, Ford began shooting medium shots. Son was holding a red and white guidon, which kept spooking his horse. "Let 'em be nervous," Ford said, pushing the horse's rump. "Now, Dick, you look up that canyon." Ford began giving the actors their line readings, something that actors abhor and directors know is an insult to the actors.

"You say, 'Plumtree! I don't like the looks of it. Take a look up that canyon.' Ben, you hold off a second.

"Then Dick, you say 'Jones, you go with him.'" Ford then paused and said (doing Widmark), "Jones! JONES!" Ford then pointed to Dobe. Then you say, 'Name's *Smith*, sir.'" Then Ford pointed to Widmark. Then you say, 'Oh. Well, go with him.'"

Chewing on his trademark handkerchief, Ford said to Dobe, "When he calls out 'Jones' the second time, Dobe, you look around behind you. You're thinkin' 'who the hell's Jones?' Then, 'JONES!' Point to yourself. 'Name's Smith, sir.' Ben, take a look like ya hate like hell to ride up there – rise up in your stirrups."

When the camera rolled, Widmark did as he was told and when he shouted "JONES!" Dobe said, "My name's Smith, sir!"

Ford growled. "'Name's Smith, sir! Don't try to pad your part!"

Dobe, realizing that this was one of those moments when Ford could turn on him – and realizing he was only just now back in the old man's graces – nodded nervously. "Yes, sir."

On the second take, Dobe made the same mistake, saying, "My name's Smith, sir!"

"Your name's NOT Smith!" Ford yelled. "Stop tryin' to steal the scene from old Ben there!"

Dobe, now very nervous, nodded. On the third take, he said, "The name's Smith, sir!"

A silence descended over the company, and Ford glowered. On the fourth take, Dobe got it right. Ford merely glared at him and grunted. Then Son stabbed the guidon into the dirt and the two men galloped off down the canyon. At that point, Ford said his trademark, "That's well!"[2]

In another scene, Son and Carey were to charge their horses across a river. Son usually rode his own horses in movies, but early in the shooting Son's horse was severely injured and had to be put down. Son was forced to ride another horse, which Carey said was "second rate."[3] Carey relished the opportunity to actually outride Son in a scene for a change.

Ford told the two men to charge through the mud full out. Son, who never liked to be second place in anything, took Carey aside and warned him about riding full tilt through a patch of blue mud. When they began their charge into the mud, Carey pulled his horse up and Son charged right by him "like it was the Santa Anita race track..."[4]

In 1994, Carey recalled working on the film as a "happy experience."[5]

Cheyenne Autumn was Ford's last Western, released on October 3, 1964.

While Son had little to do on the film, he was in the right place at the right time.

During the filming of *Cheyenne Autumn,* a young journalist and film maker named Peter Bogdanovich came to interview Ford. Ford shunned him, but Bogdanovich befriended actress Carroll Baker, the film's star, and her husband, director Jack Garfein. Garfein interceded and convinced Ford to talk to Bogdanovich.[6]

Richard D. Jensen

Bogdanovich was one of the new generation of film directors and auteurs who viewed Ford as a genius. The usually publicity shy Ford took a liking to Bogdanovich and his documentary film crew. During this process, Bogdanovich became acquainted with Son. This would prove to be fortuitous.

"He seemed like a nice boy," Son said of Bogdanovich. The young would-be film director told Son that one day he wanted to cast Son in a movie. "I'd heard that before," Son said.

Within a decade Bogdanovich would cast Son as Sam the Lion in *The Last Picture Show*, a role which would win Son the coveted Academy Award for Best Supporting Actor.

But first, Sam Peckinpah would reappear and cast son in a handful of movies that would ever-alter Son's career path and his legacy.

The Nicest Fella - The Life of Ben Johnson

Young Ben Johnson, age 10 or 11, when he first dreamed of the cowboy life. He went to work for the famed 101 Ranch not long after this photo was taken.

Fred Beeson and Ben Johnson about to compete in a roping contest, 1920.

Richard D. Jensen

Ben Johnson and Ollie Workmon on their wedding day in 1917. Ollie was part Osage Indian.

Francis Benjamin Johnson, Jr., known as "Son" by those who loved him, at age two months.

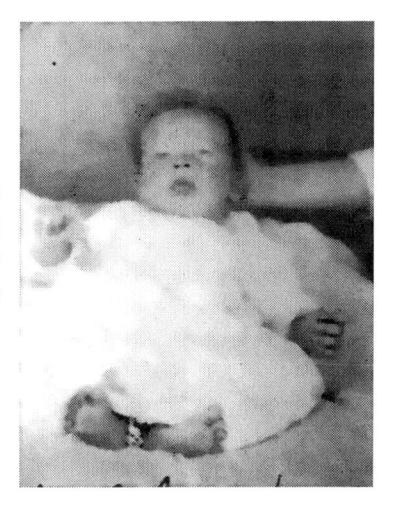

The Nicest Fella - The Life of Ben Johnson

Ben Johnson, front, in 1920 working on a ranch in the Tall Grass Prairie of Oklahoma.

Son and Maryann, his beloved "Sis." They were very close and Son was devastated by her early death from a stroke.

Richard D. Jensen

Ben Johnson, winner of Cheyenne Frontier Days, 1923, when that title was considered rodeo's world championship.

Ben Johnson winning the top prize at the famous Miller Brothers' 101 Ranch in Bliss, Oklahoma.

The Nicest Fella - The Life of Ben Johnson

Hugo Milde pins the prize on Ben's shirt. As a teen, Ben had worked on the famous ranch as a cowhand and also as the bunkhouse barber.

Son at Rice Creek School, standing far left.

Richard D. Jensen

Maryann Johnson in a formal school portrait.

Ben "Son" Johnson's formal school portrait.

The Nicest Fella - The Life of Ben Johnson

Son and high school sweetheart Georgia Martin Wright.

Ben Johnson, center, with Horace Barnard and John Chapman of the enormous Chapman Barnard Ranch in Pawhuska, Oklahoma. The ranch is now the Tall Grass Prairie Preserve.

Richard D. Jensen

Son, bottom left, and behind him stands Carol, Faye, Ben, and Ben's mother, Anne. Uncles Arch and Max and cousin Donnie Johnson kneel in foreground.

Son as a stuntman with superstar Tarzan Johnny Weissmuller, a former Olympic Gold medal swimmer, on the set of *Tarzan's Desert Mystery* (1943).

She Wore A Yellow Ribbon (1949). Son is center with John Wayne, Harry Carey, Jr., John Agar and George O'Brien.

Son, as Sgt. Tyree. Son hated doing dialog, preferring to ride horses and do stunts. Director John Ford thought Son was the best natural actor -- and the best horseman -- he'd ever seen.

Richard D. Jensen

Son, left, with Maureen O'Hara, Claude Jarman, Jr., and Dobe Carey in the climactic scene of *Rio Grande* (1950). O'Hara thought Ford's treatment of Son was deplorable, and she defended his refusal to take Ford's verbal abuse.

Son poses on the set of *Rio Grande* (1950). During production, Son refused to allow director John Ford to insult him. Ford thereafter blacklisted him for 11 years.

The Nicest Fella - The Life of Ben Johnson

Son on the set of *Mighty Joe Young* (1949) with Carol and his mother, Ollie. Son insisted on these photos because the studio was taking publicity photos of Son and co-star Terry Moore and trying to hint at a romance to promote the film. Son was happily married and demanded the studio drop the PR campaign.

Son, right, with Dobe Carey, center, and songwriter Stan Jones at the Pawhuska, Oklahoma opening of *Wagonmaster* (1950).

Richard D. Jensen

The bucking horse scene in *Wagonmaster* (1950). Joanne Dru, right, has thrown a bucket of water from her wagon, causing Son's horse to buck. Dobe Carey looks on.

Happy and successful, on the Oklahoma prairie in the early 1950s.

The Nicest Fella - The Life of Ben Johnson

Son in Pendleton, Oregon in 1949, when he set a world record in calf roping.

Son roping a calf in record time at a rodeo in Yuma, Arizona in 1952.

Richard D. Jensen

Always hands-on with his horses, Son directs a blacksmith while Dobe Carey watches from his mount.

Son does his own stunts in *Fort Bowie* (1958).

The Nicest Fella - The Life of Ben Johnson

Son and Marlon Brando in a scene from Brando's only directorial effort entitled *One Eyed Jacks* (1961). The film exposed Son to a new generation of film fans who didn't normally watch Westerns.

The two actors clown for the camera. Son rarely drank. The long production schedule resulted in lots of practical jokes to kill time.

Richard D. Jensen

Son roping a calf in California, 1953.

Son behind the chutes before a rodeo in the early 1950s.

RCA World Champion Cowboy 1953.

Still winning prize money even as he entered his 60s, Son began organizing celebrity rodeo events to raise money for charity.

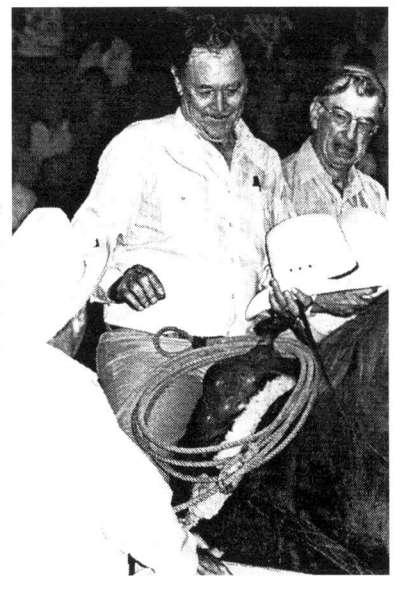

Richard D. Jensen

Sam Peckinpah's masterpiece, *The Wild Bunch* (1969), featured a new kind of performance from Son -- a harsh, colder-than-death outlaw.

"Sam the Lion" recalls a lost love in the water tank scene that garnered Son his Oscar for Best Supporting Actor in *The Last Picture Show* (1971).

The Nicest Fella - The Life of Ben Johnson

Son, right, with the New York Film Critic's Award for *The Last Picture Show* in 1972, with co-star Cybill Shepherd and director Peter Bogdanovich.

A major star at age 54, Son is heralded as a serious actor capable of turning in performances of honesty and realism.

Richard D. Jensen

Winning the Best Supporting Actor Oscar for *The Last Picture Show*. Son joked, "it couldn't happen to a nicer fella."

On the set of *Chisum* (1970), with the stuntmen, including "Bad Chuck" Roberson, far right.

The funeral scene in *Chisum* (1970), with Duke Wayne and Lynda Day George.

The Train Robbers (1973) poker scene, with Jerry Gatlin, Rod Taylor, Chris George, Duke Wayne, Son and Bobby Vinton.

Richard D. Jensen

Son arrives on the set of *The Train Robbers* (1973) in Durango, Mexico, after winning his Oscar.

John Wayne and Son in *The Train Robbers* (1973). The two men were in the cattle business together, but Wayne did not hire Son for a movie role from 1950 until 1969. Many believed Wayne didn't want to run afoul of John Ford's temper.

The Nicest Fella - The Life of Ben Johnson

Son on the set of *Soggy Bottom, U.S.A.* The 1980 film was produced in Oklahoma. Son worked for years to bring movie productions to his home state in hopes of bringing jobs and prosperity to the region.

A movie poster from *The Swarm* (1978). Son is billed above Fred MacMurray and Henry Fonda. He stunt-doubled both actors in the 1940s.

Richard D. Jensen

Oscar-winners Son and Olivia de Havilland socialize on the set of *The Swarm* (1978).

With Fred MacMurray in *The Swarm* (1978). Son had stunt-doubled MacMurray in *Smoky* (1946) and was now a bigger star.

The Nicest Fella - The Life of Ben Johnson

Son and Carol shortly before she became ill.
Her death hit Son hard. He died two years later.

After Carol's death. Son's smile was never as bright. Without children of their own, Son devoted himself to raising money for children's charities.

Richard D. Jensen

Son was garlanded with many honors,
including many film and charitable awards.

Son and Ollie at the dedication of the
Ben Johnson Cowboy Trail in Osage County, Oklahoma.

The Nicest Fella - The Life of Ben Johnson

With Dobe Carey in Italy in 1996. The two men had ridden into movie history as co-stars of some of the most critically acclaimed and beloved Western movies of all time. They were also the best of friends for over 50 years.

Dobe presents Son and Marino Amoroso with Wrangler Awards at the National Cowboy Western Heritage Museum.

Richard D. Jensen

How Son viewed himself: Pendleton Roundup, 1949. Son set the record time against this Who's Who of rodeo greats. From left to right, Buck Sorrells, Jim Snively, Vern Castro, Homer Pettigrew, Jack Skipworth, Son, Shoat Webster, Toots Mansfield, Everett Shaw and Carl Arnold. Son often told friends that his 1953 World Championship buckle meant more to him than his Oscar.

How Son viewed himself part two: Family and friends were the most important thing to Son. From left to right, Ben Alan Christenson, Marion Miller, Ann Briggs, Lee Briggs, Gene Hensley, owner of Ruidoso Downs Racetrack, Son and Carol, Son's sister Helen Christenson, and Son's nephew, John Miller. Standing behind in the center is Helen's husband, Dale Christenson, and to his right is their son, Dale Christenson, Jr.

CHAPTER FIFTEEN
PECKINPAH AND A NEW GENERATION

Careers in show business are cyclical. Actors struggle for years, then achieve success, often rise to critical acclaim, and then inexplicably find themselves in career Siberia, struggling to make a living.

Like a great many people in the entertainment industry, Ben Johnson had several careers in Hollywood. He arrived as a cowboy-wrangler, used his amazing skills as a horseman and rodeo cowboy to transition to stuntman, then used his good looks, charm and talent to transition again into an actor.

After his initial brush with fame and leading man roles under John Ford's tutelage, Son had worked his way back down the corporate ladder of stardom, returning to stuntwork and work as a character actor, mostly on TV. His work in *Shane* and *One-Eyed Jacks* had raised his profile as a serious actor, but the bulk of his work was still in small character parts and on television as a "guest-star," usually in Westerns. And his latest work with John Ford was as a lowly extra.

Richard D. Jensen

After nearly working together on *One-Eyed Jacks*, Son and Sam Peckinpah finally got together on a new film Peckinpah planned to make in Mexico.

In 1964 Peckinpah was planning a cavalry epic to star Charlton Heston. *Major Dundee* was Peckinpah's first big-budget film. The screenplay was written by Harry Julian Fink (who would later write *Dirty Harry* and many films for John Wayne). Producer Jerry Breslin liked Fink's script but Peckinpah hated it.

Heston was lukewarm about the script. "The characters are there, and the bones of the story, but there's a lot of excess mishmash, as well as the kind of theatrically seriocomic violence you find in part of Ford's work (and not the best part, at that)..." Heston wrote in his diary.[1]

Son initially turned down an offer from Peckinpah to do the film.

"The first time I met him was when he asked me to appear in *Major Dundee*, with Charlton Heston," Son said. "I went to his office to meet him, and I was sitting across the desk from Sam when a stunt-man comes in. Well, Sam abused him something terrible, yelling at him. He did it there, in front of me, and when the man walked out, I just said, 'I can't work for you.' He said, 'Why not?'

"I says, 'By God, if you did to me what you did to that man there, I'd hit you right in the damn nose and you'd run me out of the business, and I'm not ready to leave..' 'Well,' he says, 'I'm not that bad. I was just trying to scare him a little.'"[2]

Amazingly, the two men would work well together for years to come.

An iconoclast, Peckinpah liked other iconoclasts, and, just like Son, he hated Hollywood pretension. Additionally, Peckinpah had grown up on a ranch and he liked real cowboys and liked hanging out with them.

Anthony Quinn was approached for the part of Tyree, but he was unavailable. Steve McQueen was also approached for the part, which Heston thought was a better choice.[3] The role eventually went to Richard Harris, who proved to be a giant pain in the ass while on location. Lee Marvin was slated to play Potts, but the role went to James Coburn. Omar Shariff was to play Gomez, but the role went to Mario Adorf.[4]

As he assembled his cast, Peckinpah began rehearsals. On January 28, 1964, he called for his actors to be test as to their equestrian abilities. Heston wrote in his journal that day that the only actor besides himself that could ride was James Coburn.[5] One can only assume that Ben Johnson wasn't present for that event!

Peckinpah took his cast and crew to Mexico by private jet. Heston, still unhappy with the script, was pressuring the director to make changes. Peckinpah decided he would rewrite the script as the film was being shot.[5]

This on-the-fly rewriting enraged producer Breslin both because Breslin liked Fink's script and because the process was causing the film to go over budget.

While Durango, Mexico was one of John Wayne's favorite locations, indeed he invested heavily in his productions there, Heston found Durango to be "not very much."

Richard D. Jensen

Peckinpah fought with everyone, but not Son. Peckinpah liked to hang out with men whose lives did not revolve around the ego-driven world of Hollywood. The director preferred men with scars and faces weathered by real life experiences. Peckinpah found in Son an actor of remarkable authenticity. Additionally, Peckinpah was a notorious bully on the set in the tradition of John Ford. He liked to hire actors who would stand up to him in an argument, work well under tough conditions, and be fiercely loyal. Interestingly, a famous as Peckinpah was for his gonzo film-making and bullying of actors and crew, he never turned his wrath onto Son. Peckinpah knew well of the legendary day that Son told Ford to go to hell, and he respected Son for it. The tension between Peckinpah and the studio boiled over and the result was a difficult production. Heston and Peckinpah respected each other's professionalism, but the two men struggled to remain cordial to each other. Their relationship soured greatly when Heston refused to join Peckinpah on a nightly soiree at a local brothel. Thereafter Peckinpah viewed Heston as a stuffed shirt and taunted him mercilessly. During the filming of a battle sequence in which Heston was mounted on a horse, Heston finally got so sick of Peckinpah's behavior that he tried to run Peckinpah down and stab him with a cavalry saber.[6]

To make matters worse, early in the production Heston fell off a horse while clowning around in front of his kids, injuring his left elbow badly.[7] He would have trouble with the arm for the remainder of the shoot, including having to have help even mounting his horse.[8] This difficulty further soured his demeanor.

Actors and crew fell ill, especially Warren Oates, who got so ill he nearly had to be flown to the U.S. for treatment. Actor L.Q. Jones summed it up succinctly when he said, "Major Dundee was a hard shoot." This was because the day the crew arrived on location, the studio ordered the production time cut by 15 days.[9]

Even worse, Peckinpah was drinking, taking drugs and whoring throughout the entire shoot. Ironically, it was Son who often rescued Peckinpah from trouble and became his protector.

While Peckinpah lived his life at full burn, fueled by alcohol and cocaine and a relentless drive to raise hell, Son lived quietly, eschewing drink and Hollywood parties for quiet nights at home with his beloved Carol. On the *Major Dundee* shoot, Son very often became Peckinpah's "designated driver."

"Sam was a fatalist. He was a pretty talented guy, but he didn't care much about life, and some of what he did, he didn't care much about the outcome as long as the movie had blood and guts and thunder," Son said. " He was pretty dingy. I saved his life about a dozen times, I guess. He'd start drinking whiskey and taking pills and he'd go crazy. He'd go into a bar, walk through the place and find the biggest guy there, and pick a fight with him. He was crazy."[10]

Son played Sgt. Chillum, and true to form, he showed up each day on the set ready to do his scene and stay out of the fray. He worked hard, turned in a solid performance, and kept out of the line of fire, except for one incident that is well documented during the filming of the scene where the Indians ambush Dundee's troop.

Richard D. Jensen

"It was a hellacious master shot," actor L.Q. Jones recalled. "At the end Ben and I were on the outskirts and the Indians were making an escape. We took off after them. He heard, 'Cut' – and then [Peckinpah] started in on us. 'You ignorant cocksuckers,' etc. He was on our case and got a little hostile. We rode back to the platform where he was and I started climbing up to kick his ass. I told him he didn't have the talent to direct me to the men's room. The next line should have been, 'You're on the bus,' when he fired me. But it wasn't. You couldn't back off with Sam or he'd be on you like a duck on a June bug."[11]

The already difficult shoot was made all the more so by Richard Harris, who was a constant source of delay and irritation. He refused to come to the set until all of the actors were in place for his scenes, including Heston, who was the star. This egotism caused as much as a half-hour of delay every day of filming. One of the cardinal rules of film acting is that an actor must do the exact same performance in camera take after camera take so the editor can match the shots. Harris violated this often. In one scene, he used a different rifle in two takes, which caused costly retakes.[12]

Heston said of Harris, "he's something of a fuck-up, no question."[13]

Son had no desire to get into the daily dramas, especially the friction between Peckinpah and Heston, but he made sure he stood his ground whenever Peckinpah went on a rampage – which was often.

While Peckinpah fought with the studio over the budget and the shooting schedule, the actors suffered in the heat, dust and mosquito-laden atmosphere.

Many of the actors and crew spent all of their free time cavorting in the local brothels, drinking and using drugs to pass the free time.

After four weeks in Durango, the production flew to Mexico City. Mexican star Cantinflas sent his private jet to help carry the company to the capitol.[14]

Peckinpah wanted *Major Dundee* to be the antithesis of the John Ford cavalry epic. He wanted to debunk Ford's glamorization of the horse soldier and replace it with a gritty realism. He shot the movie with a meticulous eye, going over schedule (not hard since the studio had cut the shooting time drastically) and over budget.

When producer Jerry Bresler decided to fire Peckinpah from the film, Heston threatened to quit the movie. Son joined Harris, Jones, Oates and R.G. Armstrong in supporting Peckinpah. Heston sweetened the deal by giving up his $200,000 salary for the film if the studio would keep Peckinpah on as director. The ploy worked and Peckinpah remained. Heston later regretted his largesse, when the studio slashed the film to ribbons and it was a financial and critical failure.[15]

Major Dundee was completed over budget and when it was released it was a disaster. The studio had cut Peckinpah's masterpiece to shreds, excising over 40 minutes of the movie from the final cut. James Powers, the Hollywood Reporter critic, called it "bewildering… stuck together with no continuity." [16]

The film has since been restored to its proper length and has been hailed as a landmark film. It would be tragic to think that such labor resulted in the horrible patchwork of the theatrical version, especially when

Richard D. Jensen

one considers actor Armstrong's words, "We thought we wouldn't get out of Mexico alive."

Heston concurred. "I've never been so glad to finish a location."[17]

Son went back to the mythical Shiloh Ranch of *The Virginian* after finishing *Major Dundee* and was cast in an episode entitled *Dangerous Road*. During the shoot he worked with a young stuntman named Dean Smith. Son and Smith would work together often thereafter. The episode aired on March 17, 1965.

One of the strangest things about an actor's career is he never knows who will hire him. Son had worked with Tarzan, a giant gorilla, Abbott and Costello and in 1965 Son was cast in *Bob Hope's Chrysler Theater* production of *March from Camp Tyler*. The show featured Broderick Crawford, who had won an Oscar for his portrayal of the corrupt politician in the film version of *All The King's Men*. The cast also included Peter Lawford, the musical comedy actor who was married to Patricia Kennedy the sister of the late President John F. Kennedy. Lawford would divorce Kennedy in 1966 and embark on the carefree life of a sexually ambiguous flower child playboy. A one-time member of Frank Sinatra's infamous Rat Pack, Lawford would have a falling out with Sinatra and his career would never recover.

Son never discussed working on this program, but one wonders how Son must have felt working with Crawford, a notoriously egotistical and difficult actor, and Lawford, a hipster playboy of 1960s.

After finishing the Bob Hope show, Son went to work with Chuck Connors on his new TV series *Branded*. A former basketball player who played with the Boston Celtics and then switched professional baseball with the Brooklyn Dodgers and Chicago Cubs, Connors had hit it big as a Western TV star in *The Rifleman*, which ran from 1958 until 1963. The show co-starred Paul Fix as Micah Torrance, the marshal. Fix was father in law to Son's pal, Dobe Carey, who had married Fix's daughter Marilyn in the mid-1940s.

When *Branded* began its second season, Son was cast as a notorious gunfighter in an episode entitled *McCord's Way*. Directed by Republic Studios alumni and B-Western legend William Witney, the episode features a conflict between Son and Jason McCord, Connors' character. McCord has killed a young gunman, and the boy's father is a notorious gunfighter. *Branded* had 30-minute episodes, so there is little character development, and the show is perfunctory. Son is out of place as the gunslinger, and his costume is oddly ill-fitting, especially the hat. Son, by this time 48 years of age, does his best to bring menace to the role of Bill Latigo, the vengeful gunman. The show aired on January 30, 1966.

Director Andrew McLaglen then cast Son in a Jimmy Stewart Western called *The Rare Breed* which filmed in late 1965. Based on the true story of when English Hereford cattle were crossbred with Texas longhorns, the movie features Stewart as an old-line cowboy who helps a British woman (Maureen O'Hara) with the cattle breeding.

The Rare Breed boasts a superb cast. In addition to Stewart and O'Hara, the cast including Brian Keith, Dobe Carey, Jack Elam and Juliet Mills.

The film was the first time Son worked with O'Hara since Son's disastrous fall from grace with John Ford on *Rio Grande* 16 years before. They had a warm reunion and the years melted away. Son had a great respect for O'Hara, and O'Hara had tremendous affection and respect for Son. She never forgave Ford for his cruelty to Son, and made sure Son knew it.

The Rare Breed is markedly old Hollywood Western, the kind of star-laden Western epic so commonly made in the 1960s with Stewart, or Kirk Douglas or John Wayne. It suffers because the story's main conflict is whether or not the two breeds of cattle will mate and produce offspring. The film is set bound, using studio sound stages for many of the exterior shots. The film is hampered further by MacLaglen's languid direction, which saps the movie of any real movement. Keith's performance is over the top, and he steals as much camera time as possible in all of his scenes. Son has little to do in the film, but he lends it some needed authenticity. *The Rare Breed* was released on February 25, 1966 to moderate success and mixed reviews.

Peckinpah, who had directed Son in *Major Dundee*, approached ABC about producing a TV movie he wanted to make called *Noon Wine*. When ABC approved the film, Peckinpah hired Son to play the part of the sheriff in the drama. Son took the part more out of loyalty to Peckinpah than anything else. The film aired November 23, 1966 and was soon forgotten, except by Peckinpah scholars and devotees.

CHAPTER SIXTEEN
A TV SERIES – THE MONROES

As 1966 began Son was approached about taking a role in a TV series.

It is common for character actors to accept roles in series television because it is steady work. Character actors are not the star of the show, and they risk nothing if the show fails and have everything to gain if the show is a success. If a show is a failure, the blame is usually laid at the feet of the lead actors. Such blame never filters down to the character actors, who most often are looked upon as having done all they could as seasoned performers to make a show work. The down side of this steady work is the long hours and the potential to miss lucrative film roles.

So, as fate would have it, Son was offered the part of Sleeve in a Western series called *The Monroes*.

The show starred 24-year-old Michael Anderson, Jr. and Barbara Hershey, who was just 18 years old. The plot revolved around five orphans trying to live and survive in the high country in Wyoming.

Richard D. Jensen

The young cast was ably supported by both Dub Taylor and his son, Buck Taylor, who would later go on to fame as Deputy Newly O'Brien on the long-running series *Gunsmoke*, and also become a noted Western watercolor artist. Ron Soble was cast as Dirty Jim, an Indian friend. Soble would later rise to the presidency of the Screen Actors Guild.

The show was wholesome family entertainment, with engaging young actors in the lead roles and lovable character actors playing the supporting roles. Exterior sequences were filmed in Wyoming but the bulk of the show was shot in Hollywood and Culver City, California. Stunts were handled by stunt legend Yakima Canutt's sons, Joe and Tap Canutt, both of whom would become stunt legends as well.

The initial episode, entitled *The Intruders*, was shot and presented to ABC. The network gave the show a green light and 26 episodes were ordered.

Hopes were high for the new show, which was directed by the much-loved television director Bernard Kowalski.

To everyone on the show's amazement, ABC decided to run the show opposite two ratings leaders – *The Beverly Hillbillies* and *The Virginian*. Many in Hollywood said quietly the show wouldn't last a half-season, but the cast and crew forged on.

The Intruder aired on September 7, 1966. The ratings weren't great, but they weren't horrible either.

The second episode, entitled *Night of the Wolf*, aired on September 14, 1966. James Gammon appeared in the episode. He would develop his career in the following decade and become one of America's best loved character actors.

The third episode was directed by Earl Bellamy, the seasoned actor and director. *Ride With Terror* had Claude Akin as guest star and aired on September 21, 1966.

Warren Oates was brought in to guest star in the fourth episode, entitled *The Forest Devil*. Son had worked with Oates on Peckinpah's cavalry epic *Major Dundee* and the two would work together for Peckinpah, and also for director John Milius, in the next decade. Son and Oates developed a warm, friendly working relationship and each enjoyed the other's no-bullshit way of life. *The Forest Devil* aired on September 28, 1966.

The fifth episode was entitled *Wild Dog Of The Tetons* and aired on October 5, 1966. The episode featured character actor Albert Salmi as guest star. Salmi's career had taken off in 1958 in *The Brothers Karamazov* and then in John Huston's Western *Unforgiven*. Salmi would work steadily for decades until his tragic suicide in 1990.

Incident At Hanging Tree was the sixth episode of *The Monroes*, and aired on October 12, 1966. James Brolin appeared as guest star. He would later become a major television star and marry legendary superstar Barbra Streisand.

The seventh episode was entitled *Ordeal By Hope*, and aired on October 19, 1966. Edward Faulkner appeared in the episode. Faulkner became a favorite supporting player in John Wayne's circle of actors, as did Son, and Faulkner and Son would later work together on *The Undefeated* and *Chisum* with Wayne.

The eighth episode of *The Monroes* was entitled *The Hunter* and aired on October 26, 1966. It was directed by Tom Gries, who would later cast Son in his classic Western *Will Penny*. Character actor Bing Russell appeared in the episode. Russell, an actor popular with producers and directors for supporting roles, is now best remembered as the father of superstar Kurt Russell.

War Arrow was the ninth episode. It aired on November 2, 1966 and featured Dub Taylor and veteran movie villain Morgan Woodward.

The tenth episode was entitled *The Friendly Enemy* and aired on November 9, 1966.

Court Martial was the eleventh episode, and featured Buck Taylor and Robert Fuller, the star of TVs *Laramie*. It aired on November 16, 1966.

The twelfth episode was entitled *Silent Night, Deadly Night* and again featured Brolin. Ray Teal, who is best remembered as the sheriff on TV's *Bonanza,* appeared in the episode, which aired on November 23, 1966.

Lost In The Wilderness was the thirteenth episode of *The Monroes* and it aired on November 30, 1966. It featured Noah Beery, Jr., one of a long line of famous character actors. Beery's father, Noah Sr., and uncle, Wallace Beery, were both major stars in the 1920s and 1930s. Beery, Jr. would become best remembered as James Garner's father on the hit TV series *The Rockford Files*. Shug Fisher, an alum of the John Ford company, appeared in the episode, which aired on November 30, 1966. The episode was directed by Ray Kellogg, the

The Nicest Fella - The Life of Ben Johnson

legendary director who worked on nearly every single hit television show of the 1950s, 1960s and early 1970s.

A lull in the production schedule of *The Monroes* gave Son the opportunity to work again with director Bernie Kowalski again, only this time not on *The Monroes* but instead on *Gunsmoke*. The episode was entitled *Quaker Girl* and aired on December 10, 1966.

Son then went back to continue his work on *The Monroes* with episode fourteen, entitled *Gold Fever*. The episode featured Dan Duryea, who was famous for his portrayals of seamy, slimy villains in dozens of Westerns. The episode aired on December 14, 1966.

The fifteenth episode of *The Monroes* was entitled *Range War* and featured James Brolin again. It aired on December 21, 1966.

The sixteenth episode featured Argentinian actor Alejandro Rey, who went on to star as the priest in the Flying Nun with Sally Field. The episode was entitled *Pawnee Warrior* and was aired on December 28, 1966.

The Mark of Death was the seventeenth episode, and featured James Brolin. The episode aired on January 4, 1967.

The eighteenth episode was entitled *To Break A Colt* and featured Son's rodeo pal Casey Tibbs. The two men had become close friends during their rodeo careers, and both were world champions. Indeed, Tibbs won nine world championships in his amazing rodeo career.

Son made sure Tibbs worked often as an actor, and the two men appeared together often on film.

The Monroes' nineteenth episode was entitled *Race for the Rainbow*, which aired on January 18, 1967.

Richard D. Jensen

Gun Bound was the show's twentieth episode, and featured Buck Taylor, Nick Adams and John Dehner. It aired on January 25, 1967. Adams was the kind of actor Son never liked or understood. Obsessed with the perks of being a star, Adams was neurotic in the extreme. He was rumored to be a gay hustler and was, without question, a heavy drug user. That said, he was very popular with audiences and had a hit TV series called *The Rebel*. He was also good friends with James Dean and Elvis Presley. In less than a year from his appearance on *The Monroes*, Adams was found dead of a drug overdose.

The twentieth episode of *The Monroes* was entitled *Killer Cougar*, and featured performances by a handful of Hollywood's best character actors. Robert Wilke, the rotund movie villain, and Robert Walker, Jr. appeared, along with Rance Howard, who would become best known as the father of actor and prolific director Ron Howard and Clint Howard, a noted character actor. *Killer Cougar* aired on February 1, 1967.

By the time *Killer Cougar* was broadcast, the ratings for *The Monroes* had slipped to a distant third place. This was at a time when there were three broadcast networks - ABC, CBS and NBC. Thus, being in third place was simply dead last.

The cast and crew of the show knew the handwriting was on the wall and the show would not be renewed at the end of the season. Still, they labored on.

Episode 22 was entitled *Wild Bull* and aired on February 15, 1967. It featured Dub Taylor, one of Son's closest Hollywood friends.

The twenty-third episode of *The Monroes* was entitled *Trapped* and featured Buck Taylor as well. It aired on February 22, 1967.

Stalwart actor Robert Lansing, who had starred on TV's *87th Precinct* and appeared on *Twelve O'Clock High* and many other hit televisions series, was the guest star of episode 24, entitled *Manhunt,* which aired on March 1, 1967.

Rance Howard returned for episode 25, entitled *Teaching the Tiger to Purr,* which aired on March 15, 1967.

The final episode of *The Monroes* was *Ghosts of Paradox.* Actor X Brands, most famous for his portrayal of Pahoo-Ka-Ta-Wah, the Indian sidekick of Yancy Derringer in the hit TV series of that same name. Brands was famous for his portrayals of Indians, despite have no Indian blood. Richard Kiel, the enormously tall actor who became famous as the villain "Jaws" in the James Bond movies, also appeared. *Ghosts of Paradox* aired on March 15, 1967.

The Monroes was cancelled.

As soon as Son finished work on *The Monroes*, he went to work for one of the shows that killed *The Monroes – The Virginian.* Son was cast in an episode entitled Johnny Munn, which aired on October 11, 1967.

Son then went to Bishop, California in the dead of winter to make one of the greatest Western movies of all time.

CHAPTER SEVENTEEN
SON'S STAR RISES AGAIN

While writer/director Tom Gries was working on *The Monroes* with Son, he was also working hard to complete his story *Will Penny* for the screen. When he was finished he took a deep breath and sent it to Charlton Heston's agent. He felt Heston was perfect for the part of the down on his luck, aging cowhand. Heston was not in the mood to make another Western, and was unreceptive. The agent prevailed on Heston to read the script. Heston was blown away. "The script for *Will Penny* was one of the best I ever read," Heston said.[1]

Gries had been fascinated with the story concept for a long time. He had actually filmed an earlier version of the script once before, in an episode of the TV series *The Westerner*, entitled *Line Camp*.

Once Heston was on board, Paramount Pictures decided to back the film. Son was cast as Alex, the foreman of the Flat Iron Ranch, who hires Will to run a line camp during a brutal winter. Lee Majors and Anthony Zerbe signed on as Will's cowboy pals and Donald Pleasance and Bruce Dern were hired to play the villains.

Son appears only briefly in the film, but his character is pivotal. The stern foreman issues a hard set of rules for Will to follow, rules which become important in the story. Will is not to allow squatters on Flat Iron land, a rule he breaks almost immediately when he encounters a stranded woman and her son.

Will Penny is one of the best Westerns ever made, and it is beautifully photographed by Lucien Ballard in the high desert around Bishop, California.

Interestingly, Son had worked with Heston on *Major Dundee* and again on *Will Penny*, and they were cordial with each other, but never became friends. Heston was one of Hollywood's royalty, an actor who was comfortable in the pantheon of Tinseltown society either in New York or Los Angeles. He spent considerable time working on location in foreign countries, and styled himself as a man of the theater. Heston often referred to the fact that Hollywood and New York City elitists called the land between New York and California "fly-over country." Heston prided himself on his reputation as a classical actor.

Son was from that "fly-over country" and didn't think of himself as an actor at all. Indeed, he didn't believe he *could* act, merely that he was cowboy lucky enough to work and fake acting. Son disliked the Hollywood scene intensely. He preferred the company of non-actors, people who worked outside of the permissive leftist culture so prevalent in and around Hollywood. Son involved himself in many business activities outside of the film business, and all of them involved ranching and real estate interests far from the tinsel and glitter (and sex, alcoholism and drug use) of show business.

Heston had little in common with Son, and since Heston was consumed with the Hollywood lifestyle, they likely had little to talk about.

That said, when the *Will Penny* retrospective, *The Cowboys of Will Penny*, was filmed, Heston said Son was "marvelous. Of course, Ben is a real cowboy, and he couldn't have been better."[2]

Will Penny was shot in the middle of winter. The winter is integral to the story. It adds tremendous dimension to the film. The cowboy's life is de-glamorized and there is a sincere character study in the film. There are tremendous performances in the movie. Joan Hackett is perfect as the woman stranded in the line camp with Will. Majors, who would later become famous on TV's Western hit *The Big Valley*, is good as Blue, Will's pal. Son's old pal Slim Pickens is in the film, and Dern is particularly good as the son of the maniacal killer.

Heston would later say that *Will Penny* was one of his favorite roles.

The film premiered in Finland on February 16, 1968 and in the U.S. on August 10, 1968. It was hailed as an instant classic by critics worldwide.

After working on the traditional Western *Will Penny*, Son was hired by Clint Eastwood to co-star in *Hang 'Em High*, Eastwood's first American-made spaghetti Western. Eastwood, a TV star in the late-1950s and early 1960s on the show *Rawhide*, leapt to superstardom in the quirky Italian-made *A Fistful of Dollars* (1965). The film single-handedly revived interest in Westerns in the Vietnam War era. Audiences, now cynical after two decades of the Cold War and general disillusionment with modern civil society, didn't buy the outmoded pre-war concept of the chivalrous cowboy hero. The anti-hero was now in vogue, and Eastwood's Man With No Name character was a cool, sexualized protagonist, capable of greed and avarice.

Hang 'Em High is a revenge tale, ably directed by Ted Post. Eastwood plays Cooper, a man who is wrongfully lynched for rustling and survives to seek revenge against those who tried to kill him. Son plays Marshal Dave Bliss, who rescues Cooper from the noose and later must kill a deranged man (Dennis Hopper). While not a big part, Son's character drives the story as Bliss takes Cooper to territorial courthouse, where a judge (Pat Hingle) gives Cooper a job as marshal, giving his vengeance the color of lawfulness.

Son's initial scene in the movie is terrific. He discovers Eastwood hanging from the tree and rides up at a gallop, sliding his black horse to a stop as only a true horseman can – and all of this before the opening credits. The shooting of the escaping psychopath is dramatic and Son is seen close up as he wrestles with the moral justification of shooting the fleeing man. It is a very dramatic scene and Son is terrific in it.

One note of film trivia: The old cowboy who asks, "Are we gonna hang him or beat him to death?" in the hanging scene is former silent and early talkie cowboy star Bob Steele, who went on to do many character parts in films as he aged.

Hang 'Em High premiered on August 3, 1968 to strong reviews and huge success.

Richard D. Jensen

Both *Will Penny* and *Hang 'Em High* were successful films. In Hollywood, an actor is only as good as the films he's in, and being associated with two hits is good for the career. Nearly 30 years after his arrival in California, Son was working steadily on screen, getting good parts in top quality films and working with top Hollywood stars. Little did Son know that his best work was yet to come.

Son kept busy working and went right back to TV as soon as his work on *Will Penny* and *Hang 'Em High* was finished.

He co-starred on *The Virginian*, in an episode entitled *Vision of Blindness*, which featured John Saxon and David Hartman, who later hosted *Good Morning America* for 11 years. The musical group, The Irish Rovers, also appeared. They had the hit song *Unicorn* that year.

The episode aired on October 9, 1968.

Son then enjoyed working with long-time friends on a *Disney* TV episode entitled *Ride A Northbound Horse*, a two-part episode. The episode featured old pals Dobe Carey, Andy Devine, Jack Elam, Dub Taylor and starred Carroll O'Connor. In just two years O'Connor would become the biggest star on television as the bigoted Archie Bunker on CBS' *All In The Family*.

Sunday, March 16, 1969 must have seemed like Ben Johnson Night on television, because the first installment of *Ride A Northbound Horse* aired that night and an episode of *Bonanza* featuring Son, entitled *The Deserter*, aired that same night.

The second installment of *Ride a Northbound Horse* aired on March 23, 1969.

CHAPTER EIGHTEEN
THE WILD BUNCH

When Sam Peckinpah set about casting *The Wild Bunch*, he made sure there was a part for Ben Johnson. Casting the main roles proved difficult for the director. He initially wanted to hire James Drury for the lead role of Pike. Drury was the immensely popular star of TV's Western hit, *The Virginian*. Drury was obligated to a heavy shooting schedule for the series and could not break away. Peckinpah then tried to hire Lee Marvin, the war hero turned leading character actor, but Marvin was off making *Paint Your Wagon*, and obligated to immediately film the war movie *Hell In The Pacific*. Marvin had wanted to make *The Wild Bunch* badly, but producer Josh Logan had offered Marvin a cool $1 million to star in the musical – something Marvin could not turn down.[1]

Peckinpah then tried to hire James Stewart, Robert Mitchum, Burt Lancaster, Sterling Hayden, Richard Boone and Gregory Peck, but all turned him down.[2] Peckinpah again tried to hire Charlton Heston. The two men had such bad blood from the making of *Major Dundee* that Heston declined.[3]

Richard D. Jensen

The movie project was about to be shelved when William Holden agreed to star in *The Wild Bunch*. The studio was not thrilled. Holden's career was on the decline, fueled by his alcoholism and back to back films which had failed at the box office. The studio agreed to Holden only after Holden agreed to cut his salary from $400,000 down to $250,000 – a substantially lower amount.[4] Getting a big star, even a fading one, for $250,000 made *The Wild Bunch* a worthwhile risk.

Keeping with his desire to film movies as a far away from studio brass as possible, Peckinpah planned to shoot the film in his beloved Mexico. Son was hired to play Tector Gorch. Also in the cast were star Ernest Borgnine, Robert Ryan, Edmond O'Brien, Dub Taylor, Strother Martin and L.Q. Jones.

The cast and crew arrived in Durango, Mexico in the spring of 1968. Peckinpah was his usual out-of-control self, raising hell on the set as he strived for cinematic perfection, and raising hell at night, brawling and whoring in the brothels. As audacious as he was, one actor on set out-classed Peckinpah's reputation for violence and for debauchery.

"If there was one person who could've given Sam lessons in debauchery, it was Emilio Fernandez. Emilio was a true original, a real one-off. I don't know whether this was before or after he'd shot a producer, but there was an awesome aura about the man. He had brought this harem, some 50 teenage girls who lived with him at his hacienda outside Mexico City. Yes, Emilio was perfect for the part of the insane scumbag Mapache,"assistant director Cliff Coleman said.[5]

As production progressed, the actors realized that Peckinpah was striving for something new. Peckinpah was working hard to focus on the blood and gore of violence.

Since the dawn of film-making, dying was portrayed as a nearly bloodless event. Between censorship and the belief that the public wanted its entertainment sanitized, studios eschewed blood and guts in favor of clean death. Peckinpah saw a lyrical quality to the act of dying, and he wanted to show the horrific bond between those who kill and those who are killed. Indeed, Fernandez provided Peckinpah with the idea for one of the movie's most carnal moments, the ants vs. scorpions sequence, which gave the film its intensely violent tone.[6]

When production went smoothly, Peckinpah was manic. When things went awry, he was a madman. Sometimes, he was so overtaken with emotion he would burst into tears.

Son was swept along in the production, and as a result of this he ended up doing some scenes he would end up regretting. It was an interesting time for him. He felt uncomfortable with the growing usage of nudity, violence and profanity in films, but here he was starring in the most violent movie made to date, filled with nudity and profanity. Indeed, Son has a scene cavorting in a brothel with a nearly naked Mexican woman.

Peckinpah shot the film more efficiently than he shot *Major Dundee*. He chose locations close to civilization, shooting many of the key sequences within eyesight of major roads, but carefully constructing his shots to great effect.

Peckinpah completed the movie and began editing it. When he was done, the film ran 3 hours and 45 minutes. Legendary director Martin Scorcese, who saw the original edit, said *The Wild Bunch* was "the greatest American movie ever made."

The studio disagreed. The prevailing wisdom was the movie was too long. Cuts were ordered. When the slashing of *The Wild Bunch* was finished, and the film was shown to preview audiences, the reaction was overwhelmingly negative. The studio had cut the film too much, excising all of Peckinpah's lyrical storytelling and ending up with a violent shoot 'em up.

Amazingly, when the much-edited version was released, it became a cult hit. Audiences flocked to see the new, ultra-violent western. All of the actors involved in *The Wild Bunch* got an enormous career boost from the film. L.Q. Jones said, "On *The Wild Bunch*, [Peckinpah] coaxed extraordinary work out of the people. Eddie O'Brien was thought of as a blind, drunk has-been by most critics. Then they started talking about how brilliant he was in *The Wild Bunch* and writing that he still had the magic that made him so memorable in *DOA*. And Ernie Borgnine, who'd gotten a reputation, undeserved in my opinion, of being an old ham since winning his Oscar; in Sam's hands he became a legend all over again. As for us younger guys, Warren, Ben, Strother, me, we built our careers on having been in *The Wild Bunch*. It opened doors. People who wouldn't return our agent's calls were now asking us out to dinner. Of course, cause we were Sam's boys we'd always go to lunches in our work gear; Stetsons, ponchos, leather jackets. It must have looked weird, us cowboys eating canapés with the suit and tie brigade."[7]

Son's performance in *The Wild Bunch* is a marvel. Gone is the folksy, aw-shucks persona. In its place is a steely hardness. Son is colder, darker and more menacing than at any other time on screen. He sheds his affable personable nature and is as cold as death, his eyes narrowed to slits, his face covered in a dark beard. Son's character is on the edge of violence throughout the entirety of the film, and it is striking to watch.

"The good thing about Sam Peckinpah as a director was that he could get unexpectedly good performances out of people who were more or less stereotypes. Somebody like Ben Johnson, for example, and Edmond O'Brien – someone who people before *The Wild Bunch* remembered only as the protagonist in *D.O.A.*" James Dickey, the novelist, said.[8] Critics often mention the scene where Son is toying with the bird on a string, a small bit of business that makes a contrast between the inherent violence of the outlaws and the gentle bird.

"Johnson with that bird on the string, that was Peckinpah's," assistant director Cliff Coleman said. "He would do things like that, he would come up with things that guys would do."[9]

When the movie came out, Son put his extended family and friends on notice that they shouldn't go see it. He was uncomfortable with his kinfolk seeing the violence and nudity in it, especially the scene in which he cavorts in a bathtub where he is groping the breasts of naked and nearly naked Mexican prostitutes.

Son recalled in 1992 that in order to do that scene he got drunk.

"When Warren and I did the scene in the wine vat in *The Wild Bunch*, we asked Sam you know 'What do you want us to do?' and he said, 'Well, what would you do in a wine vat with a bunch of these gals?' So, this morning he gave each one of us a fifth of brandy. He says, 'I'm gonna shoot this, this afternoon.' So we drank most of that brandy and then we got in the wine vat with those gals and I haven't been able to get back to Mexico by myself since. My wife won't let me go."[10]

Son insisted that the folks in Oklahoma avoid *The Wild Bunch*. "We were told we weren't supposed to see *The Wild Bunch*," Son's niece Anne Whitehorn recalled.

The Wild Bunch was released on August 7, 1969 and caused an uproar. Film critics either loved it and hailed it an instant classic or hated it and decried it as an orgy of violence. Audiences rushed to see what all the fuss was about.

John Wayne expressed disgust when he saw it, amazed that there was so much blood in the film. Amazingly, in the following years he would have to follow suit, as audiences now took for granted – indeed, wanted – such realistic violence in movies. *Big Jake* (1971) was Wayne's most violent movie, made in the wake of *The Wild Bunch*. It contained shotgun killings, brutal pitchfork stabbings and more – a level of violence that Wayne would have refused to do prior to the release of *The Wild Bunch*.

The movie industry was evolving with the times. Whether Son or John Wayne liked it or not, the increasing violence, nudity and sexual content were here to stay. Wayne, by virtue of his age and superstar status, was able to avoid the inclusion of nudity in his films, but not the violence. Son would make his mark in two films that contained graphic violence and graphic nudity and sexual content – *The Wild Bunch* and *The Last Picture Show*. Ironically, he would never assail the orgy of violence or nudity in *The Wild Bunch*, but he would refer to the *The Last Picture Show*, which contained no graphic violence but several sex scenes and blatant nudity as "a dirty movie" for the rest of his life.

CHAPTER NINETEEN
WITH WAYNE ON TWO NOT-GOOD PICTURES.

Immediately after John Wayne won his Oscar for *True Grit* (1969), demand for Wayne's formula westerns grew considerably. Unfortunately, Wayne was stuck in a time warp, unable to recognize that his age and weight – and his obduracy about what kind of characters he'd play – were resulting in formulaic films which were little more than an opportunity for Wayne to be John Wayne.

Hollywood had embraced the new generation of film makers, most of them dope-smoking, free-lovin' hippies and leftists who were bringing much-needed life and creativity to film. This included Westerns, which were now mostly "spaghetti Westerns," Italian-made horse operas shot in Almería, Spain. These highly stylized, terribly inaccurate Westerns featured anti-heroes. They were as far from traditional Westerns – and the real west – as a Western could be.

"Well, I can't handle phony people, and there are a lot of them in Hollywood," Son said. "I've built my life around the principles of honesty, realism and respect, and if the people in Hollywood are so pumped up on themselves they can't deal with that, I say the hell with 'em. I think I've won the respect of some people over there and I think I managed to stay real."[1]

While the old guard had been sent packing, and many actors, directors, producers and studio executive of Wayne's generation had been pink-slipped (or relegated to television), Wayne doggedly hung on. This was mainly because Wayne had his own production company, Batjac, ostensibly run by Wayne's eldest son Michael. The studios continued to green light Wayne's films because he shot them cheaply, on time and under budget. There was still enough interest in Wayne, due to his Mount Rushmore-like status and his recent Oscar, to warrant bank-rolling a John Wayne western – if the film came in cheaply.

Wayne, responsible for an enormous family and a cadre of employees at Batjac, continued to work. Indeed, many friends knew Wayne continued working far harder than he needed to merely to get away from home.

Wayne's marriage to third wife Pilar had deteriorated, and they fought constantly. He insisted on shooting in the wilds of remote Mexico, where he could hide from his wife's tantrums and avoid their arguments. He often brooded about growing old, and, according to director Burt Kennedy, had become despondent about his age and weight.[2] To lessen his ennui, Wayne had spent years surrounding himself with a cadre of actors he used repeatedly, in the model of John Ford's stock company. After years of being ignored by Wayne, Son was included in that group.

Son arrived on the set of *The Undefeated* in Louisiana on February 4, 1969. As soon as the Louisiana locations were finished, the company moved to Durango, Mexico. Production proceeded at a leisurely pace for roughly three months. Dobe Carey was cast in the film as well, and from all reports Son enjoyed working with Wayne and Dobe again after nearly 20 years.

The Undefeated is a stodgy western about post-Civil War Confederate patriots, led by Rock Hudson, to find a new Eden in Mexico. Wayne is the Union commander who is driving horses to Mexico to sell. The two cross paths and join forces against outlaws and a corrupt Mexican general.

Hudson was excited about making the film, and he was grateful to Wayne for giving him the part. His career had been on the skids and he knew that co-starring with John Wayne would be a shot in the arm.[3] For all of Wayne's largesse in giving the role to Hudson, he was jealous of Hudson's good looks and youthful appearance. Behind Hudson's back, Wayne often groused with envy about how handsome Hudson was, and referred to Hudson as a "queer," even doing so in front of Wayne's daughter, Aissa.[4]

Son had become vocal with his anti-gay opinions as well. Calling homosexuals "sick," Son admitted to a journalist that he was "for shipping the gay people off to their own island and letting them stay there. Some of these people are as likely to come flying by as they are walking by. That's the way I feel and I'm not afraid to speak out."[5]

It is unknown if Son expressed these feelings to Rock Hudson, but it is unlikely.

Son, having worked in Durango, Mexico for Peckinpah on *Major Dundee* and *The Wild Bunch*, adapted easily to the surroundings and enjoyed the relaxed pace of the shoot.

Character actor Robert Donner had a scene with Son in *The Undefeated* in which the two men are fishing at a picnic and end up in a fist fight.

"There's a scene in the picture where Ben Johnson and I get into a fight. We're sitting and fishing and the next thing you know we are fighting. Now it was cold in Durango, but Andy [McLaglen, the director] would go down there and feel the water. He's say, 'No, no, not today.' The water wasn't cold enough for him. As I recall he'd drag Duke into it. 'Duke what do you think?' Duke would say, 'No, no! It's not cold enough.' So this went on for days. Well, one day they decided it was cold enough. Believe me, it was cold! And they finally decided to send 'them two boys' into it to see how it worked. Ben Johnson can tell you. It was cold!"[6]

The Undefeated was released on November 27, 1969. John Wayne fans flocked to the theater but critics were less than kind.

The Undefeated was completed in May 1969 and that fall Son joined Wayne for *Chisum*, loosely based on the Lincoln County Wars and the exploits of Billy the Kid.

Produced by Wayne's company, Batjac, and produced by Wayne's eldest son, Michael, all in attendance knew that the casting of Billy the Kid was pivotal.

Richard D. Jensen

Story editor Tom Kane recalled that Wayne attended a pre-production meeting in Los Angeles and told Michael to cast Son as Billy the Kid. When he was reminded that Son was roughly 50 years old, Wayne was perplexed.[7] Wayne, like his movies, were stuck in a time warp, reliving as much as he could the good ol' days when he worked on A-list Westerns for directors like Howard Hawks and John Ford.

Son saw that the formula was entrenched . "By the time we were doing those films with Andy (McLaglen), it was all pretty much the same film. The only thing that changed was Duke's weight, which went up and down. I was just happy to be working." That said, Son admitted that *The Undefeated* and *Chisum* "weren't good pictures."[8]

MacLaglen said that *Chisum* was one of his two favorite John Wayne films which he'd directed, mainly because of the scenes in which Son and Wayne bicker at each other.[9] The film was shot on location in Durango, Mexico from October 6, to mid-December 1969.

Son was enjoying the relaxed atmosphere of working on *Chisum* when he received the terrible news of the sudden death of his sister, Mary, who Son referred to as "Sis." Mary Ann Johnson Miller, had died suddenly at age 48. John Wayne arranged for Son to fly out of Durango on a private jet to Oklahoma.

"My Sis lived here in Pawhuska - north of town. She and her husband, Marion, had gone to a family reunion of his family in Ramona. She complained of a terrific headache and passed out. They took her to Jane Phillips Hospital in Bartlesville where it was confirmed she had an aneurism in her brain and she never regained consciousness," Helen remembered.[10]

John Miller said the family was stunned by his mother's sudden death. "She had been healthy her whole life," Miller said.[11] Mary Ann Johnson Miller was buried on October 15, 1969.[12]

Deeply saddened at the loss of his Sis, Son flew back to Mexico and stoically finished work on *Chisum*.

Like most character actors, Son knew that any time John Wayne assembled his troupe of actors for a shoot in Mexico, it was a good two or three months of easy-going work, a sort of working vacation. And Son was always an affable addition to the cast. Never one to show his temper, Son handled disputes with a steely calm, such as the incident with John Ford on the set of *Rio Grande*.

Actor Ed Faulkner recalled an tense incident during the production of *Chisum*. One of the teamsters charged with driving the actors to the set in Durango arrived at the third-rate hotel where the cast was staying. An argument ensued in the parking lot between the driver and another man. They were right in front of Son's hotel room, where he and wife Carol were getting ready for the day.

When the teamster began to shout epithets at the other man, Faulkner said the language reached a point of severe profanity. Suddenly Son's hotel room door opened and Son sauntered out, eyeing the teamster with a cold, steely glint in his eye. Without raising his voice, Son went over to the teamster and said, "Now, my wife is in that room and if you don't stop with your barn talk you and I'll have a go and I'll give you something to remember me by."

The teamster took one look at Ben's cold glare and stood mutely nodding his head.[13]

Helen said her brother's distaste for profanity was a Johnson trait. "My dad didn't allow barn talk, and neither did Son." She said, contrary to popular conceptions about cowboys, most of them didn't ever utter a curse word, even when angry.

Of course, this is contrasted by many accounts of Hollywood actors who relate tales of Son cursing. It is likely that Son kept to the cowboy code of not cursing in front of women, children and old people. As Helen was Son's baby sister, he likely never cursed around her.

Chisum opened on July 29, 1970. The general consensus among critics was John Wayne had made two formula Westerns back-to-back.

Son returned from Durango, Mexico in late 1970 and went to work on *Bonanza*, in an episode entitled *Top Hand*. Fellow former stuntman Richard Farnsworth also appeared in the episode as a character named Sourdough. The show aired on January 24, 1971.

Son's life had seemingly come full circle. He had spent the past year working with John Wayne again after a 19-year period. He was working both in film and television and seemed to have no trouble making a living as a character actor.

Little did Son know that in short order he would be one of the most talked about, most famous and most critically acclaimed actors in the movies.

CHAPTER TWENTY
THE LAST PICTURE SHOW

Son didn't want to do *The Last Picture Show*.

He especially didn't like the language in the script. It didn't matter to him if the dialog rang true, Son – at least in public – held to his father's edict that a man didn't use "barn talk," especially in front of women and child and old folks. *The Last Picture Show* was full of it. It also was chock full of nudity and sex.

Larry McMurtry had written a terrific book about small town Texas, and director Peter Bogdanovich wanted the film to breathe with realism. He knew that the character of Sam the Lion was the moral center of the story, and in order to accomplish his goal Bogdanovich knew he had to have an actor so intrinsically tied to the region that his performance would resonate with authenticity.

Bogdanovich wanted to make a gritty black and white film, capturing on celluloid images reminiscent of Ford's signature work. He'd gotten the idea to make *The Last Picture Show* in black and white from Orson Welles, the brilliant cinema auteur who encouraged Bogdanovich to use the film for its depth of field.[1]

Bogdanovich said that color film "romanticizes" the action on screen, and he wanted gritty realism.[2]

A devout disciple of John Ford's films, Bogdanovich was a big fan on Son's and knew that only Ben Johnson could play the part of Sam the Lion, the owner of the cinema and pool room in the dying Texas town.

Son did not want to play the role. It was too verbose and he simply could not utter the profanities in the script on film. To add to Son's unease about the language, Bogdanovich was a largely untried director. He had only directed three infinitesimally small-budget independent films. Son turned Bogdanovich down flat.

"He kept saying too many words! Too many words!" Bogdanovich recalled.[3]

Faced with Son's turning down the role, Bogdanovich began reading other actors, but his heart was set on Son. Son's heart was set on *not* doing the picture.

Bogdanovich was testing actors all over the country. During one session, he read a young actor named John Ritter for one of the lead juvenile roads. Ritter was the charmingly boyish son of singing cowboy icon Tex Ritter and would later go on to stardom in TV's *Three's Company*.[4] Bogdanovich realized when he met Tex Ritter that the singing cowboy had aged into a persona of a gravelly-voiced elder Texan. Ritter had also won an Oscar for his rendition of the theme song for *High Noon*. A native of Panola County, Texas, he was as quintessentially Western as Ben Johnson.

As production loomed, Tex Ritter seemed closer and closer to winning the part of Sam the Lion. That said, Bogdanovich wanted Son. He kept up the pressure. He thought he could wear Son down with money. He offered Son 10% of the film's gross, an unheard of sum, but a gamble because the picture could lose money.

"He'd say, 'I don't want to say all those dirty words,'" Bogdanovich said.

Son still turned Bogdanovich down. The studio began pushing the director to approach both Jimmy Stewart and John Wayne. Bogdanovich felt both men could do the role, but they "wouldn't be right."[5]

He decided to play his trump card – John Ford.

Bogdanovich, who spent as much time writing about films as he did making them, had spent years interviewing Ford and the two men had gotten to know each other fairly well by this time.

Bogdanovich contacted Ford and asked Ford to intercede.

Ford called Son and told him to do Bogdanovich's film.

"Pete knew I wouldn't turn Mr. Ford down, so he got Mr. Ford to ask me to do the show as a favor. I said, 'Yes, sir, I will,'" Son said.[6]

Bogdanovich said Son called and said, "'You put the old man on me.'"

Son came to Bogdanovich's office three days later for a meeting.

"He'd say, 'I don't want to say all those dirty words,'" Bogdanovich said. "He came up with any goddamn reason he could to not do the picture. I said, 'Ben, you don't understand. In this role you're gonna get the Academy Award.'

"He yelled, 'Why the hell do you say that?' And I said, 'I don't know. You'll at least get a nomination. In

Richard D. Jensen

this role you'll be dynamite.' He slammed the script shut. 'All right, I'll do the damned thing.'"

Son had capitulated, but he had a card to play as well. "I didn't want to do a movie that I wouldn't want my mother to see. There were too many dirty words and a lot of nakedness," Son said.[7]

Son held out for one perk. He insisted on rewriting his dialog to remove the profanity. Bogdanovich caved in. Son told Bogdanovich he'd have his agent call to work out the financial details.

Son called his agent, Herb Tobias, and told him to tell Bogdanovich he wanted double his salary, believing no one would pay that amount. Again, Son was stunned when Bogdanovich agreed.

"I knew nobody'd pay Ben Johnson that much money but sure enough they did," Son said.[8]

The production was based in the Texas Panhandle town of Wichita Falls, Texas, and filming began in and around Archer City, Texas, the hometown of author Larry McMurtry. Bogdanovich assembled a cast of talented newcomers, including the feisty Cybill Shepherd, a model from Memphis, Tennessee who would later become an Emmy-winning television star. Jeff Bridges, son of TV star Lloyd Bridges, and brothers Sam and Timothy Bottoms were cast as the brothers.

The arrival of the film company was met with some trepidation by the locals in Archer City. The story of *The Last Picture Show* is essentially a coming-of-age tale of sexually precocious high school students and their amorous high-jinks with each other and with the sexually frustrated wives of local citizens. One Baptist minister in Archer City railed against the film company, exhorting his flock to reject the actors and filmmakers as "pornographers." This prompted the local school board to hold a vote to decide whether they would allow the studio to shoot at the local high school, a vote that was narrowly approved.[9]

Indeed, the highly-touted nude party scene at the swimming pool proved particularly difficult. While many wealthy north Texas ranchers and oilmen had swimming pools which would suffice for the scene, most of them who were approached by the studio flatly refused to allow the film makers to use their pools for the scene.[10]

Shot in wide-screen, the film opens with Timothy Bottoms starting a dilapidated truck and arriving at a pool room owned by Sam the Lion. Son's initial appearance in the film is seemingly innocuous, but his arrival breathes authenticity into the proceedings. He is dressed in a drab sweater, his curly hair over-long and unkempt. He is a force to reckon with.

Son was characteristically humble and down-to-earth about his preparation for the role. "I know a lot of people down in Oklahoma who left their farms to live in small towns, I just put two or three of them together in my mind to play the part. Once I made up my mind to appear in the picture, I did my best."[11]

The Last Picture Show is a marvel. Ahead of its time in the depiction of youthful sexual exploration, it is also an eerily accurate portrayal of post World War II small town life. The film has no central crisis to over-dramatize. It is a slice of life, as accurate as newsreel footage.

Richard D. Jensen

Son's portrayal of Sam the Lion grounds the film, giving it a conscience. When the boys trick young Billy, a mentally slow boy, into an encounter with a mean-spirited whore, Sam gives them a lecture about decency that is riveting.

The scene at the water tank where Sam the Lion reminisces about his lost love and his faded youth is mesmerizing. With a simplicity few actors can accomplish, Son delivers a monologue of such authenticity and such sincerity that it is breath-taking.

Bogdanovich shot the scene in one long take. The sky was cloudy and the ever-present wind was stirring. As Son delivers his lines, the sun peaks through and back lights the scene, giving it a luminescence. Bogdanovich said as the scene was shot, he got a feeling it would be a one-take shot and he'd yell "Cut! Print!" Suddenly, silence descended as Timothy Bottoms failed to say his line to cue the remainder of Son's speech. Bogdanovich said he waited for at least 20 seconds before he shouted the line to Bottoms, who still didn't speak.

Frustrated, Bogdanovich ordered a second take, realizing Son's perfect first take was marred.

When the second take was finished, Bogdanovich ordered the first take printed and scrapped the second take. He later edited out Bottom's awkward pause. Thus, Son delivered the scene that won him the Oscar on the first take. And this from an actor who hated dialog and insisted he could never remember his lines.

Bogdanovich knew that Son hated dialog. "[John] Ford had told me when they were shooting together Ben always complained of 'too many words.' [Ford] said: 'If

Ben heard he had lines to speak, he would go off and sulk. If he only had to ride the horse, he was happy.'

"But Ben, of course, not only said all those words in *Picture Show*, he said them brilliantly. Most of stuff was gotten on the first or second take. He is a complete natural and a great professional. Working with him was one of the lovely experiences of my life and I will always treasure the memory and the result. Ben's performance was like a wonderful present he gave to me and to all of us," Bogdanovich said.[12]

Eileen Brennan, the actress who played Genevieve the tragic waitress in the film, recalled, "He used to say to me, 'I'd rather ride my horse a thousand miles than say any of these goddamned words.' He hated to talk."

Brennan's recollection is that Son used profanity in her presence. This is intriguing solely because Son seemed to use profanity on film sets, around the rodeo and ranch cowboys, but never around women.

Son continued to decry profanity in movies and often walked out of a movie if it contained too much cursing. He didn't allow it around his home or in the presence of women. Indeed, during one dinner at home with Carol and fellow actor David Huddleston and his wife, Son refused to watch Mel Brooks' comedy *Blazing Saddles* because of the cursing.[13]

When *The Last Picture Show* was released on October 22, 1971. The reviews were all glowing. Suddenly, Son was being hailed as a serious actor.

"I didn't know you had to make a dirty movie to get noticed so much," Son said.[14]

And then, to Son's amazement, he was indeed nominated for an Oscar, along with Bogdanovich,

Richard D. Jensen

Bridges, Burstyn and Leachman. Oscar nominations are good for business, and the studio immediately put the publicity machine for *The Last Picture Show* into overdrive.

Bogdanovich began a heavily promoted interview tour, traveling from city to city. He quickly grew weary of the banality of reporter's questions, chiefly being related to the film being shot in black and white.

Son joined Bogdanovich on the tour in Atlanta. By this point, Bogdanovich had become downright surly while being interviewed.

"We were having drinks late in the day with two major local newspaper critics, and as I'd just got back from Europe and the same old routine. Ben, who'd only just started the trip, was trying to distract them from my ill humor and mono-syllable answers," Bogdanovich recalled. "The Academy Awards were coming around, Ben had been nominated, and after several weighty questions and about three drinks, he leaned back expansively and said to the two journalists, 'Why don't y'all come on out fer the Oscars an' get some a that Hollywood puss?' One of the writers was in mid-swallow, I think, and nearly had a bad moment all over the table but, to their credit, they rapidly collapsed, with me and Ben, into total hilarity, and there wasn't another serious question the rest of the night. If only Ben could always be around."[15]

Downplaying his critical acclaim in his usual self-deprecating style, Son summed up his acting by saying, "nobody can play Ben Johnson as well as Ben Johnson."[16]

In reality, *The Last Picture Show* was only one of three films in which Son liked his own performance. "I've never seen myself to do anything I really liked on the screen. Then I saw *Picture Show* and I sort of liked it. I sort of liked myself in *One-Eyed Jacks* and *Shane*, but not much else."[17]

In addition to his Oscar nomination, Son was nominated for – and won -- the New York Film Critic's Award and the Golden Globe. These honors were for his performance in a film that he candidly admitted he didn't like.

"It might be all right for some of these freaks, but it's not somethin' for real people to see. I would not want to take my wife to see it," Ben said.[18]

Son's negative reaction to the film mirrored the reaction of the people of Archer City, Texas, who uniformly hated the film because it portrayed the town as being filled with flawed, failed and listless people, bent on drunken lust.

Helen recalled that Son told the family not to go see it, which of course made her and the rest of the extended family want to rush off to see what the fuss was about.

Son's nephew and also a famous rodeo cowboy, Dale Christenson, Jr., said he was forbidden from seeing his uncle's Oscar-winning performance. "I was 32 years old before I saw *The Last Picture Show*. We were never allowed to watch it."[19]

Son's niece, Ann Whitehorn, said she was discouraged from seeing the movie as well.[20] Helen's lifelong friend, Frances Jo Brooks, said she finally saw the movie years after its release and felt that it was only worth watching because Son was in it. "After his part was over, there was nothing to it," she said.[21]

Nita Salmon Jones, whose father Sol worked alongside Ben at Chapman Barnard Ranch and who is also a lifelong friend of Helen's, said she thought, "Son was great in it, but the movie was bad."[22]

It is intriguing that *The Wild Bunch* and *The Last Picture Show,* the two films which garnered Son the most attention and praise for his work – and made him more marketable for future film projects – were two films with the profanity, violence and nudity that Son abhorred.

The irony was not lost on Son, who for years afterward would decry *The Last Picture Show* as a "dirty movie."

CHAPTER TWENTY ONE
BACK TO TV

No sooner had shooting wrapped on *The Last Picture Show* than the buzz around Hollywood was that Cloris Leachman, Ellen Burstyn, Jeff Bridges, Cybill Shepherd and Son had turned in Oscar-caliber performances. Son didn't buy the hype. He'd been in the business for 30 years and he knew that Hollywood was notorious for building up the expectations of actors, only to dash them. While many actors would suddenly position themselves as worthy only of other films of import,

Son did what he'd always done when he finished one job, he went right on to the next one. Being in a film of the scope and magnitude of *The Last Picture Show* didn't stop Son from going right back to guest roles on TV shows and character parts in movies.

Son went from the sublime and somewhat surreal world of working on *The Last Picture Show* back to familiar territory. He signed on to work with director Andrew McLaglen in a Western entitled *Something Big*, starring Dean Martin and Brian Keith.

The film was written by James Lee Barrett, the screenwriter who was one of John Wayne's favorites, and was famous for writing such movies as *Shenandoah* (1965), *Bandolero* (1968), *The Green Berets* (1968), *The Undefeated* (1969) and *Cheyenne Social Club* (1970).

Something Big is a quirky, fun Western, in which Dino brings his ring-a-ding-ding insouciance and plays the film for some laughs. Dino is Joe Baker, who kidnaps the wife of a cavalry colonel (Keith) with unpredictable results.

Dobe Carey, Edward Faulkner, Paul Fix and Bob Steele are along for ride, as is Honor Blackman, who played "Pussy Galore" in the James Bond epic *Goldfinger* (1964).

Something Big was released to mediocre reviews on December 1, 1971.

Son then jumped right into working on another episode of *Gunsmoke,* where he appeared in an episode entitled *Drago*. Also appearing in the episode were Buddy Ebsen, Edward Faulkner and Pat Hingle. The episode aired on November 22, 1971.

After finishing *Gunsmoke*, Son was hired by director Leonard Horn to appear in a low-budget movie about stock car racing entitled *Corky*. The film starred Robert Blake, the former child actor with whom Son had worked with often at Republic Studios in the 1940s. Blake had reinvigorated his career as a now grown actor with a terrifying performance in the film version of Truman Capote's *In Cold Blood* (1967). Blake, who was born Michael James Vincenzo Gubitosi, was a brilliant, if somewhat tortured actor whose career was boom and bust until 2001 when he was accused of murdering a woman he had recently married. When he was acquitted in 2005, he disappeared from public sight, vowing never to be a victim of the media again.

In *Corky*, Blake is a ne'er do well country boy who wants to be a race car driver. He has the bad luck to get into scrapes and squabbles, and ends up killing a man and ends up dying in a crash during a demolition derby. Son took the part of Boland, and did so as much because the film was set for location shooting in Arlington, Texas. The film also featured racing legends Richard Petty, Cale Yarbrough, Donnie Allison and Bobby Allison.

Corky and John Boorman's landmark film *Deliverance* were the first of many films shot in the South featuring quintessentially Southern stories. The popularity of Southern-themed shows on TV, such as *The Andy Griffith Show, Green Acres, Mayberry RFD* and others – and the growth of country music in Nashville, especially dramatic songs like *The Night The Lights Went Out In Georgia*, a 1972 hit for singer Vicki Lawrence – showed Hollywood producers that there was market in the South for entertainment product especially geared to Southern audiences.

Many of these films were low-budget, but they often captured with considerable accuracy life in the American South in the 1970s. Burt Reynolds, the first truly Southern movie superstar, would make his mark in *Deliverance* (1972), then follow it up with *White Lightning* (1973), *Gator* (1976), *Smokey and the Bandit* (1977), and many other Southern-themed films. Max Baer, the handsome actor who played Jethro for laughs in TV's *The Beverly Hillbillies*, turned a low-budget,

Richard D. Jensen

redneck chase film entitled *Macon County Line* into one of the biggest money-makers of 1974.

Moonrunners, a 1975 micro-budget film by independent producer Gy Waldron, was the original *Dukes of Hazzard* and was three years later sanitized and turned into a hit TV series.

Corky was released in March of 1972 and was one of the first of such films, and in the next decade Westerns would decline in popularity while Southern-oriented films would become enormously popular – and Son would be increasingly cast in these Southern bred films, including *The Sugarland Express* (1974), *The Town That Dreaded Sundown* (1976), and *Soggy Bottom U.S.A* (1980),

CHAPTER TWENTY TWO
A HOUSEHOLD NAME AND OSCAR

When *The Last Picture Show* was released, critical acclaim began to pour in for Son. After 30 years in the business, Son was now hailed as a serious actor, an iconic veteran actor capable of performances with depth and resonance.

Not only that, Son was suddenly a household name. For decades Son had been a favorite actor of Western fans, but the elitists of blue state America largely were unaware of Son or his work.

This became clear to Son when he received overtures from the big talk shows for personal appearances. During the 30 years that Johnny Carson hosted the *Tonight Show* on NBC, he was the king of late night television. For 90 minutes, Carson ruled the night. If a performer was asked to guest on his show that was a sign that the performer was a star.

Son was invited to appear on the *Tonight Show* February 17, 1972 along with superstar actor Michael Caine. Carson joked with Son, asking him if he really

Richard D. Jensen

turned down *The Last Picture Show* because of the profanity. Son said he had. Carson asked why and Son told him, "Well, Mr. Carson, I reckon I'm from the old school, but I don't think we ought to use such language in front of our women and children."

Carson then asked Son if he cursed when he got thrown off a horse. Son smiled broadly and answered, "Oh, I use them four letter words, all right, all of 'em. But out there we ain't got any women and children around."[1]

For the first time in his long career, his opinions were suddenly of interest to the general public. The 1960s and 1970s were turbulent times, and the subject of politics and current events often came up in interviews.

Son thought it all a little silly. "The Academy Award changed my whole life," he said.. "You win one of those Oscars and all at once people think you know something. You don't know any more than you did before, but they think you do. And the studios offer you more jobs for a lot more money."[2]

Like fellow cowboy icon John Wayne, Son's politics tilted hard to the right in the wake of the Vietnam War. As with many traditionalists of Son's generation, the rise of the hippie movement and the growth of the drug culture unnerved him. "This is a farce," Son said. "All these vote-seekers tryin' to legalize marijuana and this dope. I think they oughta be hung up by their leg in the town square or somethin.' Anybody that tries to legalize dope for these kids, I think, is way off base.

"We need somebody runnin' our country who can say 'no' and mean it. We don't need any of these jellyfish. It's like puttin' these sex offenders in jail and turnin' 'em out in 30 days. It's a terrible thing to say, but I think they just oughta kill 'em on the first offense, then they wouldn't have so much of it."³

Son began to openly call the younger generation "freaks" and "longhairs." His affable nature often soured when he was asked in interviews about it.

"They ought to dip 'em the way they used to dip cattle," Son said. "Whenever one of them guys burns his draft card, he's done lost my business."

This patriotic bravura was reminiscent of John Wayne, who made similar statements at the time. Ironically, because both men sat out World War II, many on the left in Hollywood viewed such comments with derision.

Son took a hard line against gun control as well. "Let's don't leave 'em with the hoods and take 'em away from the rest of us."⁴

Son recognized at the time that he and Wayne were to the right of most of Hollywood. "They stay mad at John Wayne out there a lot of the time. He makes fun of the hippies and when he's asked to talk at colleges he pokes fun at their long hair and says, 'why don't you go to work?'"⁵

Son did his best to ignore the hype about his star status and kept working.

The TV show *The Virginian* was known for its 90-minute episodes, each a veritable TV movie in its own right, with the main characters remaining and a steady stream of guest stars. In early 1972, the producers planned a two-part special entitled *The Bull of the West*. Directors Jerry Hopper and Paul Stanley hired Charles

Richard D. Jensen

Bronson, Brian Keith, George Kennedy (fresh from his Oscar for *Cool Hand Luke*), *Star Trek*'s DeForest Kelley and Son for the three-hour episode.

The result was a curious mishmash. Despite the presence of the regular cast of the show, including James Drury starring as *The Virginian*, Doug McClure as *Trampas* and Lee J. Cobb as the judge, the movie was over-long and confusing. This was, no doubt, due to the fact that two directors worked on two separate sections, and the continuity was often lost in the mess. It aired on April 14, 1972.

CHAPTER TWENTY THREE
BACK WITH PECKINPAH

After working on two average John Wayne Westerns, a redneck race car movie, and a handful of TV shows – all in the wake of the critical acclaim from *The Last Picture Show*, Son was summoned by Sam Peckinpah to join the cast of *Junior Bonner*. The legendary director's homage to rodeo cowboys was a fitting film for Son, whose status as a former rodeo world champion lends credibility to the film.

Languidly paced, the film is a character study and gives a glimpse of the lives of rodeo cowboys in the 1970s, before corporate sponsorships inflated the prize money cowboys could win.

In *Junior Bonner*, Son is cast as a rodeo promoter. Junior Bonner (Steve McQueen) is a down-on-his-luck former champion bull rider who needs a win. He offers a bribe to Buck, Son's character: Junior will give half of his prize money to Buck if Buck can rig the draw and make certain that Junior will draw a certain bull that Junior knows he can ride to win.

The film was shot mostly on location in Prescott, Arizona, and the setting lends considerable authenticity to the tale. The result is a slice-of-life look at the world of rodeo and the lives of rodeo cowboys and their families. It is also a good glimpse of what Arizona was like at the time. One scene was shot in the famous Palace Bar, a popular local haunt for cowboys. The weather was particularly hot that week and the bar's air-conditioning couldn't keep up with the desert heat and the added heat of the movie lights. When the studio was unable to locate an air-conditioning system for the bar scenes, Son contacted John Wayne, who had equipment which Wayne used often on his desert locations. Wayne sent up one of his special trucks which contained a giant air-conditioning system used by Wayne on Batjac productions.

McQueen turns in a wonderfully understated performance as Junior. Like Son, he preferred as little dialogue as possible, choosing to pare down his words and let his acting tell the story.

McQueen spent the bulk of his time off-camera in bed with starlet Barbara Leigh, who was dating rock music icon Elvis Presley at the time. Presley came to Prescott on at least one occasion to try to win Leigh back, to no avail. McQueen would dump later Leigh for Ali McGraw when the two co-starred in Peckinpah's next film – *The Getaway*.

During the filming of *Junior Bonner*, Son began considering Arizona as the place to live when he retired from motion pictures. For years he'd talked only of returning to Oklahoma, but the warm caresses of the desert winds baked his aches and pains, earned from years of stunt work on horses.

"Uncle Ben got hooked on Arizona during *Junior Bonner*," nephew John Miller said. "He loved the weather and the frontier people. My brother and I lived around here."

Miller said Son moved to Mesa in early 1973 shortly after Ollie moved to a Mesa area retirement village called Leisure World.[1]

The *Junior Bonner* shoot was more leisurely than the other Peckinpah productions Son had worked on. The director, normally manic one minute and enraged the next, was in good humor throughout the process. He got along well with all of the cast, with the exception of Joe Don Baker, who played Junior's money-grabbing brother, Curly. Peckinpah hated Baker on sight. No one knows why, but from Baker's first day on the set, Peckinpah made his dislike of Baker known. He ordered the prop man to take away Baker's folding chair. Every actor on the set had one but Baker. "Fuck him," Peckinpah growled at each mention of Baker's name.[2]

Junior Bonner, which was one of a handful of feature films produced by the ABC television network, was released on August 2, 1972. It bombed. Peckinpah groused that the critics would savage him for violence in his films, but when he made a film without violence, no one came to see it.

Penelope Gilliatt of New Yorker said *Junior Bonner* was "typical of the best of Peckinpah's work," while Newsweek's Paul D. Zimmerman called it "... ponderously slow" and "tiresome."

Director Monte Hellman, who had originally been approached about making the film, turned it down because he thought the script wasn't any good. That said, he thought Peckinpah had done the best any director could have done bringing it to the screen.[3]

McQueen thought that ABC made a strategic blunder releasing *Junior Bonner* nationwide. He argued that the film should be released like an art film, with limited theaters until the word-of-mouth about the film had grown. Others blame the flood of rodeo films released that same month. Cliff Robertson's *J.W. Coop* and James Coburn's *The Honkers* were in direct competition with *Junior Bonner*.

Most fans of Westerns wanted shoot 'em ups, and by 1972 the hottest Western star was Clint Eastwood, whose initial spaghetti Westerns for director Sergio Leone had caused an avalanche of imitators. Now Eastwood was making Westerns in the United States, but using the elements of the Italian-made films, and he was king of the Western. John Wayne, despite his Oscar for *True Grit*, was no longer at the top of the Western movie heap.

Rodeo movies tended to focus not just on the competition in the arena, but on the leisurely lifestyle of the traveling rodeo cowboys, and their drinking and romancing. The films focused more on the slice-of-life elements than on larger than life conflicts. Audiences stayed away in droves.

At the Dallas premiere of *Junior Bonner*, Son told an interviewer that he was trying to put together the deal to make the long dormant Larry McMurtry script *Streets of Laredo*.[4]

McMurtry, who had written *The Last Picture Show* and *Hud*, had a script about two aging Texas Rangers who decide to take one last hurrah and go to Montana on a cattle drive. The Texas-born novelist wanted John Wayne to play Capt. Woodrow Call and Jimmy Stewart to play Augustus McCrae. Son was being considered for the role of Jake Spoon. Peter Bogdanovich was committed to directing the film and the only holdout was John Wayne, who thought Call was too stern a character for him. (Apparently Wayne had forgotten the critical and financial success of *Red River* and *The Searchers*, two movies in which he played tyrannical anti-heroes.) The film script would eventually grow into the Pulitzer Prize-winning novel *Lonesome Dove*, which would thereafter be made into a television movie with Tommy Lee Jones as Call and Robert Duvall as Gus. It is hailed as perhaps the greatest Western movie ever made.

Almost immediately thereafter, Peckinpah hired Son for *The Getaway* (1972), and gave him a meatier part than in *Junior Bonner*. Steve McQueen is Doc and Ali McGraw is Carol, his girlfriend and partner in crime. Son is cast as the double-crossing politician Jack Benyon, who forces Carol to sleep with him in order for her to rescue her boyfriend, Doc, from prison.

Son is very good as the seamy Texas honcho. He delivers the right amount of malice when he invites Carol for a drink – the implication being that she will end up sleeping with Benyon against her will to save her man from prison. There is tense scene when Doc and Benyon take a boat down San Antonio's Riverwalk to discuss a bank heist. Later, when Doc realizes that Benyon has slept with his girl, there is a shootout with a surprise climax.

Richard D. Jensen

The Getaway is Peckinpah at the top of his form. Sardonic, sly, languidly paced but filled with tension, it palpably realistic. It also contains Peckpinpah's wry sense of humor. Peckinpah stages a scene where Doc and Carol take a romantic stroll through a garbage dump. When Doc ambushes a henchman who has turned on him, his girl (Sally Struthers) begins to wail plaintively. Doc matter-of-factly punches her in the face, knocking her out and bringing blessed silence.

The Getaway is classic of the genre, and Son is a major player in the film.

The publicity for *The Getaway* took on a surreal tone when McQueen and McGraw became romantically involved. McGraw had been living with Paramount studio head Robert Evans, a powerhouse film producer and studio executive. McQueen had been hot and heavy with Barbara Leigh.

That said, from day one on set the sexual tension between the two actors was palpable, on screen and off. McQueen's laconic cool smouldered and McGraw's breezy sexuality was intoxicating. When the gossip columnists got a hold of the story, it spread like wildfire. By the time *The Getaway* was released, the word of mouth about the film was so powerful that it was a smash hit, critically and financially.[5]

For Son, the smashing success of *The Last Picture Show, The Wild Bunch* and *The Getaway* had raised his profile considerably. Considered as a cowboy actor for decades, Son now had the reputation as an actor of substance who just happened to be a cowboy. *The Getaway* also exposed Son to the new breed of producers and directors who had taken over Hollywood in the late 1960s.

The old guard, many left over from the old days of the studio system, had been pushed out in favor of young, often completely inexperienced, film makers in the wake of the success of *Easy Rider*. *Easy Rider* was the first smash hit movie of the Vietnam War generation, a buddy flick with anti-war, hippie-era overtones. The film sent shockwaves through Hollywood, where the greying, balding old guard was presiding over the death of the film industry by making un-hip films which were out of step with the mood of the nation.

Peter Fonda, son of iconic actor Henry Fonda, had made *Easy Rider* on a shoestring and it had grossed hundreds of millions of dollars. Studios had immediately done the time-honored Hollywood thing – jumped on the hippie bandwagon. Suddenly young film students with little to no experience were directing major Hollywood films.

The new guard in Hollywood all flocked to *The Getaway* when it was released on December 13, 1972. The movie starred their favorite anti-hero, McQueen, and their favorite flower child, McGraw. In doing so, these young film makers saw Ben Johnson deliver a solid performance as a dirty villain. Such roles would add years – and luster – to Son's career.

Having finished *Junior Bonner* and *The Getaway* for Peckinpah, Son was already making plans to join John Wayne in Mexico for his latest western. Written and directed by stalwart Burt Kennedy, *The Train Robbers* told the story of a hunt for stolen loot. Almost as soon

Richard D. Jensen

as he arrived, Son had to leave and ended up making history.

Son arrived in Durango, Mexico on Thursday, March 23, 1972 to begin work on the film. John Wayne's sets were always relaxed and leisurely and had an atmosphere of camaraderie, so long as everyone did their job.

Kennedy had some battles with producer Michael Wayne over the train used in the climax of the movie, and Kennedy wasn't enamored of co-star Rod Taylor, but overall production was a pleasant experience.[6]

Just two weeks after his arrival on set, on Thursday, April 6, 1972, Son flew with Ann-Margret to Hollywood from Durango aboard John Wayne's new private jet. He had been summoned to Hollywood for the telecast of the Academy Awards on television. It's a not so well-kept film industry secret that if you are called and encouraged to attend the Oscar ceremony that it's an inside hint that you've won. Son got the call on Saturday, April 1, 1972, and one has to wonder if he thought it was an April Fool's joke.

"We were making *The Train Robbers* in 1972. That's when they called me from Hollywood and said I better get back there because I *might* win an Academy Award. Well I was a cowboy and no cowboy had ever won an Academy Award, so I knew I could. Well, anyhow, Duke lent Ann-Margret and me his new airplane to go to the awards. We come up there and I win that old Oscar. That's the big thing in my life. I'm the only cowboy who ever won a World Championship in the rodeo and won an Oscar in the movies. I don't know if it means anything or not, but I like to hear myself tell it anyway," Son said.[7]

When Son accepted his Oscar, he strode to the podium with a gee-whiz smile on his face. He reached the microphone and gave an acceptance speech that went down in history.

"Wa'll ain't that purty," Son drawled. "What I'm about to say will start a controversy around the world. This couldn't have happened to a nicer fella."

Son had tried to write a speech, but was frustrated by the phoniness of his prepared remarks. By speaking from the heart, he showed both his humor and self-effacing personality.

Back in Durango, Mexico, the cast of *The Train Robbers* was busy working on the night scene where Christopher George's horse is trapped under a fallen tree when word reached the cast the Son had won his Oscar.[8]

Son joked that when he started his speech, he looked down at Carol and could see she was nervous for him. "She thought I was gonna talk about the hippies or something," he laughed.[9]

Dobe Carey recalled that he was in Rome filming a *Trinity* western with Terrence Hill. As he made his way to breakfast at his hotel, Dobe noticed that all of the newspapers in a newsstand had Son's photo and the caption about his "nicer fella" comment. Dobe was struck by the impact of the moment, that his pal had won an Oscar and was now famous the world over.[10]

As Son basked in the glow of the praise of his peers, he was still mindful that he was in many ways not a part of the scene. "Those things are pretty cold," Son said. "You feel a little like a man without a country at those things."[11]

Son didn't think he'd win the Oscar, but he had been hopeful. "If I got the better part, I wanted to win it. If someone else did the better job, I wanted them to win it. I'm not interested in the politics in it. I've been around too long to start playing games."[12]

From the sublime to the ridiculous – later that same year, an earthquake rumbled through Westlake Village, where Son and Carol lived. Their home was severely damaged.

"The earthquake broke my swimming hole in half and caused havoc in my house. It cost me $15,000 to get it put back together again," Son said. "Only our beds and half of the sofa didn't turn over. When it ended there were only six drinking glasses not shattered."

Son was literally rattled by the incident. "I don't scare easy, but earthquakes scare me."[13]

CHAPTER TWENTY FOUR
A "SERIOUS" ACTOR

With his Oscar for *The Last Picture Show* firmly in hand, Son flew back to Durango, Mexico on Wednesday, April 12, 1972 aboard John Wayne's private plane. He was again accompanied on the return trip by Ann-Margret, whose spirits were less buoyant than Son's after losing to Cloris Leachman for her performance in *The Last Picture Show*.

The first scene they shot upon arrival was the famous scene in which Ann-Margret falls off a horse into a river and nearly drowns while Son and Wayne chat amiably on the riverbank and then have to rescue her. In the rescue scene, Son does his own stunts, while Wayne is doubled by "Bad Chuck" Roberson.[1]

When Son arrived back in the dry Mexican desert he found Wayne genuinely happy for his success, but wistful about the future of their careers. Wayne, like many of the old stars, felt lost in the new youth-driven film industry with it's leftist values.

"He felt out of place in modern society," Son said. "He'd not changed his ideas on life, and he didn't like the way films were 'growing up.' He saw modern films as being morally repugnant. But, hell, the American public had watched the Vietnam War on their TVs and there was no going back to the kind of illusions of the old days of cinema.

"If people couldn't believe a film was being realistic, they didn't go. Even I [knew] that. I did *The Last Picture Show* and I got myself an Oscar as Best Supporting Actor. I said to Wayne, 'Duke, what do you think of that? I never ever thought I was an actor.' He said, 'I'm delighted for you, Ben. You're a really fine actor and you don't like to admit it. But what kind of movies are these damn people making?'

"I said, 'Duke, there's nothing wrong with the movie. You just won't stop living in the past. Life isn't a John Ford picture.' He said, 'You're right, but I can't help feeling lost.' I felt sorry for Duke. Very sad. It seemed to me he had become lonely. Things were bad between him and Pilar, although they were trying to keep their marriage problems out of the public eye. But everyone who knew them also knew it was over between them. Very sad indeed."[2]

Son knew that Wayne was right. The old days of Western movies being made with actors who were real cowboys were gone. The old days when movies starred former real cowboys such as Tom Mix, Buck Jones and Hoot Gibson were gone. The old-time Western movies were based upon many real-life experiences of real cowboys and ranchers. The modern Westerns were often ridiculous charades written by writers who didn't know a horse from a goat, starring actors who didn't know anything about the real West.

"It's hard to find young people in the business who know anything about the real West," Son said. "A lot of them don't know whether a horse roosts in a hole or a tree. Most actors can't ride well enough to get in and out of a scene. They're about as western as my poodle."[3]

Son had two cherished dogs at this time, a part Bengal and part Australian shepherd named Frank and a poodle named Jody. Son often joked that Carol would have an easier time replacing him than the poodle.[4]

During the location shooting for *The Train Robbers*, director Burt Kennedy spent a lot of free time riding horses in the desert with Wayne when the cameras weren't rolling. They wouldn't talk much, just ride together much the same way that the Duke's legendary screen characters would ride the west, saying little, deep in thought. Kennedy recalled at the time that Wayne was despondent over his now acrimonious relationship with his wife. Kennedy could see that Wayne knew that his marriage was over. "I think he hates his wife," Kennedy recorded in his diary after one of those rides.[5]

Son realized that after nearly 35 years in the film business he was suddenly accepted as a "serious actor." It reminded him of the way critics suddenly began taking John Wayne seriously as an actor in 1947 when Howard Hawks' classic *Red River* was released. In this brilliant cowboy version of *Mutiny On The Bounty*, Wayne plays the maniacal Tom Dunson, the cattle baron version of Captain Bligh.

"There was John Ford, putting Duke into secondary roles and telling him what a lousy actor he was, and all of a sudden the critics were raving about Duke's performance in *Red River*," Son said. "People were suddenly asking, why was it that John Wayne has been in the business for two decades and that instead of going into decline, he had suddenly become a major attraction? Ford suddenly comes up with an answer which he claims he knew all along. He said, 'Duke is the best actor in Hollywood, that's why.' He suddenly puts Duke into the starring role in *She Wore A Yellow Ribbon* which again proved that Duke was a really fine actor. I can tell you that the reason he had been so successful, and became even more successful, was because he was the hardest-working actor I ever knew. He worked damned hard to prove himself. But still, even with *Red River* he was being shunned by his peers. He should have been nominated for an Oscar, but he wasn't."[6]

One thing is certain, Oscar-winner John Wayne was the star of *The Train Robbers* and Oscar-winner Ben Johnson was playing, once again, second fiddle to the Duke. Once again, their byplay on screen was magical.

Kennedy was glad to have Son on the shoot, noting in his diary that when he learned that Son would make the film was his "lucky day."[7]

As he always did, Son added an extra dimension of realism to the film. Because he was a championship roper, Ben could be counted on to display his skill with a lariat on camera, roping a horse or cow or other object in a tight camera shot, thus adding additional realism to the film. Many actors, Wayne included, could ride well enough to convince audiences that they were "real"cowboys, but few could actually cowboy. Son was one of them.

The Train Robbers is an iconic John Wayne western, full of the imagery that made John Wayne the king of the modern western film. It's opening scene steals shamelessly from *Once Upon A Time In The West*, and Son is the first person you see as he waits for the train bearing Wayne and Ann-Margret. Wayne arrives and immediately punches out "Grady" (Rod Taylor) when Christopher George mouths off to him. Taylor, the much-younger and stouter Australian born he-man, is clearly physically able to beat the hell out of the aging Wayne, but that's not the point. This is a John Wayne film, and he stand tall, playing as Taylor's character calls him, "... that big ol' Lane."

Son's underplayed style of acting gives great credibility to the film. He anchors the film with a sense of gritty reality.

Some of the performances, especially that of singer Bobby Vinton, weaken the film, but Son's austerity centers the characters, making the entire adventure seem quite real.

Son's character, "Jesse," is the conscience of the film. He warns Lane that the adventure could get the widow, "Mrs. Lowe," killed. Later, during a campfire sequence, Son provides the back story, telling the woman that Lane, Grady and he had ridden together since the Civil War, riding up various hills in battle. He tells that Lane's wife's died after the war and the two men "went up that hill with him, too." In this simple, understated scene, Ben Johnson proves that he is a gifted natural actor.

Richard D. Jensen

Son always asserted that he never acted in films, rather he just "played Ben Johnson better than anyone else." This is a self-effacing over-simplification. Acting on film is the most difficult of tasks, requiring an ability to convey sincerity and realism while playing pretend. Son became famous as Ben Johnson the actor not because Son was a thespian in the classical sense, but because he learned early on that by playing roles with which he could identify, he could turn in performances of incredible resonance.

Son returned from Mexico and *The Train Robbers* set in early June 1972 and began work for Robert Totten, the director of many Western TV series and movies, in a TV adaptation of the John Steinbeck classic, *The Red Pony*. The cast included Henry Fonda, Maureen O'Hara, Jack Elam, Clint Howard and his dad, Rance Howard.

The Train Robbers premiered on February 7, 1973, and did solid business.

The Red Pony aired on March 18, 1973 to critical acclaim and an Emmy nomination for its screenplay.

The spring of 1973 was good for Son. He had a popular movie in the theaters, *The Train Robbers*, and a well-received and critically acclaimed TV movie, *The Red Pony*, airing on television.

When *The Red Pony* premiered on television, Son wasn't watching. He was back in his hometown of Pawhuska, Oklahoma, escorting Oklahoma Gov. David Hall to the Barnsdall High School commencement exercises. Son's sister, Helen, who was now the elected Osage County Court Clerk, accompanied the group of dignitaries, which included Osage County Sheriff

George Wayman, Barnsdall Mayor Bert Lewis, Senator John Dahl of Barnsdall and State Rep. Bill Kennedy.[8]

Son stayed in Oklahoma to work on his latest film, *Dillinger*, the saga of the famous bank robber. The film was directed by John Milius and starred Warren Oates as the infamous John Dillinger. Son was cast as FBI agent Melvin Purvis, the man who headed the manhunt for Dillinger. Son was happy to be working on the film location in Ardmore, Oklahoma. He was always pushing Oklahoma as a movie location. Also, shooting *Dillinger* in Oklahoma meant Son was working on another movie in which he didn't have to work in Hollywood. And Son was happy to be working with Oates, a fellow alum of *The Wild Bunch*.

The film is uniformly good, and Son is quite good as Purvis, even if the film portrays Purvis inaccurately. Son is a big, aging, cowboy. Purvis was a small, effete Southerner of considerable wealth who over-dressed and even had a manservant while serving in the FBI. He was actually a disaster as the leader of the FBI's war on crime, but he was kept in place because FBI director J. Edgar Hoover, a closet homosexual, had a crush on Purvis. This information was recently revealed in declassified documents. Their relationship is only now being reevaluated in the wake of this newly declassified material.

The film, which was released on July 20, 1973, also co-starred Cloris Leachman, fresh from her Oscar for *The Last Picture Show*, Harry Dean Stanton, and a young actor named Richard Dreyfuss as Baby Face Nelson. Steve Kanaly, who would later co-star in the hit

TV series *Dallas*, played Pretty Boy Floyd. Amazingly, the real J. Edgar Hoover played himself!

Son had agreed to star in *Dillinger* for American International, a low-budget company, because the company agreed to film the movie in Oklahoma. Son continued to hope – and work for – the establishment of Oklahoma as a film center. "If people will really go along with this company and try to help them, and not rob them, we might get some others," Son said.[9]

During the filming of *Dillinger*, Oates told the Associated Press that he had tremendous admiration and respect for Son. "I want to be like Ben Johnson. Not just Ben Johnson on the screen, but Ben Johnson in every aspect of life. He's a straight, wonderful, natural performer. A purist."[10]

Interestingly, Milius used much of the stock footage from *Dillinger* to make a sequel entitled *Melvin Purvis, G-Man,* which was released the following year. It is unknown why Milius recast the role of Purvis and hired former cowboy star (and Oklahoman) Dale Robertson to replace Son as the famous FBI agent. It is most likely that Son had committed to work with Stephen Spielberg on *The Sugarland Express,* a feature film. Further, Milius' sequel was to finish shooting in California and Son preferred working on location. Spielberg was shooting his movie in Texas. It could also be a matter of money. Robertson's career was faltering, and thus he worked cheaper than Son, who was charging top dollar for his services, thanks to his Oscar for *The Last Picture Show.*

Son continued to get offers for many films, including a Western set to star Gregory Peck, entitled *Billy Two*

Hats. Son turned down the film because it was to be shot in Israel, and he didn't trust "the upscuffle over there" between the Israelis and Palestinians. He also turned it down because Carol and he hated flying.[11]

When Son finished *Dillinger*, TV director David Lowell Rich offered son a starring role in a TV movie entitled *Runaway!* Disaster films were the rage in the early 1970s, and *Runaway!* was made to cash in on the trend. Filled with 1970s TV stars and character actors such as Ben Murphy (*Alias Smith and Jones*), Ed Nelson, Martin Milner (*Adam 12*), and Kip Niven, the movie also featured Vera Miles, the actress best known for her work in John Ford's *The Searchers* (1956) and *The Man Who Shot Liberty Valance* (1962).

The film was shot on location in the Rocky Mountains around Denver, Colorado and aired on September 29, 1973.

After completing *Runaway!*, Son was cast in *Blood Sport,* a remarkably good TV movie about a father who is pushing his son to become a high school football star.

It is obvious that Son's portrayal of Sam the Lion in *The Last Picture Show* and its subtext of high school football, played a part in Son's casting.

Son was cast as the father and Gary Busey was cast as the son. Larry Hagman, the star of *I Dream Of Jeannie* and later the megahit TV series *Dallas,* played the conniving football coach determined to win at all costs.

Writer/director Jerrold Freedman's film focuses less on theatrics and more on the emotional toll of pushy parents and coaches. *Blood Sport* is a very good socially conscious TV movie and Son, Busey and Hagman are extremely good in it. *Blood Sport* aired on December 5, 1973.

Keeping with his practice of taking film roles that enabled him to work away from Los Angeles, Son signed on to play Capt. Tanner, the leader of a Texas manhunt for a young couple that has kidnaped a highway patrolman in *The Sugarland Express* (1973). Goldie Hawn starred as Lou Jean Poplin, a country girl who breaks her husband out of work release so they can get their baby back from child welfare authorities. Directed by a bright young newcomer named Steven Spielberg, who would go on to become a powerhouse filmmaker and win Oscars for *Schindler's List* and *Saving Private Ryan*, the film is shot on location in south Texas.

Son adds considerable authenticity to the movie. It begins as a light-hearted romp, with the young couple becoming modern-day folk heroes, but takes on a serious tone when the law steps in to rescue the kidnaped officer.

Son infuses Capt. Tanner with the right mix of devotion to duty and world-weariness. His role is pivotal. He is the catalyst that grounds the light-hearted romp in reality, and we realize the gravity of the situation as Tanner's unease foreshadows the violent reality of the coming climax. Tanner knows that the folk hero status that Lou Jean and her husband (played with charm by William Atherton) will be short-lived when the authorities catch up to the kidnappers.

The Sugarland Express is a good film, made better by the austerity of the location filming, and a bevy of locals enlisted to play the townspeople. Indeed, Buster

Daniels is hysterical as the drunk in the squad car haranguing the highway patrolman (Michael Sacks) who eventually is kidnaped.

The final shot, beautifully filmed by cinematographer Vilmos Zsigmond, is a backlit scene at sunset. The light shimmers across the rushing waters of a river as Son approaches and returns the highway patrolman's gun to him. It is a lyrical shot, and because it is shot in silhouette we focus on the emotion of the moment, instead of the actors.

During the filming of the movie, Spielberg's first, the media focused as much on Son's participation in it as they did Hawn, who had achieved stardom on the hit TV series *Laugh In.* As a recent Oscar-winner for a film about Texans, Son's arrival to make another movie in Texas was big news. This was especially so because Son was so affable. The quintessential everyman, Son evoked memories of fellow Oklahoman Will Rogers, who never met a stranger. Son was always friendly, always accessible. He stopped to talk to anyone who crossed his path. This quality endeared Son to the locals wherever he worked, and was key to his popularity with audiences.

While filming one day on location for *The Sugarland Express,* Son was being interviewed by a reporter when a young girl rode by on a horse. She had come from a nearby farm to watch the filming, but she was a poor rider and her horse was acting up, shying and spooking at the cameras and equipment. Son brow furrowed with concern and he became fixated on watching the girl, explaining to the reporter that the girl was perilously close to being badly hurt. He found it difficult to

Richard D. Jensen

continue the interview because of his concern for the girl's safety. Like a protective uncle, Son kept his eye on the girl the entire time, poised to come to her aid if the situation went from bad to worse.[12]

This episode is typical of Son. Childless himself, he was known as a doting father figure. He would never step in and take over as an authoritarian, but he would be ever-ready to lend a helping hand or a guiding word of advice. This was especially true when it came to young people and their horses.

The Sugarland Express premiered on April 5, 1974 and was an immediate hit, and Son received even more exposure to an even more youthful audience.

When 20th Century Fox was planning *Kid Blue*, a new Western with *Easy Rider* star Dennis Hopper, Son was cast as Mean John Simpson the sheriff who pursues Hopper. A comedic and wry Western, *Kid Blue* was shot in Mexico and co-starred Warren Oates, Peter Boyle, Ralph Waite and Clifton James.

Son brought his mother, Ollie, and Carol with him when he went on location for the shoot.

During filming in Mexico, Son, Carol and Ollie were invited to visit Pancho Villa's widow at the dead revolutionary's hacienda. This visit was the highlight of the entire production.

Kid Blue was released the following year, on May 2, 1974.

As soon as they returned from Mexico, Son and Carol went to Pawhuksa, where Son played in the Osage Golf Course Benefit Tournament on Saturday, May 20, 1973. Son was virtually unrecognizable, dressed in a pair of plaid pants, a long-sleeve dress shirt and a ball cap. The tournament benefitted the Oklahoma Lung Research and Development program.[13]

During the summer of 1973, word spread throughout Hollywood that John Ford's health was failing. Years of over-indulgence of alcohol, cigars, poor diet and depression had taken its toll on the visionary, but troubled, filmmaker.

Son went to see Ford sometime in early August, and knew the end was near. He sat by Ford's bed for a long while, and Ford seemed to be searching for something to say. He finally looked up at Son and said, quietly, "Ben, don't forget to stay real"

"I never forgot that," Son said.[14]

Ford died of cancer on August 31, 1973.

Son finished 1973 working on charity events and spending time hunting and fishing with friends.

Son went home to Oklahoma and met up with pal Dub Taylor and hunted quail along with Dub's son, Buck Taylor, the star of *Gunsmoke*, and western movie star Dale Robertson at the National Quail Hunt in Pawhuska. After the hunt, the roughly 40 hunters in attendance gathered at Harold Groendyke's lodge, dined on roast pig and spare ribs. The media attended and the event received lots of local press.[15]

The year 1975 brought with it two film roles that would further cement Son's reputation as a seasoned, gifted actor.

One film was the brainchild of a laconic and gifted Hollywood director known for historical blockbusters, and the other was a return to working with the brilliant Tom Gries, with whom Son had worked on *Will Penny* (1968).

Richard D. Jensen

One of the best movies Son co-starred in after his Oscar win was the incredible *Bite the Bullet*, starring Gene Hackman. The film takes place after the turn of the 20th Century. We see clearly that it is the last days of the West. Autos are replacing horses. Electric wires and telegraph lines abound.

A cross-country endurance horse race is held and the contestants vie for a huge jackpot.

There is much intrigue, drama and excitement as the various riders cross mountains and deserts, dodging bandits and escaped convicts. Candice Bergen plays a gorgeous woman who enters the race, but only to further a prison escape.

James Coburn and Jan-Michael Vincent are also in the cast of this better-than-usual Western, which also features Mario Arteaga as a valiant Mexican charro, who competes despite a terrible jaw infection.

In the movie, Son plays an aging cowboy who enters the grueling cross-country horse race. He meets his death shortly after he falls into a frozen river. As he lays by a fire, the cowboy tells Gene Hackman that he is willing to risk his life to win the race, in order to be "somebody."

Bite the Bullet was written and directed by Richard Brooks, the tall, lanky, pipe-smoking, multi-Oscar-winning film-maker who was responsible for such film classics as *Cat On A Hot Tin Roof* (1958) and *Elmer Gantry* (1960). Most notably, Brooks also wrote and directed the exquisite Western *The Professionals* (1966) which starred Lee Marvin, Burt Lancaster, Woody Strode, Jack Palance and Ralph Bellamy. *Bite the Bullet* has the same gritty realism of *The Professionals* and

The Wild Bunch, and also has the same dramatic sense of loss as larger-than-life heroes outlive their time and struggle to find adventures that will bring back the heroics of their youth.

The year 1975 continued to be a banner year for Son when he joined superstar Charles Bronson and the cast of *Breakheart Pass,* a film adaptation of Alistair MacLean's novel of murder and intrigue an a train in the Old West. A diptheria epidemic has supposedly broken out at a distant fort, but it's all a ruse.

Shot on location in Idaho during the winter, the film features the historic Camas Prairie Railroad.

The film also featured actress Jill Ireland, Bronson's real wife and frequent co-star, TV great Richard Crenna, and a host of well-known and beloved character actors, including Charles Durning, Ed Lauter, Bill McKinney, and David Huddleston.

Breakheart Pass is a taut, exciting Western, uniquely set in the dead of winter. Very few Westerns reflect that much of the American West is in the High Country, where snow is prevalent throughout the winter. This makes *Breakheart Pass* visually striking and adds considerable dimension to the story. Lucien Ballard's cinematography captures the inspiring Idaho landscape and the film is a cut above the standard Western.

Basically a Western version of Agatha Christie's *Ten Little Indians*, the film is just plain fun. The stunts are well executed, especially the thrilling train wreck. It is also notable for being the final film of legendary stuntman Yakima Canutt, whose son Joe also worked on the film.

Richard D. Jensen

Also in the cast is rodeo great Casey Tibbs, a contemporary of Son's from his rodeo days.

Son's participation in Robert Aldrich's seamy crime drama *Hustle* is puzzling. After working on two big budget, traditional Westerns, this film is an odd choice. Most likely Son was offered the choice part and wanted to work with its star, Burt Reynolds, which whom Son had worked on the original *Gunsmoke* episodes. The movie, however, contains all the raw, cynical elements Son disliked about the new Hollywood movies.

Hustle is a gritty film, starring Reynolds as a police lieutenant and Catherine Deneuve as his prostitute girlfriend. Eddie Albert plays the corrupt lawyer who is deeply involved in organized crime.

The cast included Oscar-winner Ernest Borgnine, Son's co-star from *The Wild Bunch* (1971).

Donald "Red" Barry has a bit part as a bartender in a scene in which he and Reynolds eye an Asian temptress in a bar and make lewd comments about her.. Barry starred as Red Ryder in the 1940s Westerns for Republic Studios and his career lasted decades, but never reached the stardom his talent deserved. Barry was one of those incredibly talented actors whose ego ruined his career. Similar to Jimmy Cagney in stature and demeanor, he could have been a superstar. Unfortunately, the banty Texan alienated so many directors his career nearly ended more than once. He made a living by taking minor roles, and had worked with Son in 1972 on Peckinpah's *Junior Bonner.*

Barry committed suicide on July 17, 1980. This author had a genial conversation with Barry on the backlot at Warner Brothers' Burbank Studios only days before his death. He was amiable and flattered that I knew who he was and remembered his work.

Catherine Bach, who went on to stardom as Daisy Duke on TV's hit show, *The Dukes of Hazzard*, plays a hooker and appears semi-nude in several scenes.

Hustle is a striking example of the kind of film Son decried. A seamy, downbeat film about corruption, prostitution and pornography. The movie is far more graphic than *The Last Picture Show,* and one wonders if Son didn't feel the need to decry its contents because it was a flop at the box office and few people saw it.

That said, Son is terrific in the film. Son plays a Korean War veteran suffering from post traumatic stress disorder who becomes bent on revenge when his daughter turns up dead. He curses and rages and punches out cops and stalks mobsters in a strip club. He buys a gun at a pawn shop and plans the murders of the men who destroyed his daughter.

The scene where Son's character is forced to watch his late daughter performing in a porn film is harrowing. Son's face goes slack, his eyes glaze into a icy coldness. He goes on a rampage against the underworld that dragged his daughter into prostitution and porn. When he finally guns down the crooked mob lawyer, he is catatonic.

By 1975 Son was constantly telling the press that he was disgusted with modern Hollywood. He often decried the anti-war hippies and their opposition to the Vietnam War. A son of the Oklahoma prairie, Son's beliefs mirrored many of his Hollywood contemporaries. He was a conservative as John Wayne,

Richard D. Jensen

John Ford, Ward Bond, as were many other Western actors. He was also a patriotic and a traditionalist.

Son seemed to be a paradox after winning the Oscar for *The Last Picture Show*. Having won acclaim for what Son called "a dirty movie," Son's credibility as an actor stemmed from his participation in big budget feature films directed by the new breed in Hollywood. Bogdanovich had directed Son in *The Last Picture Show* (1971). Peckinpah had directed Son in *Major Dundee* (1965), *The Wild Bunch* (1969), *Junior Bonner* (1972) and *The Getaway* (1972). John Milius had directed Son in *Dillinger* (1973). Steven Spielberg had directed Son in *The Sugarland Express* (1974). And now Aldrich was directing Son in *Hustle*.

That said, Son preferred to work with old-line directors who made more traditional films.

The problem was Son was offered piles of cash to work with these new directors, and it was money that Son, a shrewd businessman, couldn't turn down.

Son's stardom had risen so much after his Oscar that he was suddenly in demand by talk shows. On January 19, 1978 Son was a guest on the *Mike Douglas Show*. Douglas was a G-rated version of Johnny Carson, a genial singer and everyman whose syndicated daytime talk show was a television mainstay for more than 20 years. Son appeared alongside comedian Robert Klein and actress Barbara Parkins.

In keeping with his desire to work in film but not work in the modern Hollywood, Son accepted the lead in a low-budget suspense/horror film produced and directed by a maverick film-maker named Charles B. Pierce. Pierce was making a serial killer film called *The*

Town That Dreaded Sundown, which was based on a true story. Son's interest in the project was cemented when he realized it was to be filmed in Garland City, Arkansas, not far from the border with his beloved Oklahoma.

Son plays police Capt. J.D. Morales, a small town cop trying to capture a serial killer who strikes terror when he goes on a nightly rampage. The film is the epitome of the drive-in movie slasher film, the kind of movie modern iconic director Quentin Tarrantino heralds in his *Grindhouse* films.

Andrew Prine, who had worked with Son and John Wayne in *Chisum* in 1970, co-starred as Son's deputy. Dawn Wells, who played sweet, virginal Mary Anne in the hit TV series *Gilligan's Island*, was cast as a woman who falls victim to the killer.

The movie is quite good, and very scary. It's low budget and location shooting give it an air of realism, as does Son's flinty portrayal of the cop trying to catch the serial killer.

The film was so cheap to make that it made a profit and when Pierce would come calling the following year seeking Son's participation in *Greyeagle*, a remake of John Ford's *The Searchers,* Son agreed to star.

Disaster films continued to be the rage in the mid-1970s, and Son wrapped *The Town That Dreaded Sundown* and jumped immediately into the starring role in *The Savage Bees* (1976).

The run-of-the-mill disaster film starred Son as a sheriff trying to figure out why killer bees are swarming and killing people. The film co-stars Michael Parks, star of TV's *Then Came Bronson*, and James Best, the character actor who would gain everlasting fame as Sheriff Roscoe P. Coltrane on TV's *The Dukes of Hazzard*.

Director Tom Gries then asked Son to play a cameo in *The Greatest*, a terrible film starring Muhammad Ali as himself.

When Charles B. Pierce called Son and asked him to take on the John Wayne role in his remake of John Ford's classic *The Searchers*, Son agreed. Son wanted to work, and he wanted to make Westerns, and he wanted to do so outside of Hollywood. Pierce planned to make the film in the Helena National Forest around Helena, Montana.

In a public relations play to make audiences take notice, the film co-starred Lana Wood, sister of Natalie Wood (who played the kidnaped daughter in the original.)

After Pierce hired Son to play the John Wayne part, he then cast Iron Eyes Cody, the Indian actor famous for the Keep America Beautiful commercials. Jack Elam was hired as well.

The film, entitled *Greyeagle*, began production in the spring of 1977. During the filming in Montana, the cast noticed that a section of the script was left blank. Cody began a quest to determine why. Pierce told the cast the blank pages were for a secret scene, and Cody got cranky. "What do you have me doing in it, scalping somebody's genitals? Using bad language – an Indian for the first time on screen using bad language?" Cody groused.

Cody said Son was standing nearby, and drawled, "Hail, don't worry about that. I used dirty language and got an Academy Award for it. I'll swear on the screen but I'll be a son of a bitch if I'll appear naked."[16]

The film is not at all as good as Ford's classic, but it is an occasionally interesting Western. Pierce's talent as a director is workman-like at best, and the film succeeds only because of the veteran actors and the marvelous Montana scenery. Paul Fix, the veteran character actor who is most famous as Sheriff Micah from The Rifleman TV series, plays the Indian known as "Running Wolf." Fix was one of the close circle of Western stalwarts, an actor in John Wayne's inner circle. Fix was also the father of Marilyn Fix Carey, the wife of Son's good friend Dobe Carey.

Popular Western actor Alex Cord played the title character of Greyeagle, the Indian who kidnaps Beth, the character played by Lana Wood.

The film suffers greatly because Wood can't act. Indeed, she is abominable. Cord is badly miscast as the titular Indian. The film's major flaw is the use on non-Indian actors in Indian roles. Son is a joy to watch in *Greyeagle*, and his presence carries much of the film.

CHAPTER TWENTY FIVE
WORKING HARD FOR CHARITY

Son continued to invest his movie money into non-movie investments, but the results were often mixed. On June 1, 1978, he incorporated Ben Johnson's Montana Properties in Montana to sell a real estate development in Ennis, Montana. The state assigned the company an identification number of L011298. The registered office for the company was Son's office located at 2659 Townsgate Road, Suite 115, Westlake, Ca. 91361. Son renewed the corporate certificate on July 1, 1992, but the corporation would dissolve after Son's death. The development would eventually lose money and Son would donate the land to charity.

Son was much in demand by social and charitable organizations, as well as professional groups. On June 30, 1978, Son was elected to the Board of Trustees of the Prorodeo Hall of Champions in Denver, Colorado.[1]

Disaster films still dominated the box office in 1978 when Son was cast in *The Swarm*, Warner Brothers' big-budget killer bee movie. The film was the brainchild of disaster epic director Irwin Allen, and was headlined by superstar Michael Caine. As was common in the

1970s, such disaster films are packed with aging movie giants, and this film co-starred a galaxy of Hollywood's Golden Era greats, including Richard Widmark, Olivia de Havilland, Henry Fonda and Fred MacMurray. Additionally, TV stars Richard Chamberlain, Patty Duke, Lee Grant, Bradford Dillman and Cameron Mitchell were on hand.

Son enjoyed working again with fellow rodeo star-turned-actor Slim Pickens, and had a warm reunion with Fred MacMurray, whom Son had stunt doubled for on the Western classic *Smoky* in 1946. MacMurray always credited Son with much of the success of the movie. An inept horseman and no cowboy, MacMurray relied on Son to make him look good and was always grateful. *The Swarm* was typical of the bloated disaster flicks of the day, and is more memorable for its cast than it's story or special effects.

When he heard about the project, Son jumped at the chance to work on the TV-movie adaptation of Louis L'Amour's classic Western novels *Sackett* and *The Daybreakers*.

Titled *The Sacketts*, the film was scheduled to be a four-hour mini-series, and was intended to be a faithful adaptation of the legendary books.

The producers chose two popular TV stars, Sam Elliott and Tom Selleck as Tell and Orrin Sackett, and cast newcomer Jeff Osterhage as Ty Sackett. Western icon Glenn Ford was cast as Tom Sunday. Son was hired to play Cap Roundtree.

The film is full of Western characters known and beloved by Western fans. Gilbert Roland, the original *Cisco Kid,* was cast as Don Luis. The beloved stray-eyed geezer Jack Elam was hired, along with burly Gene Evans, Son's rodeo pal Slim Pickens, and Gene Autry sidekick Pat Buttram.

Many of the new breed of Western character actors were brought on board as well, including L.Q. Jones, Paul Koslo, James Gammon and Buck Taylor. Taylor was now well-known from his nearly 15 years playing Newly on TV's "Gunsmoke." Taylor, the son of character actor Dub Taylor, one of Son's good friends and a frequent co-star and hunting buddy, is also a noted Western painter.

The film also featured Shug Fisher, the stuttering bit part actor used often by John Ford in his Westerns. Ruth Roman and Mercedes McCambridge, two major stars in the 1950s, were also cast.

The Sacketts is a landmark TV western. It attempts to faithfully capture the scope of L'Amour's book, and nearly succeeds. It's only drawback is its length. Stretching the story to four hours makes for uneven pacing. Some scenes are crisp and striking, while others are languid and without movement. The film is further weakened by sloppy editing and a weak musical score.

That said, the film is head and shoulders above other TV-movie Westerns of that time. It's Canon City, Colorado locations are awe-inspiring.

Selleck and Elliott turn in star-making performances. Both men would etch out a place in the pantheon of Western TV-movie stars in the next two decades.

Son is perfect as Cap Roundtree, and his performance resonates with gritty realism.

When the first installment of *The Sacketts* was aired on May 15, 1979, it was highly rated. Television was chock full of modern sitcoms, such as the highly-rated *Laverne and Shirley* and *Three's Company*, and quirky shows like *Charlie's Angels*. Primetime was dominated by soap operas like *Dynasty* and *Dallas.*

Audiences were starved for a good solid TV Western, and *The Sacketts* was just what audiences wanted.

The success of *The Sacketts* was dulled for Son when, a mere 26 days later, John Wayne succumbed to cancer.

"When I heard he died, it was losing part of [my] family. I felt kind of the same way when John Ford died six years earlier," Son said. "But unlike Duke, I got to see John Ford when he was on his deathbed."[2]

"Duke was the Rock of Gibraltar for me," Son said. "He helped me a heck of a lot in the picture business. I doubled Duke way back in the 1940s, right after I first came out here. He was very professional and he was a great guy to work with.

"Duke was from the old school. It was honesty, realism and respect. He had a lot of respect for himself and a lot of respect for women and children.

"I like that philosophy, and that's what I live my life by. I was always glad someone else felt and thought the same way. He sure helped an awful lot of people throughout the years. He was an all-around good fella and helped a lot of kids all over the world, lots of under-privileged kids. I liked that, too," Son said.[3]

Son's next film grew out of his friendship with Oklahoma's billionaire media mogul Edward Gaylord, II, owner of the *Daily Oklahoman* newspaper, Opryland,

Richard D. Jensen

Gaylord Entertainment Company, the Nashville Network, Country Music Television (CMT), the Lazy E Arena in Oklahoma City, and much more. He wanted to dabble in film-making. Both Son and Gaylord wanted to make movies in Oklahoma, and nearby.

Shot in Marshall, Texas and produced by Gaylord, *Soggy Bottom USA* was initially filmed as *The Swamp Rats*. The film was produced to ride the trend of comic redneck chase movies which began with *Smokey and the Bandit* and culminated with TV's *Dukes of Hazzard*.

Son starred with Dub Taylor, Jack Elam and Lois Nettleton. Son thought that Gaylord had a silly script, but what the heck. Redneck movies were popular and they were essentially family pictures. Son wanted to make a family film. Son wanted to bring movie productions to Oklahoma. He hoped to benefit his home state with a steady stream of film companies coming to the state and bringing much-needed revenue to the state – and jobs for Oklahomans.

Ultimately, the movie was shot in southern Oklahoma and across the border in Texas.

Soggy Bottom USA is an awful, silly movie, disjointed and as banal as *The Dukes of Hazzard*, but it is harmless entertainment. It plays with the same easy-going silliness of an episode of *Dukes of Hazzard*, with the characters behaving in as illogical a manner as in any redneck comedy. It even has a farting dog that we are lead to believe stinks so bad that federal agents run from its smell.

Son's easy charm is on display here, but we sense he is too old to play the role of the sheriff. In one scene, he and girlfriend Lois Nettleton avoid the stereotypical sex scene with a simple plot device. Son has an episode of erectile dysfunction, allegedly brought on by the stress of revenue agents prowling the bayou. This is an odd moment for a family-oriented movie, but it rescues Son from another embarrassing *The Wild Bunch* moment.

They struggle with the sheriff's inability to commit to marrying, and an argument ensues. It is an odd scene, out of place in such a silly comedy, and Son is awkward in it. There is another scene in which the townspeople welcome a famous country singer to town for a coon dog race. As the gaudily dressed starlet is introduced to the sheriff, she makes a crack about her dog and "bitches in heat." These two scenes are awkward, and one wonders why Son – who had helped put this film deal together and made it happen – included them in the film.

Given Son's considerable unease with the increasing profanity and sexuality in films, it is curious that these scenes exist in the movie at all.

As low budget and silly as *Soggy Bottom USA* is, there are some fine moments in the movie. The opening sequence where Son rides a big grey horse, galloping through the dense woods while Dub Taylor gives chase in a Model T is pure fun. Old cowboy pal Hank Worden is on hand in one scene, barely missing being bitten by a large alligator as it crosses the road. Dub Taylor is hysterical throughout the film as the wise-cracking moonshiner.

When Son hit the road to promote the film's release. Gaylord's *Daily Oklahoman* gave it the big push. Asked about the film, Son quipped, somewhat disingenuously, "This is a funny movie. It'll be a show you can take your whole family to see. It has a lot of class and it's all low."[4]

CHAPTER TWENTY SIX
WESTERNS ANATHEMA, EXCEPT ON TV

The year 1980 heralded the near-death experience of the Western, thanks to a talented film director who rose to prominence with *The Deer Hunter*, then snubbed the dying John Wayne at the Oscars when it won Best Picture, then bankrupted United Artists with a pseudo-Western called *Heaven's Gate*.

Heaven's Gate cost $30 million to make (it had been budgeted at $11 million) and another $10 million to market and grossed only $3.4 million. The result was the death of UA, a healthy studio.

"When they made *Heaven's Gate*, they invested $50 or $60 million in it, and it busted all those people. They called it a western, so after that anytime somebody mentioned a western, they all ran backwards," Son said. "It's very expensive to make an authentic western. It's almost impossible to afford to have 1,000 head of cattle in a movie. It is just very difficult to finance, produce, direct and act out a good western."

Son knew this first-hand. In 1973 he had purchased the rights to a book by Clair Huffaker entitled *The Cowboy and the Cossack*. Huffaker had written books and screenplays for years, including *Flaming Star* (1960), *The Comancheros* (1961), *Rio Conchos* (1964), *Tarzan and the Valley of Gold* (1966), and *The War Wagon* (1967). Son was never able to obtain the financing to make the film a reality.

While Hollywood film producers ran from Westerns like they were the plague, television producers were reevaluating the genre.

With the success of *The Sacketts*, television networks and producers were looking for more Western books to adapt into miniseries.

When Brian Garfield's novel *Wild Times* was published, Metromedia Productions bought the rights and turned it into a three and a half hour miniseries.

The film starred Sam Elliott as sharpshooter Hugh Cardiff and Son as Doc Bogardus, his # 1 rival. Son's character is a blend of two real-life shooters, William Frank "Doc" Carver and Capt. Adam Henry Bogardus, who competed against each other in the 1880s. Son and Elliott enjoyed working together on *The Sacketts* and enjoyed their reunion on *Wild Times*.

Timothy Scott, who had co-starred with Robert Redford in *Electric Horseman* (1979) the year before and who would rise to fame as Pea Eye in *Lonesome Dove* (1989), co-stars as Caleb Rice, Cardiff's saddle pal. TV star Bruce Boxleitner (*How The West Was Won*) also co-starred.

Wild Times also features Son's good friend Dobe Carey, as well as veteran character actors Gene Evans, Pat Hingle, L.Q. Jones and Buck Taylor. Cameron

Richard D. Jensen

Mitchell and Leif Erickson who co-starred in TV's epic Western series *High Chaparral* also appear.

Son is terrific in *Wild Times*, dressed in an silk brocade vest and an open crown black cowboy hat. Elliott is excellent as Cardiff. The film suffers from the same woes as *The Sacketts*. It is overlong, and slows often to a snail's pace. Otherwise, it is uniformly excellent, with superb art direction, costuming, period styling and a sense of realism. The streets are muddy, the cowboys drab.

After finishing *Wild Times*, Son was cast by Buzz Kulik to co-star with Steve McQueen in *The Hunter*, a film based on the life of real-life bounty hunter Ralph "Papa" Thorson.

McQueen and Son had worked together on *Junior Bonner* (1972) and *The Getaway* (1972), both for director Sam Peckinpah. McQueen was a no bullshit guy, and he liked working with Son, who was also a no bullshit guy. Both men were without gall or ego, and both men looked at acting as merely a job. Neither took themselves too seriously, and both men enjoyed working away from Hollywood. They were easygoing on the set, and neither had that all-too common self-absorption of film actors.

Like Son, McQueen was a vocal supporter of the Vietnam War. Indeed, McQueen never understood how hip teenagers considered him "cool," when he was over 40 and a pro-Nixon Republican. This, despite some numbskull in Nixon's White House putting him on Nixon's enemies list.

During the making of *The Hunter*, it was obvious to the entire cast and crew that McQueen was very ill.

His weight was down and his energy was sapped. The reality that McQueen was dying of lung cancer cast a bittersweet pall over the film set.

Son played Sheriff Strong, and his work on the film was over quickly. He appears in one pivotal sequence in which he threatens to shoot McQueen in the groin if he persists in trying to serve a bail-jumping warrant on Strong's son.

When the film wrapped McQueen went home and never made another film. *The Hunter* premiered on August 1, 1980 and McQueen died on November 7, 1980 in Juarez, Mexico, where he had traveled in a desperate attempt to obtain some holistic treatment that would cure his cancer.

The Hunter began a phase of Son's career that would continue until his death. No longer would Son be offered lead roles. He would be offered only featured parts in movies starring other – often much younger – stars.

Son was in his 60s by this time and his face was lined with heavy creases and wrinkles. He looked like what he was – a real cowboy, aged by the sun and years of life experience.

Son's career had taken the path of many actors before him. He had been a stuntman, then a stuntman-turned-actor, then an actor who did stunts, then an in-demand character actor, then suddenly a serious Oscar-winning actor, then an Oscar-winning leading man, then an aging Oscar-winning character actor.

This final phase of Son's career gives us a glimpse of how John Wayne's career would likely have wound up had the Duke lived another decade.

CHAPTER TWENTY SEVEN
OUT OF STEP WITH THE TIMES AND ITS MOVIES

When Son began the 1980s, he began spending less time working on films and more time on his various business ventures. Son kept his personal wealth quiet, but it was clear he owned ranches in California, Arizona, Montana and Oklahoma. He raised quarter horses in Arizona, and real estate developments in California and Montana, where in one subdivision he reportedly had 600 houses being built at one time. Some financial reporters estimated Son was worth somewhere around $100 million.[1]

Nephew John Miller said this estimate was "bullshit. That $100 million was bullshit. How can you be worth that when you give everything away? He was living in Westlake. He was worth 100 million?

"He was frugal. If you look back, he didn't make that much money at that time. He had four or five good movies. He told me the government took half of what he earned.

"He had a couple of investment that went sour on him. Montana properties was good until he gave it away to the Boy Scouts. The value of that land, well, $300,000 is very conservative. I think the Boy Scouts got a whole lot more use out of it than that."[2]

Son's real estate developments, ranching and other ventures took up a great deal of his time, but he also spent more time doing charity work and traveling, enjoying the company of family and friends.

He and Carol often went to visit friends and Son's involvement with various celebrity roping events kept him busy – and out of Hollywood.

"I've never mingled too much," Son said. "I've always had the idea I might be bothering someone so I kind of stayed off to myself. I never did care for too much drinking or carousing around so I didn't go to many parties. I've seen a lot of people take the jug route and they don't last long. I think that's how many insecure people start out. They're looking for jobs so they start drinking with this guy or that one. And, the first thing you know, they're on the jug. And I never had any desire to go that route."[3]

Son and Carol preferred barbecues at home, and Son only occasionally had a glass of bourbon and water. He joked that he couldn't tell the taste of one liquor from another.[4]

Son also avoided going out with Carol because he didn't want the bad publicity if something went wrong.

"Carol and I are homebodies. We hate to go out for an evening because, in all probability, there will be an obnoxious person sitting across the room from us using four-letter words. If you go over and try to shut him up, you end up getting in a fracas and receiving bad publicity for being a square," Son said.[5]

Son and Carol usually went together everywhere. Even after 40 years together, they still adored each other. They traveled together, went camping together, raised flowers together. Carol said that Son "knew when to laugh. Humor's a big thing." Carol said another important reason their love lasted was they never dwelt on the other's mistakes.

One thing they did not have in common was sleep schedules. Son was an early riser, while Carol slept late.[6]

For relaxation, Son took up golf and discovered he liked it. He was, admittedly, terrible at it, but he loved it just the same. He also loved hunting, and often went with close pal, actor Dub Taylor, to Montana to hunt. Both men owned land near the small town of Ennis. Indeed, Taylor owned an enormous 23,000 acre ranch there. The two would bird hunt and fish, as far away from Hollywood as possible.[7]

The roles Son was being offered didn't suit him, but Son was always keen to work. He felt driven to earn money. Having grown up in the hardscrabble world of ranching during the lean years of the 1920s and 1930s, Son was always ready to work – even in cameo roles.

Cameos are roles that contain only two or three scenes in a film, but they are pivotal. Stars like cameos because they can charge a pretty penny for what is usually a few days work.

Studios love using stars for cameos because they get to put the actor's marquee name on the film but not pay a fortune for the star's work.

Son finished work on *The Hunter* and headed to Canada to film *Terror Train*, a modern day horror film starring Jamie Lee Curtis. Curtis, the daughter of movie star Tony Curtis and Janet Leigh, had carved herself a big career as the Queen of modern horror films.

The film is an oddity. It features TV actor Hart Bochner, magician David Copperfield, and Vanity, the actress whose biggest claim to fame was dating the singer Prince.

It is neither memorable nor commendable as a film. Son turns in a solid performance as the conductor, but the film is forgettable.

Son then moved on to play a bit part in *Ruckus* (1981) a low-budget film starring TV actor Dirk Benedict, star of *Battlestar Gallactica* (1978) and Linda Blair, star of the ground-breaking horror film *The Exorcist* (1973).

The plot revolves around a hapless Vietnam veteran who comes to a small town and becomes the target of local bullies. The result is a ruckus when the young ex-soldier becomes the focus of a manhunt.

Benedict's limited talent and lack of charisma sink this film, and Son is given little to do, as is fellow cowboy and fellow former stuntman Richard Farnsworth. Farnsworth had graduated to the ranks of serious actor in 1978 when he garnered an Oscar nomination as the aging cowboy in Alan J. Pakula's *Comes A Horseman*.

Surely it must have occurred to Son and to Farnsworth that these two veterans – both Oscar-quality actors who had started life as real cowboys, then become stuntmen, and were now venerated actors – were now appearing in a film with two of the most forgettable actors of the 1980s.

Ruckus is a low-budget *Rambo-First Blood* clone, and plays to all the worst media stereotypes about Vietnam vets. The protagonist is a broken down man, unable to function after having returned to the United States.

Son was next cast in *Tex,* the highly-touted film adaptation of S.E. Hinton's novel about two boys coming of age in hard times. The film stars Matt Dillon and Emilio Estevez, both up-and-coming teen actors, as two boys abandoned by their father in Oklahoma in the wake of their mother's death.

The film was produced by Walt Disney Productions and was shot on location around Tulsa, Oklahoma, a stone's throw from Son's hometown of Pawhuska. Son and Carol were able to spend their free time visiting with family and friends, and having them visit the movie set.

Son was happy to work in Oklahoma, and he continued to push the state as a film center. Burt Reynolds was busy doing the same for Georgia at the time. Studios liked both states because they were right-to-work states and this meant the powerful film unions and their expensive rules couldn't drive up the cost of production.

That said, Son was a strong union man when it came to actors. He was a vocal supporter of the Screen Actor's Guild and told this author once in a 1984 conversation that all film actors needed the Screen Actor's Guild to protect them from unscrupulous film producers.

Tex was released on July 30, 1982.

On April 24, 1982, Son and fellow rodeo cowboy and actor Slim Pickens were inducted in the Hall of Great Western Performers at the National Cowboy Hall of Fame, now called the National Cowboy and Western Heritage Museum, in Oklahoma City. A portrait of Son and Slim was commissioned. The 18" x 20" painting by artist John Howard Sanden was entitled *Night Stage*. It is a marvelous work of art, featuring both men atop a stage coach. Slim is driving and Son is riding shotgun. A full moon looms in the background. Fans can buy prints of this painting from the museum's store.

On August 19, 1983 Son attended the annual Golden Boot Awards, benefitting the Motion Picture and Television Fund, which provides health care for ailing actors. Gene Autry, Joel McCrea, Roy Rogers, Dale Evans, Sunset Carson, Slim Pickens, Bob Steele, Charles Starrett, Eddie Dean, Lash Larue, Monte Hale, James Garner, Sug fisher, Lee Majors, Clayton Moore, Rex Allen, and Jack Elam were in attendance that night. Pat Buttram served as master of ceremonies.

Son was back on comfortable, familiar territory when CBS and his long-time pal, director Andrew MacLaglen cast Son in the TV movie adaptation of Louis L'Amour's novel, *The Shadow Riders*.

Eager to repeat the success of *The Sacketts*, L'Amour insisted on recasting Tom Selleck, Sam Elliott, Jeff Osterhage and Ben Johnson for the new film. Dobe Carey and Gene Evans and Katherine Ross (Elliott's wife) were also cast.

It was a pleasant reunion for all the actors in involved. They arrived on location in Columbia,

California and enjoyed working together on the film, which seemed like an extended vacation in which they were also making a top notch TV-movie.

MacLaglen, a methodical director who had directed Son in *Chisum* and *The Undefeated*, kept the atmosphere genial and the film was a joy to work on for all involved.

The Shadow Riders was aired on September 28, 1992.

Director John Irvin cast Son in his inspirational film *Champions*, based on the true story of Bob Champion, the jockey who was diagnosed with testicular cancer in 1979, overcame the disease and went on to ride Aldaniti in the 1981 Grand National steeple chase and win. He later went on to found a cancer charity that raised millions for cancer research.

Champion had written the film along with Jonathan Powell. The movie features John Hurt as Champion, who turns in a searingly painful and inspired performance at the ailing jockey. The movie also features an up-and-coming young actress named Kirstie Alley – who at her sexiest best here. British actor Edward Woodward, who went on to star in TV's *The Equalizer*, is also in the cast.

Son again has several scenes in the film as a Kentucky horse trainer named Burly Cocks. He wears a mustache and a Great Gatsby hat in the initial scene, in which he encourages Champion to remain in Kentucky and jockey for him. Later, Burly helps Champion ascertain if still has his senses. We see Son in this scene as we've come to know him, in a gleaming white Stetson. The film chronicles Champion's grueling battle to overcome his cancer and retain his competitive spirit. It is a very good movie, full of unflinching details about the ravages of cancer and moving examples of courage and the indomitable human spirit.

Son is terrific as the trainer, encouraging Champion to return to racing as he recovers from the ravages of chemotherapy. The scene in which Champion discovers his hair growing back and asks Burly to touch his head is both moving and humorous at the same time. Son gives Burly the right balance of enthusiasm and no-nonsense pragmatism.

Champions was well received at the Berlin International Film Festival when it was released on April 20, 1984 and Irvin was nominated for Best Director by the festival.

That same month Son was the guest of honor at The Masquers Club, an elite Hollywood social organization that raises money for charity. On Friday, April 27, 1984, a gala of Hollywood stars saluted Son. The dais included Richard Dreyfuss, George Montgomery, Gene Autry, Lee Meriwether, Sam Peckinpah, Richard Brooks,, Monte Hale, Montie Montana, Richard Farnsworth, Casey Tibbs. Jock Mahoney, Dobe Carey and Bruce Boxleitner. Peter Bogdanovich and Dub Taylor were supposed to attend, but both were delayed by film production schedules.

Son had only recently been honored by President Ronald Reagan with an invitation to join the National Republican Senatorial Inner Circle. Many Republican leaders from western states were encouraging Son to run for political office. Son always turned them down.

Richard D. Jensen

Son then returned to Oklahoma to take part in the Oklahoma Motion Picture Hall of Fame gala honoring Dale Robertson, the cowboy star. Governor George Nigh said Son's attendance at the event made the event a success.[8]

Son was ever on the move.

When not filming a movie, he was busy raising money for charity. He sponsored and promoted celebrity roping events which were huge successes.

Son and Texas oilman Red Adair held an enormous fundraiser in Fort Worth, Texas during the weekend of July 14-15, 1984. A concert by Charlie Daniels was followed by a celebrity roping which featured stars such as Robert Duvall, Dale Robertson, James Drury, Doug McClure, Buck Taylor, Jeff Osterhage, and rodeo greats Casey Tibbs, Jim Shoulders, Walt Garrison, and Son's nephews John and Ben Miller.

Director John Milius, who had directed Son in *Dillinger*, hired Son for his latest film, a thriller entitled *Red Dawn*. The film centers on a Soviet-backed invasion of the United States by Cuban soldiers.

The movie takes place in the fictional town of Calumet, Colorado, and stars Patrick Swayze, Charlie Sheen, C. Thomas Howell, Darren Dalton and Doug Toby as teenagers who form a home-grown guerilla unit to fight the invaders.

The film was shot in and around Las Vegas, New Mexico. Son plays a rancher whom the guerilla teens turn to for supplies and information. Son has only three scenes, two interior scenes in a ranch house and one exterior scene at the barn. The two interior scenes are mere exposition and the scene at the barn serves to provide the horses for the guerillas. Clearly, Son's work on the film amounted to only a few days.

Milius said often that the film was inspired by the mujahedin resistance to the Soviets in Afghanistan. Indeed, the film is an Americanization of that story of struggle. The teens flee an invasion, then arm themselves and after hiding out in the mountains, return to their hometown to discover their parents imprisoned. When the Soviets and Cubans begin executing the civilians, the teens fight a guerilla war.

Red Dawn was made for a budget of $4.2 million. Essentially a low budget film, it has the feel of a quickly-made action film. Many of the shots are without any real composition. In the scene where Son gives the teens horses to ride, Milius has Son's back to the camera, robbing the moment between Swayze and Son of any emotional impact.

The only scene which is lit and composed well is the medium shot of the mayor (Lane Smith) reacting to the slaughter of his townspeople.

The geography of northern New Mexico is gorgeous, and the scenes of the guerillas on horseback harken to the best of Westerns, but the overall pace and milieu of *Red Dawn* is drab.

There are some excellent moments. When the invading paratroopers parachute into the school yard on a quiet, wind-swept day, it is a striking moment. The disbelief on the faces of the students and the teacher (Frank McRae) is palpable. The scene where the teens ambush the invaders are well constructed, as is the scene where the guerillas find the boxes of food lying on the road, unaware that they are walking (and riding) into an ambush. Also, stuntman turned character actor Roy Jenson has a great bit part as the gas station owner.

The performances of the teen actors are sincere, but amateurish at best, especially during scenes of anguish, during which the teens all overact. Swayze, Sheen and Howell all show early signs of talent and charisma, but this is clearly the earliest of work for all three and they are inexperienced actors here. Most of the young stars would hone their craft and go on to major stardom.

Son is excellent as the rancher, grounding the somewhat surreal story in reality with two expository scenes in which he describes the invasion and the rise of a militant movement. This is the type of scene Son did well. It is similar in tone to his campfire scenes in *The Train Robbers* and *Bite the Bullet*.

Red Dawn was released on August 10, 1984. Marketed heavily to teen moviegoers, the film was a smash hit, earning $38 million at the box office. In July 2009, superstar Kurt Russell announced a planned remake of *Red Dawn*, to be directed by former stunt man Dan Bradley.

After finishing *Red Dawn*, Son headed to Ennis, Montana where his Ben Johnson Montana Properties· was losing money. While there, Son donated 320 acres of land to the Montana Boy Scouts. The land was publicly valued at $300,000 and located on the east side of the Gravelly Mountains in Madison Valley.[9]

Son then headed north to Sheridan, Wyoming to co-star with country music superstar Kenny Rogers and TV sitcom star Pam Dawber in a TV-movie entitled *Wild Horses*. Rogers had scored a massive hit record with a story-song called *The Gambler*, which had a famous refrain of "you've got to know when to hold 'em, know when to fold 'em, know when to walk away, know when to run. You've never count your money when you're sittin' at the table, they'll be time enough for countin' when the dealin's done." The song was parlayed into a TV-movie of the same title, a Western that is memorable more for Rogers' charm and personality. The success of that telefilm lead to several others, and *Wild Horses* was one of them.

A smart entertainer who knew how to please his audience, Rogers made sure his TV-movies gave audiences what they wanted, traditional Westerns for the entire family to watch. *Wild Horses* is the tale of an ex-rodeo champion (Rogers) who is long past his prime. He has a job working on an assembly line, but gets fired.

 He decides to return to his cowboy heritage and goes to the high country of Wyoming to herd mustangs. Son plays a veteran mustanger who hires Rogers and his pal. Richard Farnsworth plays an old rancher who befriends Rogers and Dawber plays the rancher's daughter.

Buck Taylor and the cowboy music group Riders In the Sky also appear in *Wild Horses*, which is low-key and enjoyable family entertainment.

Wild Horses aired on November 12, 1985.

In 1985, Son held the first of many Ben Johnson Pro Celebrity Team Roping and Penning at the Lazy E Arena in Oklahoma City, Oklahoma. The event became an annual tradition, raising money for Children's Hospital of Oklahoma and Children's Medical Research, Inc.

Richard D. Jensen

Son then signed on to make a brief appearance in *Trespasses*, a low-budget independent film about a small Texas town and two rapists. Written and starring Lou Diamond Phillips, the film was produced by XIT Productions. It is curious that Son would agree to appear in the film, which is amateurish and altogether grim. Son plays the rape victim's father, and his appearance in the film is brief. Perhaps Son agreed to the film because it was shot on location in Bastrop, Texas, just outside of Austin. XIT Productions is no longer in business, and one wonders if the company was affiliated with the XIT Ranch or its offshoot corporations, many of which are located in Dumas and Dalhart, Texas, north of Amarillo.

In any event, *Trespasses* came and went from the theaters quickly when it was released on January 1, 1987.

When director Dick Lowry began casting his new seven-hour miniseries *Dream West*, he assembled an enormous array of talent. Richard Chamberlain, who was at the time king of the television miniseries, was cast as John Charles Fremont, the man who first explored and mapped much of the American West.

Son was given the role of Jim Bridger, the famous mountain man and Indian scout.

F. Murray Abraham, who had just won an Oscar for *Amadeus* and co-starred with Sean Connery in *The Name of the Rose*, was hired to play Abraham Lincoln.

Well-known TV and movie actors were added to the cast, including Jerry Orbach, G.D. Spradlin, Rip Torn, Fritz Weaver, Anthony Zerbe, Claude Akin, Mel

Ferrer, John Anderson, Cameron Mitchell, Buck Taylor and Noble Willingham.

From the first day of shooting, it was apparent the bloated miniseries was a mess and the production would be arduous. The production took place mostly in Arizona, over a lengthy six month period.

Zerbe, who co-starred with Son in *Will Penny* and later with John Wayne in *Rooster Cogburn* and was a veteran character actor, said, "I worked on the first day of the mini-series, then I left. I went away and did another mini-series. I did a play. I went through the Christmas holidays. Four months later I returned for the final week of filming. Everybody had lost 20 pounds. The only person who was totally unchanged was Richard Chamberlain."[10]

Dream West was a ratings and critical disaster when it aired on April 13-15, 1986.

Son was then cast in *Let's Get Harry*, a drama about a kidnaped engineer (Mark Harmon) who is taken hostage in Colombia. Son has a bit part as Harmon's father. The film was a disaster from the start, so much so that the director of the film is listed as Alan Smithee, a pseudonym used by directors who don't want their name associated with the film.

Stuart Rosenberg actually directed the movie. Famous for such classics as *Cool Hand Luke*, this turkey must have been a bitter experience for him.

Let's Get Harry was released on October 31, 1986.

Son and Dobe Carey were both hired to appear in a strange science fiction film called *Cherry 2000*, about a man whose android wife breaks and he goes in search of a new robot bride.

Richard D. Jensen

Sexually graphic at times, inane the rest of the time, the film is an oddity. It has a smug, seedy tone to it. A weird blend of sci fi and western shtick, the film has a Western town named Glory Hole, which is a pornographic reference.

The cheesiness of the tone of this film permeates it, except in the few scenes in which Son appears. Son plays "Six-Fingered Jake," a hermit who lives in a subterranean cave alongside an underground river underneath a hydroelectric dam. He wears a miner's helmet an leads a mule around. It is as if Son has taken on the mantle of Walter Huston's miner character in *Treasure of the Sierra Madre*.

When we first see Son, he is staring down a rifle at Melanie Griffith and David Andrews, who have arrived at his cave by spectacular means. We learn that Jake is Griffith's uncle.

The movie is just awful, and its only moments of credibility come from the scenes in which Son's character pontificates on the meaning of life. As Son did so memorably in *The Last Picture Show, Bite the Bullet* and *The Train Robbers*, he delivers the moral center of the film. In two key scenes, Son's credibility is all that gives the movies any import at all. In one exchange, Son's character, Jake, decries the decay of the modern society, where men marry robots and have pretend relationships.

And, in a scene similar to that of Son's death scene in *Bite the Bullet*, Son's character, Jake, reflects on death:

"When your time comes... your time, my time... it's like you turn into a little part of the world... wind, maybe. Yeah. A little stream of wind. Sometimes I feel like I know the whole story. Then other times, I feel like it's completely out of control."

Then, after this rare scene in which the film finally begins to gain some credibility, the plot takes a weird twist. Dobe's character, Snappy, and his female accomplice shoot Jake in the back, killing him.

There is a funny moment in the film in which Son, Griffith and Andrews first encounter Dobe. Dobe's character, Snappy, pops out of a refrigerator, surprising Griffith and Andrews. At one point, Snappy tells his female accomplice, "You can go shit in your hat." Son ad libs, "You shouldn't curse that'a way."

Cherry 2000 was considered such a disaster by distributor Orion Pictures that is was released in Europe and never released in the United States. It was eventually released to cable TV in February 1988 and later on video.

Tommy Lee Jones was cast to star in TV-movie entitled *Stranger On My Land*, about a Vietnam vet who comes home only to find the U.S. military trying to take his ranch for a new base.

Son was cast in a bit part in the production, as was Barry Corbin, who would work with Jones again in *Lonesome Dove* and *No Country for Old Men*. The film was shot on location in picturesque Park City, Utah.

The film was not critically well received and when it aired was quickly forgotten.

Son then went to work for Kingpin Productions on *Dark Before Dawn*. The company was working with Eddie Gaylord, II, the Oklahoma billionaire who had produced *Soggy Bottom U.S.A.* with Son in 1980. The film was set for production in Edmond, Oklahoma.

The film was directed by Robert Totten

Doug McClure, Buck Taylor and veteran screen villain Morgan Woodward co-starred. Oklahoman Rex Linn, who would go on to appear in every major Western movie and TV movie of the 1980s and co-star with Jackie Chan in *Rush Hour* (1988) also appears in the film.

Son then appeared in a Western short entitled *The Last Ride*, which was written by co-star Thomas F. Wilson and directed by Bill Russ. The 23-minute film was about a dying cowboy's last wish.

Son most likely agreed to star in *Back to Back*, an odd mystery film, because it was shot not too far from his new home in Mesa, Arizona. It could also be because the film contained some references to Sam Peckinpah, who had directed Son in *Major Dundee, The Wild Bunch, Junior Bonner, Noon Wine* and *The Getaway.* There's even a Peckinpah reference in the film with a character named Cable Hogue, a reference to Peckinpah's film *The Ballad of Cable Hogue.*

Shot on location around Superstition Mountain and Apache Junction, Arizona, the film is the story of a fabled armored car robbery and the efforts of the son of one of the supposed robbers to either clear his father's name or find the lost millions.

Back to Back stars Texas-born Bill Paxton, who would go on to star in many hit movies, including *Tombstone* (1993) and *Twister* (1996), and the HBO hit TV series *Big Love*. Luke Askew co-stars, along with Apolonia Kotero.

Son plays an outfitter and provides the film's disjointed narration.

In the late 1980's, artist Jimmy Don Cox was commissioned to create a bronze sculpture of Son.

Cox thought the best way to depict Son was while riding a horse.

"I thought that would be the natural way to portray old Ben and I chose to mount him in the bronze on his movie horse, Blackie. Ben's nephew, Ben Miller, had Blackie running out with some other roping horses and I picked him out because he looked more like a typical ranch horse.," Cox said.

"As it turned out, Blackie was the very one that Ben rode in numerous movies including *Hang 'em High*, *The Sacketts* and several others in which Ben had co-starred with the Duke, John Wayne. Ben was much more worried about how I would make old Blackie look in the bronze rather than himself. He had made only one remark to me about that, "Just don't make my belly too big."

Cox crafted the sculpture, which was titled *Ben and Blackie: A Pair of Aces.* The sculpture was to be auctioned at a banquet at the National Cowboy and Western Heritage Museum in Oklahoma City. The proceeds would benefit the Ben Johnson Pro-Celebrity Roping.

As the auction began, Oklahoma's billionaire media mogul Eddie Gaylord, II won with a winning bid of $30,000. When Gaylord took the podium with Cox, he called Son up to the stage.

Gaylord then handed the sculpture to Son, saying, "Ben, you're the number one cowboy, so this is for you. Take it home to Carol."

Tears welled in Son's eyes as the assembled crowd erupted into thunderous applause and leapt to its feet.[11]

Son was next cast in a TV-movie entitled *The Chase*, a hostage drama starring Casey Siemaszko, who had gained fame in *Stand By Me* (1986) and *Young Guns* (1988). The story is based upon a true-life event, the climax of which became a famous televised shootout.

Siemaszko plays a bank robber who kills a Denver cop and then takes an old man hostage. The police, and the media, give chase. Son plays an old man taken hostage by the robber. The film was shot on location in Denver, and Barry Corbin also appeared, portraying the cop who is killed.

The film is awkward at first, spending way too much time on the build up. We are presented with too many characters, and the younger actors are uniformly terrible. Son has two expository scenes in which he is relating to a mentally challenged granddaughter. This humanizes his character so that in the final climax, when Son is kidnaped, his character has some import. Son's character forcefully exhorts the young thug to give himself up as he is being chased by the cops and a news helicopter.

The climactic shootout between the kidnaper and the cops faithfully recreates the final shootout.

The Chase aired on February 10, 1991.

CHAPTER TWENTY EIGHT
SON CONSIDERS HIS LEGACY

As Son aged, he became more deeply concerned about the welfare of children. Because he and Carol were childless, Son felt as if he needed to leave a legacy for the children of others.

He was active in various charity efforts, including the Ben Johnson roping events, various golf and hunting events. Son wanted to do more. He began to give large chunks of his net worth to various charities, and raise much more besides.[1]

On April 20, 1991, Son formed Ben Johnson Pro-Celebrity, Inc. in Arizona to provide charitable work for children via a fund called Cowboys For Kids Charity Fund. The Arizona Secretary of State assigned the charity identification number 102594. The charity's address was listed as P.O. Box 1811, Black Canyon Stage #1, Phoenix, Arizona 85027.

Son believed sincerely that the problem facing most teens in the post Vietnam War era was a lack of self respect.

"Young people, today, need to have three things in their lives - honesty, reality and respect," Son said. "If they'd listen to someone who is real and honest, and if they'd respect themselves, they wouldn't get involved with drugs and have so many problems."

Son didn't blame the kids, though. He blamed their parents. "The kids who get in trouble just didn't get the right kind of milk at home. They didn't get any help."

The idea of raising money for children's programs and children's charities was a good one, and before long Son was swamped with requests for help.

"We're getting calls every day from all over the country, where other folks want us to put on a rodeo for them. But, I've just about loaded my boat. I spend so much time helping get money together for other people that I can hardly take time to make a living for myself."[2]

Stuart Rosenberg, the director who had disavowed his association with *Let's Get Harry* (1986) by using the pseudonym Alan Smithee, remembered Son from the film and cast him in *My Heroes Have Always Been Cowboys*.

Son plays Jesse Dalton, the aging father of broken down rodeo cowboy H.D. Dalton, played by Scott Glenn.

Jesse is old and losing his ability to take care of himself, so much so that his daughter puts him in a nursing home. H.D. comes homes from the rodeo circuit to find Jesse in the nursing home, in a room he shares with a slightly befuddled roommate, played to the hilt by the legendary Mickey Rooney.

A note of trivia here: One of Rooney's first roles in Hollywood was that of the boy king in Tom Mix's *My Pal the King*, a 1933 classic. Remember, Mix cowboyed all around the Osage prairie on which Son was born and worked at the 101 Ranch in Bliss, Oklahoma, at the same time Son's dad worked as a young cowboy and at about the same time Mix was beginning his movie career in Oklahoma for the Selig studios.

H.D. "rescues" Jesse from the nursing home and takes him back to the ranch, where he attempts to take care of him and give him his dignity back.

My Heroes Have Always Been Cowboys was shot in Guthrie, Oklahoma. Son had encouraged the producers to make the film there.

My Heroes Have Always Been Cowboys is a frustrating film. It suffers from a lack of focus, the same lack of focus that burdened *Junior Bonner* 19 years before. One of the most noticeable things about Son's performance is that he has begun to age dramatically. His weight has ballooned, his face is now heavy with age. He seems tired and moves painfully. That said, Son makes the movie worthwhile.

Glenn is rather wooden as H.D., but Gary Busey is good as the son-in-law, and Tess Harper is fine as Jesse's frustrated daughter. The gorgeous Kate Capshaw is wonderful as H.D.'s girlfriend, and Clarence Williams, III, the former star of TV's hit series *Mod Squad* is great as the deputy sheriff.

Dub Taylor is in the film, as is Rex Linn and Clu Gulager.

The film could have been so much better. It could have focused more on Jesse's internal struggle, his frustration with losing his freedom. Instead, the film focuses on ne'er do well H.D., the selfish son who refuses to give up rodeo, even if it ruins him and his aging father in the process.

My Heroes Have Always Been Cowboys was released on March 1, 1991. The film has a large following, as it is shown often on Encore's Westerns Channel on cable TV.

Son was cast as Geronimo Bill in Richard Donner's *Radio Flyer*. Donner, famous for his *Superman* and *Lethal Weapon* monster hits, created this tale of boys suffering at the hands of a brutal stepfather who take refuge in their imaginations.

This magical film contains a terrific cameo by Son, as an old cowpoke who runs a dilapidated tourist trap in the desert, which charges passing motorists to see his pet buffalo. Son takes pity on the children in the story and lets them tour the buffalo park for free. The scene is shot in the arid desert of Arizona, but the narration provided by Tom Hanks sets the scene in Oklahoma. This was no doubt a plug by Son for his home state, as the scene is clearly not shot in the prairies of Oklahoma.

Son is at his best here, conveying down-to-earth simplicity and a heart of gold. It is a tiny cameo and he is wonderful. He wears a gray beard and a battered hat reminiscent of the high-peaked crease worn by Harry Carey and by John Wayne in *Three Godfathers*. He is the embodiment of cowboy values here.

Radio Flyer was released on February 21, 1992.

Son continued to receive praise and accolades for his rodeo, film and charity work. In 1993, Son was awarded his own star on Hollywood's famous Walk of Fame. Son's star was placed at 7083 Hollywood Blvd.

And the work continued:

Producer David Dortort, who had struck gold with the hit series *Bonanza*, which ran from 1959 to 1973, wanted to resurrect the series. In early 1988 he began putting together a deal to reprise the series with Lorne Greene returning as Ben Cartwright. Sadly, Greene died just before production began. Dotort hired John Ireland, who had appeared in many classic westerns including *Red River*, to play Aaron, Ben's brother. Michael Landon, Jr. was hired to play Little Joe Cartwright's son and Gillian Greene, Lorne Greene's daughter, was also cast. The broadcast was a success and in 1992, Dotort began plans for a second sequel.

The result was *Bonanza - The Return,* which starred Son as Bronc Evans and Michael Landon, Jr. as Benji Cartwright. Richard Roundtree and Jack Elam were both on hand for the telefilm.

Bonanza - The Return was aired on November 28, 1993 to good ratings.

Mickey Rooney has been planning to make a western he'd written entitled *Outlaws: The Legend of O.B. Taggart.* During the production of *My Heroes Have Always Been Cowboys,* Rooney asked Son to appear in the film.

The film eventually was produced by Rooney, who starred. Ned Beatty was cast, along with country singers Randy Travis and Larry Gatlin and Ernest Borgnine, with whom Son had worked on The Wild Bunch. Gloria De Haven, the legendary Hollywood actress from the heyday of MGM's musicals, also appeared.

The cast assembled on the Bonanza Creek Ranch location outside of Santa Fe, New Mexico.

Richard D. Jensen

After *Outlaws: The Legend of O.B. Taggart,* Son was cast as the owner of the California Angels in the wonderful fantasy film *Angels In The Outfield*.

No doubt Son was portraying the fictional version of cowboy star turned billionaire mogul Gene Autry, who had actually owned the team for years. The story revolved around real angels aiding the sad sack team win games after a young boy prays to God to send help for his favorite team.

The film stars Danny Glover, Tony Danza and Christopher Lloyd, as well as two young actors who would become big stars - Matthew McConaughey and Adrien Brody, who would win an Oscar in 2003 for *The Pianist* (2002). Another unknown actor, Dermot Mulrooney, appeared in the film before becoming a film star in his own right. *Angels In The Outfield* was released on July 15, 1994 and was an immediate hit.

CHAPTER TWENTY NINE
ALONE IN A NEW WILDERNESS

Son and Carol were enjoying more and more time together traveling to and from Son's charity events when suddenly Carol took a fall and broke her hip. Not long afterward the doctors found she had cancer.

John Miller, Son's nephew, said Carol went downhill quickly. "She had broken a hip and things kind of fell in on her," Miller said. "You know. She died an unfortunate death. She was too young and too vital. One of those people that everybody loved and she loved everybody.

"She was the life of the party anytime and all the time, and Uncle Ben absolutely loved her."[1]

Carol's strength gave way and she died painfully, and Son was powerless to help her. He took her death hard. They had been in love and happily married for 56 years. With no children of his own, Son had only his memories. He buried Carol in their plot in Pawhuska City Cemetery next to Ben and Aileen on Friday, April 1, 1994.

Son chose to live alone in his house in Leisure Village, a retirement village in Mesa, Arizona. His home was, on purpose, close to his mother. He kept only a handful of horses, in Arizona and a few in Pawhuska, which he would occasionally ride. Every now and then he'd rope.

John Miller said he kept close tabs on Son in the wake of Carol's passing.

"After Carol died, in fact, we were pretty dang close. About every evening at 5, I'd come in the house and call Uncle Ben," Miller said. "To this day, at 5 p.m. it's still time to call him."[2]

Miller said Son stoically went about managing his business and his charity work, burying his grief by keeping busy..

"Uncle Ben did better than I thought he'd do. He still had his mom. She outlived him. He spent a lot of time with Ollie anyway, and so they were close. He checked on her all the time."[3]

Son continued his whirlwind of charity work in the wake of Carol's death, much of it in Arizona. In November 1994, Son, Dobe Carey and 20 other movie cowboys and character actors appeared at Goldfield Ghost Town in Apache Junction, Arizona, to raise money for the AJ Youth Center and the Sunshine Acres Children's Home.

One of the founding members of the charity group Goldfield Ghost Riders, a long-time Apache Junction resident Charlotte Holmes, asked Son to come to the group's charity ride.

Son also donated his name and efforts to fundraising for Sunshine Acres Children's Home, where he often went to raise money by holding roping "lessons."

David Dortort brought Son back for another Bonanza sequel in 1994 entitled *Bonanza - Under Attack*. The telefilm once again featured Michael Landon, Jr. as Benji Cartwright, Richard Roundtree and Jack Elam, and Dirk Blocker, the son of Dan Blocker, who played Hoss in the original hit show. This marketing ploy may have worked for ratings, and the young actors here are eager, but pretty horrible, with the exception of Jeff Phillips, as A.C. Cartwright.

Leonard Nimoy also appears in the film as legendary outlaw Frank James, and Dennis Farina, who would later star in TV's *Law and Order*, played famous lawman Charley Siringo.

The performances of the veteran actors are uniformly excellent, especially Son, Nimoy and Roundtree. Indeed, Nimoy's performance is quite good. So well known for his portrayal of Mr. Spock in the Star Trek movies, it is striking to see him in a Western. He performs admirably.

Farina is awkward as an out-of-control Charley Siringo, bent on killing Frank James, who is friends with the Cartwrights. Farina nearly falls off his horse in the few riding scenes he has. The rest of the time it is obvious that his stunt double is riding for him.

In his first role after Carol's death, and nearly 77 years old at the time of production, Son shows his age and his wear and tear in this production.

That said, he brings the right amount of authority as Bronc Evans, the de facto heir to Ben Cartwright. Son is part John Wayne, part Mount Rushmore here.

The scene at the campfire when Bronc talks about his dead wife are moving. His voice cracks, and we are moved by the undeniable truth of the moment. Moments later, Bronc is seated at a desk, looking at a photo of his late wife. Son's face is ravaged with pain and loss, and it is clear he is thinking of his beloved Carol.

Bonanza - Under Attack is a frustrating TV-movie because it never reaches its full potential. A decent script overall, and some interesting plot twists that blend old West history and fiction, the story is muddled by lackluster direction and uneven performances. At various points the characters fail to use common sense in dealing with the threat of an armed group of vigilantes.

The art direction in *Bonanza - Under Attack* is uneven at best. Some of the stuntmen/actors playing the posse wear historically accurate, well-made beaver hats, but many in the cast are in horribly cheap hats and incorrect wardrobe. Even Son's hat is clearly a late 20th Century Resistol, complete with machine-driven eyelets. The worst is Farina's Siringo, who is shown in close up putting on machine-sewn gloves and then securing his pistol in a machine-sewn holster. The cast is bundled up in heavy coats for much of the film, and the actors' breath can be seen in many scenes, a testament to the chilly temperatures during filming.

Bonanza Under Attack is well worth watching merely for the performances of the veterans, if the viewer is willing to suspend disbelief of its flaws.

The film also references Tom Mix. The story takes place after the election of Teddy Roosevelt, circa 1905. Frank James tells Bronc about Tom Mix wanting to make this new fangled thing called moving pictures. It's intriguing to think of Son, a cowboy and actor from Pawhuska, Oklahoma, playing a fictional character who is talking about another cowboy and actor from the same part of Oklahoma.

Bonanza - Under Attack also has some cameo appearances by veteran Western actors, such as Jack Elam as Buckshot, the Ponderosa's cook and Don Collier ("High Chapparal") in a bit part as the U.S. Marshal after the shootout.

Bonanza - Under Attack aired on January 15, 1995 on ABC.

In 1996 Son accepted a part in *Ruby Jean and Joe*, a rodeo saga produced by Tom Selleck and his TWS Productions, II and starring Selleck and Rebekah Johnson. Selleck plays an aging rodeo cowboy who must come to terms with his life. He meets Ruby Jean on the road and their unlikely friendship forces them to come to terms with their life issues. The script was written James Lee Barrett, the legendary screenwriter famous for so many John Wayne hit movies.

Son appears as Big Man, and enjoyed working on the film with Selleck, especially since the film was shot in Arizona, close to Son's Mesa home.

Richard D. Jensen

Ruby Jean and Joe aired on August 11, 1996, and quickly faded from public sight and is not seen on cable TV, nor is it available on DVD or video.

Son's final appearance on film was in *The Evening Star*, the sequel to *Terms of Endearment*, the 1983 hit movie. Both were based upon novels by Larry McMurtry. In *The Evening Star*, the story takes up with Aurora Greenway after the death of her daughter, Emma. Jack Nicholson appears in the film, reprising his role as the gregarious Garrett Breedlove.

The Evening Star was released on Christmas Day 1996, eight months after Son's death.

CHAPTER THIRTY
SON JOHNSON DIES

April 8, 1996 was a bright, sunny Monday morning in Mesa, Arizona. Son lived at 2466 Leisure World on Elegante Street. He dressed and headed down the street to have breakfast with his mother. Both Son and Ollie lived in Leisure World, a retirement community outside of Phoenix.

Son felt a little ill when he arrived at his mother's, and thought that breakfast might make him feel better.

Son felt a sick to his stomach, and headed to the bathroom. When he reached the bathroom, he collapsed. Paramedics were summoned.

Son was taken by ambulance to Valley Lutheran Hospital, where he was pronounced dead. He had died two years and seven days after the death of his beloved Carol.

John Miller recalled receiving the news of his uncle's death: "The gal that was living with Ollie called and said we just lost Uncle Ben. It was kick in the belly," Miller said. "He'd been going doing a lot of charity work and doing a lot and raising money for kids organization.

People would call him to do an appearance and he just wouldn't say no.

"We tried to talk him into slowing down but he just wouldn't do it. He was doing three or four major charity events a year for the last eight or ten years of his life. Anything he could do. No tellin' how much he raised," Miller said.

Son's body was transported to Pawhuska.

More than 400 mourners showed up for his funeral on Sunday, April 14, 1996. As a fiddler played the gospel standard, *Just A Closer Walk With Thee*, they stood silently by the casket, cowboy hats in hands placed over their hearts.[2]

Son was laid to rest on a gentle hillside at Pawhuska City Cemetery on the west side of Pawhuska, next to his beloved Carol and his father, Ben and stepmother, Aileen.

Son told a reporter in 1982 that he wanted his gravestone to read: "Here lies someone who tried to do good for the people, someone who lived by the Golden Rule."[3]

The gravestone reads: "Precious Memories."

Indeed.

EPILOGUE
LEGACY

Both Ben Johnsons were the product of their times and the red dirt of Oklahoma. They were both cowboys, raised in the deeply rooted ranch culture of the Tall Grass Prairie. They were tall grass cowboys, plain and simple.

Ben Johnson was a rodeo champion and ranch foreman at a time when both jobs were the stuff of legend. Ben's reputation in Oklahoma is only dimmed by the passage of time and the faltering memories of those who are still alive and knew him. Were it not for his daughter, Helen, Ben Johnson's memory would be all but faded – mere statistics in rodeo time sheets and stories in old newspaper archives.

Were it not for the existence of mass media, Ben "Son" Johnson would have had the same faded legacy, a mere statistic in the rodeo records. Like his dad, Son would have been remembered as former rodeo champion whose dad was also a champion.

But Son came of age in a time when the bulk of American movie entertainment was Westerns. Who else was better suited to portray the true cowboy on film than Son?

Had Son come to Hollywood a mere 20 years later, his career would have been markedly different. He would have likely been a stuntman and movie wrangler, but by that end of the 1950s, Westerns were in decline. Son would likely never have been given the chance to earn his spurs as an actor and become a movie star and Oscar-winner.

There are many legacies left by a man. There is his professional legacy, his personal legacy, and the impact his life had on the world community.

Ben Johnson, Jr., known as Son Johnson to those who knew him best, known as actor Ben Johnson to the world, left the world knowing that he had lead a charmed life.

"I think probably that I'm the luckiest 'actor,' if that's what you wanna call me, that's ever hit Hollywood because my character – well, people have accepted it. You know, everybody in town is a better actor than I am, but nobody can play Ben Johnson as good as I can."[1]

Dobe Carey said that in the 45 years of his friendship with Son, their friendship had grown because Son was simply a great person.

"Ben Johnson has been my friend for 45 years," Carey said. "As you get old, you realize that there are not too many people you can say that about. Our friendship has grown over the years, and we accept each other's shortcomings. That seems to make the bond between us even stronger. Ben Johnson was the only member of the Ford Stock Company who didn't have a screw loose somewhere."

"Ben's not a drunk, and he's not given to fits of temper or depression. Ben made it because of his incredible horsemanship, his humor, and then Ford found out he could really act."[2]

When asked once to summarize his life, Son said, "I've done pretty good for a cowpuncher."[3]

When asked how he'd like to be remembered, Son said, "There's three things we've lost in this country - honest, realism and respect. I'd like to be remembered for my honest, my realism and my respect."[4]

Louis L'Amour, the legendary Western novelist, said, "When they ask me what the western man was like I tell them to look at Ben Johnson."[5]

Perhaps, Son said it best:

"You know, when I left Oklahoma I wasn't even sure which direction Hollywood was, but I could ride a horse pretty good. I had no formal education to speak of. I was a cowboy from the time I hit the ground. I knew if a cow weighed 1,000 pounds and bought $10 a hundred, I knew how much that was," Son said. " But, I was fortunate because people accepted my character. I ran my life a certain way. I didn't hobnob with the elites because I didn't do drugs and I didn't drink a lot of whiskey. oh, I might take a drink now and then, but you know what I mean. I think I got a lot respect from people in the business because of my honesty. Honesty is like a good horse, you know it'll work anyplace you hook it."[6]

BEN JOHNSON FILMOGRAPHY

The Fighting Gringo (1939) (RKO Radio Pictures)
Director: David Howard
Writer: Oliver Drake (story)
Release Date: 8 August 1939
Cast:
George O'Brien ... Wade Barton
Lupita Tovar ... Anita 'Nita' del Campo
Lucio Villegas ... Don Aliso del Campo
William Royle ... Ben Wallace
Glenn Strange ... Rance Potter
Slim Whitaker ... Monty Bates (as Slim Whittaker)
LeRoy Mason ... John Courtney
Mary Field ... Sandra Courtney
Martin Garralaga ... Pedro, Ranch Foreman
Dick Botiller ... Jose, del Campo Vaquero
Bill Cody ... Sheriff Fred Warren (as Bill Cody Sr.)
Cactus Mack ... Utah Jones
Chris-Pin Martin ... Felipe, the Barber

Hank Bell ... Wallace Henchman Shot by Wade (uncredited)
Ben Corbett ... Shorty (uncredited)
Billy Franey ... Tom, Courtney's Cook (uncredited)
Oscar Gahan ... Barton Rider (uncredited)
Al Haskell ... Manuel, del Campo Vaquero (uncredited)
Ben Johnson ... Mexican Barfly (uncredited)
Sid Jordan ... Buck, Stage Driver (uncredited)
Forrest Taylor ... Foreman of Coroner's Jury (uncredited)
59 min
Black and White
Filming Locations: Iverson Ranch, Chatsworth, California

The Durango Kid (1940) (Columbia Pictures Corporation)
Director: Lambert Hillyer
Writer: Paul Franklin (original screenplay)
Release Date:15 August 1940
Cast:
Charles Starrett ... Bill Lowry / The Durango Kid
Luana Walters ... Nancy Winslow
Kenneth MacDonald ... Mace Ballard
Francis Walker ... Henchman Steve
Forrest Taylor ... Ben Winslow
Melvin Lang ... Marshal Dan Trayboe
Bob Nolan ... Bob - Member of Sons of the Pioneers
Pat Brady ... Pat - Member of Sons of the Pioneers
Frank LaRue ... Sam Lowry
Sons of the Pioneers ... Ranch Hands and Musicians
Silver Tip Baker ... Piute City Townsman (uncredited)
Steve Clark ... Henchman Bixby (uncredited)
Jack Evans ... Nester (uncredited)
Hugh Farr ... Singer with Sons of the Pioneers (uncredited)
Karl Farr ... Guitarist with Sons of the Pioneers (uncredited)

Roger Gray ... Henchman Jergens (uncredited)
Lloyd Perryman ... Lloyd - Member of Sons of the Pioneers (uncredited)
Ralph Peters ... Taylor (uncredited)
Raider ... Durango Kid's Horse (uncredited)
Jack Rockwell ... Jud Evans (uncredited)
George Russell ... Henchman (uncredited)
Marin Sais ... Mrs. Evans (uncredited)
Tim Spencer ... Tim - Member of Sons of the Pioneers (uncredited)
Ben Taggart ... Flynn (uncredited)
John Tyrrell ... Hank Banning (uncredited)
Runtime:61 min
Black and White
Filming Locations: Agoura Ranch, Agoura, California, USA

The Outlaw (1943) (Howard Hughes Productions)
Director:Howard Hughes
Writer:Jules Furthman (screenplay)
Release Date:13 June 1948
Cast:
Jack Buetel ... Billy the Kid (as Jack Beutel)
Jane Russell ... Rio McDonald
Thomas Mitchell ... Pat Garrett
Walter Huston ... Doc Holliday
Mimi Aguglia ... Guadalupe
Joe Sawyer ... Charley
Gene Rizzi ... Stranger
rest of cast listed alphabetically:
Bobby Callahan ... Boy (uncredited)
Martin Garralaga ... Mike - Waiter (uncredited)

John Howard ... Face on Wanted Poster, from Texas Rangers Ride Again (uncredited)
Ben Johnson ... (uncredited)
Dickie Jones ... Boy (uncredited)
Cecil Kellogg ... Officer (uncredited)
Ethan Laidlaw ... Deputy (uncredited)
Ted Mapes ... Guard (uncredited)
William Newell ... Drunken Cowboy (uncredited)
Emory Parnell ... Dolan - Man Entering Saloon (uncredited)
Edward Peil Sr. ... Swanson (uncredited)
Wallace Reid Jr. ... Bystander (uncredited)
Julian Rivero ... Pablo (uncredited)
Lee Shumway ... Card Dealer (uncredited)
William Steele ... Deputy (uncredited)
Harry Strang ... Townsman at Sheriff's Office (uncredited)
Frank Ward ... Boy (uncredited)
Pat West ... Bartender (uncredited)
Runtime:116 min
Black and White
Filming Locations:General Service Studios - 1040 N. Las Palmas, Hollywood, Los Angeles, California, USA

Riders of the Northwest Mounted (1943) (Columbia Pictures Corporation)
Director: William Berke
Writer: Fred Myton (writer)
Release Date:15 February 1943
Cast:
Russell Hayden ... Lucky Lawson

Dub Taylor ... Cannonball
Bob Wills ... Mountie Bob Wills (Texas Playboys Band Leader)
The Texas Playboys ... Mounties
Richard Bailey ... Henchman Remy (uncredited)
Dick Curtis ... Victor Renaud (uncredited)
Joe Holley ... Mountie / Texas Playboys Band Member (uncredited)
Harley Huggins ... Mountie / Texas Playboys Band Member (uncredited)
Jack Ingram ... Henchman Jacques (uncredited)
Millard Kelso ... Mountie / Texas Playboys Band Member (uncredited)
Adele Mara ... Gabrielle Renaud (uncredited)
Leon McAuliffe ... Mountie Chuck / Texas Playboys Band Member (uncredited)
Vernon Steele ... Captain Blair (uncredited)
Luke Wills ... Mountie / Texas Playboys Band Member (uncredited)
Wen Wright ... Trapper (uncredited)
Ben Johnson .... stunt double: Russell Hayden (uncredited)
Runtime:57 min
Black and White
Filming Locations: Big Bear Lake, California, USA

Riders of the Rio Grande (1943) (Republic Pictures)
Director:Howard Bretherton
Writers:William Colt MacDonald (characters)
Albert DeMond (original screenplay)
Release Date:21 May 1943
Cast:
Bob Steele ... Tucson Smith

Tom Tyler ... Stony Brooke
Jimmie Dodd ... Lullaby Joslin
Lorraine Miller ... Janet Owens
Edward Van Sloan ... Pop Owens
Rick Vallin ... Tom Owens
Harry Worth ... Sam Skelly
Roy Barcroft ... Sarsaparilla, 1st 'Cherokee Boy'
Charles King ... Thumber, 2nd 'Cherokee Boy'
Jack Ingram ... Berger, a henchman
Roy Bucko ... Card player (uncredited)
Fred Burns ... Townsman (uncredited)
Budd Buster ... Jed, bank manager (uncredited)
Yakima Canutt ... Deputy (uncredited)
Lane Chandler ... Townsman (uncredited)
Chester Conklin ... Barfly (uncredited)
Curley Dresden ... Bar Patron who gets Socked (uncredited)
Bob Kortman ... Zeke, a henchman (uncredited)
Nolan Leary ... Jailer (uncredited)
Rex Lease ... Father of twins (uncredited)
Frank McCarroll ... Card player (uncredited)
Frank O'Connor ... Man exiting saloon (uncredited)
Bud Osborne ... Sheriff Glenn (uncredited)
Jack O'Shea ... Butch, 3rd 'Cherokee Boy' (uncredited)
Cliff Parkinson ... Deputy (uncredited)
Hal Price ... Man owing money (uncredited)
Charles Sullivan ... Bartender (uncredited)
Ted Wells ... Deputy (uncredited)
Runtime:55 min
Black and White
Filming Locations:Iverson Ranch, Chatsworth, Los Angeles, California, USA

Bordertown Gun Fighters (1943) (Republic Pictures)
Director: Howard Bretherton
Writer: Norman S. Hall (original screenplay)
Release Date: 8 July 1943
Cast:
Bill Elliott ... Wild Bill Elliott (as Wild Bill Elliott)
George 'Gabby' Hayes ... Gabby Hayes
Anne Jeffreys ... Anita Shelby
Ian Keith ... Cameo Shelby
Harry Woods ... Dave Strickland
Edward Earle ... Dan Forrester
Karl Hackett ... Frank Holden
Roy Barcroft ... Jack Gatling
Bud Geary ... Henchman Buck Newcombe
Carl Sepulveda ... Henchman Red Dailey
Nino Bellini ... Roulette Croupier (uncredited)
Ralph Bucko ... Townsman (uncredited)
Fred Burns ... Townsman (uncredited)
Budd Buster ... Barfly (uncredited)
Foxy Callahan ... Townsman (uncredited)
Wheaton Chambers ... Roland Clark (uncredited)
Neal Hart ... Townsman (uncredited)
Al Haskell ... Townsman (uncredited)
Ben Johnson ... Messenger (uncredited)
Charles King ... Sheriff Barnes (uncredited)
Jack Kinney ... Train Conductor (uncredited)
Jim Massey ... Townsman (uncredited)
Frank McCarroll ... Henchman (uncredited)
James Mitchell ... Townsman (uncredited)
Post Park ... Stage Driver (uncredited)
Pascale Perry ... Barfly (uncredited)
Rose Plumer ... Townswoman (uncredited)

Marshall Reed ... Townsman (uncredited)
Jack Rockwell ... Gambler (uncredited)
Frosty Royce ... Townsman (uncredited)
Charles Sullivan ... Henchman Grady (uncredited)
Ken Terrell ... Stevens - Train Rowdy (uncredited)
Herman Willingham ... Man at Roulette Table (uncredited)
Bill Wolfe ... Townsman (uncredited)
Runtime:56 min
Black and White
Filming Locations: Iverson Ranch, Chatsworth, Los Angeles, California

The Pinto Bandit (1944) (Alexander-Stern Productions)
Director:Elmer Clifton
Writer:Elmer Clifton (original story and screenplay)
Release Date:27 April 1944
Cast:
Dave O'Brien ... Tex Wyatt (as Dave 'Tex' O'Brien)
James Newill ... Jim Steele (as Jim Newill)
Guy Wilkerson ... Panhandle Perkins
Mady Lawrence ... Kitty Collins
James Martin ... Walter Collins
Jack Ingram ... Tom Torrant
Ed Cassidy ... Doc Carson (as Edward Cassidy)
Budd Buster ... P. T.Heneberry
Karl Hackett ... Sheriff Bisbee
Bob Kortman ... Draw Dudley, Henchman (as Robert Kortman)
Charles King ... Spur Sneely, Henchman (as Charles King Jr.)
Jimmy Aubrey ... Bartender Tommy (uncredited)

Herman Hack ... Barfly (uncredited)
Ray Henderson ... Barfly (uncredited)
Ben Johnson ... Race Contestant (uncredited)
Carl Mathews ... Barfly (uncredited)
Kermit Maynard ... Relay Rider (uncredited)
Don Weston ... Relay Rider (uncredited)
Carl Mathews .... stunt double (uncredited)
Kermit Maynard .... stunt double (uncredited)
Wally West .... stunt double (uncredited)
Runtime:56 min
Black and White
Filming Locations:Corriganville, Ray Corrigan Ranch, Simi Valley, California

Arizona Trail (1943) (Universal Pictures)
Director:Vernon Keays
Writer:William Lively (original screenplay)
Cast:
Tex Ritter ... Johnnie Trent
Fuzzy Knight ... Kansas
Dennis Moore ... Wayne Carson
Janet Shaw ... Martha Brooks
Jack Ingram ... Ace Vincent
Erville Alderson ... Dan Trent
Joseph J. Greene ... Dr. J.D. 'Doc' Wallace (as Joseph Greene)
Glenn Strange ... Henchman Matt
Dan White ... Sheriff Jones
Art Fowler ... Henchman Curley
Johnny Bond ... Red, (leader of the Red River Valley Boys)
Red River Valley Boys ... Musicians, Cowhands

Roy Brent ... Ben Gorman, Detective (uncredited)
Jimmie Dean ... Member, Red River Valley Boys (uncredited)
George Gray ... Fake blind man (uncredited)
Ray Jones ... Stage Guard (uncredited)
Art Mix ... Henchman (uncredited)
Paul Sells ... Member, Red River Valley Boys (uncredited)
Wesley Tuttle ... Member, Red River Valley Boys (uncredited)
Blackie Whiteford ... Townsman (uncredited)
Bill Wolfe ... Townsman (uncredited)
William Yip ... Chinese Waiter (uncredited)
Ben Johnson .... stunt double (uncredited)
Cliff Lyons .... stunt double (uncredited)
Henry Wills .... stunt double (uncredited)
Runtime: 57 min
Black and White
Company:Universal Pictures

Blazing Guns (1943) (Monogram Pictures Corporation)
Director:Robert Emmett Tansey
Writers:Gina Kaus (story)
Frances Kavanaugh (writer)
Release Date:8 October 1943
Cast:
Ken Maynard ... Marshal Ken Maynard
Hoot Gibson ... Marshal Hoot Gibson
LeRoy Mason ... Duke Wade
Emmett Lynn ... Eagle-Eye
Weldon Heyburn ... Henchman Vic
Roy Brent ... Jim Wade

Eddie Gribbon ... Cactus Joe
Lloyd Ingraham ... Governon Bryden
George Kamel ... Weasel (as Geo. Kamel)
Cay Forrester ... Mary (as Kay Forrester)
Robbie Kavanaugh ... Virginia
Frank Ellis ... Lefty
Charles King ... Henchman Westy
Kenne Duncan ... Henchman Red Higgins (as Ken Duncan)
Dan White ... Henchman Trigger
Ben Corbett .... stunt double
Ben Johnson .... stunts (uncredited)
Cliff Lyons .... stunt double (uncredited)
Wally West .... stunts (uncredited)
Runtime:54 min
Black and White
Filming Locations: Corriganville, Ray Corrigan Ranch, Simi Valley, California

Tarzan's Desert Mystery (1943) (RKO/Sol Lesser Productions)
Director:Wilhelm Thiele
Writers: Edgar Rice Burroughs (characters)
Edward T. Lowe Jr. (writer)
Release Date:15 April 1944
Johnny Weissmuller ... Tarzan
Nancy Kelly ... Connie Bryce
Johnny Sheffield ... Boy
Otto Kruger ... Paul Hendrix
Joe Sawyer ... Karl Straeder
Lloyd Corrigan ... Sheik Abdul El Khim
Robert Lowery ... Prince Selim
Frank Puglia ... Magistrate

Philip Van Zandt ... Kushmet
Bobby Barber ... Turban Vendor (uncredited)
John Berkes ... Charlie (uncredited)
Dice ... Jaynar (uncredited)
Frank Faylen ... Achmed (uncredited)
George J. Lewis ... Ali Baba Hassan (uncredited)
Nestor Paiva ... Prison Guard (uncredited)
Ben Johnson .... stunt double (uncredited)
Paul Stader .... stunts (uncredited)
Runtime:70 min
Black and White
Filming Locations:Alabama Hills, Lone Pine, California

Tall in the Saddle (1944) (RKO Radio Pictures)
Director:Edwin L. Marin
Writers:Gordon Ray Young (story)
Michael Hogan (screenplay)
Release Date:29 September 1944
Genre:Mystery | Western | Romance more
Cast:
John Wayne ... Rocklin
Ella Raines ... Arleta 'Arly' Harolday
Ward Bond ... 'Judge' Robert Garvey
George 'Gabby' Hayes ... Dave
Audrey Long ... Clara Cardell
Elisabeth Risdon ... Miss Elizabeth Martin
Donald Douglas ... Harolday (as Don Douglas)
Paul Fix ... Bob Clews
Russell Wade ... Clint Harolday
Emory Parnell ... Sheriff Jackson
Raymond Hatton ... Zeke
Harry Woods ... George Clews

Erville Alderson ... Wells Fargo Clerk (uncredited)
Walter Baldwin ... Stan (depot master) (uncredited)
Hank Bell ... Hotel Clerk (uncredited)
Clem Bevans ... Card game spectator (uncredited)
Wheaton Chambers ... Ab Jenkins (uncredited)
George Chandler ... Saddle Maker (uncredited)
Victor Cox ... Townsman (uncredited)
Frank Darien ... Train Station Master (uncredited)
William Desmond ... Town Citizen (uncredited)
Russell Hopton ... Wagon Driver (uncredited)
Ben Johnson ... Townsman (uncredited)
Cy Kendall ... Cap, Bartender (uncredited)
Sam McDaniel ... Servant (uncredited)
Robert McKenzie ... Doc Riding (uncredited)
Frank Orth ... 'Shorty' Davis (uncredited)
Frank Puglia ... Talo (uncredited)
Russell Simpson ... Pat Foster (uncredited)
Tom Smith ... Townsman (uncredited)
Eddy Waller ... Santa Inez Depot Master (uncredited)
Runtime:87 min
Black and White
Filming Locations:Agoura Ranch, Agoura, California

The Old Texas Trail (1944) (Universal Pictures)
Director:Lewis D. Collins
Writer:William Lively (original screenplay)
Release Date:November 1944
Cast:
Rod Cameron ... Jim Wiley, posing as Rawhide Carney
Eddie Dew ... Dave Stone
Fuzzy Knight ... H. Pinkerton 'Pinky' Pinkley
Ray Whitley ... Amarillo

Virginia Christine ... Queenie Leone
Joseph J. Greene ... Jefferson Talbot
Marjorie Clements ... Mary Lane
George Eldredge ... Sparks Diamond
Edmund Cobb ... Joe Gardner, posing as Jim Wiley
Jack Clifford ... Sheriff Thomas
The Bar-6 Cowboys ... Musicians (as The Bar Six Cowboys)
William Desmond ... Townsman (uncredited)
Art Fowler ... Rawhide Carney (uncredited)
Terry Frost ... Henchman Nevada (uncredited)
Herman Hack ... Bartender (uncredited)
Tex Harper ... Road Worker (uncredited)
Ray Jones ... Road Worker (uncredited)
Frank McCarroll ... Camp Cook (uncredited)
George Plues ... Stagecoach Driver (uncredited)
George Sowards ... Barfly (uncredited)
Harry Strang ... Howard Lane (uncredited)
Merle Travis ... Musician Jake (uncredited)
George Turner ... Henchman Pete (uncredited)
Michael Vallon ... Warren (uncredited)
Henry Wills ... Barfly (uncredited)
Ben Johnson .... stunts (uncredited)
Cliff Lyons .... stunts (uncredited)
Frank McCarroll .... stunts (uncredited)
Henry Wills .... stunts (uncredited)
Runtime:60 min
Black and White

Nevada (1944) (RKO Radio Pictures)
Director:Edward Killy
Writers:Zane Grey (novel)
Norman Houston (writer)

Release Date:25 December 1944
Cast:
Robert Mitchum ... Jim 'Nevada' Lacy (as Bob Mitchum)
Anne Jeffreys ... Julie Dexter
Guinn 'Big Boy' Williams ... Dusty
Nancy Gates ... Hattie Ide
Richard Martin ... Chito Jose Gonzales Bustamante Rafferty
Craig Reynolds ... Cash Burridge
Harry Woods ... Joe Powell
Edmund Glover ... Ed Nelson, Assayer
Alan Ward ... Sheriff William H. Brewer
Harry McKim ... Marvie Ide
Larry Wheat ... Ben Ide
Jack Overman ... Croupier Red Berry
Emmett Lynn ... 'Pancake' Comstock
Virginia Belmont ... Dancer (uncredited)
Sammy Blum ... Gold Hill Bartender (uncredited)
Patti Brill ... Dancer (uncredited)
Ralph Bucko ... Barfly (uncredited)
Wheaton Chambers ... Doctor Burton (uncredited)
George DeNormand ... Red Berry's Bartender (uncredited)
Mary Halsey ... Dancer (uncredited)
Russell Hopton ... Henchman (uncredited)
Ben Johnson ... Saloon Patron (uncredited)
Bert Moorhouse ... Sandy Bowers - townsman (uncredited)
Philip Morris ... Prospector Ed (uncredited)
Margie Stewart ... Dancer (uncredited)
Bryant Washburn ... Townsman (uncredited)
George DeNormand .... stunts (uncredited)
Fred Graham .... stunt double: Harry Woods & Craig Reynolds (uncredited)

Ben Johnson .... stunt double: Robert Mitchum (uncredited)
Runtime:62 min
Black and White
Filming Locations: Alabama Hills, Lone Pine, California

Corpus Christi Bandits (1945). (Republic Pictures)
Director:Wallace Grissell
Writer:Norman S. Hall (original screenplay)
Release Date:20 April 1945
Cast:
Allan Lane ... Captain James Christi / Corpus Christi Jim
Helen Talbot ... Dorothy Adams
Jack Kirk ... Editor Lon Adams
Twinkle Watts ... Nancy Christi
Roy Barcroft ... Wade Larkin
Tom London ... Henchman Rocky
Kenne Duncan ... Henchman Spade
Robert J. Wilke ... Henchman Steve (as Bob Wilke)
Ruth Lee ... Mom Christi
Francis McDonald ... Dad Christi
Ed Cassidy ... Marshal Dan Adams
Emmett Vogan ... Texas Governor
Freddie Chapman ... Stinky, a young boy
Dickie Dillon ... Brush, a young boy
Shelby Bacon ... Moonlight, a young boy
George Bell ... Stage Driver (uncredited)
Roy Bucko ... Barfly (uncredited)
Foxy Callahan ... Townsman (uncredited)
Horace B. Carpenter ... Townsman (uncredited)

Frank Ellis ... Henchman (uncredited)
Jack Evans ... Barfly (uncredited)
Carl Faulkner ... Bartender, Lone Star Saloon (uncredited)
Herman Hack ... Barfly (uncredited)
Neal Hart ... Townsman (uncredited)
Ben Johnson ... 2nd Stage Driver (uncredited)
Frank McCarroll ... Henchman Tom (uncredited)
Rose Marie Morel ... Saloon Girl (uncredited)
Lew Morphy ... Barfly (uncredited)
Eva Novak ... Stage Passenger (uncredited)
Cliff Parkinson ... Henchman Red (uncredited)
Post Park ... 1st Stage Driver (uncredited)
Hal Price ... Townsman Harvey (uncredited)
Henry Wills ... Henchman / 2nd Stage Guard (uncredited)
Ben Johnson .... stunts (uncredited)
Frank McCarroll .... stunts (uncredited)
Eddie Parker .... stunt double: Roy Barcroft (uncredited)
Tom Steele .... stunt double: Allan Lane (uncredited)
Henry Wills .... stunts (uncredited)
Runtime:56 min
Black and White
Filming Locations:Iverson Ranch, Chatsworth, Los Angeles, California

The Naughty Nineties (1945) (Universal Pictures)
Director:Jean Yarbrough
Writers: Edmund L. Hartmann (screenplay) &
John Grant (screenplay) ...
Release Date:6 July 1945

Cast (Complete credited cast)
Bud Abbott ... Dexter Broadhurst
Lou Costello ... Sebastian Dinwiddle
Alan Curtis ... Mr. Crawford
Rita Johnson ... Bonita Farrow
Henry Travers ... Capt. Sam Jackson
Lois Collier ... Miss Caroline Jackson
Joe Sawyer ... Bailey
Joe Kirk ... Croupier
Rainbow Four ... Themselves
Bill Alcorn ... Specialty dancer (uncredited)
Audley Anderson ... Card player (uncredited)
Jack Barbee ... Himself (Rainbow Four member) (uncredited)
Suzanne Lee Bastian ... Baby (uncredited)
Gladys Blake ... Girl in garter gag (uncredited)
Milt Bronson ... Gambler (uncredited)
Douglas Carter ... Croupier (uncredited)
Jack Chefe ... Gilded Cage waiter (uncredited)
Jack Coffey ... Specialty dancer (uncredited)
Bing Conley ... Croupier (uncredited)
Tony Dell ... Croupier (uncredited)
William Desmond ... (uncredited)
Dolores Evers ... Girl in high-wire act (uncredited)
Tom Fadden ... Wounded gambler (uncredited)
Sid Fields ... (uncredited)
Jack Frack ... Croupier (uncredited)
Jack Frost ... Himself (Rainbow Four member) (uncredited)
Edward Gargan ... Baxter (saloon bartender) (uncredited)
Parker Garvie ... Croupier (uncredited)
Rita Gould ... Girl in water gag (uncredited)

William E. Green ... Minstrel (uncredited)
John Hamilton ... Sheriff of Ironville (uncredited)
Carol Hughes ... Tessie (uncredited)
John Indrisano ... Croupier (uncredited)
Warren Jackson ... Card player (uncredited)
Ben Johnson ... Coach driver (uncredited)
Ralph Johns ... Croupier (uncredited)
Shirley Karnes ... Hatcheck girl (uncredited)
Donald Kerr ... Croupier (uncredited)
William W. Larsen ... Magician (uncredited)
Perc Launders ... Card player (uncredited)
Ann Lawrence ... Girl in garter gag (uncredited)
Rex Lease ... Sheriff Wright (uncredited)
Ruth Lee ... (uncredited)
Arthur Loft ... Billy Boy (uncredited)
Chick Madden ... Himself (Rainbow Four member) (uncredited)
Sam McDaniel ... Matt (cook-waiter) (uncredited)
Charles McNally ... Waiter (uncredited)
Mantan Moreland ... (uncredited)
Jack Norton ... Drunk at the Gilded Cage (uncredited)
Bud O'Connor ... Croupier (uncredited)
Jack Overman ... Gambling Room guard (uncredited)
Barbara Pepper ... Gilded Cage hostess (uncredited)
Charles Phillips ... Croupier (uncredited)
Torchy Rand ... Singing specialty (uncredited)
Jack Rice ... Waiter (uncredited)
Cyril Ring ... Man in water gag (uncredited)
Sue Robin ... Topsy (uncredited)
Henry Russell ... Croupier (uncredited)
Sarah Selby ... Mrs. Hawkins (uncredited)
Arthur 'Fiddlin' Smith ... Fiddle Player (uncredited)

Ronald Stanton ... Specialty dancer (uncredited)
Irene Thomas ... Specialty dancer (uncredited)
Emmett Vogan ... Henry (Ironville citizen) (uncredited)
Bill Ward ... Boy (uncredited)
Bud Wolfe ... Croupier (uncredited)
Jack Worth ... Croupier (uncredited)
Lillian Yarbo ... Effie (Bonita's cook) (uncredited)
Runtime:76 min
Black and White

Santa Fe Saddlemates (1945) (Republic Pictures)
Director:Thomas Carr
Writer:Bennett Cohen (original screenplay)
Release Date:2 June 1945
Cast (Complete credited cast)
Sunset Carson ... Sunset Carson
Linda Stirling ... Ann Morton
Olin Howland ... Dead Eye (as Olin Howlin)
Roy Barcroft ... John Gant
Bud Geary ... Spur Brannon
Kenne Duncan ... Brazos Kane
George Chesebro ... Fred Loder
Robert J. Wilke ... Henchman Rawhide (as Bob Wilke)
Henry Wills ... Henchman Denver
Forbes Murray ... Inspector Burke
Frank Jaquet ... Governor L. Bradford Prince
Johnny Carpenter ... Henchman Mills (as Josh Carpenter)
Rex Lease ... Smiley - jewel cutter
Ralph Bucko ... Exits saloon (uncredited)
Horace B. Carpenter ... Town Lamplighter (uncredited)
Edmund Cobb ... Border Guard Hank (uncredited)
Fred Graham ... Burke's 1st guard (uncredited)

Chick Hannon ... Barfly (uncredited)
Neal Hart ... Barfly (uncredited)
Carol Henry ... Townsman (uncredited)
Nolan Leary ... Doctor (uncredited)
George Magrill ... Man in Hallway (uncredited)
Kansas Moehring ... Barfly (uncredited)
Bill Nestell ... Brawler (uncredited)
Frank O'Connor ... Townsman (uncredited)
Jack O'Shea ... Bartender Charlie (uncredited)
Rose Plumer ... Townswoman (uncredited)
Bob Reeves ... Barfly (uncredited)
Duke Taylor ... Henchman (uncredited)
Sailor Vincent ... Saloon Waiter (uncredited)
Bill Wolfe ... Barfly (uncredited)
Johnny Carpenter .... stunts (uncredited)
Fred Graham .... stunt double (uncredited)
Carol Henry .... stunts (uncredited)
Ben Johnson .... stunt double (uncredited)
Duke Taylor .... stunt double (uncredited)
Runtime:58 min
Black and White
Filming Locations: Iverson Ranch, Chatsworth, Los Angeles, California

California Gold Rush (1946) (Republic Pictures)
Director:R.G. Springsteen
Writers:Fred Harman (character)
Robert Creighton Williams (original screenplay)
Release Date:4 February 1946
Cast:
Bill Elliott ... Red Ryder (as Wild Bill Elliott)
Robert Blake ... Little Beaver (as Bobby Blake)

Alice Fleming ... Duchess Wentworth, Red's Aunt
Peggy Stewart ... Hazel Parker
Russell Simpson ... Colonel Parker
Dick Curtis ... Chopin - the Harmonica killer
Joel Friedkin ... Murphy
Kenne Duncan ... Felton
Tom London ... Sheriff Peabody
Monte Hale ... Pete - driver that quits
Wen Wright ... The Idaho Kid
Dickie Dillon ... Broken Arrow
Mary Arden ... Stage Passenger
Jack Kirk ... Stage passenger
Roy Bucko ... Deputy Ted (uncredited)
Budd Buster ... Desk Clerk (uncredited)
Jess Cavin ... Townsman (uncredited)
Freddie Chapman ... Young Boy (uncredited)
Frank Ellis ... Man in lobby (uncredited)
Frances Gladwin ... Girl (uncredited)
Herman Hack ... Posse rider (uncredited)
Neal Hart ... Townsman (uncredited)
Marian Kerrigan ... Girl (uncredited)
Nolan Leary ... Refuses to ride on stage (uncredited)
James Mitchell ... Townsman (uncredited)
Kansas Moehring ... Townsman (uncredited)
Bud Osborne ... Henchman Frank (uncredited)
Cliff Parkinson ... Stage hand Bill (uncredited)
Post Park ... New stage driver (uncredited)
Pascale Perry ... Deputy (uncredited)
Beverly Reedy ... Girl (uncredited)
Dorothy Stevens ... Girl (uncredited)
Henry Wills ... Henchman (uncredited)
Bill Yrigoyen ... Driver Ted Parker (uncredited) \l

Ben Johnson .... stunt double (uncredited)
Henry Wills .... stunts (uncredited)
Bill Yrigoyen .... stunts (uncredited)
Runtime:56 min
Black and White
Filming Locations:Studio City, Los Angeles, California

Badman's Territory (1946) (RKO Radio Pictures)
Director:Tim Whelan
Writers:Jack Natteford (story) and
Luci Ward (story)
Release Date:1 April 1946
Cast:
Randolph Scott ... Sheriff Mark Rowley
George 'Gabby' Hayes ... Honest Jim Badger / The Coyote Kid
Ann Richards ... Henryetta Alcott
Ray Collins ... Colonel Farewell / Narrator
James Warren ... Deputy John Rowley
Morgan Conway ... Captain William 'Bill' Hampton
Virginia Sale ... Meg
John Halloran ... Hank 'Mac' McGee
Andrew Tombes ... Doc Quillan aka Doc Grant
Richard Hale ... Ben Wade
Harry Holman ... Hodge
Chief Thundercloud ... Chief Tahlequah
Lawrence Tierney ... Jesse James
Tom Tyler ... Frank James
Steve Brodie ... Bob Dalton
Fred Aldrich ... Townsman at Dance (uncredited)
Bonnie Blair ... Daisy (uncredited)

Budd Buster ... Doc's Friend (uncredited)
George Chesebro ... Johnny, Baggage Man (uncredited)
Jack Clifford ... Team Owner (uncredited)
Tex Cooper ... Tex - Townsman (uncredited)
John Elliott ... Brother Hooker (uncredited)
Carl Faulkner ... Deputy Marshal (uncredited)
Herman Hack ... Townsman (uncredited)
Chuck Hamilton ... Indian (uncredited)
John Hamilton ... Commissioner Taylor (uncredited)
Carl Eric Hansen ... Bill Doolin (uncredited)
Neal Hart ... Townsman (uncredited)
Harry Harvey ... Station Master (uncredited)
Robert Homans ... Judge (uncredited)
Ben Johnson ... Deputy Marshal (uncredited)
Ethan Laidlaw ... Lieutenant Patton (uncredited)
Frank LaRue ... Jury Foreman (uncredited)
Elmo Lincoln ... Dick Broadwell (uncredited)
Theodore Lorch ... Citizen's Committee Member (uncredited)
Jack Low ... Cowboy (uncredited)
Wilbur Mack ... Cattle Baron (uncredited)
Kermit Maynard ... Carson, Patton's Deputy (uncredited)
Glenn McCarthy ... Charles Bryant (uncredited)
Frank Meredith ... Deputy Marshal (uncredited)
Frank Mills ... Townsman (uncredited)
Monte Montague ... Bartender / Scoreboard Watcher (uncredited)
Alex Montoya ... Indian (uncredited)
Philip Morris ... Deputy Allen (uncredited)
Elmer Napier ... Dan (uncredited)
William J. O'Brien ... Man in Barber Chair (uncredited)
Frank O'Connor ... Townsman (uncredited)

Artie Ortego ... Townsman (uncredited)
Bud Osborne ... Deputy Dan Mercer (uncredited)
Emory Parnell ... Bitter Creek (uncredited)
Frank Pharr ... Joe, the Bartender (uncredited)
'Snub' Pollard ... Town Barber (uncredited)
Bob Reeves ... Townsman (uncredited)
Jason Robards Sr. ... Alert Coffeyville Citizen (uncredited)
Buddy Roosevelt ... Lieutenant Lake (uncredited)
Sherman Sanders ... Caller (uncredited)
Harry Semels ... Bettor (uncredited)
Boyd Stockman ... William McElheney (uncredited)
Brick Sullivan ... Deputy Marshal (uncredited)
Larry Wheat ... Custer, Hotel Clerk (uncredited)
Dave White ... Deputy Marshal (uncredited)
Robert J. Wilke ... Deputy Marshal (uncredited)
Chuck Hamilton .... stunts (uncredited)
Ben Johnson .... stunts (uncredited)
Kermit Maynard .... stunts (uncredited)
Glenn McCarthy .... stunts (uncredited)
Buddy Roosevelt .... stunts (uncredited)
Boyd Stockman .... stunts (uncredited)
Runtime:97 min | USA:79 min (re-edited version) (re-release)
Black and White

Smoky (1946) (Twentieth Century Fox Film Corporation)
Director: Louis King
Writers: Dwight Cummins (screenplay)
Lillie Hayward (screenplay)
Release Date:July 1946
Cast:

Fred MacMurray ... Clint Barkley
Anne Baxter ... Julie Richards
Bruce Cabot ... Frank Denton
Esther Dale ... Mrs. 'Gram' Richards
Roy Roberts ... Jeff
J. Farrell MacDonald ... Jim, the Cook
Burl Ives ... Willie (as The Singing Troubadour Burl Ives)
Robert Adler ... Scrubby (uncredited)
Stanley Andrews ... Fred Kramer - Rancher (uncredited)
Guy Beach ... Sheriff (uncredited)
Harry Carter ... Bud (uncredited)
Bud Geary ... Peters (uncredited)
Herbert Heywood ... Livery Stable Proprietor (uncredited)
Victor Kilian ... J. P. Mingo, Junkman (uncredited)
Howard Negley ... Nelson (uncredited)
Douglas Spencer ... Gambler (uncredited)
Max Wagner ... Bart (uncredited)
Ben Johnson .... stunts (uncredited)
Runtime: 87 min
Color
Filming Locations: Utah

Out California Way (1946) (Republic Pictures)
Director: Lesley Selander
Writers: Barry Shipman (story)
Betty Burbridge (screenplay)
Release Date: 5 December 1946
Cast:
Monte Hale ... Monte Hale
Lorna Gray ... Gloria McCoy (as Adrian Booth)
Robert Blake ... Danny McCoy (as Bobby Blake)

John Dehner ... Rod Mason
Nolan Leary ... George Sheridan
Fred Graham ... Ace Hanlon
Tom London ... Johnny
Jimmy Starr ... Jimmy Starr, Radio Commentator
Edward Keane ... E.J. Pearson
St. Luke's Episcopal Church Choristers ... Boy Choir (as St. Luke's Choristers)
Foy Willing ... Foy
Riders of the Purple Sage ... The Riders of the Purple Sage
Roy Rogers ... Himself
Trigger ... Trigger, Roy's Horse
Allan Lane ... Himself
Rod Bacon ... (uncredited)
George Bamby ... Musician (uncredited)
Brooks Benedict ... Cameraman (uncredited)
Ed Cassidy ... Veterinarian (uncredited)
Mary Gleason ... Dark Haired Leading Lady (uncredited)
Donald Kerr ... Reporter (uncredited)
Jack Kirk ... Tom, movie scene cowboy (uncredited)
Diana Mumby ... Blonde Leading Lady (uncredited)
Frank O'Connor ... Gateman (uncredited)
Tom Quinn ... Andy, Casting Director (uncredited)
Darol Rice ... Musician (uncredited)
Al Sloey ... Accordion player (uncredited)
Ken Terrell ... Movie Scene Sheriff (uncredited)
Robert J. Wilke ... Nate, Assistant director (uncredited)
Ben Johnson .... stunt double: Monte Hale (uncredited)
Tom Steele .... stunt double: John Dehner (uncredited)
Runtime:67 min
Color

Filming Locations: Chatsworth Reservoir, Chatsworth, Los Angeles, California

Angel and the Badman (1947) (John Wayne Productions)
Director:James Edward Grant
Writer:James Edward Grant (written by)
Release Date:15 February 1947 (USA) more
Cast:
John Wayne ... Quirt Evans
Gail Russell ... Penelope Worth
Harry Carey ... Territorial Marshal Wistful McClintock
Bruce Cabot ... Laredo Stevens
Irene Rich ... Mrs. Worth
Lee Dixon ... Randy McCall - Quirt's Partner
Stephen Grant ... Johnny Worth
Tom Powers ... Dr. Mangram
Paul Hurst ... Frederick Carson - Worth's Neighbor
Olin Howland ... Bradley - Town Telegrapher (as Olin Howlin)
John Halloran ... Thomas Worth
Joan Barton ... Lila Neal - Saloon Singer ("The Western Nightingale") in Red Rock
Craig Woods ... Ward Withers
Marshall Reed ... Nelson - Quaker Blacksmith
Doc Adams ... Quaker (uncredited)
Rosemary Bertrand ... Christine Taylor (uncredited)
Symona Boniface ... Dance Hall Madam (uncredited)
Bob Burns ... Quaker Meeting Member (uncredited)
Wade Crosby ... Baker Brother #2 (uncredited)
Steve Darrell ... Gambler (uncredited)
Kenne Duncan ... Gambler (uncredited)

Geraldine Farnum ... Saloon Girl (uncredited)
Louis Faust ... Hondo JeffriesPaul Fix ... Mouse Marr (uncredited)
Pat Flaherty ... Baker Brother (uncredited)
Lew Harvey ... Gambler (uncredited)
Jack Kirk ... Carson Ranchhand (uncredited)
Rex Lease ... Roulette Croupier (uncredited)
Cactus Mack ... Quaker (uncredited)
LeRoy Mason ... Lefty Wilson (uncredited)
Jack Montgomery ... Carson Ranchhand (uncredited)
Bert Moorhouse ... Gambler (uncredited)
Al Murphy ... Bartender (uncredited)
William Newell ... Headwaiter (uncredited)
Jack O'Shea ... Barfly (uncredited)
Eddie Parker ... Baker Brother (uncredited)
Stanley Price ... Gambler (uncredited)
John Shay ... Gambler (uncredited)
Jack Stoney ... Baker Brother (uncredited)
Ken Terrell ... Brawl Spectator (uncredited)
Tony Travers ... Hernan (uncredited)
Crane Whitley ... Townsman (uncredited)
Norman Willis ... Gambler (uncredited)
Hank Worden ... Townsman (uncredited)
Richard Farnsworth .... stunts (uncredited)
Fred Graham .... stunt double: John Wayne (uncredited)
John Hudkins .... stunts (uncredited)
Ben Johnson .... stunt double (uncredited)
Chuck Roberson .... stunts (uncredited)
Jack Stoney .... stunts (uncredited)
Ken Terrell .... stunts (uncredited)
Henry Wills .... stunts (uncredited)
Runtime:100 min

Color
Filming Locations: Sedona, Arizona

Ramrod (1947) (Enterprise Productions)
Director: André De Toth
Writers: Luke Short (novel)
Jack Moffitt (writer) ...
Release Date:2 May 1947
Cast:
Joel McCrea ... Dave Nash
Veronica Lake ... Connie Dickason
Don DeFore ... Bill Schell
Donald Crisp ... Sheriff Jim Crew
Preston Foster ... Frank Ivey
Arleen Whelan ... Rose Leland
Charles Ruggles ... Ben Dickason (as Charlie Ruggles)
Lloyd Bridges ... Red Cates
Nestor Paiva ... Curley
Ray Teal ... Ed Burma
Houseley Stevenson ... George Smedley
Ward Wood ... Link Thomas
Ian MacDonald ... Walt Shipley
Wally Cassell ... Virg Lea
Sarah Padden ... Mrs. Parks
Trevor Bardette ... Bailey - Circle 66 Hand (uncredited)
Lane Bradford ... Ivey Ranch Hand (uncredited)
Rose Higgins ... Annie - Connie's Maid (uncredited)
Cliff Parkinson ... Tom Peebles - Circle 66 Hand (uncredited)
Chick York ... Dr. Parks (uncredited)
Ben Johnson .... stunts (uncredited)
Cliff Parkinson .... stunts (uncredited)

Cal Spencer .... stunt double: Lloyd Bridges (uncredited)
Runtime:95 min
Black and White
Filming Locations: Zion National Park, Springdale, Utah, USA

Wyoming (1947) (Republic Pictures)
Director: Joseph Kane
Writers: Lawrence Hazard (screenplay) and
Gerald Geraghty (screenplay)
Release Date:28 July 1947
Cast:
Bill Elliott ... Charles Alderson (as William Elliott)
Vera Ralston ... Karen Alderson
John Carroll ... Glenn Forrester
George 'Gabby' Hayes ... Windy Gibson
Albert Dekker ... Duke Lassiter
Virginia Grey ... Lila Regan
Maria Ouspenskaya ... Maria (as Mme. Maria Ouspenskaya)
Grant Withers ... Joe Sublette
Harry Woods ... Ben Jackson
Minna Gombell ... Queenie Lassiter
Dick Curtis ... Ed Lassiter
Roy Barcroft ... Sheriff Niles
Trevor Bardette ... Timmons
Paul Harvey ... Judge Sheridan
Louise Kane ... Karen, at age 9
Eddie Acuff ... Nester (uncredited)
James Archuletta ... Indian boy (uncredited)
Tex Cooper ... Townsman (uncredited)
Dale Fink ... Boy (uncredited)

Olin Howland ... Nester (uncredited)
Charles King ... Nester (uncredited)
Rex Lease ... Store Clerk (uncredited)
Charles Middleton ... Rev, Withers (uncredited)
Charles Morton ... Nester (uncredited)
Edward Peil Sr. ... Rancher (uncredited)
Marshall Reed ... Cowhand (uncredited)
Lee Shumway ... Rancher (uncredited)
Glenn Strange ... Rustler (uncredited)
Tex Terry ... Morrison (uncredited)
Eddy Waller ... Drifter (uncredited)
David Williams ... Hotel Clerk (uncredited)
Roque Ybarra ... Indian Boy (uncredited)
Bobbie Dorree .... stunts (uncredited)
Fred Graham .... stunts (uncredited)
Ben Johnson .... stunts (uncredited)
Chuck Roberson .... stunts (uncredited)
Tom Steele .... stunts (uncredited)
Runtime: 84 min
Black and White
Locations: Kernville, California, USA

Fort Apache (1948) Argosy Pictures
Director: John Ford
Writers: Frank S. Nugent (screenplay)
James Warner Bellah (suggested by the story "Massacre")
Release Date: 9 March 1948
Cast:
John Wayne ... Capt. Kirby York
Henry Fonda ... Lt. Col. Owen Thursday
Shirley Temple ... Philadelphia Thursday
Pedro Armendáriz ... Sgt. Beaufort (as Pedro Armendariz)

Ward Bond ... Sgt. Maj. Michael O'Rourke
George O'Brien ... Capt. Sam Collingwood
Victor McLaglen ... Sgt. Festus Mulcahy
Anna Lee ... Mrs. Emily Collingwood
Irene Rich ... Mrs. Mary O'Rourke
Dick Foran ... Sgt. Quincannon
Guy Kibbee ... Capt. Dr. Wilkens
Grant Withers ... Silas Meacham
Jack Pennick ... Sgt. Daniel Schattuck
Ray Hyke ... Lt. Gates (Adjutant)
Movita ... Guadalupe (Col. Thursday's cook)
Cliff Clark ... Stage driver (uncredited)
Frank Ferguson ... Newspaperman (uncredited)
Francis Ford ... Fen (stage guard) (uncredited)
William Forrest ... Reporter (uncredited)
Art Gilmore ... Trailer Narrator (voice) (uncredited)
Fred Graham ... Cavalryman (uncredited)
Frank McGrath ... Cpl. Derice (bugler) (uncredited)
Mickey Simpson ... NCO at dance (uncredited)
Harry Tenbrook ... Tom O'Feeney (courier) (uncredited)
Archie Twitchell ... Reporter (uncredited)
Frank Baker .... stunts (uncredited)
Fred Carson .... stunts (uncredited)
John Epper .... stunts (uncredited)
Richard Farnsworth .... stunts (uncredited)
Fred Graham .... stunts (uncredited)
John Hudkins .... stunts (uncredited)
Ben Johnson .... stunts (uncredited)
Walt La Rue .... stunts (uncredited)
Cliff Lyons .... stunts (uncredited)
Frank McGrath .... stunts (uncredited)
Gil Perkins .... stunts (uncredited)

Bob Rose .... stunts (uncredited)
Danny Sands .... stunts (uncredited)
Barlow Simpson .... stunts (uncredited)
Jack Williams .... stunts (uncredited)
Henry Wills .... stunts (uncredited)
Runtime:125 min
Black and White
Filming Locations: Arches National Park, Moab, Utah, USA more

The Gallant Legion (1948) (Republic Pictures)
Director: Joseph Kane
Writers: John K. Butler (story) and
Gerald Geraghty (story) ...
Release Date:24 May 1948
Cast (Cast overview, first billed only)
Bill Elliott ... Gary Conway (as William Elliott)
Lorna Gray ... Connie Faulkner (as Adrian Booth)
Joseph Schildkraut ... Clarke Faulkner
Bruce Cabot ... Beau Laroux
Andy Devine ... Windy Hornblower
Jack Holt ... Texas Ranger Captain Banner
Grant Withers ... Wesley Hardin
Adele Mara ... Catalina
James Brown ... Texas Ranger Tom Banner
Harold Landon ... Chuck Conway (as Hal Landon)
Tex Terry ... Sergeant Clint Mason
Lester Sharpe ... Matt Kirby
Hal Taliaferro ... Billy Smith
Russell Hicks ... Sen. Beale
Herbert Rawlinson ... Major Grant
William Bailey (as William Norton Bailey)

Roy Barcroft ... (uncredited)
Trevor Bardette ... (uncredited)
Hank Bell ... (uncredited)
John L. Cason ... Henchman (uncredited)
George Chesebro ... (uncredited)
Iron Eyes Cody ... Indian Warrior (uncredited)
Joseph Crehan ... State Official (uncredited)
Augie Gomez ... Indian (uncredited)
Lloyd Hagarty ... (uncredited)
John Hamilton ... State Official (uncredited)
Jack Ingram ... (uncredited)
Ben Johnson ... Texas Ranger (uncredited)
Noble Johnson ... Chief Black Eagle (uncredited)
Jack Kirk ... (uncredited)
Fred Kohler Jr. ... (uncredited)
Rex Lease ... (uncredited)
Cactus Mack ... (uncredited)
Kermit Maynard ... (uncredited)
Merrill McCormick ... (uncredited)
Bud Osborne ... (uncredited)
Peter Perkins ... (uncredited)
Jack Perrin ... (uncredited)
Gene Roth ... Agitator (uncredited)
Jack Sparks ... (uncredited)
Glenn Strange ... (uncredited)
Ferris Taylor ... (uncredited)
Emmett Vogan ... (uncredited)
Chief Yowlachie ... Indian Warrior (uncredited)
Runtime:88 min
Color:Black and White
Filming Locations:Vasquez Rocks Natural Area Park - Agua Dulce, California, USA

Red River (1948) Charles K. Feldman Group
Directors: Howard Hawks
Arthur Rosson (co-director)
Writers: Borden Chase (Saturday Evening Post story)
Borden Chase (screenplay) ...
Release Date: 30 September 1948 (USA) more
Cast:
John Wayne ... Thomas Dunson
Montgomery Clift ... Matthew 'Matt' Garth
Joanne Dru ... Tess Millay
Walter Brennan ... 'Groot' Nadine
Coleen Gray ... Fen (also as Colleen Gray)
Harry Carey ... Mr. Melville (as Harry Carey Sr.)
John Ireland ... Cherry Valance
Noah Beery Jr. ... Buster McGee
Harry Carey Jr. ... Dan Latimer
Chief Yowlachie ... Quo (as Chief Yowlatchie)
Paul Fix ... Teeler Yacey
Hank Worden ... Simms Reeves
Mickey Kuhn ... Matt, as a boy
Ray Hyke ... Walt Jergens
Hal Taliaferro ... Old Leather (as Hal Talliaferro)
Paul Fierro ... Fernandez (as Paul Fiero)
Ivan Parry ... Bunk Kenneally
William Self ... Wounded Wrangler (as Billie Self)
Lane Chandler ... Colonel (uncredited)
Davison Clark ... Mr. Meeker (uncredited)
Harry Cording ... Gambler (uncredited)
Richard Farnsworth ... Dunston Rider (uncredited)
George Lloyd ... Rider with Mr. Melville (uncredited)
Pierce Lyden ... Colonel's Trail Boss (uncredited)
John Merton ... Settler (uncredited)

Lee Phelps ... Gambler (uncredited)
Glenn Strange ... Naylor (uncredited)
Tom Tyler ... The Quitter (uncredited)
Dan White ... Laredo (uncredited)
Shelley Winters ... Dance Hall Girl in Wagon Train (uncredited)
Richard Farnsworth .... stunts (uncredited)
Ben Johnson .... stunts (uncredited)
Fred Kennedy .... stunts (uncredited)
Danny Sands .... stunts (uncredited)
Jack Williams .... stunts (uncredited)
Carlos Albert ... Footman (uncredited)
Nana Bryant ... Nun (uncredited)
Joe Dominguez ... Francisco (uncredited)
Sally Forrest ... Dancer (uncredited)
Byron Foulger ... Grandee (uncredited)
Captain Garcia ... Coachman (uncredited)
Norma Gentner ... Convent Girl (uncredited)
Fred Gilman ... Pedro (uncredited)
Ginny Jackson ... Convent Girl (uncredited)
Michael Kostrick ... Juan (uncredited)
Mitchell Lewis ... Fernando (uncredited)
Gerö Mály ... Advisor (uncredited)
Jack Manolas ... Grandee (uncredited)
Margaret Martin ... Rosita (uncredited)
Henry Mirelez ... Pepito, 8 Years Old (uncredited)
Alex Montoya ... Bandit (uncredited)
Alberto Morin ... Lotso (uncredited)
Leo Mostovoy ... Advisor (uncredited)
Carl Pitti ... Whip Expert (uncredited)
Pedro Regas ... Esteban (uncredited)
Suzanne Ridgeway ... Guest (uncredited)

Julian Rivero ... Postman (uncredited)
Nick Thompson ... Pablo (uncredited)
Candy Toxton ... Bit Role (uncredited)
Wilson Wood ... Advisor (uncredited)
Ben Johnson .... stunts (uncredited)
Runtime:133 min
Black and White
Filming Locations: Elgin, Arizona, USA

The Kissing Bandit (1948) (MGM)
Director :Laslo Benedek
Writers: John Briard Harding (writer)
Isobel Lennart (writer)
Release Date:January 1949 (USA) more
Cast:
Frank Sinatra ... Ricardo
Kathryn Grayson ... Teresa
J. Carrol Naish ... Chico
Mildred Natwick ... Isabella
Mikhail Rasumny ... Don Jose
Billy Gilbert ... General Felipe Toro
Sono Osato ... Bianca
Clinton Sundberg ... Colonel Gomez
Carleton G. Young ... Count Ricardo Belmonte
Ricardo Montalban ... Fiesta Specialty Dancer
Ann Miller ... Fiesta Specialty Dancer
Cyd Charisse ... Fiesta Specialty Dancer
Edna Skinner ... Juanita
Vicente Gómez ... Mexican Guitarist
Carlos Albert ... Footman (uncredited)
Nana Bryant ... Nun (uncredited)
Joe Dominguez ... Francisco (uncredited)

Sally Forrest ... Dancer (uncredited)
Byron Foulger ... Grandee (uncredited)
Captain Garcia ... Coachman (uncredited)
Norma Gentner ... Convent Girl (uncredited)
Fred Gilman ... Pedro (uncredited)
Ginny Jackson ... Convent Girl (uncredited)
Michael Kostrick ... Juan (uncredited)
Mitchell Lewis ... Fernando (uncredited)
Gerö Mály ... Advisor (uncredited)
Jack Manolas ... Grandee (uncredited)
Margaret Martin ... Rosita (uncredited)
Henry Mirelez ... Pepito, 8 Years Old (uncredited)
Alex Montoya ... Bandit (uncredited)
Alberto Morin ... Lotso (uncredited)
Leo Mostovoy ... Advisor (uncredited)
Carl Pitti ... Whip Expert (uncredited)
Pedro Regas ... Esteban (uncredited)
Suzanne Ridgeway ... Guest (uncredited)
Julian Rivero ... Postman (uncredited)
Nick Thompson ... Pablo (uncredited)
Candy Toxton ... Bit Role (uncredited)
Wilson Wood ... Advisor (uncredited)
Runtime:100 min
Color
Filming Locations: California, USA

Three Godfathers (1948) (Argosy Pictures)
Director: John Ford
Writers :Laurence Stallings (screenplay) and
Frank S. Nugent (screenplay)
Release Date:1 December 1948
Cast:

John Wayne ... Robert Marmaduke Hightower
Pedro Armendáriz ... Pedro 'Pete' Roca Fuerte (as Pedro Armendariz)
Harry Carey Jr. ... William Kearney ('The Abilene Kid')
Ward Bond ... Perley 'Buck' Sweet
Mae Marsh ... Mrs. Perley Sweet
Mildred Natwick ... The Mother
Jane Darwell ... Miss Florie
Guy Kibbee ... Judge
Dorothy Ford ... Ruby Latham
Ben Johnson ... Posse man #1
Charles Halton ... Oliver Latham
Hank Worden ... Deputy Curly
Jack Pennick ... Luke (the conductor)
Fred Libby ... Deputy
Michael Dugan ... Posse man #2
Gertrude Astor ... Townswoman (uncredited)
Ruth Clifford ... Woman in bar (uncredited)
Jack Curtis ... Bartender (uncredited)
Francis Ford ... Drunken oldtimer at bar (uncredited)
Richard Hageman ... Saloon pianist (uncredited)
Cliff Lyons ... Guard at Mojave Tanks (uncredited)
Eva Novak ... Townswoman (uncredited)
Harry Tenbrook ... Bartender #2 (uncredited)
Amelia Yelda ... Robert William Pedro Hightower (the Baby) (uncredited)
Michael Dugan .... stunts (uncredited)
Bryan 'Slim' Hightower .... stunts (uncredited)
Ben Johnson .... stunts (uncredited)
Cliff Lyons .... stunts (uncredited)

Frank McGrath .... stunt double: Pedro Armendariz (uncredited)
Jack Montgomery .... stunts (uncredited)
Jack Williams .... stunts (uncredited)
Runtime:106 min
Color
Filming Locations: Alabama Hills, Lone Pine, California, USA

Mighty Joe Young (1949) (Argosy Pictures)
Director: Ernest B. Schoedsack
Writers: Merian C. Cooper (story)
Ruth Rose (screenplay)
Release Date:29 August 1949
Cast:
Terry Moore ... Jill Young
Ben Johnson ... Gregg
Robert Armstrong ... Max O'Hara
Frank McHugh ... Windy
Douglas Fowley ... Jones
Denis Green ... Crawford
Paul Guilfoyle ... Smith
Nestor Paiva ... Brown
Regis Toomey ... John Young
Lora Lee Michel ... Jill Young, as a Girl
James Flavin ... Schultz
Mary Gordon ... Old Woman (unconfirmed)
Iris Adrian ... Woman (uncredited)
Bobby Barber ... Diner Customer (uncredited)
Ian Batchelor ... Strongman (uncredited)
Primo Carnera ... Strongman (uncredited)
Cliff Clark ... Police Guard Moran (uncredited)

Frank Conroy ... Reporter (uncredited)
Ellen Corby ... Ophanage Woman (uncredited)
James Craven ... First Man at Bar (uncredited)
Karl 'Killer' Davis ... Strongman (uncredited)
William 'Wee Willie' Davis ... Strongman (uncredited)
Man Mountain Dean ... Strongman (uncredited)
Joe Devlin ... Reporter (uncredited)
Eddie Dunn ... First Bartender (uncredited)
Mary Field ... O'Hara's Secretary (uncredited)
Bess Flowers ... Nightclub Patron behind Drunks (uncredited)
Lee Tung Foo ... Waiter (uncredited)
Edward Gargan ... Bar Patron (uncredited)
Selmer Jackson ... Judge (uncredited)
Donald Kerr ... Diner Proprietor (uncredited)
Henry Kulky ... Strongman (uncredited)
Charles Lane ... Bar Patron (uncredited)
Richard Lane ... Attorney (uncredited)
Kermit Maynard ... Cowboy (uncredited)
Sammy Menacker ... Strongman (uncredited)
Anne Nagel ... Brunette at Bar (uncredited)
William Newell ... Man at Bar (uncredited)
Phil Olafsson ... Swedish Angel (uncredited)
Garry Owen ... Second Bartender (uncredited)
Jack Pennick ... Truck driver (uncredited)
Ivan Rasputin ... Strongman (uncredited)
Irene Ryan ... Girl at the bar (uncredited)
William Schallert ... Gas Station Attendant (uncredited)
Charles Sherlock ... Policeman (uncredited)
Sammy Stein ... Strongman (uncredited)
Harry Strang ... Policeman With Tramp (uncredited)
Madame Sul-Te-Wan ... Young family servant (uncredited)

Archie Twitchell ... Reporter (uncredited)
Dale Van Sickel ... Undetermined Role (uncredited)
Ray Walker ... Reporter (uncredited)
Max Willenz ... Sketch artist (uncredited)
Norman Willis ... Man with Mustache at Bar (uncredited)
Richard Farnsworth .... stunts (uncredited)
Joe Gray .... stunts (uncredited)
Fred Kennedy .... stunts (uncredited)
Carey Loftin .... stunts (uncredited)
Kermit Maynard .... stunts (uncredited)
Eddie Parker .... stunts (uncredited)
David Sharpe .... stunts (uncredited)
Paul Stader .... stunts (uncredited)
Tom Steele .... stunts (uncredited)
Dale Van Sickel .... stunts (uncredited)
Bud Wolfe .... stunts (uncredited)
Runtime:94 min | USA:84 min
Black and White

She Wore a Yellow Ribbon (1949) (Argosy Pictures)
Director: John Ford
Writers: James Warner Bellah (story)
Frank S. Nugent (screenplay)
Release Date:22 October 1949
Cast:
John Wayne ... Capt. Nathan Cutting Brittles
Joanne Dru ... Olivia Dandridge
John Agar ... Lt. Flint Cohill
Ben Johnson ... Sgt. Tyree
Harry Carey Jr. ... 2nd Lt. Ross Pennell
Victor McLaglen ... Top Sgt. Quincannon
Mildred Natwick ... Abby Allshard aka Old Iron Pants

George O'Brien ... Major Mac Allshard, Commanding Officer Fort Starke
Arthur Shields ... Dr. O'Laughlin
Michael Dugan ... Sgt. Hochbauer
Chief John Big Tree ... Chief Pony That Walks
Fred Graham ... Sgt. Hench
Chief Sky Eagle ... Chief Sky Eagle
Tom Tyler ... Cpl. Mike Quayne, Leader of Paradise River Patrol
Noble Johnson ... Chief Red Shirt
Rudy Bowman ... Pvt. John Smith aka Rome Clay (uncredited)
Lee Bradley ... Interpreter (uncredited)
Paul Fix ... Gun-runner (uncredited)
Francis Ford ... Connelly, Fort Stark Suttlers Barman (uncredited)
Art Gilmore ... Trailer Narrator (voice) (uncredited)
Ray Hyke ... Trooper McCarthy (uncredited)
Billy Jones ... Courier (uncredited)
Fred Kennedy ... Badger (uncredited)
Fred Libby ... Cpl. Krumrein (uncredited)
Cliff Lyons ... Trooper Cliff (uncredited)
Frank McGrath ... Bugler / Indian (uncredited)
Post Park ... Officer (uncredited)
Jack Pennick ... Sergeant Major (uncredited)
Irving Pichel ... Narrator (uncredited)
Mickey Simpson ... Cpl. Wagner (blacksmith) (uncredited)
William Steele ... Officer (uncredited)
Don Summers ... Jenkins (uncredited)
Dan White ... Trooper (uncredited)
Harry Woods ... Licensed Suttler Karl Rynders (uncredited)

Roydon Clark .... stunts (uncredited)
Everett Creach .... stunts (uncredited)
Michael Dugan .... stunts (uncredited)
John Epper .... stunts (uncredited)
Fred Graham .... stunts (uncredited)
Chuck Hayward .... stunts (uncredited)
Bryan 'Slim' Hightower .... stunts (uncredited)
John Hudkins .... stunts (uncredited)
Billy Jones .... stunts (uncredited)
Fred Kennedy .... stunts (uncredited)
Cliff Lyons .... stunts (uncredited)
Frank McGrath .... stunts (uncredited)
Don Nagel .... stunts (uncredited)
Post Park .... stunts (uncredited)
Gil Perkins .... stunts (uncredited)
Bob Rose .... stunts (uncredited)
Norm Taylor .... stunt double: Indian (uncredited)
Jack N. Young .... stunts (uncredited)
Runtime:103 min
Color
Filming Locations: Kanab Movie Fort, Kanab, Utah, USA

Wagon Master (1950) (Argosy Pictures)
Director: John Ford
Writers: Patrick Ford (written by)
Frank S. Nugent (written by)
Release Date:19 April 1950
Cast:
Ben Johnson ... Travis Blue
Joanne Dru ... Denver
Harry Carey Jr. ... Sandy

Ward Bond ... Elder Wiggs
Charles Kemper ... Uncle Shiloh Clegg
Alan Mowbray ... Dr. A. Locksley Hall
Jane Darwell ... Sister Ledeyard
Ruth Clifford ... Fleuretty Phyffe
Russell Simpson ... Adam Perkins
Kathleen O'Malley ... Prudence Perkins
James Arness ... Floyd Clegg
Francis Ford ... Mr. Peachtree
Fred Libby ... Reese Clegg
Jim Thorpe ... Navajo
Mickey Simpson ... Jesse Clegg
Chuck Hayward ... Jackson (uncredited)
Frank McGrath ... Posse member (uncredited)
Chuck Hayward .... stunts (uncredited)
Bryan 'Slim' Hightower .... stunts (uncredited)
Billy Jones .... stunts (uncredited)
Eddie Juaregui .... stunts (uncredited)
Fred Kennedy .... stunts (uncredited)
Cliff Lyons .... stunts (uncredited)
Frank McGrath .... stunts (uncredited)
Post Park .... stunts (uncredited)
Gil Perkins .... stunts (uncredited)
Ray Thomas .... stunts (uncredited)
Runtime:86 min
Black and White
Filming Locations: Colorado River, Moab, Utah, USA

Rio Grande (1950) (Argosy Pictures)
Director: John Ford
Writers: James Warner Bellah (story)
James Kevin McGuinness (screenplay)

Release Date:15 November 1950
Cast:
John Wayne ... Lt. Col. Kirby Yorke
Maureen O'Hara ... Mrs. Kathleen Yorke
Ben Johnson ... Trooper Travis Tyree
Claude Jarman Jr. ... Trooper Jefferson 'Jeff' Yorke
Harry Carey Jr. ... Trooper Daniel 'Sandy' Boone
Chill Wills ... Dr. Wilkins (regimental surgeon)
J. Carrol Naish ... Lt. Gen. Philip Sheridan
Victor McLaglen ... Sgt. Maj. Timothy Quincannon
Grant Withers ... U.S. Deputy Marshal
Peter Ortiz ... Capt. St. Jacques
Steve Pendleton ... Capt. Prescott
Karolyn Grimes ... Margaret Mary
Alberto Morin ... Lieutenant
Stan Jones ... Sergeant
Fred Kennedy ... Trooper Heinze
Sons of the Pioneers ... Regimental Musicians
Ken Curtis ... Donnelly (regimental singer) (uncredited)
Tommy Doss ... Regimental singer (uncredited)
Hugh Farr ... Regimental singer (uncredited)
Karl Farr ... Regimental singer (uncredited)
Shug Fisher ... Regimental singer / Bugler (uncredited)
Cliff Lyons ... Soldier (uncredited)
Lee Morgan ... (uncredited)
Jack Pennick ... Sergeant (uncredited)
Lloyd Perryman ... Regimental singer (uncredited)
Chuck Roberson ... Officer / Indian who fires arrow into Col. York's chest (uncredited)
Barlow Simpson ... Indian chief (uncredited)
Patrick Wayne ... Boy (uncredited)

Jerry Brown .... stunts (uncredited)
Everett Creach .... stunts (uncredited)
Chuck Hayward .... stunts (uncredited)
John Hudkins .... stunts (uncredited)
Fred Kennedy .... stunts (uncredited)
Cliff Lyons .... stunts (uncredited)
Frank McGrath .... stunts (uncredited)
Chuck Roberson .... stunts (uncredited)
Bob Rose .... stunts (uncredited)
Barlow Simpson .... stunts (uncredited)
Norm Taylor .... stunt double (uncredited)
Terry Wilson .... stunts (uncredited)
Jack N. Young .... stunts (uncredited)
Runtime:105 min
Black and White
Filming Locations:Colorado River, Moab, Utah, USA more

Fort Defiance (1951) (Ventura Pictures Corporation)
Director: John Rawlins
Writer: Louis Lantz (writer)
Release Date:9 October 1951
Cast:Dane Clark ... Johnny Tallon
Ben Johnson ... Ben Shelby
Peter Graves ... Ned Tallon
Tracey Roberts ... Julie Morse
George Cleveland ... Uncle Charlie Tallon
Ralph Sanford ... Jed Brown, Stagecoach Driver
Iron Eyes Cody ... Brave Bear (as Iron Eyes)
Dennis Moore ... Lt. Lucas
Craig Woods ... Dave Parker
Dick Elliott ... Kincaid

Bryan 'Slim' Hightower ... Hankey (as Bryan Hightower)
Phil Rawlins ... Les (as David Rawlins)
Jerry Ambler ... Cheyenne
Kit Guard ... Tracy, Barfly
Wes Hudman ... Stranger (as Wesley Hudman)
Runtime:82 min
Color
Filming Locations: Gallup, New Mexico

Wild Stallion (1952) (Monogram Pictures Corporation)
Director:Lewis D. Collins
Writer:Daniel B. Ullman
Release Date:27 April 1952
Cast:
Ben Johnson ... Dan Light
Edgar Buchanan ... John Wintergreen
Martha Hyer ... Caroline Cullen
Hayden Rorke ... Major Cullen
Hugh Beaumont ... Captain Wilmurt
Orley Lindgren ... Young Dan Light
Don Haggerty ... Sgt. Keach
Susan Odin ... Caroline as a Child
I. Stanford Jolley ... Bill Cole
John Halloran ... John Light
Barbara Woodell ... Abigail Light
Don Garner ... (uncredited)
John Hart ... Cavalry Corporal (uncredited)
Perc Launders ... Army Doctor (uncredited)
Elizabeth Russell ... Dan's School Teacher (uncredited)
Runtime:70 min
Color

Shane (1953) (Paramount Pictures)
Director:George Stevens
Writers:Jack Schaefer (novel)
A.B. Guthrie Jr. (screenplay)
Release Date:24 September 1953
Cast:
Alan Ladd ... Shane
Jean Arthur ... Marian Starrett
Van Heflin ... Joe Starrett
Brandon De Wilde ... Joey Starrett
Jack Palance ... Jack Wilson (as Walter Jack Palance)
Ben Johnson ... Chris Calloway
Edgar Buchanan ... Fred Lewis
Emile Meyer ... Rufus Ryker
Elisha Cook Jr. ... Frank 'Stonewall' Torrey
Douglas Spencer ... Axel 'Swede' Shipstead
John Dierkes ... Morgan Ryker
Ellen Corby ... Mrs. Liz Torrey
Paul McVey ... Sam Grafton
John Miller ... Will Atkey, bartender
Edith Evanson ... Mrs. Shipstead
Runtime:118 min
Color
Filming Locations: Big Bear Lake, California

Oklahoma! (1955) (:Magna Theatre Corporation)
Director: Fred Zinnemann
Writers: Lynn Riggs (play)
Oscar Hammerstein II (play)
Release Date:9 January 1956
Cast:
Gordon MacRae ... Curly McLain

Gloria Grahame ... Ado Annie Carnes
Gene Nelson ... Will Parker
Charlotte Greenwood ... Aunt Eller Murphy
Shirley Jones ... Laurey Williams
Eddie Albert ... Ali Hakim
James Whitmore ... Andrew Carnes
Rod Steiger ... Jud Fry
Barbara Lawrence ... Gertie Cummings
Jay C. Flippen ... Ike Skidmore
Roy Barcroft ... Marshal Cord Elam
James Mitchell ... Dream Curly
Bambi Linn ... Dream Laurey
Jennie Workman ... Dancer
Virginia Bosler ... Dancer
Jerry Dealey ... Dancer (uncredited)
Al Ferguson ... Cowboy at auction (uncredited)
Ben Johnson ... Wrangler (uncredited)
Donald Kerr ... Farmer at dance (uncredited)
Nancy Kilgas ... Dancer (uncredited)
Rory Mallinson ... Young cowboy at box lunch auction (uncredited)
Buddy Roosevelt ... Cowboy at Auction (uncredited)
Russell Simpson ... The minister (uncredited)
Ben Johnson .... stunt double (uncredited)
Runtime:145 min
Color
Filming Locations: Amado, Arizona

Rebel in Town (1956) (Schenck-Koch Productions)
Director: Alfred L. Werker
Writer: Danny Arnold (writer)
Release Date:30 July 1956

Cast:
John Payne ... John Willoughby
Ruth Roman ... Nora Willoughby
J. Carrol Naish ... Bedloe Mason
Ben Cooper ... Gray Mason
John Smith ... Wesley Mason
James Griffith ... Marshal Adam Russell
Mary Adams ... Grandmaw Ackstadt
Bobby Clark ... Peter Willoughby
Mimi Gibson ... Lisbeth Ackstadt
Sterling Franck ... Cain Mason
Joel Ashley ... Doctor
Ben Johnson ... Frank Mason
Runtime:USA:78 min
Color:Black and White
Filming Locations: Jack Ingram Ranch, Woodland Hills, California

"Cavalcade of America" Once a Hero (1956)
Director: Lee Sholem
Writers: John Dunkel (teleplay)
Jack Schaefer (original story)
TV Series:"Cavalcade of America" (1952)
Original Air Date:11 December 1956 (Season 5, Episode 12)
Cast:
Ward Bond ... Harvey Kendall
Ben Johnson ... Cal Bennett
Richard Eyer ... Timmy Kendall
Sarah Selby ... Susan Kendall
Michael Winkelman ... Mike
Christopher Olsen ... Randy (as Chris Olsen)
Robert Eyer ... Sam

David McMahon ... Dolph
Dan White ... Stan
Ralph Peters ... Man
Pamela Jayson ... Clara
Bob Burrows ... Cowboy (as Robert Burrows)
Bob Folkerson ... Cowboy (as Robert Folkerson)

War Drums (1957) (Schenck-Koch Productions)
Director: Reginald Le Borg
Writer: Gerald Drayson Adams (writer)
Release Date:21 March 1957 (USA) more
Cast (Credited cast)
Lex Barker ... Mangas Coloradas
Joan Taylor ... Riva
Ben Johnson ... Luke Fargo
Larry Chance ... Ponce
Richard H. Cutting ... Bolton (as Richard Cutting)
John Pickard ... Sheriff Bullard
James Parnell ... Arizona
John Colicos ... Chino
Tom Monroe ... Dutch Herman
Jil Jarmyn ... Nona
Jeanne Carmen ... Yellow Moon
Mauritz Hugo ... Clay Staub
Ward Ellis ... Delgadito
Runtime:75 min
Color
Filming Locations: Johnson Canyon, Kanab, Utah, USA

Slim Carter (1957) (Universal International Pictures)
Director: Richard Bartlett
Writers: David Bramson (story)

Mary C. McCall Jr. (story)
Cast:
Jock Mahoney ... Slim Carter / Hughie Mack
Julie Adams ... Clover Doyle
Tim Hovey ... Leo Gallaher
William Hopper ... Joe Brewster
Ben Johnson ... Montana Burriss
Joanna Moore ... Charlene Carroll
Walter Reed ... Richard L. Howard
Margaret Field ... Hat Check Girl
Roxanne Arlen ... Cigarette girl
Jim Healy ... M.C.
Bill Williams ... Frank Hanneman
Barbara Hale ... Allie Hanneman
Runtime:82 min
Color

Fort Bowie (1958) (Aubrey Schenck Productions)
Director: Howard W. Koch
Writer: Maurice Tombragel (screenplay)
Release Date:1 February 1958
Cast:
Ben Johnson ... Capt. Thomas Thompson
Jan Harrison ... Alison Garrett
Kent Taylor ... Col. James Garrett
Maureen Hingert ... Chanzana (as Jana Davi)
Peter Mamakos ... Sgt Kukas
Larry Chance ... Victorio
J. Ian Douglas ... Maj. Wharton
Jerry Frank ... Capt. Maywood
Barbara Parry ... Mrs. Maywood
Runtime:80 min

Black and White
Filming Locations: Kanab Movie Fort, Kanab, Utah, USA

"The Adventures of Ozzie & Harriet" Top Gun (1958)
(Stage Five Productions)
Director: Ozzie Nelson
Writers: Dick Bensfield (screenplay)
Perry Grant (screenplay)
Original Air Date:2 April 1958 (Season 6, Episode 26)
Cast:
Ozzie Nelson ... Ozzie Nelson
Harriet Hilliard ... Harriet Nelson
David Nelson ... David Nelson
Ricky Nelson ... Ricky Nelson
Frank Cady ... Dr. Williams
Gordon Jones ... Butch
Ben Johnson ... Tex Barton
John Doucette ... Laramie Kid
Anthony C. Montenaro ... Tony (as Tony Montenaro Jr.)
Stu Wilson ... Manager
Bill McLean ... Bartender (as William McLean)
Frank Richards ... Winslow
Stanley Livingston ... Small Boy
Callen John Thomas Jr. ... Small Boy (as Callen Thomas Jr.)
Paul Cotton ... Small Boy
Runtime:30 min
Black and White

"Navy Log" Florida Weekend (1958)
Director: Samuel Gallu
Original Air Date:21 August 1958 (Season 3, Episode 28)

Cast:
Richard Webb ... Kenwood Hollister
Robert Rockwell ... Sandy Bridges
Ben Johnson ... Border Patrol Officer
Abel Fernandez ... Indian
Ralph Smiley ... Indian Chief
Robert Carson ... Narrator (voice)

"The Restless Gun" No Way to Kill (1958)
Director: Edward Ludwig
Writers: Frank Burt (character)
John Falvo (writer)
Original Air Date:24 November 1958 (Season 2, Episode 9)
Cast:
John Payne ... Vint Bonner
Ben Johnson ... Sheriff Tim Malachy
Jeanne Bates ... Mary Jepson
Don Grady ... Donny Madison
Ronald Sorensen ... Kyle Jepson
Henry Corden ... Will Gerrard
Guy Kingsford ... Nat Madison
Don Kennedy ... Wade Calley
Austin Green ... Doc Seton

"Alfred Hitchcock Presents" And the Desert Shall Blossom (1958)
Director: Arthur Hiller
Writers: Loren Good (story)
Bernard C. Schoenfeld (teleplay)
TV Series:"Alfred Hitchcock Presents" (1955)
Original Air Date:21 December 1958 (Season 4, Episode 11)
Cast:

Alfred Hitchcock ... Himself - Host
Roscoe Ates ... Ben White
William Demarest ... Tom Akins
Ben Johnson ... Sheriff
Mike Kellin ... Fugitive Thug
Wesley Lau ... Deputy
Runtime:30 min
Black and White
Filming Locations: CBS Studio Center - Studio City, California, USA

"Border Patrol" Everglades Story (1959)
Director: Samuel Gallu
Writer: Allan Sloane (writer)
Original Air Date:10 March 1959 (Season 1, Episode 1)
Cast:
Richard Webb ... Deputy Chief Don Jagger
Ben Johnson ... Hank Colman
Victor Millan ... Johnny Wildcat
Rico Alaniz ... Vargas
Robert Cabal ... Julio
Pepe Hern ... Algusto Herrera
Ralph Smiley ... Seminole Chief
Joseph Sargent ... Pilot
Jim Hayward ... Crocker
Skip Killmond ... Beach Boy
K.L. Smith ... Game Warden Kurt Elkins

"Laramie" Hour After Dawn (1960)
Original Air Date:15 March 1960 (Season 1, Episode 25)
Cast:
John Smith ... Slim Sherman

Robert Fuller ... Jess Harper
Irving Bacon
Anne Barton
Bruce Bennett
Ben Johnson
Robert Osterloh
Gloria Talbott

"Have Gun - Will Travel" A Head of Hair (1960)
Director: Andrew V. McLaglen
Writers: Harry Julian Fink (writer)
Herb Meadow (creator)
Original Air Date:24 September 1960 (Season 4, Episode 3)
Cast:
Richard Boone ... Paladin
Ben Johnson ... John Anderson
Lisa Lu ... Hey Girl
Trevor Bardette ... Chagra
George Kennedy ... Lt. Bryson
Chuck Hayward ... Cheyup
Donna Brooks ... Mary
Olan Soule ... Manager
Filming Locations: Paramount Studios, Los Angeles, California

Ten Who Dared (1960) (Walt Disney Productions)
Director: William Beaudine
Writers: John Wesley Powell (journal)
Lawrence Edward Watkin (writer)
Release Date:1 November 1960
Cast:
Brian Keith ... William 'Bill' Dunn

John Beal ... Maj. John Wesley Powell
James Drury ... Walter Powell
R.G. Armstrong ... Oramel Howland
Ben Johnson ... George Bradley
L.Q. Jones ... Billy 'Missouri' Hawkins
Dan Sheridan ... Jack Sumner
David Stollery ... Andrew 'Andy' Hall
Stan Jones ... Seneca Howland
David Frankham ... Frank Goodman
Roy Barcroft ... Jim Baker (uncredited)
Jack Big Head ... Ashtishkel (uncredited)
Pat Hogan ... Indian chief (uncredited)
Dawn Little Sky ... Indian woman (uncredited)
Ray Walker ... McSpadden (uncredited)
Runtime:92 min
Color
Filming Locations:Dead Horse Point State Park - Moab, Utah

"Laramie" A Sound of Bells (1960)
Original Air Date:27 December 1960 (Season 2, Episode 13)
Cast:
John Smith ... Slim Sherman
Robert Fuller ... Jess Harper
Rachel Ames
Mara Corday ... Rose
Dick Foran ... Tom
Kim Hector ... Neil Hunter
Ben Johnson ... Driver
Ross Martin ... Angel
Robert J. Wilke

One-Eyed Jacks (1961) (Pennebaker Productions)
Director:Marlon Brando
Writers:Charles Neider (novel)
Guy Trosper (writer)
Release Date:30 March 1961
Cast:
Marlon Brando ... Rio
Karl Malden ... Sheriff Dad Longworth
Katy Jurado ... Maria Longworth
Pina Pellicer ... Louisa
Ben Johnson ... Bob Amory
Slim Pickens ... Deputy Lon Dedrick
Larry Duran ... Chico Modesto
Sam Gilman ... Harvey Johnson
Timothy Carey ... Howard Tetley
Miriam Colon ... Redhead
Elisha Cook Jr. ... Carvey (as Elisha Cook)
Rodolfo Acosta ... Mexican rurale captain (as Rudolph Acosta)
Joan Petrone ... Flower girl
Tom Webb ... Farmer's son
Ray Teal ... Barney
Nesdon Booth ... Townsman (uncredited)
Sheryl Deauville ... Marina (uncredited)
Joe Dominguez ... Corral keeper (uncredited)
Mickey Finn ... Blacksmith (uncredited)
Nacho Galindo ... Mexican townsman (uncredited)
Augie Gomez ... Townsman (uncredited)
Al Haskell ... Townsman (uncredited)
Fenton Jones ... Square-dance caller (uncredited)
Margarita Martín ... Mexican vendor (uncredited)
Jorge Moreno ... Bouncer in shack (uncredited)

'Snub' Pollard ... Townsman (uncredited)
John Michael Quijada ... Mexican rurale sergeant (uncredited)
Francy Scott ... Cantina girl (uncredited)
Shichizo Takeda ... Owner of cantina at beach (uncredited)
Felipe Turich ... Card sharp (uncredited)
Henry Wills ... Ephraim, Stableman (uncredited)
Runtime:141 min
Color
Filming Locations:Big Sur, California

Tomboy and the Champ (1961) (Signal Productions)
Director:Francis D. Lyon
Writers:Virginia M. Cooke (writer)
William Lightfoot (story)
Release Date:1 April 1961
Cast:
Candy Moore ... Tommy Jo
Ben Johnson ... Uncle Jim
Jesse White ... Windy Skiles
Jess Kirkpatrick ... Model T. Parson
Christine Smith ... Aunt Sarah
Paul Bernath ... Jaspar Stockton
Norman Sherry ... Fowler Stockton
Johnny Carpenter ... Fred Anderson (as John Carpenter)
Wally Phillips ... Hi Fi Club Announcer
Ralph Fischer ... 4-H Club President
Larry Hickie ... Curly Cone
Rex Allen ... Rex Allen
Casey Tibbs ... Casey Tibbs

Jerry Naill ... Jerry Naill
Runtime:92 min
Color
Filming Locations:Chicago, Illinois

"Laramie" Widow in White (1961)
Original Air Date:13 June 1961 (Season 2, Episode 33)
Cast:
John Smith ... Slim Sherman
Robert Fuller ... Jess Harper
Rayford Barnes ... Birch
Richard Coogan ... Sheriff
Ross Elliott ... Collins
Sue England ... Sheila Dawson
Ben Johnson ... Tarp
George Keymas ... Stover
Ed Prentiss ... Bailey

"Have Gun - Will Travel" The Race (1961)
Writers:Herb Meadow (creator)
Sam Rolfe (creator)
Original Air Date:28 October 1961 (Season 5, Episode 7)
Cast:
Richard Boone - Paladin
Ben Johnson ... Sam Crabbe
Michael Pate ... Tamasun
Stewart East
Filming Locations - Paramount Studios, Los Angeles, California

"Route 66" A Long Piece of Mischief (1962)
Director: David Lowell Rich
Writer: Stirling Silliphant (writer)

Original Air Date:19 January 1962 (Season 2, Episode 15)
Cast:
Sonny Dewberry ... Cowboy
Neal Gay ... Rodeo Boss
Carelgean Gilley ... Cowgirl
Ben Johnson ... Del
Ray Lackland ... Announcer
George Maharis ... Buz Murdock
Martin Milner ... Tod Stiles
Slim Pickens ... Jud
Denver Pyle ... Wylie
Albert Salmi ... Ollie Crump
Audrey Totter ... Babe Hunter
Filming Locations: Mesquite, Texas

"Bonanza" The Gamble (1962)
Director: William Witney
Writers: Frank Cleaver; David Dortort (creator)
Original Air Date:1 April 1962 (Season 3, Episode 27)
Cast:
Lorne Greene ... Ben Cartwright
Pernell Roberts ... Adam Cartwright
Dan Blocker ... Eric 'Hoss' Cartwright
Michael Landon ... Joseph 'Little Joe' Cartwright
Morris Ankrum ... Mr. Mason
Robert Foulk ... Clem, Deputy Sheriff
Raymond Greenleaf ... Judge Jackson
Jan Harrison ... Joyce
Ben Johnson ... Deputy Sheriff Stan Mace
I. Stanford Jolley ... Harry
Charles McGraw ... Sheriff Gains
Robert Sampson ... Artie Clay

363

Joseph Walsh ... Billy Tyler (as Joey Walsh)

"Have Gun - Will Travel" The Fifth Bullet (1962)
Director: Andrew V. McLaglen
Writers: Herb Meadow (creator)
Sam Rolfe (creator)
Original Air Date:29 September 1962 (Season 6, Episode 3)
Cast:
Richard Boone ... Paladin
Peter Boone ... Johnny Bartlett
Dorothy Dells ... Emmy Bartlett
Shug Fisher
Ben Johnson ... John Bartlett

"Stoney Burke" Point of Honor (1962)
Director :Leslie Stevens
Writer: Leslie Stevens (writer)
Original Air Date:22 October 1962 (Season 1, Episode 4)
Cast:
Patricia Breslin ... Lee Anne Hewitt
Lew Brown ... Trooper
Ben Johnson ... Rex Donally
Jack Lord ... Stoney Burke
Scott Marlowe ... Soames Hewitt
Bill Mullikin ... Leroy Sutter
Harry Dean Stanton ... Dell Tindall (as Dean Stanton)
Casey Tibbs ... Rodeo Judge
Ian Wolfe ... Judge Hewitt

"The Virginian" Duel at Shiloh (1963)
Director: Jerry Hopper

Writers :D.D. Beauchamp (teleplay)
Borden Chase (teleplay)
Original Air Date:2 January 1963 (Season 1, Episode 15)
Cast:
Lee J. Cobb ... Judge Henry Garth
Geraldine Brooks ... Georgia Price
Lew Brown ... Dowdy
Gary Clarke ... Steve Hill
Perry Cook ... Cook
John Daheim ... Brakeman (as John Day)
James Drury ... The Virginian
Roy Engel ... Loomis
Richard Garland ... Texan
Ben Johnson ... Spinner
Brian Keith ... Johnny Wade
DeForest Kelley ... Ben Tully
Mort Mills ... Deputy Bender
Roberta Shore ... Betsy Garth
Russell Thorson ... Sheriff Tybee
Pippa Scott ... Molly Wood
Randy Boone ... Randy Benton
Jan Stine ... Eddie

"Gunsmoke" Quint-Cident (1963)
Director: Andrew V. McLaglen
Writer: Kathleen Hite (writer)
Original Air Date:27 April 1963 (Season 8, Episode 33)
Cast:
James Arness ... Marshal Matt Dillon
Milburn Stone ... Dr. Galen 'Doc' Adams
Amanda Blake ... Kitty Russell
Burt Reynolds ... Quint Asper

Mary LaRoche ... Willa Devlin (as Mary La Roche)
Ben Johnson ... Ben Crown
Don Keefer ... Nally
Catherine McLeod ... Lizzie
Ollie O'Toole ... Telegrapher
Dabbs Greer ... Wilbur Jonas
Hank Patterson ... Hank Miller
Roy Roberts ... Harry Bodkin

Cheyenne Autumn (1964) (Warner Brothers Pictures)
Director: John Ford
Writers: Mari Sandoz (novel)
James R. Webb (screenplay)
Release Date:3 October 1964
Cast:
Richard Widmark ... Capt. Thomas Archer
Carroll Baker ... Deborah Wright
Karl Malden ... Capt. Wessels
Sal Mineo ... Red Shirt
Dolores del Rio ... Spanish Woman (as Dolores Del Rio)
Ricardo Montalban ... Little Wolf
Gilbert Roland ... Dull Knife
Arthur Kennedy ... Doc Holliday
Patrick Wayne ... Second Lieut. Scott
Elizabeth Allen ... Miss Plantagenet
John Carradine ... Jeff Blair
Victor Jory ... Tall Tree
Mike Mazurki ... Sr. First Sergeant
George O'Brien ... Major Braden
Sean McClory ... Dr. O'Carberry

Walter Baldwin ... Jeremy Wright (Deborah's uncle) (uncredited)
Danny Borzage ... Trooper (uncredited)
Willis Bouchey ... Colonel at Victory Cave (uncredited)
Lee Bradley ... Cheyenne (uncredited)
Harry Carey Jr. ... Trooper Smith (uncredited)
Dan Carr ... Trooper (uncredited)
Jeannie Epper ... Entertainer (uncredited)
Stephanie Epper ... Entertainer (uncredited)
Shug Fisher ... Skinny (Texas cattle drover) (uncredited)
James Flavin ... Ft. Robinson sergeant of the guard (uncredited)
William Forrest ... Senator (uncredited)
Donna Hall ... Entertainer (uncredited)
Sam Harris ... Dodge City townsman (uncredited)
Chuck Hayward ... Trooper (uncredited)
William Henry ... Infantry captain (uncredited)
Harry Hickox ... Bartender (uncredited)
Harry Holcombe ... Senator (uncredited)
Nancy Hsueh ... Little Bird (uncredited)
Ben Johnson ... Trooper Plumtree (uncredited)
Steven Manymules ... Point man (uncredited)
Ted Mapes ... Trooper (uncredited)
Mae Marsh ... Woman (uncredited)
Philo McCullough ... Man (uncredited)
John McKee ... Trooper (uncredited)
David Miller ... Trooper (uncredited)
Louise Montana ... Woman (uncredited)
Nanomba 'Moonbeam' Morton ... Running Deer (uncredited)
Many Muleson ... Medicine Man (uncredited)

James O'Hara ... Trooper (uncredited)
Denver Pyle ... Sen. Henry (uncredited)
Walter Reed ... Lt. Peterson (Ft. Robinson) (uncredited)
Chuck Roberson ... Jessie (Texas trail boss) (uncredited)
Bing Russell ... Braden's Telegraph Operator (uncredited)
Charles Seel ... Newspaper publisher (uncredited)
Mary Statler ... Entertainer (uncredited)
Carleton Young ... Aide to Carl Schurz (uncredited)
Runtime:154 min
Color
Filming Locations:Arches National Park, Moab, Utah

"Perry Mason" The Case of the Reckless Rockhound (1964)
Original Air Date:26 November 1964 (Season 8, Episode 10)
Cast:
Raymond Burr ... Perry Mason
Barbara Hale ... Della Street
William Hopper ... Paul Drake
Roy Barcroft ... Murphy
Bruce Bennett ... Malone
Donald Buka ... Clark
Elisha Cook Jr. ... Reelin' Pete (as Elisha Cook)
Jeff Corey ... Carl Bascom
Ted de Corsia ... Polek
Robert C. Gormley ... Guard
Ben Johnson ... Kelly
Douglas Lambert ... Kinder
Ralph Moody ... Jenkins
Nick Nicholson ... Police Sergeant

Lenore Shanewise ... Mrs. Munger
Harry Stanton ... Judge
Audrey Totter ... Reba Burgess
Filming Locations: Bronson Canyon, Los Angeles, California

Major Dundee (1965) (Columbia Pictures Corporation)
Director: Sam Peckinpah
Writers: Harry Julian Fink (story)
Harry Julian Fink (screenplay) ...
Release Date:15 March 1965
Cast:
Charlton Heston ... Major Amos Charles Dundee
Richard Harris ... Captain Benjamin Tyreen
Jim Hutton ... Lieutenant Graham
James Coburn ... Samuel Potts
Michael Anderson Jr. ... Trooper Tim Ryan
Senta Berger ... Teresa Santiago
Mario Adorf ... Sergeant Gomez
Brock Peters ... Aesop
Warren Oates ... O.W. Hadley
Ben Johnson ... Sergeant Chillum
R.G. Armstrong ... Reverend Dahlstrom
L.Q. Jones ... Arthur Hadley
Slim Pickens ... Wiley
Karl Swenson ... Captain Waller
Michael Pate ... Sierra Charriba
Whitey Hughes ... Confederate trooper (uncredited)
Cliff Lyons ... (uncredited)
Jody McCrea ... Lt. Brannin (uncredited)
Dennis Patrick ... (uncredited)
Rockne Tarkington ... Jefferson (uncredited)

Runtime:123 min | 136 min (2005 restored version)
Color
Filming Locations:Chilpancingo, Guerrero, Mexico

"The Virginian" Dangerous Road (1965)
Director: Maurice Geraghty
Writers: John Hawkins and Ward Hawkins
Original Air Date:17 March 1965 (Season 3, Episode 26)
Cast:
True Boardman ... Dr. Hennesy
Lew Brown ... Kelly Jones
Frank Gerstle ... Clint Koski
Gilbert Green ... Judge Porter
Ben Johnson ... Jim Brandt
Jimmy Joyce ... Clerk
Simon Oakland ... Bob Coulter
Robert Pine ... Young Bob Coulter
Tom Reese ... Hans Wollsack
Tom Simcox ... Deputy Fenton
Robin Watts ... Waitress
Will J. White ... Dr. Blackburn
Bobby Clark .... stunts
George Orrison .... stunts
Dean Smith .... stunts

"Bob Hope Presents the Chrysler Theatre" March from Camp Tyler (1965)
Original Air Date:6 October 1965 (Season 3, Episode 3)
Cast:
Broderick Crawford ... Colonel Harper
Ben Johnson ... Burt Wade
Leroy Johnson ... Two Birds (as LeRoy Johnson)

Peter Lawford ... Lieutenant Philip Cannon
Bethel Leslie ... Clarissa
Charles McGraw ... Sergeant Goss
James Murdock ... Corporal Milton
David Renard ... Miranda
Dan Tobin ... Porteus

"Branded" McCord's Way (1966)
Director: William Witney
Writers: Borden Chase (writer)
Larry Cohen (creator)
Original Air Date:30 January 1966 (Season 2, Episode 20)
Cast:
Chuck Connors ... Jason McCord
Mona Freeman ... Dora Kendall
Tom Reese ... Jess Muhler
Willard Sage ... Wes Trent
Ben Johnson ... Bill Latigo
James Beck ... Bill Tomlin (as Jim Beck)
Robert Swan ... Bud Lee
Henry Capps ... Joe Latigo
Rocky Young ... Tommy Kendall
Craig Hundley ... Rob (as Chris Hundley)

The Rare Breed (1966) (Universal Pictures)
Director: Andrew V. McLaglen
Writer: Ric Hardman (written by)
Release Date:25 February 1966
Cast:
James Stewart ... Sam Burnett
Maureen O'Hara ... Martha Price
Brian Keith ... Alexander Bowen

Juliet Mills ... Hilary Price
Don Galloway ... Jamie Bowen
David Brian ... Charles Ellsworth
Jack Elam ... Deke Simons
Ben Johnson ... Jeff Harter
Harry Carey Jr. ... Ed Mabry
Perry Lopez ... Juan
Larry Domasin ... Alberto
Silvia Marino ... Conchita
Alan Caillou ... John Taylor
Gregg Palmer ... Rodenbush
Barbara Werle ... Gert
R.L. Armstrong ... Barker (uncredited)
Holly Bane ... Barker (uncredited)
Larry J. Blake ... Auctioneer (uncredited)
Joan Connors ... Cowgirl (uncredited)
Harry Fleer ... Barler (uncredited)
Bob Gravage ... Cattle Buyer (uncredited)
Frank Hagney ... Cattle Buyer (uncredited)
Chuck Hayward ... Wrangler (uncredited)
Irene Kelly ... Cowgirl (uncredited)
Charles Lampkin ... Porter (uncredited)
Ted Mapes ... Liveryman (uncredited)
John McKee ... Cattle Buyer (uncredited)
James Nusser ... Kelly - Bum at Dodge Train Depot (uncredited)
Frank J. Scannell ... Barker (uncredited)
Hal Needham .... action coordinator
Buff Brady .... stunts (uncredited)
Steven Burnett .... stunts (uncredited)
Fred Carson .... stunts (uncredited)
Roydon Clark .... stunts (uncredited)

Patty Elder .... stunts (uncredited)
Stephanie Epper .... stunts (uncredited)
John Harris .... stunts (uncredited)
Bob Herron .... stunts (uncredited)
Leroy Johnson .... stunts (uncredited)
Sharon Lucas .... stunts (uncredited)
Ted Mapes .... stunts (uncredited)
Buddy Van Horn .... stunt double (uncredited)
Buddy Van Horn .... stunts (uncredited)
Runtime:97 min
Color
Filming Locations:California

"ABC Stage 67" Noon Wine (1966)
Director: Sam Peckinpah
Writers: Sam Peckinpah (teleplay)
Katherine Anne Porter (story)
Original Air Date:23 November 1966 (Season 1, Episode 9)
Cast:
Jill Andre ... Pearl
Theodore Bikel ... Homer T. Hatch
Olivia de Havilland ... Ellie Thompson
Robert Emhardt ... Burleigh
Ben Johnson ... Sheriff Barbee
L.Q. Jones ... Deputy
Per Oscarsson ... Olaf Helton
Jason Robards ... Royal Earle Thompson
Peter Robbins ... Herbert
Steve Sanders ... Arthur
Joan Tompkins ... Meg

"The Monroes" The Intruders (1966)
Director: Bernard L. Kowalski
Writer: Otis Carney (writer)
Original Air Date:7 September 1966 (Season 1, Episode 1)
Cast:
Michael Anderson Jr. ... Clayt Monroe
Barbara Hershey ... Kathy Monroe
Keith Schultz ... Jefferson Monroe
Kevin Schultz ... Fennimore Monroe
Tammy Locke ... Amy Monroe
Liam Sullivan ... Major Mapoy
Ron Soble ... Dirty Jim
Ben Johnson ... Sleeve
Russ Conway ... Albert Monroe
John Doucette ... Buttermore
Rance Howard
James Murdock
Marilyn Stader
May Boss .... stunts
Joe Canutt .... stunts
Jack Williams .... stunts

"The Monroes" Night of the Wolf (1966)
Director: James B. Clark
Original Air Date:14 September 1966 (Season 1, Episode 2)
Cast:
Michael Anderson Jr. ... Clayt Monroe
Barbara Hershey ... Kathy Monroe
Keith Schultz ... Jefferson Monroe
Kevin Schultz ... Fennimore Monroe
Tammy Locke ... Amy Monroe

Liam Sullivan ... Major Mapoy
Ron Soble ... Dirty Jim
Ben Johnson ... Sleeve
Richard Bakalyan ... Grac
James Gammon ... Stennis
May Boss .... stunts
Joe Canutt .... stunts
Jack Williams .... stunts

"The Monroes" Ride with Terror (1966)
Director: Earl Bellamy
Writer: Penrod Smith (writer)
Original Air Date:21 September 1966 (Season 1, Episode 3)
Cast:
Michael Anderson Jr. ... Clayt Monroe
Barbara Hershey ... Kathy Monroe
Keith Schultz ... Jefferson Monroe
Kevin Schultz ... Fennimore Monroe
Tammy Locke ... Amy Monroe
Liam Sullivan ... Major Mapoy
Ron Soble ... Dirty Jim
Ben Johnson ... Sleeve
Claude Akins ... Bud Chapel
Holly Bane ... Luke (as Michael Ragan)
Joe Canutt
Tap Canutt
Jeanne Cooper ... Mae Duvall
Peter Leeds
James Stacy ... Perry Hutchins
May Boss .... stunts
Joe Canutt .... stunts

Jack Williams .... stunts
May Boss .... stunts
Joe Canutt .... stunts
Jack Williams .... stunts

"The Monroes" The Forest Devil (1966)
Director: James B. Clark
Original Air Date:28 September 1966 (Season 1, Episode 4)
Cast:
Michael Anderson Jr. ... Clayt Monroe
Barbara Hershey ... Kathy Monroe
Keith Schultz ... Jefferson Monroe
Kevin Schultz ... Fennimore Monroe
Tammy Locke ... Amy Monroe
Liam Sullivan ... Major Mapoy
Ron Soble ... Dirty Jim
Ben Johnson ... Sleeve
Ralph Moody ... Shaman
Warren Oates ... Nick Beresford
May Boss .... stunts
Joe Canutt .... stunts
Jack Williams .... stunts
May Boss .... stunts
Joe Canutt .... stunts
Jack Williams .... stunts

"The Monroes" Wild Dog of the Tetons (1966)
Director: James B. Clark
Original Air Date:5 October 1966 (Season 1, Episode 5)
Cast:
Michael Anderson Jr. ... Clayt Monroe

Barbara Hershey ... Kathy Monroe
Keith Schultz ... Jefferson Monroe
Kevin Schultz ... Fennimore Monroe
Tammy Locke ... Amy Monroe
Liam Sullivan ... Major Mapoy
Ron Soble ... Dirty Jim
Ben Johnson ... Sleeve
James Westmoreland ... Ruel Jaxon (as Jim Westmoreland)
Robert Middleton ... Barney Wales
Buck Taylor ... John "Brad" Bradford
Albert Salmi ... Hasner
May Boss .... stunts
Joe Canutt .... stunts
Jack Williams .... stunts

"The Monroes" Incident at Hanging Tree (1966)
Director: Larry Peerce
Writer: Halsted Welles (writer)
Original Air Date:12 October 1966 (Season 1, Episode 6)
Cast:
Michael Anderson Jr. ... Clayt Monroe
Barbara Hershey ... Kathy Monroe
Keith Schultz ... Jefferson Monroe
Kevin Schultz ... Fennimore Monroe
Tammy Locke ... Amy Monroe
Liam Sullivan ... Major Mapoy
Ron Soble ... Dirty Jim
Ben Johnson ... Sleeve
James Brolin
Lisa Jak
Tim O'Kelly
May Boss .... stunts

Joe Canutt .... stunts
Jack Williams .... stunts

"The Monroes" Ordeal by Hope (1966)
Director: James B. Clark
Original Air Date:19 October 1966 (Season 1, Episode 7)
Cast:
Michael Anderson Jr. ... Clayt Monroe
Barbara Hershey ... Kathy Monroe
Keith Schultz ... Jefferson Monroe
Kevin Schultz ... Fennimore Monroe
Tammy Locke ... Amy Monroe
Liam Sullivan ... Major Mapoy
Ron Soble ... Dirty Jim
Ben Johnson ... Sleeve
James Westmoreland ... Ruel Jaxon (as Jim Westmoreland)
Robert Middleton ... Barney Wales
Buck Taylor ... John "Brad" Bradford
Rico Alaniz
John Bryant ... Doctor
Edward Faulkner ... Ferris
Jack Williams ... Corporal
May Boss .... stunts
Joe Canutt .... stunts
Jack Williams .... stunts

"The Monroes" The Hunter (1966)
Director: Tom Gries
Original Air Date:26 October 1966 (Season 1, Episode 8)
Cast:
Michael Anderson Jr. ... Clayt Monroe
Barbara Hershey ... Kathy Monroe

Keith Schultz ... Jefferson Monroe
Kevin Schultz ... Fennimore Monroe
Tammy Locke ... Amy Monroe
Liam Sullivan ... Major Mapoy
Ron Soble ... Dirty Jim
Ben Johnson ... Sleeve
Rex Holman
Roy Jenson ... Vorhees
Bing Russell
Bee Tompkins
James Whitmore ... Blackmer
May Boss .... stunts
Joe Canutt .... stunts
Jack Williams .... stunts

"The Monroes" War Arrow (1966)
Original Air Date:2 November 1966 (Season 1, Episode 9)
Cast:
Michael Anderson Jr. ... Clayt Monroe
Barbara Hershey ... Kathy Monroe
Keith Schultz ... Jefferson Monroe
Kevin Schultz ... Fennimore Monroe
Tammy Locke ... Amy Monroe
Liam Sullivan ... Major Mapoy
Ron Soble ... Dirty Jim
Ben Johnson ... Sleeve
James Almanzar
Steve Gravers ... Hadley
Anna Navarro ... Wahkonda
Dub Taylor ... Cyrus
Morgan Woodward ... Crocker
May Boss .... stunts
Joe Canutt .... stunts
Jack Williams .... stunts

"The Monroes" The Friendly Enemy (1966)
Director: James B. Clark
Original Air Date:9 November 1966 (Season 1, Episode 10)
Cast:
Michael Anderson Jr. ... Clayt Monroe
Barbara Hershey ... Kathy Monroe
Keith Schultz ... Jefferson Monroe
Kevin Schultz ... Fennimore Monroe
Tammy Locke ... Amy Monroe
Liam Sullivan ... Major Mapoy
Ron Soble ... Dirty Jim
Ben Johnson ... Sleeve
Harry Townes ... Joe Smith
May Boss .... stunts
Joe Canutt .... stunts
Jack Williams .... stunts

"The Monroes" Court Martial (1966)
Director: Robert L. Friend
Original Air Date:16 November 1966 (Season 1, Episode 11)
Cast:
Michael Anderson Jr. ... Clayt Monroe
Barbara Hershey ... Kathy Monroe
Keith Schultz ... Jefferson Monroe
Kevin Schultz ... Fennimore Monroe
Tammy Locke ... Amy Monroe
Liam Sullivan ... Major Mapoy
Ron Soble ... Dirty Jim
Ben Johnson ... Sleeve
James Westmoreland ... Ruel Jaxon (as Jim Westmoreland)
Robert Middleton ... Barney Wales
Buck Taylor ... John "Brad" Bradford
William Bryant

Burt Douglas
Robert Fuller ... Captain Geoffrey Stone
James Griffith ... Henri 'Fox' Bonnard (as James G. Griffith)
Warren J. Kemmerling ... Colonel Malcomm (as Warren Kemmerling)
John McLiam ... Sergeant Duncan McMurdoch
May Boss .... stunts
Joe Canutt .... stunts
Jack Williams .... stunts

"The Monroes" Silent Night, Deadly Night (1966)
Director: Norman Foster
Writer: Kathleen Hite (writer)
Original Air Date:23 November 1966 (Season 1, Episode 12)
Cast:
Michael Anderson Jr. ... Clayt Monroe
Barbara Hershey ... Kathy Monroe
Keith Schultz ... Jefferson Monroe
Kevin Schultz ... Fennimore Monroe
Tammy Locke ... Amy Monroe
Liam Sullivan ... Major Mapoy
Ron Soble ... Dirty Jim
Ben Johnson ... Sleeve
James Brolin
Hampton Fancher
Tim O'Kelly
Ray Teal
May Boss .... stunts
Joe Canutt .... stunts
Jack Williams .... stunts

"The Monroes" Lost in the Wilderness (1966)

Director: Ray Kellogg

Writer: Antony Ellis

Original Air Date:30 November 1966 (Season 1, Episode 13)

Cast:Michael Anderson Jr. ... Clayt Monroe

Barbara Hershey ... Kathy Monroe

Keith Schultz ... Jefferson Monroe

Kevin Schultz ... Fennimore Monroe

Tammy Locke ... Amy Monroe

Liam Sullivan ... Major Mapoy (credit only)

Ron Soble ... Dirty Jim

Ben Johnson ... Sleeve (credit only)

Noah Beery Jr. ... Alkali Tom

Shug Fisher ... Zeph (as George C. Fisher)

May Boss .... stunts

Joe Canutt .... stunts

Jack Williams .... stunts

"Gunsmoke" Quaker Girl (1966)

Director: Bernard L. Kowalski

Writer: Preston Wood

Original Air Date:10 December 1966 (Season 12, Episode 12)

Cast:

James Arness ... Marshal Matt Dillon

Milburn Stone ... Dr. Galen 'Doc' Adams

Amanda Blake ... Kitty Russell

Ken Curtis ... Festus Haggen

Roger Ewing ... Thad Greenwood

Joseph Breen ... George

William Bryant ... Kesler

Timothy Carey ... Charles 'Buster' Rilla
Ben Johnson ... Vern Morland
Anna Karen ... Woman #1
Nancy Marshall ... Woman #2
Ed McCready ... Henry
Tom Reese ... Dave Westerfield
William Shatner ... Fred Bateman
Glenn Strange ... Sam Noonan
Liam Sullivan ... Benjamin Ellis
Warren Vanders ... John Thenly
 Wilbur Jonas
Hank Patterson ... Hank Miller
Roy Roberts ... Harry Bodkin
Charles Seel ... Barney Danches

"The Monroes" Gold Fever (1966)
Director: James B. Clark
Writer: Jack Turley (writer)
Original Air Date: 14 December 1966 (Season 1, Episode 14)
Cast:
Michael Anderson Jr. ... Clayt Monroe
Barbara Hershey ... Kathy Monroe
Keith Schultz ... Jefferson Monroe
Kevin Schultz ... Fennimore Monroe
Tammy Locke ... Amy Monroe
Liam Sullivan ... Major Mapoy
Ron Soble ... Dirty Jim
Ben Johnson ... Sleeve
James Westmoreland ... Ruel Jaxon (as Jim Westmoreland)
Robert Middleton ... Barney Wales
Buck Taylor ... John "Brad" Bradford

Hardie Albright
Alan Baxter ... Stargis
Hank Brandt ... Langdon
Dan Duryea ... T.J. Elderbush
May Boss .... stunts
Joe Canutt .... stunts
Jack Williams .... stunts

"The Monroes" Range War (1966)
Director:Larry Peerce
Writer:Antony Ellis (writer)
Original Air Date:21 December 1966 (Season 1, Episode 15)
Cast-
Michael Anderson Jr. ... Clayt Monroe
Barbara Hershey ... Kathy Monroe
Keith Schultz ... Jefferson Monroe
Kevin Schultz ... Fennimore Monroe
Tammy Locke ... Amy Monroe
Liam Sullivan ... Major Mapoy
Ron Soble ... Dirty Jim
Ben Johnson ... Sleeve
James Brolin
Tim O'Kelly
Gordon Wescourt
May Boss .... stunts
Joe Canutt .... stunts
Jack Williams .... stunts

"The Monroes" Pawnee Warrior (1966)
Directed by Harmon Jones
Writing: James Leighton

Original Air Date: 28 December 1966 (Season 1, Episode 16)
Cast:
Michael Anderson Jr. ... Clayt Monroe
Barbara Hershey ... Kathy Monroe
Keith Schultz ... Jefferson Monroe
Kevin Schultz ... Fennimore Monroe
Tammy Locke ... Amy Monroe
Liam Sullivan ... Major Mapoy (credit only)
Ron Soble ... Dirty Jim
Ben Johnson ... Sleeve (credit only)
James Westmoreland ... Ruel Jaxon
Alejandro Rey ... Komatah
May Boss .... stunts
Joe Canutt .... stunts
Jack Williams .... stunts

"The Monroes" Mark of Death (1967)
Original Air Date: 4 January 1967 (Season 1, Episode 17)
Cast:
Michael Anderson Jr. ... Clayt Monroe
Barbara Hershey ... Kathy Monroe
Keith Schultz ... Jefferson Monroe
Kevin Schultz ... Fennimore Monroe
Tammy Locke ... Amy Monroe
Liam Sullivan ... Major Mapoy
Ron Soble ... Dirty Jim
Ben Johnson ... Sleeve
James Westmoreland ... Ruel Jaxon (as Jim Westmoreland)
Robert Middleton ... Barney Wales
Buck Taylor ... John "Brad" Bradford

Mario Alcalde ... Poza
James Brolin
Tim O'Kelly
May Boss .... stunts
Joe Canutt .... stunts
Jack Williams .... stunts

"The Monroes" To Break a Colt (1967)
Directed by Norman Foster
Writing: Thomas Thompson
Cast:
Michael Anderson Jr. ... Clayt Monroe
Barbara Hershey ... Kathy Monroe
Keith Schultz ... Jefferson Monroe
Kevin Schultz ... Fennimore Monroe
Tammy Locke ... Amy Monroe
Liam Sullivan ... Major Mapoy
Ron Soble ... Dirty Jim
Ben Johnson ... Sleeve
James Westmoreland ... Ruel Jaxon (as Jim Westmoreland)
Robert Middleton ... Barney Wales
Buck Taylor ... John "Brad" Bradford
Elisha Cook Jr. ... Jed
Casey Tibbs
Fredd Wayne ... Winton
May Boss .... stunts
Joe Canutt .... stunts
Jack Williams .... stunts

"The Monroes" Race for the Rainbow (1967)
Director: Norman Foster
Writer: John Furia

Original Air Date:18 January 1967 (Season 1, Episode 19)
Cast:
Michael Anderson Jr. ... Clayt Monroe
Barbara Hershey ... Kathy Monroe
Keith Schultz ... Jefferson Monroe
Kevin Schultz ... Fennimore Monroe
Tammy Locke ... Amy Monroe
Liam Sullivan ... Major Mapoy
Ron Soble ... Dirty Jim
Ben Johnson ... Sleeve
Lisa Jak
John Wilder ... Michael Duquesne
May Boss .... stunts
Joe Canutt .... stunts
Jack Williams .... stunts

"The Monroes" Gun Bound (1967)
Director: William Wiard
Writer: Howard Dimsdale
Original Air Date:25 January 1967 (Season 1, Episode 20)
Cast (Episode Credited cast)
Michael Anderson Jr. ... Clayt Monroe
Barbara Hershey ... Kathy Monroe
Keith Schultz ... Jefferson Monroe
Kevin Schultz ... Fennimore Monroe
Tammy Locke ... Amy Monroe
Liam Sullivan ... Major Mapoy
Ron Soble ... Dirty Jim
Ben Johnson ... Sleeve
James Westmoreland ... Ruel Jaxon (as Jim Westmoreland)
Robert Middleton ... Barney Wales
Buck Taylor ... John "Brad" Bradford

Nick Adams ... Dave
John Dehner ... Pete Lamson
Michael Greene ... Joel
May Boss .... stunts
Joe Canutt .... stunts
Jack Williams .... stunts

"The Monroes" Killer Cougar (1967)
Director: R.G. Springsteen
Writer: Louis Pelletier (writer)
Original Air Date:1 February 1967 (Season 1, Episode 21)
Cast:
Michael Anderson Jr. ... Clayt Monroe
Barbara Hershey ... Kathy Monroe
Keith Schultz ... Jefferson Monroe
Kevin Schultz ... Fennimore Monroe
Tammy Locke ... Amy Monroe
Liam Sullivan ... Major Mapoy
Ron Soble ... Dirty Jim
Ben Johnson ... Sleeve
James Westmoreland ... Ruel Jaxon (as Jim Westmoreland)
Robert Middleton ... Barney Wales
Buck Taylor ... John "Brad" Bradford
Rance Howard
Robert Walker Jr. ... Quint Gregger (as Robert Walker)
Robert J. Wilke ... Len Gregger
May Boss .... stunts
Joe Canutt .... stunts
Jack Williams .... stunts

"The Monroes" Wild Bull (1967)
Director: Robert Douglas

Writer: William Tunberg (writer)
Original Air Date:15 February 1967 (Season 1, Episode 22)
Cast:
Michael Anderson Jr. ... Clayt Monroe
Jeffrey Hunter ... Ed Stanley
Barbara Hershey ... Kathy Monroe
Keith Schultz ... Jefferson Monroe
Kevin Schultz ... Fennimore Monroe
Tammy Locke ... Amy Monroe
Liam Sullivan ... Major Mapoy
Ron Soble ... Dirty Jim
Ben Johnson ... Sleeve
Stanley Adams
Med Flory
Dub Taylor
May Boss .... stunts
Joe Canutt .... stunts
Jack Williams .... stunts

"The Monroes" Trapped (1967)
Director: Norman Foster
Original Air Date:22 February 1967 (Season 1, Episode 23)
Cast:
Michael Anderson Jr. ... Clayt Monroe
Barbara Hershey ... Kathy Monroe
Keith Schultz ... Jefferson Monroe
Kevin Schultz ... Fennimore Monroe
Tammy Locke ... Amy Monroe
Liam Sullivan ... Major Mapoy
Ron Soble ... Dirty Jim
Ben Johnson ... Sleeve
James Westmoreland ... Ruel Jaxon (as Jim Westmoreland)

Robert Middleton ... Barney Wales
Buck Taylor ... John "Brad" Bradford
May Boss .... stunts
Joe Canutt .... stunts
Jack Williams .... stunts

"The Monroes" Manhunt (1967)
Director: Robert Douglas
Writer: Howard Dimsdale
Original Air Date:1 March 1967 (Season 1, Episode 24)
Cast:
Michael Anderson Jr. ... Clayt Monroe
Barbara Hershey ... Kathy Monroe
Keith Schultz ... Jefferson Monroe
Kevin Schultz ... Fennimore Monroe
Tammy Locke ... Amy Monroe
Liam Sullivan ... Major Mapoy
Ron Soble ... Dirty Jim
Ben Johnson ... Sleeve
Billie Hayes
Robert Lansing ... Jonas Prine
J. Martin Wyler ... Devery
May Boss .... stunts
Joe Canutt .... stunts
Jack Williams .... stunts

"The Monroes" Teaching the Tiger to Purr (1967)
Director: Norman Foster
Writer: Barbara Chain
Original Air Date:15 March 1967 (Season 1, Episode 25)
Cast:
Michael Anderson Jr. ... Clayt Monroe

Barbara Hershey ... Kathy Monroe
Keith Schultz ... Jefferson Monroe
Kevin Schultz ... Fennimore Monroe
Tammy Locke ... Amy Monroe
Liam Sullivan ... Major Mapoy
Ron Soble ... Dirty Jim
Ben Johnson ... Sleeve
Anne Ayars
Carolyn Conwell
Clint Howard ... Jody Hillman
Rance Howard
Ron Howard ... Timothy Prescott (as Ronny Howard)
Kay Lenz ... Maudie (as Kay Ann Kemper)
Eddie Sallia
May Boss .... stunts
Joe Canutt .... stunts
Jack Williams .... stunts

"The Monroes" Ghosts of Paradox (1967)
Director: William Wiard
Writer: Otis Carney
Original Air Date:15 March 1967 (Season 1, Episode 26)
Cast :
Michael Anderson Jr. ... Clayt Monroe
Barbara Hershey ... Kathy Monroe
Keith Schultz ... Jefferson Monroe
Kevin Schultz ... Fennimore Monroe
Tammy Locke ... Amy Monroe
Liam Sullivan ... Major Mapoy
Ron Soble ... Dirty Jim
Ben Johnson ... Sleeve
James Westmoreland ... Ruel Jaxon (as Jim Westmoreland)

Robert Middleton ... Barney Wales
Buck Taylor ... John "Brad" Bradford
Jack Bailey
X. Brands
Ahna Capri ... Polly Deaver (as Anna Capri)
John 'Bud' Cardos (as Johnny Cardos)
Michael Dunn ... Nemo
Bob Gunderson
Richard Kiel ... Casmir
May Boss .... stunts
Joe Canutt .... stunts
Jack Williams .... stunts

"The Virginian" Johnny Moon (1967)
Director: Abner Biberman
Writers: Stanford Whitmore (writer)
Owen Wister (novel)
Original Air Date:11 October 1967 (Season 6, Episode 5)
Cast:
Tom Bell ... Cpl. Johnny Moon
George Brenlin ... Sammyjay
John Bryant ... Dr. Spaulding
James Drury ... The Virginian
Harper Flaherty ... Skinner
Michael Higgins ... Lawson
Bo Hopkins ... Will
Ben Johnson ... Joe Hogan
Sara Lane ... Elizabeth Grainger
Norman Leavitt ... Storekeeper
Cliff Potts ... Wes (as Cliff Potter)
Don Quine ... Stacey Grainger
Bobby Clark .... stunts

George Orrison .... stunts
Dean Smith .... stunts

Will Penny (1968) (Paramount Pictures)
Director: Tom Gries
Writer: Tom Gries (writer)
Release Date:10 April 1968
Cast:
Charlton Heston ... Will Penny
Joan Hackett ... Catherine Allen
Donald Pleasence ... Preacher Quint
Lee Majors ... Blue
Bruce Dern ... Rafe Quint
Ben Johnson ... Alex (Flat Iron Ranch foreman)
Slim Pickens ... Ike Walterstein
Clifton James ... Catron
Anthony Zerbe ... Dutchy
Roy Jenson ... Boetius Sullivan
G.D. Spradlin ... Anse Howard
Quentin Dean ... Jennie
William Schallert ... Dr. Fraker
Lydia Clarke ... Mrs. Fraker
Robert Luster ... Shem Bodine
Calvin Brown .... stunts (uncredited)
Joe Canutt .... stunt coordinator (uncredited)
Ross Dollarhyde .... stunts (uncredited)
Jerry Gatlin .... stunts (uncredited)
Rock A. Walker .... stunts (uncredited)
Jack Williams .... stunts (uncredited)
Joe Yrigoyen .... stunts (uncredited)
Runtime:108 min
Color

Filming Locations: Bishop, California

Hang 'Em High (1968) (Leonard Freeman Production)
Director: Ted Post
Writers: Leonard Freeman and Mel Goldberg
Release Date:3 August 1968
Cast:
Clint Eastwood ... Marshal Jed Cooper
Inger Stevens ... Rachel Warren
Ed Begley ... Captain Wilson, Cooper Hanging Party
Pat Hingle ... Judge Adam Fenton
Ben Johnson ... Marshal Dave Bliss
Charles McGraw ... Sheriff Ray Calhoun, Red Creek
Ruth White ... Madame 'Peaches' Sophie
Bruce Dern ... Miller, One of the 3 rustlers, and murderer
Alan Hale Jr. ... Matt Stone, Cooper Hanging Party
Arlene Golonka ... Jennifer, the Prostitute
James Westerfield ... Prisoner
Dennis Hopper ... The Prophet
L.Q. Jones ... Loomis, Cooper Hanging Party
Michael O'Sullivan ... Francis Elroy Duffy, Prisoner
Joseph Sirola ... Reno, Cooper Hanging Party
Steven Burnett .... stunts (uncredited)
Walter Scott .... stunts (uncredited)
Runtime:114 min
Color
Filming Locations: Las Cruces, New Mexico

"The Virginian" Vision of Blindness (1968)
Director: Abner Biberman

Writers: James Menzies (teleplay), Gerald Sanford (story)
Original Air Date: 9 October 1968 (Season 7, Episode 4)
Cast:
Rosalyn Burbage ... Sarah
James Drury ... The Virginian
Kimberley Farr ... Martha
David Hartman ... David Sutton
The Irish Rovers ... Themselves
Ben Johnson ... Jed Cooper
Sara Lane ... Elizabeth Grainger
Doug McClure ... Trampas
John Saxon ... Ben Oakes
May Boss .... stunts
Joe Canutt .... stunts
Jack Williams .... stunts

"Disneyland" Ride a Northbound Horse: Part 1 (1969)

Director: Robert Totten
Writer: Herman Groves
Original Air Date: 16 March 1969 (Season 15, Episode 21)
Cast:
Carroll O'Connor
Michael Shea
Ben Johnson
Andy Devine
Edith Atwater
Jack Elam
Harry Carey Jr.
Dub Taylor ... Purse

"Bonanza" Deserter, the (II) (1969)
Director: Leon Benson
Writers: David Dortort; John Dunkel
Original Air Date:16 March 1969 (Season 10, Episode 24)
Cast:
Lorne Greene ... Ben Cartwright
Michael Landon ... Joseph 'Little Joe' Cartwright
David Canary ... 'Candy' Canaday
Christian Anderson ... Turner
Robert V. Barron ... Cavalry Trooper
Ellen Davalos ... Nanita Bellis
Lincoln Demyan ... Trooper
Ken Drake ... Leatham
Duane Grey ... Henderson
Ben Johnson ... Sgt. Samuel Bellis
Todd Martin ... Denton
Ford Rainey ... Capt. Arnholt
Bing Russell ... Deputy Clem Foster

Disneyland" Ride a Northbound Horse: Part 2 (1969)
Director: Robert Totten
Writer: Herman Groves (writer)
Original Air Date:23 March 1969 (Season 15, Episode 22)
Cast: Carroll O'Connor
Michael Shea
Ben Johnson
Andy Devine
Edith Atwater
Jack Elam
Harry Carey Jr.

Dub Taylor ... Purse

The Wild Bunch (1969) (Warner Brothers/Seven Arts)
Director: Sam Peckinpah
Writers: Walon Green (story) and Roy N. Sickner (story) ...
Release Date: 7 August 1969
Cast:
William Holden ... Pike Bishop
Ernest Borgnine ... Dutch Engstrom
Robert Ryan ... Deke Thornton
Edmond O'Brien ... Freddie Sykes
Warren Oates ... Lyle Gorch
Jaime Sánchez ... Angel (as Jaime Sanchez)
Ben Johnson ... Tector Gorch
Emilio Fernández ... Gen. Mapache (as Emilio Fernandez)
Strother Martin ... Coffer
L.Q. Jones ... T.C
Albert Dekker ... Pat Harrigan
Bo Hopkins ... Clarence 'Crazy' Lee
Dub Taylor ... Rev. Wainscoat
Paul Harper ... Ross
Jorge Russek ... Maj. Zamorra
Alfonso Arau ... Lt. Herrera
Chano Urueta ... Don Jose
Elsa Cárdenas ... Elsa (as Elsa Cardenas)
Bill Hart ... Jess
Rayford Barnes ... Buck
Stephen Ferry ... Sgt. McHale (as Steve Ferry)
Sonia Amelio ... Teresa
Aurora Clavel ... Aurora
Enrique Lucero ... Ignacio

Elizabeth Dupeyrón ... Rocio (as Elizabeth Dupeyron)
Yolanda Ponce ... Yolis
José Chávez ... Juan Jose (as Jose Chavez)
René Dupeyrón ... Juan (as Rene Dupeyron)
Pedro Galván ... Mr. Benson (as Pedro Galvan)
Graciela Doring ... Emma
Major Perez ... Perez
Fernando Wagner ... Cmdr. Frederick Mohr
Jorge Rado ... Ernst
Ivan Scott ... Paymaster
Señora Madero ... Margaret (as Sra. Madero)
Margarito Luna ... Luna
Chalo González ... Gonzalez (as Chalo Gonzalez)
Lilia Castillo ... Lilia
Elizabeth Unda ... Carmen
Julio Corona ... Julio
Buck Holland ... Thornton Posse Rider (uncredited)
Matthew Peckinpah ... Young boy watching robber scoop up moneybag (uncredited)
Denny Arnold .... stunts (uncredited)
Norman Bishop .... stunts (uncredited)
Steven Burnett .... stunts (uncredited)
Archie Butler .... stunt coordinator (uncredited)
Joe Canutt .... stunts (uncredited)
Tap Canutt .... stunts (uncredited)
John 'Bud' Cardos .... stunts (uncredited)
Gary Combs .... stunts (uncredited)
Louie Elias .... stunts (uncredited)
Tony Epper .... stunts (uncredited)
Chad Evans .... stunts (uncredited)
Joe Finnegan .... stunts (uncredited)
Mickey Gilbert .... stunts (uncredited)

Bill Hart .... stunts (uncredited)
Robert 'Buzz' Henry .... stunts (uncredited)
'Chema' Hernandez .... stunts (uncredited)
Bob Herron .... stunts (uncredited)
Billy E. Hughes .... stunts (uncredited)
Whitey Hughes .... stunts (uncredited)
Gary McLarty .... stunts (uncredited)
Bob Orrison .... stunts (uncredited)
Danny Sands .... stunts (uncredited)
Bill Shannon .... stunts (uncredited)
Jim Sheppard .... stunts (uncredited)
Roy N. Sickner .... stunts (uncredited)
Jack Williams .... stunts (uncredited)
Joe Yrigoyen .... stunts (uncredited)
Runtime:134 min | USA:145 min (1995 re-release)
Color
Filming Locations: Durango, Mexico

The Undefeated (1969) (Twentieth Century-Fox Film Corporation)
Director: Andrew V. McLaglen
Writers: James Lee Barrett (screenplay)
Stanley Hough (story)
Release Date:27 November 1969
Cast:
John Wayne ... Col. John Henry Thomas
Rock Hudson ... Col. James Langdon
Antonio Aguilar ... Juarista Gen. Rojas (as Tony Aguilar)
Roman Gabriel ... Blue Boy (John Henry's Cherokee Indian adopted son)
Marian McCargo ... Ann Langdon
Lee Meriwether ... Margaret Langdon

Merlin Olsen ... Cpl. Little George, CSA
Melissa Newman ... Charlotte Langdon
Bruce Cabot ... Sgt. Jeff Newby CSA
Jan-Michael Vincent ... Lt. Bubba Wilkes CSA (as Michael Vincent)
Ben Johnson ... Short Grub
Edward Faulkner ... Capt. Anderson, CSA (Col. Langdon's aide)
Harry Carey Jr. ... Soloman Webster (Thomas rider)
Paul Fix ... Gen. Joe Masters
Royal Dano ... Maj. Sanders, CSA (one-armed major)
Richard Mulligan ... Dan Morse
Carlos Rivas ... Diaz
John Agar ... Christian
Guy Raymond ... D.J. Giles (government purchasing agent)
Don Collier ... Goodyear (Thomas rider)
Big John Hamilton ... July Mudlow (cowardly Langdon party member)
Dub Taylor ... McCartney (Thomas outfit cook)
Henry Beckman ... Thad Benedict (carpetbagger who tries to buy Langdon plantation)
Víctor Junco ... Maj. Tapia
Robert Donner ... Judd Mailer
Pedro Armendáriz Jr. ... Escalante (as Pedro Armendariz Jr.)
James Dobson ... Cpl. Jamison, CSA
Rudy Diaz ... Sanchez
Richard Angarola ... Mr. Petain (Maximilian's representative)
James McEachin ... Jimmy Collins (black carpetbagger with Benedict)

Gregg Palmer ... Ezra Parker (government purchasing agent)
Juan García ... Col. Gomez
Bob Gravage ... Bobby Jo Hicks (Thomas rider) (uncredited)
Kiel Martin ... Union corporal who brings message that the war is over (uncredited)
Hal Needham ... Yankee corporal at river crossing (uncredited)
Chuck Roberson ... Yankee sergeant at river (uncredited)
Hal Needham .... stunt coordinator
Denny Arnold .... stunts (uncredited)
Stan Barrett .... stunts (uncredited)
Dick Bullock .... stunts (uncredited)
Jim Burk .... stunts (uncredited)
William H. Burton .... stunts (uncredited)
Tap Canutt .... stunts (uncredited)
Roydon Clark .... stunts (uncredited)
Bill Couch .... stunts (uncredited)
Chuck Couch .... stunts (uncredited)
Jerry Gatlin .... stunts (uncredited)
Alan Gibbs .... stunts (uncredited)
Mickey Gilbert .... stunts (uncredited)
Kent Hays .... stunts (uncredited)
John Hudkins .... stunts (uncredited)
Clyde Hudkins Jr. .... stunts (uncredited)
Gary McLarty .... stunts (uncredited)
Hal Needham .... stunts (uncredited)
Paul Nuckles .... stunts (uncredited)
Bob Orrison .... stunts (uncredited)
Gil Perkins .... stunts (uncredited)

Chuck Roberson .... stunts (uncredited)
J.N. Roberts .... stunts (uncredited)
George Robotham .... stunts (uncredited)
Wally Rose .... stunts (uncredited)
Danny Sands .... stunts (uncredited)
Fred M. Waugh .... stunts (uncredited)
Walter Wyatt .... stunts (uncredited)
Dick Ziker .... stunts (uncredited)
Runtime:119 min
Color
Filming Locations: Baton Rouge, Louisiana, Durango, Mexico

Chisum (1970)
Director: Andrew V. McLaglen
Writer: Andrew J. Fenady
Release Date:29 July 1970
Cast:
John Wayne ... John Simpson Chisum
Forrest Tucker ... Lawrence Murphy
Christopher George ... Dan Nodeen
Ben Johnson ... James Pepper
Glenn Corbett ... Pat Garrett
Bruce Cabot ... Sheriff Brady
Andrew Prine ... Alex McSween
Patric Knowles ... J. Henry Tunstall
Richard Jaeckel ... Jess Evans
Lynda Day George ... Sue McSween (as Lynda Day)
Geoffrey Deuel ... Billy 'The Kid' Bonney
Pamela McMyler ... Sallie Chisum
John Agar ... Amos Patton
Lloyd Battista ... Neemo

Robert Donner ... Bradley Morton - Deputy sheriff
Ray Teal ... Justice J.B. Wilson
Edward Faulkner ... James J. Dolan
Ron Soble ... Charley Bowdre
John Mitchum ... Baker (deputy sheriff)
Glenn Langan ... Colonel Nathan Dudley
Alan Baxter ... Gov. Sam Axtell
Alberto Morin ... Juan Delgado
William Bryant ... Jeff - Head Wrangler
Pedro Armendáriz Jr. ... Ben (as Pedro Armendariz Jr.)
Christopher Mitchum ... Tom O'Folliard
John Pickard ... Sgt. Braddock
Abraham Sofaer ... Chief White Buffalo
Gregg Palmer ... Karl Riker
Hank Worden ... Stationmaster Elwood
Pedro Gonzalez Gonzalez ... Mexican rancher
Jim Burk ... Trace - a Wrangler
Eddy Donno ... Cass
Bob Morgan ... Pegleg on Street
William Conrad ... Narrator - Opening Credits (voice) (uncredited)
José Ángel Espinosa 'Ferrusquilla' ... Governor's Aide (uncredited)
Ron Fletcher ... Doctor (uncredited)
John Kelly ... Minister (uncredited)
Cliff Lyons ... Wrangler (uncredited)
Josh McLaglen ... Young boy loading wagon (uncredited)
Mary McLaglen ... Young girl (uncredited)
Chuck Roberson ... Trail herder (uncredited)
José Torvay ... Mexican Blacksmith (uncredited)

Trinidad Villa ... Blacksmith (uncredited)
Ralph Volkie ... Blacksmith (uncredited)
Henry Wills ... Extra (uncredited)
Dick Bullock .... stunts (uncredited)
Jim Burk .... stunts (uncredited)
Joe Canutt .... stunts (uncredited)
Tap Canutt .... stunts (uncredited)
Eddy Donno .... stunts (uncredited)
Chuck Hayward .... stunts (uncredited)
Cliff Lyons .... stunt coordinator (uncredited)
Cliff Lyons .... stunts (uncredited)
Gary McLarty .... stunts (uncredited)
Bob Morgan .... stunts (uncredited)
Hal Needham .... stunt coordinator (uncredited)
Bob Orrison .... stunts (uncredited)
Chuck Roberson .... stunts (uncredited)
Henry Wills .... stunts (uncredited)
Runtime:111 min
Color
Filming Locations: Durango, Mexico
Company: Batjac Productions

"Bonanza" Top Hand (1971)
Director: William F. Claxton
Writers: John Hawkins; Arthur Heinemann
Original Air Date:24 January 1971 (Season 12, Episode 17)
Cast:
Lorne Greene ... Ben Cartwright
Dan Blocker ... Eric 'Hoss' Cartwright
Michael Landon ... Joseph 'Little Joe' Cartwright
Walter Barnes ... Weatherby
Hal Burton ... Smokey

Bill Clark ... Jimpson
Roger Davis ... Bert Yates
Richard Farnsworth ... Sourdough (as Dick Farnsworth)
Jerry Gatlin ... Quincy
Ben Johnson ... Kelly James
Eddie Juaregui ... Bones (as Ed Juaregui)

The Last Picture Show (1971) (BBS Productions)
Director: Peter Bogdanovich
Writers: Larry McMurtry (novel and screenplay)
Release Date:22 October 1971
Cast:
Timothy Bottoms ... Sonny Crawford
Jeff Bridges ... Duane Jackson
Cybill Shepherd ... Jacy Farrow
Ben Johnson ... Sam the Lion
Cloris Leachman ... Ruth Popper
Ellen Burstyn ... Lois Farrow
Eileen Brennan ... Genevieve
Clu Gulager ... Abilene
Sam Bottoms ... Billy
Sharon Ullrick ... Charlene Duggs (as Sharon Taggart)
Randy Quaid ... Lester Marlow
Joe Heathcock ... The Sheriff
Bill Thurman ... Coach Popper
Barc Doyle ... Joe Bob Blanton
Jessie Lee Fulton ... Miss Mosey
Gary Brockette ... Bobby Sheen
Helena Humann ... Jimmie Sue
Loyd Catlett ... Leroy
Robert Glenn ... Gene Farrow
John Hillerman ... Teacher

Janice E. O'Malley ... Mrs. Clarg (as Janice O'Malley)
Floyd Mahaney ... Oklahoma patrolman
Kimberly Hyde ... Annie-Annie Martin
Noble Willingham ... Chester
Marjorie Jay ... Winnie Snips
Joye Hash ... Mrs. Jackson
Pamela Keller ... Jackie Lee French
Gordon Hurst ... Monroe
Mike Hosford ... Johnny
Faye Jordan ... Nurse
Charles Seybert ... Andy Fanner
Grover Lewis ... Mr. Crawford
Rebecca Ulrick ... Marlene
Merrill Shepherd ... Agnes
Buddy Wood ... Bud
Kenny Wood ... Ken
Leon Brown ... Cowboy in cafe
Bobby McGriff ... Truck driver
Jack Mueller ... Oil pumper
Robert Arnold ... Brother Blanton
Frank Marshall ... Tommy Logan
Tom Martin ... Larry
Otis Elmore ... Mechanic #1
Charles Salmon ... Roughneck driver
George Gaulden ... Cowboy
Will Morris Hannis ... Gas station man
The Leon Miller Band ... Themselves
Peter Bogdanovich ... DJ (voice)
Tom Tyler ... The Quitter in 'Red River' (archive footage)
Antonia Bogdanovich ... Singer (uncredited)
Runtime:118 min | 126 min (director's cut)

Black and White
Filming Locations: Archer City, Texas

"Gunsmoke" Drago (1971)
Director: Paul Stanley
Writer: Jim Byrnes (written by)
Original Air Date:22 November 1971 (Season 17, Episode 11)
Cast:
Amanda Blake ... Kitty Russell (credit only)
Ken Curtis ... Festus Haggen (credit only)
Buck Taylor ... Newly O'Brien
James Arness ... Marshal Matt Dillon
Buddy Ebsen ... Drago
Ben Johnson ... Hannon
Edward Faulkner ... Trask
Del Monroe ... Flagg
Richard Gates ... Gillis (as Rick Gates)
Pat Hingle ... Dr. John Chapman
Tani Guthrie ... Clara (as Tani Phelps Guthrie)
Jim Skaggs ... Sheepherder
Larry Randles ... Larry
Mitchell Silberman ... Ruben
Tom Brown ... Ed O'Connor
Hank Patterson ... Hank Miller
Roy Roberts ... Harry Bodkin
Charles Seel ... Barney Danches

Something Big (1971) (Cinema Center Films)
Director: Andrew V. McLaglen
Writer: James Lee Barrett (written by)
Release Date:1 December 1971

Cast:
Dean Martin ... Joe Baker
Brian Keith ... Col. Morgan
Carol White ... Dover McBride
Honor Blackman ... Mary Anna Morgan
Ben Johnson ... Jesse Bookbinder
Albert Salmi ... Jonny Cobb
Don Knight ... Tommy McBride
Joyce Van Patten ... Polly Standall
Denver Pyle ... Junior Frisbee
Merlin Olsen ... Sgt. Fitzsimmons
Robert Donner ... Angel Moon
Harry Carey Jr. ... Joe Pickins
Judi Meredith ... Carrie Standall
Edward Faulkner ... Capt. Tyler (as Ed Faulkner)
Paul Fix ... Chief Yellow Sun
Armand Alzamora ... Luis Munos
David Huddleston ... Malachi Morton
Bob Steele ... Teamster #3
Shirleena Manchur ... Stagecoach lady
José Ángel Espinosa 'Ferrusquilla' ... Emilio Estevez (as José Ángel Espinoza)
Juan García ... Juan Garcia
Bob Gravage ... Sam (as Robert Gravage)
Chuck Hicks ... Cpl. James
John Kelly ... Barkeeper
Enrique Lucero ... Indian spy
Lupe Amador ... Woman in village
Joe Gray ... (uncredited)
Hal Needham .... stunt coordinator
Joe Gray .... stunts (uncredited)
James M. Halty .... stunts (uncredited)

Chuck Hicks .... stunts (uncredited)
Runtime:108 min
Color

"The Tonight Show Starring Johnny Carson"
Episode dated 17 February 1972 (1972)
Cast:
Johnny Carson ... Himself - Host
Jim Bailey ... Himself
Michael Caine ... Himself
Ben Johnson ... Himself
Haruo Shimada ... Himself (as Shimada)

Corky (1972) (MGM)
Director: Leonard Horn
Writer: Eugene Price
Release Date:March 1972 (USA) more
Cast:
Robert Blake ... Corky Curtiss
Charlotte Rampling ... Corky's Wife
Patrick O'Neal ... Randy
Christopher Connelly ... Billy
Pamela Payton-Wright ... Rhonda
Ben Johnson ... Boland
Laurence Luckinbill ... Wayne
Paul Stevens ... Tobin Hayes
Kevin Abell ... L.D.
Bobby Allison ... Himself
Donnie Allison ... Himself
Buddy Baker ... Himself
Brad Breenstreet ... Reese
Charlie Briggs ... Red

Jesse R. Cox Jr. ... Leroy
Desmond Dhooge ... Smitty
Robert Dracup ... J.D.
Jack Garner ... Driver #1
John Gruber ... Steve
David Haney ... Pawnbroker
John Marriott ... Junkman
Richard Petty ... Himself
Lulu Roman ... Sue
Mario Rossi ... Himself
Frank Schaefer ... Hippie
William Vance White ... Man with Shotgun
Glen Wood ... Himself
Cale Yarborough ... Himself
Runtime:USA:88 min
Color
Filming Locations: Arlington, Texas

The Bull of the West (1971) (TV).
Directors:Jerry Hopper
Paul Stanley
Writers:Richard Fiedler ,Don Ingalls
Release Date:14 April 1972
Cast:
Charles Bronson ... Ben Justin
Geraldine Brooks ... Georgia Price
Gary Clarke ... Steve
Lee J. Cobb ... Judge Garth
James Drury ... Man from Virginia
Clu Gulager ... Deputy Emmett Ryker
Ben Johnson ... Spinner
Brian Keith ... Johnny Wade

DeForest Kelley ... Ben Tully
George Kennedy ... 'Bear' Suchette
Doug McClure ... Trampas
Lois Nettleton ... Mary Justin
Robert Random ... Will Justin
Vito Scotti ... Gilly

Junior Bonner (1972) (American Broadcasting Company)
Director: Sam Peckinpah
Writer: Jeb Rosebrook (written by)
Release Date:2 August 1972
Cast:
Steve McQueen ... Junior 'JR' Bonner
Robert Preston ... Ace Bonner
Ida Lupino ... Elvira Bonner
Ben Johnson ... Buck Roan
Joe Don Baker ... Curly Bonner
Barbara Leigh ... Charmagne
Mary Murphy ... Ruth Bonner
Bill McKinney ... Red Terwiliger (as William McKinney)
Dub Taylor ... Del
Sandra Deel ... Nurse Arlis
Don 'Red' Barry ... Homer Rutledge (as Donald Barry)
Charles H. Gray ... Burt (as Charles Gray)
Matthew Peckinpah ... Tim Bonner
Sundown Spencer ... Nick Bonner
Rita Garrison ... Flashie
Roxanne Knight ... Merla Twine
Sandra Pew ... Janene Twine
William E. Pierce ... Rodeo official
P.K. Strong ... Dudettes member
Toby Sargent ... Dudettes member

Bonnie Clausing ... Dudettes member
Francesca Jarvis ... Rodeo secretary
George Weintraub ... George
June Simpson ... Barmaid
Wayne McLaren
Lynette Carrington ... Young girl at Parade (uncredited)
James M. George ... Indian (uncredited)
Rod Hart ... (uncredited)
Johnnie Mullens ... (uncredited)
Sam Peckinpah ... Man in Palace Bar (uncredited)
Sharon Peckinpah ... Bar Patron (uncredited)
Casey Tibbs ... Parade Grand Marshal (uncredited)
Mickey Gilbert .... stunt coordinator (as R. Michael Gilbert)
Denny Arnold .... stunts (uncredited)
Floyd Baze .... stunt double (uncredited)
Autry Ward .... stunts (uncredited)
Steve Ward .... stunts (uncredited)
Troy Ward .... stunts (uncredited)
Runtime:100 min
Color
Filming Locations: Prescott, Arizona

The Getaway (1972) (National General Pictures)
Director: Sam Peckinpah
Writers: Walter Hill (screenplay); Jim Thompson (novel)
Release Date:13 December 1972
Cast:
Steve McQueen ... Doc McCoy
Ali MacGraw ... Carol McCoy
Ben Johnson ... Jack Beynon
Sally Struthers ... Fran Clinton

Al Lettieri ... Rudy Butler
Slim Pickens ... Cowboy
Richard Bright ... The Thief
Jack Dodson ... Harold Clinton
Dub Taylor ... Laughlin
Bo Hopkins ... Frank Jackson
Roy Jenson ... Cully
John Bryson ... The Accountant
Bill Hart ... Swain
Tom Runyon ... Hayhoe
Whitney Jones ... The Soldier
Raymond King ... Boy on the train
Ivan Thomas ... Boy on the train
C.W. White ... Boy's Mother
Brenda W. King ... Boy's Mother
W. Dee Kutach ... Parole Board Chairman
Brick Lowry ... Parole Board Commissioner
Martin Colley ... McCoy's Lawyer
O.S. Savage ... Field Captain
Dick Crockett ... Bank Guard
A.L. Camp ... Hardware Store Owner
Bob Veal ... TV Shop Proprietor
Bruce Bissonette ... Sporting Goods Salesman
Maggie Gonzalez ... Carhop
Jim Kannon ... Cannon
Doug Dudley ... Max
Stacy Newton ... Stacy
Tommy Bush ... Cowboy's Helper (as Tom Bush)
Hal Smith ... Various radio announcers (uncredited)
Tommy Splittgerber ... Train Station Ticket Agent (uncredited)
Gary Combs .... stunts (uncredited)

Dick Crockett .... stunts (uncredited)
Donna Garrett .... stunts (uncredited)
Bill Hart .... stunts (uncredited)
Whitey Hughes .... stunts (uncredited)
Carey Loftin .... stunts (uncredited)
Runtime:122 min
Color
Filming Locations: El Paso, Texas

The Train Robbers (1973) (Batjac Productions)
Director: Burt Kennedy
Writer: Burt Kennedy
Release Date:7 February 1973
Cast:
John Wayne ... Lane
Ann-Margret ... Mrs. Lowe
Rod Taylor ... Grady
Ben Johnson ... Jesse
Christopher George ... Calhoun
Bobby Vinton ... Ben Young
Jerry Gatlin ... Sam Turner
Ricardo Montalban ... The Pinkerton man
Cliff Lyons .... stunt coordinator
Denny Arnold .... stunts (uncredited)
Jim Burk .... stunts (uncredited)
Louie Elias .... stunts (uncredited)
Glory Fioramonti .... stunts (uncredited)
Chuck Hayward .... stunts (uncredited)
Terry Leonard .... stunts (uncredited)
Chuck Roberson .... stunts (uncredited)
Runtime:92 min
Color

Filming Locations: Durango, Mexico

The Red Pony (1973) (TV) (Omnibus Productions)
Director: Robert Totten
Writers: Ron Bishop; John Steinbeck
Release Date:18 March 1973
Cast:
Henry Fonda ... Carl Tiflin
Maureen O'Hara ... Ruth Tiflin
Ben Johnson ... Jess Taylor
Jack Elam ... Granddad
Clint Howard ... Jody Tiflin
Julian Rivero ... Gitano
Roy Jenson ... Toby
Lieux Dressler ... Dearie
Richard Jaeckel ... James Creighton
Woody Chambliss ... Orville Frye
Link Wyler ... Sonny Frye
Warren Douglas ... Barton
Rance Howard ... Sheriff Bill Smith
Yvonne Wood ... Sarah Taylor
Sally Carter-Ihnat ... Miss Willis
Runtime:101 min
Color
Filming Locations:Samuel Goldwyn Studios - West Hollywood, California

Dillinger (1973) (American International Pictures)
Director: John Milius
Writer: John Milius.
Release Date:20 July 1973
Cast:

Warren Oates ... John Dillinger
Ben Johnson ... Melvin Purvis
Michelle Phillips ... Billie Frechette
Cloris Leachman ... Anna Sage
Harry Dean Stanton ... Homer Van Meter
Geoffrey Lewis ... Harry Pierpont
John P. Ryan ... Charles Mackley (as John Ryan)
Richard Dreyfuss ... Baby Face Nelson
Steve Kanaly ... Pretty Boy Floyd
John Martino ... Eddie Martin
Roy Jenson ... Samuel Cowley
Read Morgan ... Big Jim Wollard
Frank McRae ... Reed Youngblood
David Dorr ... Leroy (uncredited)
Bob Harris ... Ed Fulton (uncredited)
J. Edgar Hoover ... Himself (post-end credits speech) (voice) (uncredited)
Terry Leonard ... Theodore 'Handsome Jack' Klutas (uncredited)
Jerry Summers ... Tommy Carroll (uncredited)
Catherine Tambini ... Leroy's girl (uncredited)
Runtime:107 min
Color
Filming Locations: Ardmore, Oklahoma, USA

Runaway! (1973) (TV) (Universal)
Director: David Lowell Rich
Writer: Gerald Di Pego
Release Date:29 September 1973
Cast:
Ben Johnson ... Holly Gibson
Ben Murphy ... Les Reever

Ed Nelson ... Nick Staffo
Darleen Carr ... Carol Lerner
Lee Montgomery ... Mark Shedd (as Lee H. Montgomery)
Martin Milner ... John Shedd
Vera Miles ... Ellen
Ray Danton ... Professor Jack Dunn
Frank Marth ... Dispatcher
Bing Russell ... Fireman
John McLiam ... Conductor
Lou Frizzell ... Brakeman
Frank Maxwell ... Chief Dispatcher
Kip Niven ... College Man
Laurette Spang ... Coed
Runtime:73 min
Color
Filming Locations:Denver, Colorado

Blood Sport (1973) (TV) (20th Century-Fox Television)
Director:Jerrold Freedman
Writer: Jerrold Freedman
Release Date:5 December 1973 (USA) more
Cast:
Ben Johnson ... Dwayne Birdsong
Gary Busey ... David Lee Birdsong
Larry Hagman ... Coach Marshall
William Lucking ... Dennis Birdsong
David Doyle ... Mr. Schmidt
Mimi Saffian ... Mary Louise Schmidt
Peggy Rea ... Mrs. Birdsong
Craig Richard Nelson ... Michael Braun
Michael Talbott ... Bubba Montgomery

Val Avery ... Frank Dorsdale
Jan Clayton ... Blanche Birdsong
Misty Rowe ... Holly
William Hansen ... Mr. Millsaps
Michael Lembeck ... Reuben
Marlyn Bingham
Asher Brauner ... C.C.
Lee Delano ... Besco
Richard Hamilton
Bert Verrall ... Football Player - Center
Runtime:90 min
Color
Company:20th Century Fox Television

The Sugarland Express (1974) (Zanuck/Brown Productions)
Director: Steven Spielberg
Writers: Steven Spielberg; Hal Barwood
Release Date:5 April 1974
Cast:
Goldie Hawn ... Lou Jean Poplin
Ben Johnson ... Captain Harlin Tanner
Michael Sacks ... Patrolman Maxwell Slide
William Atherton ... Clovis Michael Poplin
Gregory Walcott ... Patrolman Ernie Mashburn
Steve Kanaly ... Patrolman Jessup
Louise Latham ... Mrs. Looby
Harrison Zanuck ... Baby Langston Poplin
A.L. Camp ... Mr. Alvin T. Nocker
Jessie Lee Fulton ... Mrs. Nocker
Dean Smith ... Russ Berry
Ted Grossman ... Dietz

Bill Thurman ... Hunter
Kenneth Hudgins ... Standby
Buster Daniels ... Drunk (as Buster Danials)
James N. Harrell ... Mark Fenno (as Jim Harrell)
Frank Steggall ... Logan Waters
Roger Ernest ... Hot Jock #1
Guich Koock ... Hot Jock #2
Merrill Connally ... Mr. Vern Looby (as Merrill L. Connally)
Gene Rader ... Fred Mingers
Gordon Hurst ... Hubie Nocker
George Hagy ... Mr. Sparrow
Big John Hamilton ... Big John
Kenneth Crone ... Deputy
Peter Curry ... Judge (as Judge Peter Michael Curry)
Charles Conaway ... Attorney
Robert Golden ... Mechanic
Rudy Robbins ... Mechanic
Charlie Dobbs ... Local Cop
Gene Lively ... Reporter
John L. Quinlan III ... Bailiff
William Scott ... Station Man (as Bill Scott)
Ralph E. Horwedel ... Highway Patrol Houston Dispatcher
Edwin 'Frog' Isbell ... Jelly Bowl
Carey Loftin .... stunt coordinator
Max Balchowsky .... stunts (uncredited)
Ted Duncan .... stunts (uncredited)
Patty Elder .... stunts (uncredited)
Robert Golden .... stunts (uncredited)
Ted Grossman .... stunts (uncredited)
Bob Harris .... stunts (uncredited)

Carey Loftin .... stunts (uncredited)
Rudy Robbins .... stunts (uncredited)
Dean Smith .... stunts (uncredited)
Dale Van Sickel .... stunts (uncredited)
Runtime:110 min
Color
Filming Locations: Del Rio, Texas

Kid Blue (1973) (Twentieth Century-Fox Film Corporation)
Director: James Frawley
Writer: Bud Shrake
Release Date:2 May 1974
Cast:)
Dennis Hopper ... Bickford Waner
Warren Oates ... Reese Ford
Peter Boyle ... Preacher Bob
Ben Johnson ... Sheriff 'Mean John' Simpson
Lee Purcell ... Molly Ford
Janice Rule ... Janet Conforto
Ralph Waite ... Drummer
Clifton James ... Mr. Hendricks
José Torvay ... Old Coyote (as Jose Torvay)
Mary Jackson ... Mrs. Evans
Jay Varela ... Mendoza
Jack Starrett ... Tough Guy (as Claude Ennis Starrett Jr.)
Warren Finnerty ... Wills
Owen Orr ... Train robber #1
Richard Rust ... Train robber #2
Howard Hesseman ... Confectionery man (as Howard Hessman)

M. Emmet Walsh ... Jonesy
Henry Smith ... Joe Cloudmaker
Bobby Hall ... Newton (bartender)
Mel Stewart ... Black man (as Melvin Stewart)
Eddy Donno ... Huey
Runtime:100 min
Color
Filming Locations: Mexico

Locusts (1974) (TV) (Carson Productions)
Director: Richard T. Heffron
Writer: Robert M. Young
Release Date:9 October 1974 (USA) more
Cast:
Ben Johnson ... Amos Fletcher
Ron Howard ... Donny Fletcher
Katherine Helmond ... Claire Fletcher
Lisa Gerritsen ... Sissy Fletcher (as Lisa True Gerritsen)
Belinda Balaski ... Janet Willimer
Rance Howard ... Aaron
Robert Cruse ... Cully Cullitan
William Speerstra ... Ace Teverley
Robert Koons ... Klanser
Bob W. Hoffman ... Tom
Les Kimber ... Jim
Jacqueline Dunckel ... Mrs. Hensen
Jack Goth ... Hank
Nancy Dunckel ... Lilah
Michael James ... Cory
Runtime:74 min
Color

"The Tonight Show Starring Johnny Carson"
Episode dated 27 December 1974
Cast:
Linda Bennett ... Herself
George Carlin ... Himself
Ben Johnson ... Himself
Burt Reynolds ... Himself - Guest Host
Cybill Shepherd ... Herself
Mel Tillis ... Himself

Bite the Bullet (1975) (Columbia Pictures Corporation)
Director: Richard Brooks
Writer: Richard Brooks
Release Date: 26 September 1975
Cast:
Gene Hackman ... Sam Clayton
Candice Bergen ... Miss Jones
James Coburn ... Luke Matthews
Ben Johnson ... Mister
Ian Bannen ... Sir Harry Norfolk
Jan-Michael Vincent ... Carbo
Robert Donner ... Reporter
Jean Willes ... Rosie
Mario Arteaga ... Mexican
Dabney Coleman ... Jack Parker
John McLiam ... Gebhardt
Robert F. Hoy ... Lee Christie (as Robert Hoy)
Jerry Gatlin ... The Wood Cutter
Sally Kirkland ... Honey
Walter Scott Jr. ... Steve
William H. Burton ... Billy (as Bill Burton)
Buddy Van Horn ... Slim
Joe Brooks
Lucia Canales

Darwin Lamb
Paul Stewart ... J.B. Parker (uncredited)
Jerry Gatlin .... stunts (uncredited)
Walter Scott .... stunts (uncredited)
Buddy Van Horn .... stunts (uncredited)
Runtime:132 min
Color
Filming Locations: Carson National Forest, New Mexico

Breakheart Pass (1975) (Elliott Kastner Productions)
Director: Tom Gries
Writers: Alistair MacLean (novel and screenplay)
Release Date:25 December 1975
Cast:
Charles Bronson ... Deakin
Ben Johnson ... Pearce
Richard Crenna ... Governor Fairchild
Jill Ireland ... Marica
Charles Durning ... O'Brien
Ed Lauter ... Major Claremont
Bill McKinney ... Reverend Peabody
David Huddleston ... Dr. Molyneux
Roy Jenson ... Chris Banion
Rayford Barnes ... Sergeant. Bellew
Scott Newman ... Rafferty
Robert Tessier ... Levi Calhoun
Joe Kapp ... Henry
Archie Moore ... Carlos
Sally Kirkland ... Jane-Marie
Sally Kemp ... Prostitute
Eddie Little Sky ... White Hand
Keith McConnell ... Gabriel

John Mitchum ... Red Beard
Read Morgan ... Captain Oakland
Robert Rothwell ... Lt. Newell
Casey Tibbs ... Jackson
Doug Atkins ... Jebbo
Eldon Burke ... Ferguson (uncredited)
Irv Faling ... Colonel Scoville (uncredited)
William Klein ... Seamon Devlin (uncredited)
Tony Brubaker .... stunts
Joe Canutt .... stunts
Yakima Canutt .... stunt coordinator
Howard Curtis .... stunts
Mickey Gilbert .... stunts
Terry Leonard .... stunts
Runtime:95 min
Color
Filming Locations: Camas Prairie Railroad, Lewiston, Idaho

Hustle (1975) (Paramount Pictures)
Director:Robert Aldrich
Writers:Steve Shagan (novel)
Steve Shagan (screenplay)
Release Date:25 December 1975
Cast:
Burt Reynolds ... Lieutenant Phil Gaines
Catherine Deneuve ... Nicole Britton
Ben Johnson ... Marty Hollinger
Paul Winfield ... Sergeant Louis Belgrave
Eileen Brennan ... Paula Hollinger
Eddie Albert ... Leo Sellers
Ernest Borgnine ... Santuro

Jack Carter ... Herbie Dalitz
Colleen Brennan ... Gloria Hollinger (as Sharon Kelly)
James Hampton ... Bus Driver
David Spielberg ... Bellamy
Catherine Bach ... Peggy Summers
Chuck Hayward ... Morgue Attendant
David Estridge ... Albino
Peter Brandon ... Minister
Naomi Stevens ... Woman Hostage
Med Flory ... Cop beating Albino
Steve Shaw ... Kid in Elevator
Dino Washington ... Cop in Elevator
Anthony Eldridge ... Laugher
Barry Russo ... Man in Phone Booth (as John Duke Russo)
Don Billett ... Cop in Tee Shirt
Hal Baylor ... Police captain
Nancy Bonniwell ... Girl in Airport Bar
Don 'Red' Barry ... Airport Bartender
Karl Lukas ... Charley
Gene Chronopoulos ... Bartender
Patrice Rohmer ... Linda: a dancer
Alvin Hammer ... Liquor Store clerk
Dave Willock ... Liquor Store Clerk
Queenie Smith ... Customer
Marilyn Stader ... Customer (as Marilyn Moe)
Robert Englund ... Holdup Man
George Memmoli ... Foot Fetish Man
Fred Willard ... Interrogator
Thad Geer ... Second Holdup man
Kelly Wilder ... Nancy Gaines
Ben Young ... First Detective

Tasso Bravos ... Boy on Beach
Jim Hampton ... Boy on Beach
Nathan Harding ... Boy on Beach
John Furlong ... Waiter
Jason Wingreen ... Jim Lang
Ron Nyman ... Pan Am Clerk
Victoria Carroll ... Guest
Runtime:120 min
Color
Filming Locations: Los Angeles, California

"The Mike Douglas Show"
Episode dated 19 January 1978 (1978)
Cast:
Ben Johnson ... Himself
Robert Klein ... Himself / Co-Host
Barbara Parkins ... Herself
Jay Stewart ... Announcer
Charlie Tuna ... Announcer

"Étoiles et toiles"
Episode dated 14 April 1986 (1986)
Original Air Date:14 April 1986
Cast:
Bernard Blier ... Himself
Harry Carey Jr. ... Himself
Ben Johnson ... Himself
Silvana Pampanini ... Himself

The Town That Dreaded Sundown (1976) (Filmways Pictures)
Director:Charles B. Pierce

Writer: Earl E. Smith
Cast:
Ben Johnson ... Captain J.D. Morales
Andrew Prine ... Deputy Norman Ramsey
Dawn Wells ... Helen Reed
Jimmy Clem ... Sgt. Mal Griffin
Jim Citty ... Police Chief R.J. Sullivan
Charles B. Pierce ... Patrolman A.C. Benson
Robert Aquino ... Sheriff Otis Barker
Cindy Butler ... Peggy Loomis
Christine Ellsworth ... Linda Mae Jenkins
Earl E. Smith ... Dr. Kress (as Earl E. Smith)
Steve Lyons ... Roy Allen
Joe Catalanotto ... Eddie LeDoux (as Joe Catalanatto)
Roy Lee Brown ... Rainbow Johnson
Mike Hackworth ... Sammy Fuller
Misty West ... Emma Lou Cook
Rick Hildreth ... Buddy Turner
Jason Darnell ... Capt. Gus Wells
Mike Downs ... Newspaper Reporter
Bill Dietz ... Newspaper Reporter
Carolyn Moreland ... Newspaper Reporter
Michael Brown ... Police Officer
Woody Woodman ... F.B.I. Agent
James Duff McAdams ... Sheriff's Deputy (as James D. McAdams)
John Stroud ... Dr. Preston Hickson
Mason Andres ... Rev. Harden
Richard Green ... High School Principal
Dorothy Darlene Orr ... Dispatcher
Don Adkins ... Suspect
Bud Davis ... The Phantom Killer

Vern Stierman ... Narrator (voice)
Dennis Lehane ... Texas Ranger (uncredited)
Runtime:90 min
Color
Filming Locations: Garland City, Arkansas

The Savage Bees (1976) (TV) (Alan Landsburg Productions)
Director:Bruce Geller
Writer:Guerdon Trueblood
Release Date:22 November 1976
Cast:
Ben Johnson ... Sheriff Donald McKew
Michael Parks ... Dr. Jeff DuRand
Paul Hecht ... Dr. Rufus Carter
Gretchen Corbett ... Jeannie Devereaux
Horst Buchholz ... Dr. Jorge Meuller
Bruce French ... Police Lieutenant
James Best ... Deputy Mayor Pelligrino
David L. Gray ... Coast Guard Lieutenant
Richard Charles Boyle ... Coast Guard Chief
Eliott Keener ... Freighter Boatswain
Boardman O'Connor ... Freighter Captain
Danny Barker ... Taxicab Driver
Don Hood ... Deputy Churn
Bill Holliday ... Deputy Stilt
Carol Sutton ... Mrs. Compher
Tiffany Gautier Chase ... Julie Compher
Shirl Cieutat ... Mrs. Bryant
Judy Langford ... TV Interviewer
Lyla Hay Owen ... Mrs. McKew
James Bowers ... Morgue Technician

Sylvia Kuumba Williams ... Morgue Receptionist (as Sylvia "Kuumba" Williams)
Tom Smith-Alden ... Young Priest (as Tom Smith Alden)
Christine Ellsworth ... Pirate Girl
Kenneth Lorenzen ... Pirate
Wayne Mack ... Councilman Ralston (as Wayne 'V' Mack)
Jack L. Morrison ... Councilman Tyne
Norman Gary ... Caziot (as Dr. Norman Gary)
Cary Wilmot Alden ... Mrs. Caziot
Deonna Lang ... (uncredited)
Runtime:90 min
Color
Filming Locations: New Orleans, Louisiana

The Greatest (1977) (British Lion Film Corporation)
Directors: Tom Gries; Monte Hellman
Writers: Muhammad Ali; Richard Durham
Release Date:19 May 1977
Cast:
Muhammad Ali ... Himself
Ernest Borgnine ... Angelo Dundee
Sally Bondi ... Bess
Richard Gullage ... Commission Doctor
Arthur Adams ... Cassius Clay Senior
Dorothy Meyer ... Odessa Clay
Rahaman Ali ... Himself
Howard Bingham ... Himself
Richard Venture ... Colonel
Stack Pierce ... Johnson
W. Youngblood Muhammad ... Himself

Ven Medina ... Ronnie (as Ben Medina)
Paul Mantee ... Carrara
Skip Homeier ... Major
Lloyd Wells ... Himself
George Garro ... Mr. Curtis
David Clennon ... Captain
George Cooper ... Lawyer
Ernie Wheelwright ... Bossman Jones
Pat Patterson ... Himself
James Gammon ... Mr. Harry
Gene Kilroy ... Himself
Toni Crabtree ... Hooker
Sally Gries ... Sponsor's Wife
Elizabeth Marshall ... Sponsor's Wife
Don Dunphy ... Commentator
Fernand A. Larrieu Jr. ... Grocer
Nai Bonet ... Suzie Gomez
Harold Conrad ... Himself
Alberto Martín ... Doctor
Ray Holland ... Reporter
Lucille Benson ... Mrs. Fairlie
Drew Bundini Brown ... Himself (as Drew 'Bundini' Brown)
Annazette Chase ... Belinda Ali
Robert Duvall ... Bill McDonald
Lloyd Haynes ... Herbert Muhammad
David Huddleston ... Cruikshank
Vic Hunter ... Metro Di
Ben Johnson ... Hollis
James Earl Jones ... Malcolm X
John Marley ... Dr. Ferdie Pacheco

Chip McAllister ... Young Muhammad Ali (as Phillip 'Chip' McAllister)
Jack McDermott ... Reporter
Dina Merrill ... Velvet Green
Roger E. Mosley ... Sonny Liston
Todd Rosen ... Reporter
Malachi Throne ... Payton Jory
Mira Waters ... Ruby Sanderson
Teddy Wilson ... Gardener (as Theodore R. Wilson)
Paul Winfield ... Lawyer
Joe Bugner ... Himself (archive footage) (uncredited)
Roy Firestone ... TV Reporter (uncredited)
George Foreman ... Himself (archive footage) (uncredited)
Levi Forte ... Gym boxer (uncredited)
Bob Gordon ... Reporter (uncredited)
Archie Moore ... Himself (uncredited)
Kirby Sanders ... Reporter 'can we quote you' (uncredited)
Tracy 'Chubby' Steele ... Boxer hitting heavy-bag in 5th Street Gym (uncredited)
Runtime:101 min
Color
Filming Locations: Atlanta, Georgia

Grayeagle (1977) (Charles B. Pierce Productions, Inc.)
Director: Charles B. Pierce
Writers:Brad White; Michael O. Sajbel.
Release Date:28 December 1977
Cast:
Ben Johnson ... John Colter
Iron Eyes Cody ... Standing Bear

Lana Wood ... Beth Colter
Jack Elam ... Trapper Willis
Paul Fix ... Running Wolf
Alex Cord ... Grayeagle
Jacob Daniels ... Scar
Jimmy Clem ... Abe Stroud
Cindy Butler ... Ida Coulter
Charles B. Pierce ... Bugler
Blackie Wetzell ... Medicine Man
Cheyenne Rivera ... Shoshone brave
Wayne Wells ... Shoshone brave
Bill Lafromboise ... Indian at fort
Don Wright ... Indian at fort
Runtime:104 min
Color
Filming Locations:Helena National Forest, Helena, Montana

The Swarm (1978) (Warner Brothers Pictures)
Director: Irwin Allen
Writers: Arthur Herzog Jr. (novel); Stirling Silliphant (screenplay)
Release Date:14 July 1978 (USA) more
Cast:
Michael Caine ... Dr. Bradford Crane
Katharine Ross ... Capt. Helena Anderson
Richard Widmark ... Major General Thalius Slater
Richard Chamberlain ... Dr. Hubbard
Olivia de Havilland ... Maureen Schuster (as Olivia De Havilland)
Ben Johnson ... Felix
Lee Grant ... Anne MacGregor

José Ferrer ... Dr. Andrews (as Jose Ferrer)
Patty Duke ... Rita (as Patty Duke Astin)
Slim Pickens ... Jud Hawkins
Bradford Dillman ... Major Baker
Fred MacMurray ... Mayor Clarence Tuttle
Henry Fonda ... Dr. Walter Krim
Cameron Mitchell ... General Thompson
Christian Juttner ... Paul Durant
Runtime:116 min
Color
Filming Locations: Houston, Texas

The Sacketts (1979) (TV) (M.B. Scott Productions)
Director: Robert Totten
Writers: Jim Byrnes (writer);Louis L'Amour (novels)
Release Date:15 May 1979 (USA) more
Cast:
Sam Elliott ... Tell Sackett
Tom Selleck ... Orrin Sackett
Jeff Osterhage ... Tyrel 'Ty' Sackett
Glenn Ford ... Tom Sunday
Ben Johnson ... Cap Roundtree
Gilbert Roland ... Don Luis
John Vernon ... Jonathan Pritts
Ruth Roman ... Rosie
Jack Elam ... Ira Bigelow
Gene Evans ... Benson Bigelow
L.Q. Jones ... Beldon
Paul Koslo ... Kid Newton
Mercedes McCambridge ... Ma Sackett
Slim Pickens ... Jack Bigelow
Pat Buttram ... Tuthill

433

James Gammon ... Wes Bigelow
Buck Taylor ... Reed Carney
Lee de Broux ... Simpson
Marcy Hanson ... Laura Pritts
Ana Alicia ... Drusilla Alvarado
Wendy Rastattar ... Ange Kerry
Shug Fisher ... Purgatorie Bartender
Frank Ramírez ... Juan Torress
Ramon Chavez ... Pete Romero
Henry Capps ... Boyd
Tom Waters ... Hobes
Brian Libby ... Durango
Kimo Owens ... Fetterson
Mai Gray ... Harlot
Bill Hart ... Rodale
Monique St. Pierre ... Delilah
Malcolm Watt ... Preacher
Pam Earnhardt ... Mary
James O'Connell ... Long Higgins
Don Collier ... L.P. Seeker
R.L. Tolbert
Buddy Totten
Bruce M. Fischer ... The Trapper (as Bruce Fischer)
Anakorita
Billy Cardi
Mark Wallace ... Teller (as Mark Wales)
Pat Mahoney ... Purgatorie Customer (as Patrick Mahoney)
John Copeland
Rusty Lee
Dick Kyker
Earl W. Smith ... Billy Muffin

Melvin Todd
Dave Herrera
C.B. Clark
Richard Jamison ... Miner #1
Ken Plonkey ... Miner #2
Russ Cox Jr.
James Almanzar
Louis L'Amour ... Introduction
Runtime:240 min | USA:198 min (Video Version)
Color
Filming Locations: Canon City, Colorado

Soggy Bottom, U.S.A./Swamp Rats (1980) (Gaylord Productions)
Director: Theodore J. Flicker
Writers: Joy N. Houck Jr. and Stephen C. Burnham
Release Date:9 October 1981
Cast:
Ben Johnson ... Isum Gorch
Dub Taylor ... Cottonmouth Gorch
Ann Wedgeworth ... Dusty Wheeler
Lois Nettleton ... Molly
Don Johnson ... Jacob Gorch
P.J. Soles ... Sharlene
Lane Smith ... Smilin' Jack
Anthony Zerbe ... Morgan
Dan Resin ... Rogers
Earl Boen ... Owen
Jack Elam ... Troscliar Boudreaux
Anthony James ... Raymond
Brion James ... Defalice
Hank Worden ... Old Geezer

Charles Woolf ... LeBlanc \
Severn Darden ... Horace Mouthamush
Jim Slaughter ... Mailman
Ed Holmes ... Drunk
Layne Britton ... Storekeeper
Lee Flicker ... Leroy
Harold Suggs ... Preacher
Jeff Meyer ... Buggy Man
Joe Whitley ... Big Lug
Robert Ward ... Card Player
Ric Brigman ... Photographer
Runtime:90 min
Color
Filming Locations: Caddo Lake, Texas

"Wild Times" (1980) (Metromedia Productions)
Director: Richard Compton
Writers: Don Balluck (teleplay); Brian Garfield (novel)
Release Date:24 January 1980
Cast:
Sam Elliott ... Hugh Cardiff
Ben Johnson ... Doc Bogardus
Bruce Boxleitner ... Vern Tyree
Penny Peyser ... Libby Tyree
Timothy Scott ... Caleb Rice
Cameron Mitchell ... Harry Dreier
Gene Evans ... Cletus Hatch
Harry Carey Jr. ... Fitz Bragg
Leif Erickson ... John Tyree
L.Q. Jones ... Wild Bill Hickok
Buck Taylor ... Joe McBride
Pat Hingle ... Bob Halburton

Geno Silva ... Ibran
R.L. Tolbert ... Freight Driver
Ben Zeller ... 1st Judge
Joe Massengale ... Watts
Douglas Doran ... Herm
George Stokes ... Webster
Chris Noel ... Dolly (as Chris Noel Hanks)
Arthur Wagner ... Drifter
Jonathan Bahnks ... 1st Heckler
John Gill ... 2nd Heckler (as John Richard Gill)
George Le Bow ... Betting Man (as George LeBow)
Alan Walter ... Man in Bar
Lynn Hancock ... Jessica
Harrison Sudborough ... 2nd Judge
Ralph Dotson ... Ball Boy
Dennis Hopper ... Doc Holliday
Trish Stewart ... Jeannette Fowler
Marianne Marks ... Flower
Vernon Weddle ... Roberts
George Nason ... Jacobs (as George B. Nason)
Bob Tzudiker ... Jones
Bill Hicks ... Ramon
Robert Garcia ... 1st Indian Brave
Kenny Call ... Cowboy in Show
Sheryl Brown ... Woman in Stage (uncredited)
Russ Cox Jr. ... Artist (uncredited)
Don Hann ... Blacksmith (uncredited)
Chuck Hayward ... Makeup Man (uncredited)
William Smith ... Marshal (uncredited)
Eric Sundt ... Wrangler (uncredited)
Runtime:195 min

Filming Locations: Bonanza Creek Ranch, Santa Fe, New Mexico

The Hunter (1980) (Rastar Pictures)
Director: Buzz Kulik
Writers: Christopher Keane; Ralph Thorson.
Release Date: 1 August 1980
Cast:
Steve McQueen ... Ralph 'Papa' Thorson
Eli Wallach ... Ritchie Blumenthal
Kathryn Harrold ... Dotty
LeVar Burton ... Tommy Price
Ben Johnson ... Sheriff Strong
Richard Venture ... Spota
Tracey Walter ... Rocco Mason
Thomas Rosales Jr. ... Bernardo (as Tom Rosales)
Teddy Wilson ... Winston Blue (as Theodore Wilson)
Ray Bickel ... Luke Branch
Bobby Bass ... Matthew Branch
Karl Schueneman ... Billie Joe
Margaret Mary O'Hara ... Child on Subway (as Margaret O'Hara)
James Spinks ... Angry Car Owner
Frank Delfino ... Poker Player
Zora Margolis ... La Maze Leader
Poppy Lagos ... Mrs. Bernardo
Dea St. La Mount ... Woman Bartender
Lillian Adams ... Blumenthal's Secretary
Thor Nielsen ... Man in Blumenthal's Office
Stan Wojno ... Intern (as Stan Wojno Jr.)
Jodi Moon ... Billie Joe's Girlfriend
Kathy Cunningham ... Mother on Subway

Kelly K. Learman ... Student (as Kelly Learman)
Michael D. Roberts ... Poker Player
Kevin Hagen ... Poker Player
Luis Avalos ... Poker Player
Wynn Irwin ... Informer
Frank Arno ... Poker Player
Rick DiAngelo ... Poker Player
Ralph Thorson ... Bartender
Mathilda Calnan ... Hospital Volunteer (as Matilda Calnan)
F. William Parker ... Watch Commander
Nathaniel Taylor ... Trotter
Tony Burton ... Garbageman #2
Morgan Roberts ... Garbageman #1
Frederick Sistaine ... Pimp
Taurean Blacque ... Hustler
Alex Ross ... Clief McCurdy
Patti Clifton ... Sexy Woman
Jay Scorpio ... Man on Balcony
Jeff Viola ... Young Patrolman
Christopher Keane ... Mike
Dolores Robinson ... Principal
Anthony Mannino ... Policeman at School
Joella Deffenbaugh ... Cashier
Marilyn Jones ... Barmaid
William B. Snider ... Policeman
Chris Richmond ... Bystander
Willie Lee Gaffney ... Card Player on Street
Debbie Miller ... Car Rental Girl
Robert A. Janz ... Motorman
Dan Frick ... Man in Car
Ramiro Medina ... Low Rider

Bill Hart ... Security Guard
Bill Willens ... Suspect in Jail
Nicolas Coster ... Poker player (uncredited)
Corin Rogers ... Passenger on 'L' (uncredited)
Al Ruscio ... Mr. Bernardo (uncredited)
Runtime:97 min
Color
Los Angeles, California

Terror Train (1980) (Astral Bellevue Pathé)
Director:Roger Spottiswoode
Writer:T.Y. Drake (writer)
Release Date:3 October 1980
Cast:
Ben Johnson ... Carne, Train Conductor
Jamie Lee Curtis ... Alana Maxwell
Hart Bochner ... Doc Manley
David Copperfield ... Ken, The Magician
Derek McKinnon ... Kenny Hampson (as Derek MacKinnon)
Sandee Currie ... Mitchy
Timothy Webber ... Mo
Anthony Sherwood ... Jackson
Howard Busgang ... Ed
Steve Michaels ... Charley the Brakeman
Greg Swanson ... Class President
Vanity ... Merry (as D.D. Winters) Joy Boushel ... Pet
Victor Knight ... Walter the Engineer
DonaldLamoureux...ShovelstheStoker(asDonLamoureux)
Charles Biddle Sr. ... Donnelly the Chief Porter
Elizabeth Cholette ... Maggie the Dispatcher

Thom Haverstock ... Bill Chase (as Thomas Haverstock)
Peter Feingold ... Senior
Richard Weinstein ... Pledge #1
John Busby ... Pledge #2
Roland Nincheri ... Bus Driver
Andrea Kenyon ... Bunny Girl
Elaine Lakeman ... Nurse
Gerald Eastman ... Porter #1
Charles Biddles Jr. ... Porter #2
Nadia Rona ... Corpse
Larry Cohen ... 'Crime' band member: Keyboard Vocalist
Brenda Gagnier ... 'Crime' band member: Bass Guitar
Phil Albert ... 'Crime' band member: Drummer
Runtime:97 min
Color
Filming Locations:Montréal, Québec, Canada

Ruckus (1981) (International Vision)
Director: Max Kleven
Writer: Max Kleven
Release Date: March 1981
Cast:
Dirk Benedict ... Kyle Hanson
Linda Blair ... Jenny Bellows
Richard Farnsworth ... Sheriff Jethro Pough
Matt Clark ... Cecil 'Cece' Grant
Jon Van Ness ... Deputy Dave
Taylor Lacher ... Sarge
Clifford A. Pellow ... Homer
Ben Bates ... Big Ben

Jerry Gatlin ... Bubba
Bennie E. Dobbins ... Joe
Bobby Hughes ... Bobby Bellows
A.J. Blake ... Sally the Barmaid
Melanie Weeks ... Counter Girl
Patrick Connolly ... Gas Station Attendant
Bob Peeler ... Farmer at Fair
Ken DeGusta ... Shooting Gallery Man
Sam Johnson ... Kind Man at Fair
Jeannie Medina ... Bus Driver
Ben Johnson ... Mr. Sam Bellows
Michael A. Jones ... Man at the Bar (uncredited)
Brad Bovee .... stunts
Bennie E. Dobbins .... stunts
Sue Fish .... stunts
John Hateley .... stunts (as John Hately)
Tony Jefferson .... stunts
Lane Parrish .... stunts
Dar Robinson .... stunts
Ben Scott .... stunts
John-Clay Scott .... stunts
Walter Scott .... stunt coordinator
Runtime:93 min
Color
Filming Locations:Knights Landing, California

Tex (1982) (Walt Disney Productions)
Director:Tim Hunter
Writers:S.E. Hinton (novel); Charles S. Haas (screenplay) ...
Release Date:30 July 1982
Cast:

Matt Dillon ... Tex McCormick
Jim Metzler ... Mason McCormick
Meg Tilly ... Jamie Collins
Bill McKinney ... Pop McCormick
Frances Lee McCain ... Mrs. Johnson
Ben Johnson ... Cole Collins
Phil Brock ... Lem Peters
Emilio Estevez ... Johnny Collins
Jack Thibeau ... Coach Jackson
Zeljko Ivanek ... Hitchhiker
Tom Virtue ... Bob Collins
Pamela Ludwig ... Connie
Jeff Fleury ... Roger
Suzanne Costollos ... Fortune Teller
Marilyn Redfield ... Ms. Carlson
Pamela Ludwig ... Connie
Jeff Fleury ... Roger
Suzanne Costollos ... Fortune Teller
Marilyn Redfield ... Ms. Carlson
Mark Arnott ... Kelly
Jill Clark ... Marcie
Sheryl Briedel ... Lisa
Lisa Mirkin ... Shelly
Roderick Jones ... Doctor (as Rod Jones)
Richard Krause ... Ride Operator
Don Harral ... Doctor At Hospital
Janine Burns ... Nurse
Mark Huebner ... Orderly
Ron Thulin ... Anchorman
Mary Simons ... Ms. Germanie
Francine Ringold ... Lady Reporter
Darren N. Cates ... Kid Near Tex (as Darren Cates)

Robin Winters ... Girl on Bike
Lance Parkhill ... Boy
Wayne Dorris ... Kid #2
Mike Coats ... Dave
Charles S. Haas ... Lee (as Charlie Haas)
Larry Stallsworth ... Patrolman
Adam Hubbard ... Kid #1
Scott Smith ... Biker #1
Eric Beckstrom ... Biker #2
S.E. Hinton ... Mrs. Barnes
Coralie Hunter ... Lukie
Runtime:103 min
Color
Filming Locations: Tulsa, Oklahoma

The Shadow Riders (1982) (TV) (CBS Entertainment Productions)
Director:Andrew V. McLaglen
Writers:Louis L'Amour (novel); Jim Byrnes (written for television)
Release Date:28 September 1982
Cast:
Tom Selleck ... Mac Traven
Sam Elliott ... Dal Traven
Ben Johnson ... Uncle 'Black Jack' Traven
Geoffrey Lewis ... Major Cooper Ashbury, Comanchero Leader
Jeff Osterhage ... Jesse Traven (as Jeffrey Osterhage)
Gene Evans ... Colonel Holiday Hammond, Gunrunner
Katharine Ross ... Kate Connery / Sister Katherine
R.G. Armstrong ... Sheriff Miles Gillette

Robert B. Craig ... Laird
Marshall R. Teague ... Lieutenant Butler (as Marshall Teague)
Ben Fuhrman ... Devol
Jane Greer ... Ma Traven
Harry Carey Jr. ... Pa Traven
Dominique Dunne ... Sissy Traven
Natalie May ... Heather Traven
Jeanetta Arnette ... Southern Belle
Owen Orr ... Frank King, Kate's Fiancee
Kristina David ... Renfro Damsel
Joe Capone ... Sergeant Ballock
Scanlon Gail ... Yankee Officer
Runtime:100 min
Color
Filming Locations: Columbia State Historic Park, Columbia, California

Champions (1984) (Archerwest)
Director: John Irvin
Writers: Bob Champion; Jonathan Powell.
Release Date:20 April 1984
Cast:
John Hurt ... Bob Champion
Gregory Jones ... Peter
Mick Dillon ... Snowy
Ann Bell ... Valda Embiricos
Jan Francis ... Jo
Peter Barkworth ... Nick Embiricos
Edward Woodward ... Josh Gifford
Ben Johnson ... Burly Cocks
Kirstie Alley ... Barbara

Alison Steadman ... Mary Hussey
Jonathan Newth ... Mr. Griffith Jones
Ceri Jackson ... 1st Nurse
Francesca Brill ... 2nd Nurse
Andrew Wilde ... Graham
Judy Parfitt ... Dr. Merrow
Carolyn Pickles ... Sally
Andrew Fell ... Doctor
Fiona Victory ... Helen
Julie Adams ... Emma Hussey
Michael Byrne ... Richard Hussey
Antony Carrick ... Ken
Frank Mills ... Charles
Hubert Rees ... Bill (Hiawatha)
Richard Adams ... Nicky Hussey
Stephen Jenn ... Bald Patient
Edwin Richfield ... Ashton
Les Conrad ... Masseur
Noel Dyson ... Mrs. Champion
John Woodnutt ... Mr. Champion
Richard Leech ... Beck
Anthony Dawes ... Fred
Wendy Gifford ... Althea
Trevor Clarke ... Phil
John Buckingham ... Valet
Mark Burns ... Thorne
Mark Lambert ... Sean
Graham Welcome ... Clerk of the Scales
Leonard Trolley ... Steward
John Guise ... Starter
Aldaniti ... Himself
Runtime:106 min

Color
Filming Locations: England

Red Dawn (1984) (United Artists)
Director: John Milius
Writers: John Milius (writer); Kevin Reynolds (screenplay)
Release Date: 10 August 1984
Cast:
Patrick Swayze ... Jed
C. Thomas Howell ... Robert
Lea Thompson ... Erica
Charlie Sheen ... Matt
Darren Dalton ... Daryl
Jennifer Grey ... Toni
Brad Savage ... Danny
Doug Toby ... Aardvark
Ben Johnson ... Mason
Harry Dean Stanton ... Mr. Eckert
Ron O'Neal ... Bella
William Smith ... Strelnikov
Vladek Sheybal ... Bratchenko
Powers Boothe ... Andy
Frank McRae ... Mr. Teasdale
Roy Jenson ... Mr. Morris
Pepe Serna ... Aardvark's Father
Lane Smith ... Mayor Bates
Judd Omen ... The Nicaraguan Captain
Michael D'Agosta ... Boy in Classroom
Johelen Carleton ... Girl in Classroom
George Ganchev ... Soldier #1
Waldemar Kalinowski ... Soldier #2

Sam Slovick ... Yuri
Radames Pera ... Stepan Gorsky
Lois Kimbrell ... Mrs. Mason
Elan Oberon ... Alicia
Harley Christensen ... Man on Pole
Fred Rexer ... Tank Survivor
Michael Meisner ... Russian Tanker #1
Victor Meisner ... Russian Tanker #2
Phil Mead ... Mr. Barnes
Sam Dodge ... Man at Drive-In
Ben Zeller ... Man #2 at Drive-In
Dan Sparks ... Man #3 at Drive-In
Benjamin Schick ... Russian Sergeant (as Ben Schick)
George Fisher ... KGB Major
Zitto Kazann ... Political Officer
Chuk Besher ... Door Gunner
J.D. Ruybal ... Cuban Crew Chief (as Jay Dee Ruybal)
Pacho Lane ... Firing Squad Officer
Julius L. Meyer ... Latin Soldier
Tom Ireland ... KGB #2
Krzysztof Janczar ... Soviet Soldier (as Christopher Janczar)
Tacy Norwood ... Rat Girl
Raquel Provance ... Rachel
Gene Scherer ... KGB #1
Scott Phillips ... Russian Soldier (uncredited)
Kenny Call .... stunts
Buddy L. Edmunson .... stunts
Tom Elliott .... stunts
Cindy Folkerson .... stunts
Clifford Happy .... stunts
Chris Howell .... stunts

Terry Jackson .... stunt double: Darren Dalton
Soren Jensen .... stunts
Terry Leonard .... stunt coordinator (as Terry J. Leonard)
Bob Lockrow .... stunts
Mike H. McGaughy .... stunts (as Mike McGaughy)
Jimmy Medearis .... stunts (as Jim Medearis)
Jeff Ramsey .... stunts
Glenn Randall Jr. .... stunts (as Glenn H. Randall Jr.)
Larry Randles .... stunts
Ross Reynolds .... stunts
Thomas Rosales Jr. .... stunts (as Tom Rosales)
Kerry Rossall .... stunts
Ben Scott .... stunts (as Ben R. Scott)
John-Clay Scott .... stunts
Frank James Sparks .... stunts (as Frank J. Sparks)
Runtime:114 min
Color
Filming Locations: Johnson Mesa, New Mexico

Wild Horses (1985) (TV) (Telepictures Productions)
Director: Dick Lowry
Writers: Roderick Taylor; Dan Vining
Release Date:12 November 1985 (USA) more
Cast:
Kenny Rogers ... Matt Cooper
Pam Dawber ... Daryl Reese
Ben Johnson ... Bill Ward
David Andrews ... Dean Ellis
Richard Masur ... Bob Bowne
Karen Carlson ... Ann Cooper
Richard Farnsworth ... Chuck Reese

Richard Hamilton ... Blue Houston
Jack Rader ... Dick Post
Ritch Brinkley ... Wedge Smithfield
Buck Taylor ... Cowboy
Kelly Junkerman ... Ted Holmes
Cathy Worthington ... Lynda
R.W. Hampton ... Himself
Bryan Rogers ... Matt Cooper Jr.
Jamie Fleenor ... Debbie
Dawn Holder ... Katie Cooper
John Ryan King
Roddy Salazar ... Carlos
Beckie Hinton ... Girl
Chas. H. Hunt ... Auctioneer
Dave Lowry ... Wrangler
Jay H. Zirbel ... Leon
Riders in the Sky
Runtime:USA:120 min
Color
Filming Locations: Sheridan, Wyoming

Trespasses (1986) (XIT Productions)
Directors: Loren Bivens; Adam Roarke
Writers: Loren Bivens; Lou Diamond Phillips
Cast:
Robert Kuhn ... Franklin
Van Brooks ... Richard
Mary Pillot ... Sharon Rae
Adam Roarke ... The Drifters
Lou Diamond Phillips ... The Drifters (as Lou Diamond)
Ben Johnson ... August Klein
Thom Meyers ... Johnny

Marina Rice ... Johnny's girlfriend
Deborah Neumann ... Catherine
Eleese Lester ... Maudie
George Sledge ... Gibby
KaRan Neff Reed ... Robin
John Browning ... Herschel
Martin Smith ... Sheriff
Robert Butler ... Mich
Lou Perryman ... Arnold (as Lou Perry)
Lori Lantz ... Ila Beth
Jim Bob Kuhn ... Cowboy
John Henry Faulk ... Dr. Silver
Richard 'Cactus' Pryor ... Dr. Laswell (as Cactus Pryor)
Darrell Kreitz ... Bank Examiner
Horace Newcomb ... Preacher
Ron Queen ... Bubba
Gary Carter ... Deputy
Adell Powell ... Constables
Oscar Dungan ... Constables
Mona Lee Fultz ... Molly
Aimee Guillot ... Kim
Matthew Baugh ... Kevin
Ralph Ware ... Cook at Maudie's
Natalya Wynd ... Bank Tellers
Daeb Hearrean ... Bank Tellers
Jeff Schwan ... Cowboys
David Kuhn ... Cowboys
Jim Allday ... Ambulance Attendants
Patty Kelsey ... Ambulance Attendants
Clare McGill ... Elderly Lady
Lorena Strong ... Choir
Rene Fitzgerald ... Choir

Trixie Lambert ... Choir
Charles Burton ... Choir
Sharon Kuhn ... Choir
Mary Margaret Dement ... Choir
Kim Mathis ... Prisoner's wife
Diana Bober ... Wife's cousin
Aaron Carroll ... Prisoners
Rodger D. Payne ... Prisoners
Rocky Patterson ... Prisoners
Hallmark Van Noy ... Prisoners
Runtime:90 min
Color
Filming Locations: Bastrop, Texas

"Dream West" (1986)
Director: Dick Lowry
Writers: Evan Hunter (writer); David Nevin (novel)
Release Date:13 April 1986
Cast:
Richard Chamberlain ... John Charles Fremont
Alice Krige ... Jessie Benton Fremont
F. Murray Abraham ... President Abraham Lincoln
René Enríquez ... Gen. Castro
Ben Johnson ... Jim Bridger
Jerry Orbach ... Capt. John Sutter
G.D. Spradlin ... Gen. Steven Watts Kearney
Rip Torn ... Kit Carson
Fritz Weaver ... Sen. Thomas Hart Benton
Anthony Zerbe ... Bill Williams
Claude Akins ... Tom Fitzpatrick
John Anderson ... Brig. Gen. Brooke
Lee Bergere ... 'Papa Joe' Nicollet

Jeff East ... Tim Donovan
Michael Ensign ... Karl Preuss
Mel Ferrer ... Judge Elkins
Burton Gilliam ... Martineau
John Harkins ... Secretary of State George Bancroft
Gayle Hunnicutt ... Mrs. Maria Crittenden
Matt McCoy ... Louis Freniere
Cameron Mitchell ... Cmmdre. Robert Stockton
Noble Willingham ... President James Polk
Bill Campbell ... Lt. Gaines
James Cromwell ... Maj. Gen. David Hunter
Lee de Broux ... Provost
Jonathan Frakes ... Lt. Archibald Gillespie
John Francis ... Zindel
Stefan Gierasch ... Trenor Park
Richard Hamilton ... Gen. Murdoch
Will Hare ... Dr. McClain
Dave Lowry ... Godey
Kip Niven ... Sen. John Crittenden
John Quade ... Big Fallon
Martin Rabbett ... Ned Kern
Hansford Rowe ... John Floyd
Timothy Scott ... Ezekial Merrit
Vernon Washington ... Dodson
Anna Bjorn ... Angelique
Cecile Callan ... Nicole
Nikki Creswell ... Lily Fremont
Terrence Evans ... Farmer
William Glover ... Sir Roger Dunston
Gloria Hayes ... Indian Maiden
Barton Heyman ... Judge Advocate Lee
George American Horse ... Chief

Charles Hyman ... Sgt. Riordan
Joaquín Martínez ... Sagundai
George McDaniel ... Col. Mason
Randal Patrick ... Carvalho
Buck Taylor ... Egloffstein
Helen Floyd ... Sally
Charles Bazaldua ... Mexican Officer
Marco Hernandez ... Mexican Lieutenant
Jeff Allin ... Blonde Man
Michael Crabtree ... 2nd Man on Trek 5
Joe Dorsey ... Col. Atherton
Jim Grimshaw ... 2nd Man
Dennis King ... Francis Blair
Jay Louden ... Campaign Aide
Robert Lussier ... Dr. Harris
Kelly Junkerman ... 1st Man on Trek 5
Erich Anderson
Dan Biggers
Dennis Breckner
Bob Burchette
Chris Campbell
Ritchie Copenhaver
John Countryman
Carole Davis
Bill Eudaly
Kevin Grantz
Joe Inscoe
Ken Collins ... Cavalry Officer
Bret Culpepper ... Cavalry Scout
Dirty Denny ... Union army cook (unconfirmed)
Tom Even ... Secretary of State Buchanan
Stephen Lee

Lee Lively
Fred Lloyd … Lt. John Thompson
David Midthunder
John Mingus
Glenn Morshower
Randy Mulkey
Danny Nelson
Mike Pingel … Courtroom Guard
Ron Stone … Calvary Soldier
Ken Walters … Unnamed political speaker
Sam Wells … Political Campaign Chairman
Dan Daggett … Cavalry soldier (uncredited)
Ol'Dave Nelson … Older Settler (uncredited)
John T. Wardle … Mountain Man (uncredited)
Daniel Frank Webster … Settler (uncredited)
Color
Filming Locations: Bell Rock, Sedona, Arizona

Let's Get Harry (1986) (Delphi V Productions)
Directors: Stuart Rosenberg; Alan Smithee
Writers:Charles Robert Carner (writer); Mark Feldberg (story)
Release Date:31 October 1986
Cast:Fidel Abrego … Hood #1
Jere Burns … Washington aide
Gary Busey … Jack
Cecile Callan … Theresa
Terry Camilleri … Mercenary
Elpidia Carrillo … Veronica
Matt Clark … Walt Clayton
Rodolfo De Alexandre … Pablo
Robert Duvall … Norman Shrike

Javier Estrada ... Dwarf
Glenn Frey ... Spence
Salvador Godínez ... Boat man
Bruce Gray ... Ambassador Douglas
Jerry Hardin ... Dean Reilly
Mark Harmon ... Harry Burck Jr.
David Hess ... Mercenary
Ben Johnson ... Harry Burck Sr.
Jonathan Kano ... Hood #3
James Keane ... Al King
Guillermo Lagunes ... Hood #2
Pierrino Mascarino ... Pinilla
Alfredo Ramírez ... Hood #4
Guillermo Ríos ... Carlos Ochobar
Rick Rossovich ... Kurt Klein
Michael Schoeffling ... Corey Burck
Gregory Sierra ... Alphonse
Robert Singer ... Bartender
J.W. Smith ... Mercenary
César Sobrevals ... Pinilla's man
Jon Van Ness ... Mickey
John Wesley ... Mercenary
Thomas F. Wilson ... Bob Pachowski (as Tom Wilson)
Jorge Zepeda ... MP captain
Bobby Bass .... stunt coordinator
Bobby Bass .... stunts
David Burton .... stunts
Gilbert B. Combs .... stunts
Jeffrey J. Dashnaw .... stunts
Shane Dixon .... stunts
Billy D. Lucas .... stunts (as Billy Lucar)
Jon Conrad Pochron .... stunts (as Jon Pochran)

Mic Rodgers .... stunts
David Webster .... stunts
Runtime:102 min
Color
Filming Locations: Aurora, Illinois

Cherry 2000 (1987) (ERP Productions)
Director: Steve De Jarnatt
Writers: Michael Almereyda; Lloyd Fonvielle
Release Date:5 February 1988
Cast:
David Andrews ... Sam Treadwell
Jennifer Balgobin ... Glory Hole Hotel Clerk
Marshall Bell ... Bill
Harry Carey Jr. ... Snappy Tom
Laurence Fishburne ... Glu Glu Lawyer (as Larry Fishburne)
Pamela Gidley ... Cherry 2000
Melanie Griffith ... Edith 'E.' Johnson
Michael C. Gwynne ... Slim
Brion James ... Stacy
Ben Johnson ... Six-Fingered Jake
Jeff Levine ... Marty
Jennifer Mayo ... Randa
Cameron Milzer ... Elaine aka Ginger
Howard Swain ... Jim Skeet
Jack Thibeau ... Stubby Man
Tim Thomerson ... Lester
Robert Z'Dar ... Chet
Jenny Lester-McKeon ... Robot at Slim's
Katie Greene ... Amy Meemur
Joan Riddell ... Frazzled Woman

John Tarnoff ... Lawyer
Annabel Brooks ... Glu Glu Club Patron
Ray Favaro ... Glu Glu Club Patron
Frances McCaffrey ... Glu Glu Club Patron
Sly Smith ... Bartender at Sinker Saloon in Glory Hole (as Sly-Ali Smith)
Donny Evins ... Donny
Claude Earl Jones ... Earl from Adobe Flats (uncredited)
Scott Edmund Lane ... Jack (uncredited)
Charles Croughwell .... stunts
Gene Hartline .... stunts
Terry Jackson .... stunt double: Tim Thomerson
Tony Jefferson .... stunts (as Anthony M. Jefferson)
Roy Jenson .... stunts
Sasha Jenson .... stunts
Mike Johnson .... stunts (as John Michael Johnson)
Tracy Keehn-Dashnaw .... stunts (as Tracy Keehn)
Walt La Rue .... stunts (as Walt LaRue)
Mike H. McGaughy .... stunts (as Mike McGaughy)
Kathleen O'Haco .... stunts (as Kathleen Louise O'Haco)
Carol Rees .... stunts
Thomas Rosales Jr. .... stunts
Ben Scott .... stunts (as Ben R. Scott)
John-Clay Scott .... stunts
Al Simon .... stunts
Fred Smith .... stunts
Brett Smrz .... stunts
Scott Sproule .... stunts
Kevin Swigert .... stunts
Danny Wong .... stunts

Runtime: 93 min
Color
Filming Locations: Death Valley National Park, California

Stranger on My Land (1988) (TV) (Edgar J. Scherick Associates)
Director: Larry Elikann
Writer: Edward Hume
Cast:
Tommy Lee Jones ... Bud Whitman
Jeff Allin ... Marine Captain
Richard Anderson ... Maj. Walters
Tip Boxell ... Capt. Wister
Michael Paul Chan ... Eliot
Barry Corbin ... Gil
John Daryl ... Kyle
Michael Flynn ... Brewer
Joseph Gordon-Levitt ... Rounder (as Joseph Gordon Levitt)
Natalie Gregory ... Gillian
Eric Hart ... Gil Worthy
Pat Hingle ... Judge Munson
Ben Johnson ... Vern Whitman
Stephen Joyce
Denise Kerwin ... Dancer
James Lashly
Tien Loung ... ARVN Officer
Alan Nash ... Simon Crane
Timothy J. Nelson ... Vietnam Surgeon (as Tim Nelson)
Annie O'Donnell ... Mrs. Fourchette

Jeff Olson ... Gene Stewart
Terry O'Quinn ... Connie Priest
John Perryman ... Corpsman
Ned Romero ... Doc
Michael Ruud ... Able
Don Shanks ... Construction Worker #1
George Sullivan ... Thorne
Arsenio 'Sonny' Trinidad ... Peasant Elder
Marshall Bill Turner ... Air Force Policeman
Dee Wallace ... Annie Whitman (as Dee Wallace Stone)
Lyman Ward
Mike Watkiss ... Television Reporter
Kent Williams
Robert Conder .... stunts
Bob Miles .... stunt coordinator
David Boushey .... stunts (uncredited)
Runtime::94 min
Color
Filming Locations: Park City, Utah, USA

Dark Before Dawn (1988) (Kingpin Productions)
Director: Robert Totten
Writer: Reparata Mazzola
Release Date:September 1988
Cast:
John Martin ... Sen. Henry Vance (as John L. Martin)
Clem McSpadden ... Cattleman
Francis Zickefoose ... Diaryman
Charles Dickerson ... Farmer
Rance Howard ... Logan
E.K. Gaylord II ... Grain Hauler

Gary Jordan ... Crop Duster
Charles Beecham ... Ferdie
Timothy Scott ... Ollie (as Tim Scott)
Jeff Cox ... Earl
Buck Taylor ... Charlie
Reparata Mazzola ... Jessica
Paul Newsom ... Roger
Sonny Gibson ... Jeff
Woody Watson ... Luther
Morgan Woodward ... J.B. Watson
Robert Miller ... Otis
Butch McCain ... Newsman
Tony Sellars ... Newsman
Tom Schreier ... Lou
William Donaldson ... Ed
Barbara Henson ... Red
Robert Totten ... Dusty
Jeff Osterhage ... Andy
Danny Steagall ... Shorty
Doug McClure ... Kirkland
William Buckner ... Potts
Eldon G. Hallum ... Simpson
James Potts ... Mitchell
Charles McCally ... Robbins
Billy Drago ... Cabalista Leader
Rex Linn ... Don Hayse
Ted E. Heaton ... Policeman #1
Steve Lewis ... Policeman #2 (as Steve C. Lewis)
Becky Borg ... Thelma
Ben Johnson ... The Sheriff
Gary Cooper ... Concierge
Lee Gideon ... Hitman #1
Randy Whalen ... Hitman #2
Dennis Lehane ... Overnight Driver

Ben L. McCain ... News Reporter
Joseph Fallin ... Bailiff
Dean Lewis ... Watson's Attorney
John Hendrix ... FBI Agent
Nanc T. Woodall ... Watson's Secretary
Kevin Rushing ... Senator's Aide (uncredited)
Red Steagall ... Porter (uncredited)
Runtime:95 min
Color
Filming Locations: Edmond, Oklahoma

The Last Ride (1989)
Director: Bill Russ
Writer: Thomas F. Wilson
Cast:
Ben Johnson
Thomas F. Wilson ... Buck Johnson III
Runtime:23 min
Color

Back to Back (1989) (Motion Pictures Corp. Of America)
Director: John Kincade
Writer: George Frances Skrow
Cast:
Bill Paxton ... Bo Brand
Todd Field ... Todd Brand
Apollonia Kotero ... Jesse Duro
Luke Askew ... Wade Duro
Ben Johnson ... Eli Hix
Susan Anspach ... Madeline Hix
Sal Landi ... Deputy Jackson
David Michael Sterling ... Hank Brand
Roger Rook ... Manny Duro
Tony Gaznick ... Warren Enfield

Terence Marinan ... Spider Hand (as Terry Marinan)
Edward Alberty ... Bandit #2
Cole S. McKay ... Bandit #3
Daniel O'Haco ... Bandit #4
Mildred Brion ... Hedda Niven
Thom Kahler ... Gary Mackintosh
Steven Kent ... Vulture
Earl W. Smith ... Gravedigger #1 (as Earl Smith)
Bob Hayes ... Gravedigger #2
Bill Parker ... Minister
Jay Zingler ... Lem Stanislaw
Warner McKay ... Cable Hogue
Hugh Burritt ... Young Cabel
Tony Noakes ... Young Sabatini
Steve Kelso ... Deputy #1
Curt Bortel ... Boll Weevel McKenny
Henry Kendrick ... Mitchell Sabatini
Roger Carter ... Tow Truck Driver
Eli Cross ... Herb the Fish Man (as Bryan Pryor)
Bob Schoose ... McKenny Brother #2
Pat Green ... McKenny Brother #3
Cecile Krevoy ... Looter #1
Harley Rinzler ... Looter #2
Charles Phillips ... Townie
Jennifer Childs ... Mystery Woman
Runtime:USA:95 min
Color
Filming Locations: Apache Junction, Arizona

The Chase (1991) (TV)(Steve White Productions)
Director: Paul Wendkos
Writer: :Guerdon Trueblood.

Release Date: 10 February 1991
Cast:
Casey Siemaszko ... Hutchinson
Ben Johnson ... Laurienti
Gerry Bamman ... Peter
Robert Beltran ... Mike Silva
Barry Corbin ... Wallis
Megan Follows ... Gloria
Sheila Kelley ... Roxanne
Ricki Lake ... Tammie
Anthony Tyler Quinn ... Dale
Gailard Sartain ... Hammer
Jimmie F. Skaggs ... Tom
Micole Mercurio
Nada Despotovich
Daniel Quinn ... Julian
Georgia Emelin
Paul Collins
Paul Borrillo
Susan Long
Michelle Joyner
Gil Colon
Joe Horváth
Marcia Holley (as Marcia Holly)
Bill Young
Erik Rondell
Ed Battle
Charles A. Tamburro
Runtime: 93 min
Color
Filming Locations Denver, Colorado

My Heroes Have Always Been Cowboys (1991) (Home Grown Inc.)
Director: Stuart Rosenberg
Writer: Joel Don Humphreys
Release Date:1 March 1991
Cast:
Scott Glenn ... H.D. Dalton
Kate Capshaw ... Jolie, H.D.'s Girlfriend
Tess Harper ... Cheryl
Gary Busey ... Clint Hornby
Ben Johnson ... Jesse Dalton
Balthazar Getty ... Jud, Jolie's Son
Clarence Williams III ... Deputy Sheriff Virgil
Mickey Rooney ... Junion, Jesse's Roommate at Retirement Home
Cynthia Mackey ... Ambulance attendant (as Cynthia H. Mackey)
Bill Clymer ... Rodeo announcer
Benjamin Rosenberg ... Gas Station Attendant
Megan Parlen ... Becky
Jim Robnett ... Guard at bank
Jennifer Johnson ... Secretary
Jan Hoag ... Nurse
Dub Taylor ... Gimme Cap
Harold Suggs ... Red Man
Will Hussong ... Card player
Dennis Fimple ... Straw Hat
Clu Gulager ... Dark Glasses
Terry McIlvain ... Pool Player #1
Robert Knott ... Pool Player #2
David Honeycutt Hamilton ... Singer
Theresa Bell ... Guest at Barbeque

Rex Linn ... Guest at Barbeque
Sarah Bratton ... Girl at fruit stand
Clem McSpadden ... Bullmania announcer
Don Endsley ... Bullmania announcer
Kevin Rushing ... Sheriff at the Rodeo
Richard A. Buswell ... Rodeo Fan (uncredited)
Runtime:USA:106 min
Color

Radio Flyer (1992) (Columbia Pictures Corporation)
Director: Richard Donner
Writer:David M. Evans
Release Date:21 February 1992
Cast:
Lorraine Bracco ... Mary
John Heard ... Daugherty
Adam Baldwin ... The King
Elijah Wood ... Mike
Joseph Mazzello ... Bobby
Ben Johnson ... Geronimo Bill
Sean Baca ... Fisher
Robert Munic ... Older Fisher
Garette Ratliff Henson ... Chad (as Garette Ratliff)
Thomas Ian Nicholas ... Ferdie
Noah Verduzco ... Victor Hernandez
Isaac Ocampo ... Jorge Hernandez
Kaylan Romero ... Jesus Hernandez
Abraham Verduzco ... Carlos Hernandez
T.J. Evans ... Big Raymond
Victor DiMattia ... Little Raymond
Adam Hendershott ... Boy #1
Daniel Bieber ... Boy #2

Coleby Lombardo ... Fisher Friend #1
Mike Simmrin ... Fisher Friend #2
Elden Henson ... Fisher Friend #3 (as Elden Ratliff)
Lennard Camarillo ... Fisher Friend #4
Lois Foraker ... Aunt
William J. Bonnel ... Uncle
Henry LaPlante ... Priest
Steve Kahan ... Coffee Shop Manager (as Stephen Kahan)
Steven Anthony Jones ... Postman
Paul Tuerpe ... Market Cashier (as Paul Tuerpé)
Scott Nimerfro ... Golfer (as Scott Lloyd Nimerfro)
Reye Reed ... Restaurant Patron
Susan Gale Linn ... Waitress at Coffee Shop
Dawan Scott ... Bigfoot
James Oliver ... Gas Station Attendant
Michael Maiello ... Gas Station Patron
Hattie Schwartzberg ... Ticket Taker #1
Joan Hyman ... Ticket Taker #2
John Mazzello ... School Boy
Hannah Wood ... School Girl
James W. Gavin ... Pilot
Tom Hanks ... Older Mike (uncredited)
Rob Harris ... Traffic Director (uncredited)
Daniel Trimble ... Neighborhood Kid (uncredited)
Scott Trimble ... Neighborhood Kid (uncredited)
Runtime:114 min
Color

Bonanza: The Return (1993) (TV) (Legend Entertainment)
Director: Jerry Jameson

Writers: David Dortort (characters); Michael Landon
　　Jr. (story)
Release Date:28 November 1993
Cast:
Ben Johnson ... Bronc Evans
Michael Landon Jr. ... Benjamin 'Benj' Cartwright
Emily Warfield ... Sara Cartwright
Brian Leckner ... Josh Cartwright
Richard Roundtree ... Jacob Briscoe
Jack Elam
Dirk Blocker
David Sage
Stewart Moss
Dean Stockwell ... Augustus Brandenburg
Linda Gray ... Laredo Stimmons
John Ingle ... Judge
Archie Lang ... Dr. Green
Richard Fullerton ... Head Surveyor
Charles Gunning ... Otis
Runtime:93 min
Color
Filming Locations: California

Outlaws: The Legend of O.B. Taggart (1994)
Director: Rupert Hitzig
Writer: Mickey Rooney
Cast:
Ned Beatty
Ernest Borgnine
Larry Gatlin
Ben Johnson
Mickey Rooney ... O.B. Taggart

Randy Travis
Christopher Aber ... Young Stud
Billy Barty
Gloria DeHaven
Pamela Guest
Brandon Maggart
Willie Rack
Rob Word ... Pike
Runtime:98 min
Color
Filming Locations: Bonanza Creek Ranch, Santa Fe, New Mexico

Angels in the Outfield (1994) (Caravan Pictures)
Director: William Dear
Writers: Dorothy Kingsley; George Wells
Release Date:15 July 1994
Cast:
Danny Glover ... George Knox
Brenda Fricker ... Maggie Nelson
Tony Danza ... Mel Clark
Christopher Lloyd ... Al the Boss Angel
Ben Johnson ... Hank Murphy
Jay O. Sanders ... Ranch Wilder
Joseph Gordon-Levitt ... Roger Bomman
Milton Davis Jr. ... J.P.
Taylor Negron ... David Montagne
Tony Longo ... Triscuitt Messmer
Neal McDonough ... Whitt Bass
Stoney Jackson ... Ray Mitchell
Adrien Brody ... Danny Hemmerling
Tim Conlon ... Wally

Matthew McConaughey ... Ben Williams
Israel Juarbe ... Jose Martinez
Albert Alexander Garcia ... Pablo Garcia
Dermot Mulroney ... Mr. Bomman (Roger's Dad)
Robert Clohessy ... Frank Gates
Connie Craig ... Carolyn
Jonathan Proby ... Miguel Scott
Michael Halton ... Hairy Man
Mark Conlon ... Photographer
Danny Walcoff ... Marvin (Little Boy in Sandlot Game)
James C. King ... Home Plate Umpire
Tony Reitano ... Singing Umpire
Diane Amos ... Woman Next to J.P.
Christopher Leon DiBiase ... Teenager
Robert Stuart Reed ... Guard
Ruth Beckford ... Family Court Judge
Victoria Skerritt ... Social Worker
Devon Dear ... National Anthem Singer
O.B. Babbs ... Mapel (Angels Player)
Mitchell Page ... Abascal (Angels Player)
Mark Cole ... Norton (Angels Player)
Chuck Dorsett ... Usher
Carney Lansford ... Kit 'Hit or Die' Kesey
Pamela West ... Girl Angel
Oliver Dear ... Rookie Angel
Lionel Douglass ... Brother Angel
Bundy Chanock ... Umpire
John Howard Swain ... First Base Umpire
Marc Magdaleno ... Home Plate Umpire #2
Steven Meredith ... Toronto Player
William Dear ... Toronto Manager

Matthew I. Baker ... Fan (uncredited)
David Courtney ... Anaheim Stadium P.A. Announcer (uncredited)
Shawn Flanagan ... Toronto Bluejay Player (uncredited)
David Maier ... Batboy (uncredited)
Theodore S. Maier ... Baseball Player (uncredited)
Johnny Martin ... Toronto Bluejay Player (uncredited)
Tim Meredith ... Toronto Blue Jay Player (uncredited)
Ron Roggé ... Angel's Coach (uncredited)
Tommy Savich ... Baseball Coach (uncredited)
Joseph Quinn Simpkins ... Hotdog vendor (uncredited)
Seth Smith ... Bubble Boy (uncredited)
Lew Temple ... Baseball Player (uncredited)
Fairly Tull ... Upscale Woman from Anaheim (uncredited)
Runtime:102 min
Color
Filming Locations: Alameda, California

Bonanza: Under Attack (1995) (TV) (Legend Entertainment)
Director: Mark Tinker
Writers: David Dortort (characters); Denne Bart Petitclerc (written by)
Release Date:15 January 1995
Cast:
Ben Johnson ... Bronc Evans
Michael Landon Jr. ... Benjamin 'Benj' Cartwright
Emily Warfield
Brian Leckner ... Josh Cartwright

Jeff Phillips ... Adam 'A.C.' Cartwright Jr.
Richard Roundtree ... Jacob
Jack Elam
Dirk Blocker
Dennis Farina ... Charley Siringo
Sonia Satra
James Karen
Leonard Nimoy ... Frank James
Ted Markland ... Cole
Gordon Jennison Noice ... Black Jack (as J. Gordon Noice)
Kenny Call ... Mears
Bill Yarbrough ... Lucas
Don Collier ... U.S. Marshal
Cal Bartlett ... Sheriff
Eric Lawson ... Morgan
Biff Manard ... Luke
Runtime:89 min
Color
Filming Locations: Ponderosa Ranch - Lake Tahoe, Nevada

Ruby Jean and Joe (1996) (TV) (TWS Productions II)
Director: Geoffrey Sax
Writer: James Lee Barrett
Release Date:11 August 1996
Cast:
Tom Selleck ... Joe Wade
Rebekah Johnson ... Ruby Jean
JoBeth Williams ... Rose
Ben Johnson ... Big Man
Eileen Seeley ... Margaret Johnson

John Diehl ... Harris Johnson
Margo Martindale ... Frankie
Larry Soller ... Harry
Robert Guajardo ... R.J.'s Hitchhike Driver
Robert Starr ... Motel Clerk
Forrie J. Smith ... Birthday Drunk
Ed Adams ... Bar Bully
Darwin Hall ... Annoyed Cowboy
Warner McKay ... Homer
Boots Southerland ... Telephone Cowboy
Glen Gold ... Gas Station Attendant
Shawn Howell ... Bob
Shane McCabe ... Saloon Bartender
Stan Sessoms ... Bus Driver (as Stan Sessums)
Clark Andres Rey ... 1st Rodeo Cowboy
Robert Peters ... 2nd Rodeo Cowboy
Kerry Wayne Kimbro ... 3rd Rodeo Cowboy
Leslie Peters ... 1st Prostitute
Lori Collins ... 2nd Prostitute
Eugene Cochran ... Saloon Drunk
Bob Tallman ... Rodeo Announcer
Nancy Criss ... (uncredited)
Runtime:99 min
Color
Filming Locations: Bisbee, Arizona

The Evening Star (1996) (Rysher Entertainment)
Director: Robert Harling
Writers:: Larry McMurtry (novel); Robert Harling (screenplay)
Release Date:25 December 1996
Cast:

Shirley MacLaine ... Aurora Greenway
Bill Paxton ... Jerry Bruckner
Juliette Lewis ... Melanie Horton
Miranda Richardson ... Patsy Carpenter
Ben Johnson ... Arthur Cotton
Scott Wolf ... Bruce
George Newbern ... Tommy Horton
Marion Ross ... Rosie Dunlop
Mackenzie Astin ... Teddy Horton
Donald Moffat ... Hector Scott
Jennifer Grant ... Ellen
China Kantner ... Jane
Jack Nicholson ... Garrett Breedlove
Shawn Taylor Thompson ... Bump
Jake Langerud ... Henry
Sharon Bunn ... Dolly
Clement von Franckenstein ... Pascal Ferney
Antonia Bogdanovich ... Toni
Jimmie Lee Balthazar ... Jimmie Lee
Melinda Renna ... Nurse Susan
Mark Walters ... Doctor Faulkner
Ann Hardman-Broughton ... Lola Bruckner
Woody Watson ... James
Larry Elliott ... Billy
Donny Caicedo ... Joey
Connie Cooper ... Casting Assistant
Laura Cayouette ... Sitcom Actress Becky
John McCalmont ... Bernie Steinberg
John Bennett Perry ... Sitcom Parent
Mary Gross ... Sitcom Parent
Alex Morris ... Professor Warwick
Will Wallace ... Ticket Agent

Kim Terry ... Flight Attendant
Eileen Morris ... Nurse Margaret
Christopher Ballinger ... Bump, Age 9
Austin Samuel Hembd ... Bump, Age 7
Don Burgess ... Stage Manager
Steve Danton ... Minister B. Ramsey
Robert 'Bobby Z' Zajonc ... Helicopter Pilot
J.D. Hawkins ... Airline Passenger (uncredited)
Frank Page ... Dr. Wilber (uncredited)
Brandon Porter ... Teddy's Son (uncredited)
Eric Skoy ... Opera Critic (uncredited)
Runtime:129 min
Color
Filming Locations: Galveston, Texas

END NOTES

PROLOGUE
1. Interview John "Johnny" Cochran, June 19, 1993 Cowboy Reunion.
2. Interview with Trig Meeks, 1991 Cowboy Reunion.
3. Curtis, Gene. "Only in Oklahoma: Oilman gave money away - secretly." Tulsa World, 11/13/2007.

CHAPTER 1
1. "Ben Johnson to Hall of Fame," Pawhuska Journal, 1/31/1961.
2. Wallis, Michael. The Real Wild West: The 101 Ranch and the Creation of the American West. New York: St. Martin's Press, 1999., p. 407.
3. Family photo, courtesy of Helen Christenson. Undated.
4. Wallis, Michael. The Real Wild West: The 101 Ranch and the Creation of the American West. New York: St. Martin's Press, 1999., p. 407.
5. Interview Edna Mae Olsen, 2/14/09.
6. Wallis, Michael. The Real Wild West: The 101 Ranch and the Creation of the American West. New York: St. Martin's Press, 1999., p. 407.

7. Ibid., p. 408.
8. Interview Helen Christenson, 2/14/09.
9. Undated, published letter by D.E. "Gene" Waters, Tulsa. Publication unknown.
10. Interview Nita Jones, Helen Johnson Christiansen, 2/14/2009.
11. Email from Ben Fowler, 5/8/2009.
12. Interview with Frances Jo Brooks, 2/14/09.
13. Interview with Helen Christenson, 8/23/2009
14. Interview with Nita Jones, 2/14/2009.
15. Interview with Frances Jo Brooks, 2/14/2009.
16. Published article, untitled, by Paul McGuire. Publication unknown. Undated.
17. Interview with Holton Payne, 2/14/2009.
18. Burrough, Bryan, Public Enemies. New York: Penguin, 2004., p. 19-21.
19. Interview with Dale Christenson, 2/14/2009.
20. Interview with Trig Meeks, 1991 Cowboy Reunion.
21. Interview with Dallas Poteet, 1991 Cowboy Reunion.
22. Interview with Trig Meeks, 1991 Cowboy Reunion.
23. Lutz, Aleta."Tradition of A Cowboy," Oklahoma's Orbit, 6/14/1964.
24. Interview with Holton Payne, 12/01, 2008.
25. Interview with Dallas Poteet, 1991 Cowboy Reunion.
26 Interview, Nita Jones, 2/14/09.
26. Interviews with Holton Payne, 12/1/2008 and 2/14/09.
27. Interview with Holton Payne, 12/01/2008;
28. Interview with Helen Johnson Christenson, 12/2/2008.
29. Interview with Holton Payne, 12/1/2008.
30. Interview with Holton Payne, 12/1/2008.

31. "Ben Johnson to Hall of Fame," Pawhuska Journal, 1/31/1961.
32. Interview Dale Christenson, 2/14/2009.
33. "Ben Johnson to Hall of Fame." Pawhuska Journal, 1/31/1961.
34. Interview, Nita Jones, 2/14/2009.
35. Lutz, Aleta. "Tradition of a Cowboy." Oklahoma Orbit. 6/14/1964.
36. Clancy, Fog Horn. "Oklahomans are TOPS in the Cowboy Profession." The Ranchman. May, 1941.
37. Published article. Publication/date/author unknown.
38. http://oklahombres.org/eve/forums/a/tpc/f/2876036794/m/13310153311
39. Interview with Holton Payne, 2/14/2009.
40. http://oklahombres.org/eve/forums/a/tpc/f/2876036794/m/13310153311.

CHAPTER 2
1. Scrapbook - The Family of Ollie Rider.
2. Ibid.
3. Family photos, courtesy of Helen Christenson.
4. Interview with Helen Christenson, 9/1/2009.
5. Interview, Dale Christenson, 2/14/09.
6. Interview, Helen Christenson, 2/13/2009.
7. Interview with Leon "Puny" Martin, Cowboy Reunion 1991.
8. Interview with Frederick Drummond, 2/14/2009.
9. Interview with Frederick Drummond, 2/14/2009.
10. Jackson, Wanda. "Foraker Cowboy recalls 30 years of wild cowboy stories." Foraker Review, 3/14/1985.
11. Interview with Oscar Wright, Cowboy Reunion 1991.

12. Jackson, Wanda. "Foraker Cowboy recalls 30 years of wild cowboy stories." Foraker Review, 3/14/1985.
13. Interview with Oscar Wright, 1991 Cowboy Reunion.
14. Interview, Helen Christenson, 8/30/2009.
15. Published article, untitled, by Paul McGuire. Publication unknown. Undated.

CHAPTER 3
1. Dorsey, Helen. "Ben Does It." The Richmond News Leader, 4/15/1972.
2. Gregory, Bob. "Gentle Ben."
3. Dorsey, Helen. "Ben Does It." The Richmond News Leader, 4/15/1972
4. Ibid.
5. Bean, Covey. "Ben Johnson" The Oklahomans. 11/16/1980.
6. Wallis, Michael. The Real Wild West: The 101 Ranch and the Creation of the American West. New York: St. Martin's Press, 1999., p. 408.
7. Interview with Helen Christenson, 8/5/2009.
8. Official Kay County Marriage License Records.
9. Interview with Helen Christenson, 8/4/2009.
10. Ibid.
11. Ibid.
12. Ibid.
13. Ibid.
14. Interview with Helen Christenson, 8/23/2009
15. Interview with John Miller, 8/09/2009

CHAPTER 4
1. Ben Johnson Interview with KDSM Fox 17 reporter Steve Barry. 4/13/1993.

2. Bean, Covey. "Ben Johnson" The Oklahomans. The Sunday Oklahoman. 11/16/1980.
3. Carey, Harry Jr. Company of Heroes: My Life As An Actor In The John Ford Stock Company. Metuchen: The Scarecrow Press, Inc., 1994., p. 13.
4. http://stevesomething.wordpress.com/2008/09/25/fat-jones-stables.
5. Bean, Covey. "Ben Johnson" The Oklahomans. The Sunday Oklahoman. 11/16/1980.
6. "Our Recipe for a Happy Marriage. " National Enquirer. Date Unknown.
7. "Ben Johnson ... Oklahoma Cowboy," The Peace Officer. Author Unknown. 1/1973.
8. Bean, Covey. "Ben Johnson" The Oklahomans. The Sunday Oklahoman. 11/16/1980.
9. Ben Johnson Interview with KDSM Fox 17 reporter Steve Barry.4/13/1993.
10. Published article. Publication/date/author unknown.
11. Dorsey, Helen. "Ben Does It." The Richmond News Leader, 4/15/1972.
12. Ibid.

CHAPTER 5
1. Interview with Helen Christenson, 2/14/2009.
2. Interview with Ben Johnson, 1984.
3. Cody, Iron Eyes and Collin Perry. Iron Eyes: My Life As A Hollywood Indian. New York: Everest House, 1982., p. 239.
4. Scrapbook - The Family of Ollie Rider.
5. Ibid.
6. http://www.jwayne.com/articles/benjohnson.shtml

7. Essoe, Gabe. Tarzan of the Movies. New York: Cadillac Publishing, 1968., p. 113.
8. Ibid., p. 115.
9. Ibid., p. 117
10. Scheuer, Phillip K. "Ben Johnson Feels Lucky." Publication unknown. 1/11/1948.
11. Roberson, "Bad Chuck" and Bodie Thoene. The Fall Guy: 30 Years As The Duke's Double. North Vancouver: Hancock House, 1980., p. 22.
12. Ibid., p. 24.
13. Ibid., p. 23, 24.

CHAPTER 6
1. Fagen, Herb. Duke: We're Glad We Knew You. Secaucus, Birch Lane Press, 1997., p. 76; Carey, Harry Jr. Company of Heroes: My Life As An Actor In The John Ford Stock Company. Metuchen: The Scarecrow Press, Inc., 1994., p. 14.
2. DeYong, Joe. "Home Folks." Western Horseman, 2/1951.
3. Ben Johnson interview by Marino Amoroso, AMC.
4. Fagen, Herb. Duke: We're Glad We Knew You. Secaucus, Birch Lane Press, 1997., p. 80.
5. Ibid.
6. Published article. Publication/date/author unknown.
7. http://www.jwayne.com/articles/benjohnson.shtml

CHAPTER 7
1. Author unknown. "Tulsa Rancher Finds Former Cowboy Now Top Movie Star." Tulsa World. 2/8/1948.

2. Sayre, J. Willis. "In Seattle Lights." Publication unknown. Date unknown.
3. "Mighty Joe Young Stop Action Film Has Thrills." The Hollywood Reporter. 5/24/1949.
4. Clary, Patricia. "Starring Film Roles Pile Up for Oklahoma Cowboy 'Find.'"UPI.Undated.
5. "Shy Actor Prefers Horses to Women."Publication unknown. 2/17/1949.
6. Carey, Harry Jr. Company of Heroes: My Life As An Actor In The John Ford Stock Company. Metuchen: The Scarecrow Press, Inc., 1994, p. 14.
7. Fagen, Herb. Duke: We're Glad We Knew You. Secaucus, Birch Lane Press, 1997, p. 81.
8. Eyles, Allen. John Wayne and the Movies. New York: Grossett and Dunlap, 1976., p. 288.
9. Fagen, Herb. Duke: We're Glad We Knew You. Secaucus, Birch Lane Press, 1997, p. 81.
10. Published article. Publication unknown. Dated July 17, 1948.
11. Munn, Michael. John Wayne: The Man Behind The Myth. New York: New American Library, 2003. p. 121.
12. Eyles, Eyles, Allen. John Wayne and the Movies. New York: Grossett and Dunlap, 1976., p. 290.
13. Zolotow, Zolotow, Maurice. Shooting Star: A Biography of John Wayne. New York: Simon & Shuster, 1974., p. 254.
14. Ben Johnson interview with Marino Amoroso, AMC.
15. Sinclair, Andrew. John Ford: A Biography. New York: Lorrimer Publishing, 1979, p. 157.

16. Ben Johnson interview with Marino Amoroso, AMC.
17. Carey, Harry Jr. Company of Heroes: My Life As An Actor In The John Ford Stock Company. Metuchen: The Scarecrow Press, Inc., 1994., p. 59.
18. Ben Johnson interview with Marino Amoroso, AMC.
19. Ibid.
20. Fagen, Herb. Duke: We're Glad We Knew You. Secaucus, Birch Lane Press, 1997. p. 81.
21. Carey, Harry Jr. Company of Heroes: My Life As An Actor In The John Ford Stock Company. Metuchen: The Scarecrow Press, Inc., 1994.,p. 68.
22. Ibid., p. 69.

CHAPTER 8
1. O'Hara, Maureen and John Nicoletti. 'Tis Herself. An Autobiography. New York: Simon & Shuster, 2004., p. 104.
2. Bogdanovich, Bogdanovich, Peter. Peter Bogdanovich On The Movies. New York: Arbor House, 1973., p. 171.
3. Roberson, "Bad Chuck" and Bodie Thoene. The Fall Guy: 30 Years As The Duke's Double. North Vancouver: Hancock House, 1980., p. 65.
4. O'Hara, Maureen and John Nicoletti. 'Tis Herself. An Autobiography. New York: Simon & Shuster, 2004., p. 190.
5. Ibid., p. 190.
6. Ibid., p. 187.
7. Ibid., p. 191.
8. Ibid., p. 191.

9. Wayne, Aissa. John Wayne: My Father. New York: Taylor Trade, 1998. p. 101.
10. Ibid., p. 101.
11. O'Hara, Maureen and John Nicoletti. 'Tis Herself. An Autobiography. New York: Simon & Shuster, 2004., p. 192.
12. Sinclair, Andrew. John Ford: A Biography. New York: Lorrimer Publishing, 1979., p. 150.
13. Fagen, Herb. Duke: We're Glad We Knew You. Secaucus, Birch Lane Press, 1997.p. 81.
14. Munn, Michael. John Wayne: The Man Behind The Myth. New York: New American Library, 2003. p. 121.
15. Ben Johnson interview with Marino Amoroso, AMC.
16. Carey, Harry Jr. Company of Heroes: My Life As An Actor In The John Ford Stock Company. Metuchen: The Scarecrow Press, Inc., 1994., p. 97.
17. Ibid., p. 87.
18. Ibid., p. 87.
19. Ibid., p. 105.
20. Interview with Anne Whitehorn and Helen Johnson Christenson, 2/13/2009.
21. Email from Helen Johnson Christenson, 2/21/2009.
22. Interview with Helen Christenson, 2/14/09.
23. Interview with Frances Jo Brooks, 2/14/09.
24. Everson, William K. The Hollywood Western. New York: Citadel Press, 1969, 1992., p. 238.
25. Ibid.
26. Ibid., p. 243.

CHAPTER 9
1. Carey, Harry Jr. Company of Heroes: My Life As An Actor In The John Ford Stock Company. Metuchen: The Scarecrow Press, Inc., 1994.p. 109.
2. Ibid., p. 110.
3. Ibid., p. 110.
4. Ibid., p. 112.
5. Roberson, "Bad Chuck" and Bodie Thoene. The Fall Guy: 30 Years As The Duke's Double. North Vancouver: Hancock House, 1980., p. 63.
6. Carey, Harry Jr. Company of Heroes: My Life As An Actor In The John Ford Stock Company. Metuchen: The Scarecrow Press, Inc., 1994.p. 117.
7. Roberson, "Bad Chuck" and Bodie Thoene. The Fall Guy: 30 Years As The Duke's Double. North Vancouver: Hancock House, 1980., p. 71.
8. Carey, Harry Jr. Company of Heroes: My Life As An Actor In The John Ford Stock Company. Metuchen: The Scarecrow Press, Inc., 1994., p. 117.
9. Ibid., p. 119.
10. Bogdanovich, Peter. Peter Bogdanovich On The Movies. New York: Arbor House, 1973., p. 178.
11. Ben Johnson interview with Marino Amoroso, AMC.
12. Ibid.
13. Munn, Michael. John Wayne: The Man Behind The Myth. New York: New American Library, 2003., p. 132.
14. Ben Johnson interview with Marino Amoroso, AMC.
15. Ibid.
16. Ibid.

17. Munn, Michael. John Wayne: The Man Behind The Myth. New York: New American Library, 2003. p. 132
18. Carey, Harry Jr. Company of Heroes: My Life As An Actor In The John Ford Stock Company. Metuchen: The Scarecrow Press, Inc., 1994., p. 121.
19. O'Hara, Maureen and John Nicoletti. 'Tis Herself. An Autobiography. New York: Simon & Shuster, 2004., p.139.
20. Ben Johnson interview with Marino Amoroso, AMC.
21. http://www.jwayne.com/articles/benjohnson.shtml
22. O'Hara, Maureen and John Nicoletti. 'Tis Herself. An Autobiography. New York: Simon & Shuster, 2004., p. 140.
23. Fagen, Herb. Duke: We're Glad We Knew You. Secaucus, Birch Lane Press, 1997., p. 81.

CHAPTER 10
1. Blinn, Johna. "Stuntman Has a way with Buttermilk Biscuits." The Hartford Times, 10/27/1971.
2. Everson, William K. The Hollywood Western. New York: Citadel Press, 1969, 1992., p. 242.
3. Keavy, Hubbard. "Hollywood... by Bob Thomas" by Hubbard Keavy. Publication/date unknown.
4. Blinn, Johna. "Actor Ben Johnson likes biscuits." Times Union. 10/24/1971
5. Carey, Harry Jr. Company of Heroes: My Life As An Actor In The John Ford Stock Company. Metuchen: The Scarecrow Press, Inc., 1994., p. 120.
6. Interview with Helen Christenson, 2/14/2009.

7. Lutz, Aleta."Tradition of a Cowboy." Oklahoma Orbit. 6/14/1964.

CHAPTER 11
1. Dorsey, Helen. "Ben Does It." The Richmond News Leader, 4/15/1972.
2. Ibid.
3. Interview with Helen Christenson, 2/14/2009.
4. http://www.westernhorseman.com/index.php/featured-articles/article/252-ben-johnson.html.
5. Bean, Covey. "Ben Johnson" The Oklahomans. The Sunday Oklahoman. 11/16/1980.

CHAPTER 12
1. Published article. Publication/date unknown.
2. Fine, Marshall. Bloody Sam: The Life and Films of Sam Peckinpah. New York: Miramax Books, 2005.,p.123.
3. Fagen, Herb. Duke: We're Glad We Knew You. Secaucus, Birch Lane Press, 1997.,p. 80.
4. Interview with John Hughes, 12/02/2008.
5. Fagen, Herb. Duke: We're Glad We Knew You. Secaucus, Birch Lane Press, 1997., p. 81.

CHAPTER 13

CHAPTER 14
1. Carey, Harry Jr. Company of Heroes: My Life As An Actor In The John Ford Stock Company. Metuchen: The Scarecrow Press, Inc., 1994., p. 191.
2. Bogdanovich, Peter. John Ford. Berkeley: University of California Press, 1968., p. 10, 11.

3. Carey, Harry Jr. Company of Heroes: My Life As An Actor In The John Ford Stock Company. Metuchen: The Scarecrow Press, Inc., 1994., p. 195.
4. Ibid., p. 196.
5. Ibid., p. 194.
6. Bogdanovich, Bogdanovich, Peter. Peter Bogdanovich On The Movies. New York: Arbor House, 1973., p. 169).

CHAPTER 15
1. Heston, Charlton. The Actor's Life: Journals 1956-1976. New York: Dutton, 1976., p. 182-3.
2. http://www.jwayne.com/articles/benjohnson.shtml
3. Heston, Heston, Charlton. The Actor's Life: Journals 1956-1976. New York: Dutton, 1976., p. 183.
4. Ibid., p. 183.
5. Ibid., p. 191.
6. Ibid., p. 192-193.
5. Ibid., p. 192.
6. Fine, Marshall. Bloody Sam: The Life and Films of Sam Peckinpah. New York: Miramax Books, 2005., p. 90.
7. Heston, Heston, Charlton. The Actor's Life: Journals 1956-1976. New York: Dutton, 1976.p. 193.
8. Ibid., p. 193.
9. Fine, Marshall. Bloody Sam: The Life and Films of Sam Peckinpah. New York: Miramax Books, 2005, p. 86.
10. http://www.jwayne.com/articles/benjohnson.shtml

11. Fine, Marshall. Bloody Sam: The Life and Films of Sam Peckinpah. New York: Miramax Books, 2005., p. 90
12. Heston, Charlton. The Actor's Life: Journals 1956-1976. New York: Dutton, 1976., p. 197.
13. Ibid.
14. Ibid., p. 194).
15. Weddle, David. "If They Move... Kill 'Em!" The Life and Times of Sam Peckinpah. New York: Grove Press, 1994., p. 240; Fine, Marshall. Bloody Sam: The Life and Films of Sam Peckinpah. New York: Miramax Books, 2005., p. 92).
16. Fine, Marshall. Bloody Sam: The Life and Films of Sam Peckinpah. New York: Miramax Books, 2005., p. 99.
17. Heston, Charlton. The Actor's Life: Journals 1956-1976. New York: Dutton, 1976., p. 198.

CHAPTER 16

CHAPTER 17
1. Interview with Charlton Heston. *The Cowboys of Will Penny*, DVD featurette, widescreen edition of *Will Penny*.)
2. Ibid.

CHAPTER 18
1. Weddle, David. "If They Move... Kill 'Em!" The Life and Times of Sam Peckinpah. New York: Grove Press, 1994., p. 318.
2. Ibid., p. 319.
3. Fine, Marshall. Bloody Sam: The Life and Films of Sam Peckinpah. New York: Miramax Books, 2005., p. 124.

4. Weddle, David. "If They Move... Kill 'Em!" The Life and Times of Sam Peckinpah. New York: Grove Press, 1994., p. 320.
5. Luck, Richard. The Essential Sam Peckinpah. Harpenden: Pocket Essentials, 2000., p. 37-8.
6. Ibid., p. 38.
7. Ibid., p. 37)
8. Weddle, David. "If They Move... Kill 'Em!" The Life and Times of Sam Peckinpah. New York: Grove Press, 1994., p. 339.
9. Ibid., p. 338.
10. Interview with Ben Johnson, 1992 *Sam Peckinpah's West* Documentary.

CHAPTER 19
1. http://www.jwayne.com/articles/benjohnson.shtml
2. Kennedy, Kennedy, Burt. Hollywood Trail Boss: Behind the Scenes of the Wild, Wild Western. New York: Boulevard Books, 1997., p.48
3. Munn, Michael. John Wayne: The Man Behind The Myth. New York: New American Library, 2003., p. 290.
4. Wayne, Aissa. John Wayne: My Father. New York: Taylor Trade, 1998., p. 161.
5. Warga, Wayne. "Ben Johnson's Salary Plot Fails, Leads Him to Success." Publication/date unknown.
6. Fagen, Fagen, Herb. Duke: We're Glad We Knew You. Secaucus, Birch Lane Press, 1997. p. 169.
7. Zolotow, Maurice. Shooting Star: A Biography of John Wayne. New York: Simon & Shuster, 1974., p. 321.

8. Munn, Michael. John Wayne: The Man Behind The Myth. New York: New American Library, 2003. p. 294-5.
9. Fagen, Herb. Duke: We're Glad We Knew You. Secaucus, Birch Lane Press, 1997, p. 60.
10. Interview with Helen Christenson, 8/23/2009
11. Interview with John Miller, 8/23/2009.
12. Interview with Helen Christenson, 8/30/2009.
13. Interview with Ed Faulkner, 10/2006.

CHAPTER 20
1. Interview with Peter Bogdanovich, The Last Picture Show: A Look Back.
2. Ibid.
3. Ibid.
4. Ibid.
5. Kay, Terry. "Does Oscar Wait for Ben Johnson?" Publication/date unknown.
6. Published article. Publication/Date Unknown.
7. Bean, Covey. "Ben Johnson" The Oklahomans. 11/16/1980.
8. Published article. Publication/Date unknown.
9. Bogdanovich, Peter. Peter Bogdanovich On The Movies. New York: Arbor House, 1973., p. 250.
10. Interview with Bogdanovich, The Last Picture Show: A Look Back.
11. Scott, Vernon. "Johnson Almost Refused Role Because of Four Letter Words." Herald Examiner, 2/12/1972.
12. Letter from Peter Bogdanovich to Anthony Caruso, dated April 25, 1984.
13. Gregory, Bob. "Gentle Ben." Oklahoma Monthly. Date unknown.

14. Published article. Publication/Date unknown.
15. Bogdanovich, Peter. Peter Bogdanovich On The Movies. New York: Arbor House, 1973., p. 240.
16. Bean, Covey. "Ben Johnson" The Oklahomans. The Sunday Oklahoman. 11/16/1980).
17. Warga, Wayne. "Ben Johnson's Salary Plot Fails." (Publication/date unknown.
18. "Ben Johnson... The Oklahoma Cowboy," The Peace Officer. Author Unknown. January, 1973.
19. Interview with Dale Christenson, Jr., 2/14/09.
20. Interview with Ann Whitehorn, 2/14/09.
21. Interview with Frances Jo Brooks, 2/14/09
22. Interview with Nita Salmon Jones, 2/14/09.

CHAPTER 21

CHAPTER 22.
1. Smith, Lewis. "Ben & Oscar & Howard." Publication/Date unknown.
2. http://www.westernhorseman.com/index.php/featured-articles/article/252-ben-johnson.html
3. "Ben Johnson... The Oklahoma Cowboy," The Peace Officer. Author Unknown. January, 1973.
4. Ibid.
5. Published article. Publication/Date unknown.

CHAPTER 23
1. Interview with John Miller, 8/2009.
2. Fine, Marshall. Bloody Sam: The Life and Films of Sam Peckinpah. New York: Miramax Books, 2005., p. 218.
3. Ibid., p. 216.
4. Donaldson, Bill. Showcase. Tulsa Tribune, 7/4/1972.

5. Weddle, David. "If They Move... Kill 'Em!" The Life and Times of Sam Peckinpah. New York: Grove Press, 1994., p. 441.
6. Munn, Michael. John Wayne: The Man Behind The Myth. New York: New American Library, 2003, p. 305.
7. Fagen, Herb. Duke: We're Glad We Knew You. Secaucus, Birch Lane Press, 1997., p. 81.
8. Kennedy, Burt. Hollywood Trail Boss: Behind the Scenes of the Wild, Wild Western. New York: Boulevard Books, 1997., p. 51
9. Ben Johnson interview with Marino Amoroso, AMC.
10. Ibid.
11. Dorsey, Helen. "Ben Does It." The Richmond News Leader, 4/15/1972.
12. Scott, Vernon. "Sooner Cowboy Won't Allow Family to See His New Film." UPI. 1/30/1972.)
13. Warga, Wayne. "Ben Johnson's Salary Plot Fails, Leads Him to Success." Publication/date unknown.

CHAPTER 24

1. Kennedy, Burt. Hollywood Trail Boss: Behind the Scenes of the Wild, Wild Western. New York: Boulevard Books, 1997., p. 52.
2. Munn, Michael. John Wayne: The Man Behind The Myth. New York: New American Library, 2003.p. 304
3. http://www.westernhorseman.com/index.php/featured-articles/article/252-ben-johnson.html
4. Gregory, Bob. "Gentle Ben." Oklahoma Monthly. Date unknown.

5. Kennedy, Burt. Hollywood Trail Boss: Behind the Scenes of the Wild, Wild Western. New York: Boulevard Books, 1997., p. 48.
6. Munn, Michael. John Wayne: The Man Behind The Myth. New York: New American Library, 2003., p. 120.
7. Kennedy, Burt. Hollywood Trail Boss: Behind the Scenes of the Wild, Wild Western. New York: Boulevard Books, 1997, p. 49.
8. Published Article. Publication Unknown. Dated Friday, May 18, 1973.
9. Ford, Elaine. "Ben Johnson Just Wants to Play Ben Johnson," Showcase. Date Unknown.
10. Keevil, Katherine. "Character Actor Warren Oates dies at age 52." Associated Press. Date unknown.
11. Ford, Elaine. "Ben Johnson Just Wants to Play Ben Johnson," Showcase.
12. Stowers, Carlton. "Somebody's Got To Hold The Horses." Southwest Scene/Dallas Morning News. 4/29/1973.
13. "Tee-off at the Benefit," Pawhuska Daily Journal-Capital, 5/20/1973.
14. Fagen, Herb. Duke: We're Glad We Knew You. Secaucus, Birch Lane Press, 1997., p. 82.
15. "Bobwhite Beware - Grand National Hunt Begins Today." Publication unknown. 11/29/1973).
16. Cody, Iron Eyes and Collin Perry. Iron Eyes: My Life As A Hollywood Indian. New York: Everest House, 1982., p. 273.

CHAPTER 25
1. Letter from Ken Stemler to Ben Johnson, 6/30/1978.

2. Fagen, Herb. Duke: We're Glad We Knew You. Secaucus, Birch Lane Press, 1997., p. 82.
3. Fagen, Herb. Duke: We're Glad We Knew You. Secaucus, Birch Lane Press, 1997., p. 80.
4. Bean, Covey. "Ben Johnson" The Oklahomans. The Sunday Oklahoman. 11/16/1980.

CHAPTER 26

CHAPTER 27
1. Bean, Covey. "Ben Johnson" The Oklahomans. The Sunday Oklahoman. 11/16/1980.
2. Interview with John Miller, 8/23/2009).
3 Dorsey, Helen. "Ben Does It." The Richmond News Leader, 4/15/1972.
4. Gregory, Bob. "Gentle Ben." Oklahoma Monthly. Date unknown.
5. Harwood, Nina. "Actor Johnson makes visit here."Kerrville Times, 1/17/79.
6. "Our Recipe..." National Equirer. Date unknown.
7. Gregory, Bob. "Gentle Ben."
8. LetterfromGeorgeNightoBenJohnson,dated4/27/1984.
9. "Hollywood actor gives land to Boy Scout." Publication/date unknown.
10. http://lavender.fortunecity.com/flamingos/387/richarddream.html.
11. http://www.mediajaw.com/sub_jimmydoncox/ag_bab.asp.

CHAPTER 28
1. Interview with John Miller,8/23/2009
2. http://www.westernhorseman.com/index.php/featured-articles/article/252-ben-johnson.html.

CHAPTER 29
1. Interview with John Miller, 8/23/2009.
2. Ibid.
3. Ibid.

CHAPTER 30
1. Interview with John Miller, 8/23/2009.
2. Interview with Helen Christenson, 2/14/2009.
3. McQueen, Max. "Ben Johnson - Living the Golden Rule." MT/TDN.11/21/1982.

EPILOGUE
1. Ben Johnson interview with Marino Amoroso, AMC.
2. Carey, p. 96.
3. Ben Johson interview with Marino Amoroso, AMC.
4. Ibid.
5. Handwritten note to Ben Johnson from Louis L'Amour, Date unknown.
6. http://www.jwayne.com/articles/benjohnson.shtml.

BIBLIOGRAPHY

Bogdanovich, Peter. John Ford. Berkeley: University of California Press, 1968.

Bogdanovich, Peter. Peter Bogdanovich On The Movies. New York: Arbor House, 1973.

Burrough, Bryan. Public Enemies. New York: Penguin, 2004.

Carey, Harry Jr. Company of Heroes: My Life As An Actor In The John Ford Stock Company. Metuchen: The Scarecrow Press, Inc., 1994.

Cody, Iron Eyes and Collin Perry. Iron Eyes: My Life As A Hollywood Indian. New York: Everest House, 1982.

Collings, Ellsworth and Alma Miller England. The 101 Ranch. Norman: The University of Oklahoma Press, 1937, 1989.

Essoe, Gabe. Tarzan of the Movies. New York: Cadillac Publishing, 1968.

Eyles, Allen. John Wayne and the Movies. New York: Grossett and Dunlap, 1976.

Everson, William K. The Hollywood Western. New York: Citadel Press, 1969, 1992.

Fagen, Herb. Duke: We're Glad We Knew You. Secaucus, Birch Lane Press, 1997.

Fine, Marshall. Bloody Sam: The Life and Films of Sam Peckinpah. New York: Miramax Books, 2005.

Fulwood, Neil. The Films of Sam Peckinpah. London: B.T. Basford Film Books, 2002.

Heston, Charlton. The Actor's Life: Journals 1956-1976. New York: Dutton, 1976.

Kennedy, Burt. Hollywood Trail Boss: Behind the Scenes of the Wild, Wild Western. New York: Boulevard Books, 1997.

Luck, Richard. The Essential Sam Peckinpah. Harpenden: Pocket Essentials, 2000.

Munn, Michael. John Wayne: The Man Behind The Myth. New York: New American Library, 2003.

O'Hara, Maureen and John Nicoletti. 'Tis Herself. An Autobiography. New York: Simon & Shuster, 2004.

Roberson, "Bad Chuck" and Bodie Thoene. The Fall Guy: 30 Years As The Duke's Double. North Vancouver: Hancock House, 1980.

Sinclair, Andrew. John Ford: A Biography. New York: Lorrimer Publishing, 1979.

Wallis, Michael. The Real Wild West: The 101 Ranch and the Creation of the American West. New York: St. Martin's Press, 1999.

Wayne, Aissa. John Wayne: My Father. New York: Taylor Trade, 1998.

Weddle, David. "If They Move... Kill 'Em!" The Life and Times of Sam Peckinpah. New York: Grove Press, 1994.

Yule, Andrew. Picture Shows: The Life and Films of Peter Bogdanovich. New York: Limlight Editions, 1992.

Zolotow, Maurice. Shooting Star: A Biography of John Wayne. New York: Simon & Shuster, 1974.

Printed in Great Britain
by Amazon